Python Natural Language Processing

Advanced machine learning and deep learning techniques for natural language processing

Jalaj Thanaki

BIRMINGHAM - MUMBAI

Python Natural Language Processing

First published: July 2017

Production reference: 1280717

Published by Packt Publishing Ltd.
Livery Place
35 Livery Street
Birmingham
B3 2PB, UK.
ISBN 978-1-78712-142-3

www.packtpub.com

Credits

Author
Jalaj Thanaki

Reviewers
Devesh Raj
Gayetri Thakur
Prabhanjan Tattar
Chirag Mahapatra

Commissioning Editor
Veena Pagare

Acquisition Editor
Aman Singh

Content Development Editor
Jagruti Babaria

Technical Editor
Sayli Nikalje

Copy Editor
Safis Editing

Project Coordinator
Manthan Patel

Proofreader
Safis Editing

Indexer
Tejal Daruwale Soni

Production Coordinator
Deepika Naik

Foreword

Data science is rapidly changing the world and the way we do business --be it retail, banking and financial services, publishing, pharmaceutical, manufacturing, and so on. Data of all forms is growing exponentially--quantitative, qualitative, structured, unstructured, speech, video, and so on. It is imperative to make use of this data to leverage all functions-- avoid risk and fraud, enhance customer experience, increase revenues, and streamline operations.

Organizations are moving fast to embrace data science and investing a lot into high-end data science teams. Having spent more than 12 years in the BFSI domain, I get overwhelmed with the transition that the BFSI industry has seen in embracing analytics as a business and no longer a support function. This holds especially true for the fin-tech and digital lending world of which Jalaj and myself are a part of.

I have known Jalaj since her college days and am impressed with her exuberance and self-motivation. Her research skills, perseverance, commitment, discipline, and quickness to grasp even the most difficult concepts have made her achieve success in a short span of 4 years on her corporate journey.

Jalaj is a gifted intellectual with a strong mathematical and statistical understanding and demonstrates a continuous passion for learning the new and complex analytical and statistical techniques that are emerging in the industry. She brings experience to the data science domain and I have seen her deliver impressive projects around NLP, machine learning, basic linguistic analysis, neural networks, and deep learning. The blistering pace of the work schedule that she sets for herself, coupled with the passion she puts into her work, leads to definite and measurable results for her organization.

One of her most special qualities is her readiness to solve the most basic to the most complex problem in the interest of the business. She is an excellent team player and ensures that the organization gains the maximum benefit of her exceptional talent.

In this book, Jalaj takes us on an exciting and insightful journey through the natural language processing domain. She starts with the basic concepts and moves on to the most advanced concepts, such as how machine learning and deep learning are used in NLP.

I wish Jalaj all the best in all her future endeavors.

Sarita Arora
Chief Analytics Officer, SMECorner
Mumbai, India

About the Author

Jalaj Thanaki is a data scientist by profession and data science researcher by practice. She likes to deal with data science related problems. She wants to make the world a better place using data science and artificial intelligence related technologies. Her research interest lies in natural language processing, machine learning, deep learning, and big data analytics. Besides being a data scientist, Jalaj is also a social activist, traveler, and nature-lover.

Acknowledgement

I would like to dedicate this book to my husband, Shetul Thanaki, for his constant support, encouragement, and creative suggestions.

I give deep thanks and gratitude to my parents, my in-laws, my family, and my friends, who have helped me at every stage of my life. I would also like to thank all the mentors that I've had over the years. I really appreciate the efforts by technical reviewers for reviewing this book. I would also like to thank my current organization, SMECorner, for its support. I am a big fan of open source communities and education communities, so I really want to thank communities such as Kaggel, Udacity, and Coursera who have helped me, in a direct or indirect manner, to understand the various concepts of data science. Without learning from these communities, there is not a chance I could be doing what I do today.

I would like to thank Packt Publishing and Aman Singh, who approached me to write this book. I really appreciate the effort put in by the entire Packt editorial team to make this book as good as possible. Special thanks to Aman Singh, Jagruti Babaria, Menka Bohra, Manthan Patel, Nidhi Joshi, Sayli Nikalje, Manisha Sinha, Safis, and Tania Dutta.

I would like to recognize the efforts of technical editing team, strategy and management team, marketing team, sales team, graphics designer team, pre-production team, post production team, layout coordinators team, and indexer team for making my authoring journey so smooth.

I feel really compelled to pass my knowledge on to those willing to learn.

Thank you God for being kind to me!

Cheers and Happy Reading!

About the Reviewers

Devesh Raj is a data scientist with 10 years of experience in developing algorithms and solving problems in various domains--healthcare, manufacturing, automotive, production, and so on, applying machine learning (supervised and unsupervised machine learning techniques) and deep learning on structured and unstructured data (computer vision and NLP).

Gayetri Thakur is a linguist working in the area of natural language processing. She has worked on co-developing NLP tools such as automatic grammar checker, named entity recognizer, and text-to-speech and speech-to-text systems. She currently works for Google India Pvt.Ltd. India.

She is pursuing a PhD in linguistics and has completed her masters in linguistics from Banaras Hindu University.

Prabhanjan Tattar has over 9 years of experience as a statistical analyst. Survival analysis and statistical inference are his main areas of research/interest, and he has published several research papers in peer-reviewed journals and authored three books on R: *R Statistical Application Development by Example*, Packt Publishing, *A Course in Statistics with R*, Wiley, and *Practical Data Science Cookbook*, Packt Publishing. He also maintains the R packages gpk, RSADBE, and ACSWR.

Chirag Mahapatra is a software engineer who works on applying machine learning and natural language processing to problems in trust and safety. He currently works at Trooly (acquired by Airbnb). In the past, he has worked at A9.com on the ads data platform.

www.PacktPub.com

For support files and downloads related to your book, please visit www.PacktPub.com.

Did you know that Packt offers eBook versions of every book published, with PDF and ePub files available? You can upgrade to the eBook version at www.PacktPub.com and as a print book customer, you are entitled to a discount on the eBook copy. Get in touch with us at service@packtpub.com for more details.

At www.PacktPub.com, you can also read a collection of free technical articles, sign up for a range of free newsletters and receive exclusive discounts and offers on Packt books and eBooks.

https://www.packtpub.com/mapt

Get the most in-demand software skills with Mapt. Mapt gives you full access to all Packt books and video courses, as well as industry-leading tools to help you plan your personal development and advance your career.

Why subscribe?

- Fully searchable across every book published by Packt
- Copy and paste, print, and bookmark content
- On demand and accessible via a web browser

Customer Feedback

Thanks for purchasing this Packt book. At Packt, quality is at the heart of our editorial process. To help us improve, please leave us an honest review on this book's Amazon page at `https://www.amazon.com/dp/1787121429`.

If you'd like to join our team of regular reviewers, you can e-mail us at `customerreviews@packtpub.com`. We award our regular reviewers with free eBooks and videos in exchange for their valuable feedback. Help us be relentless in improving our products!

Table of Contents

Preface

The book title, **Python Natural Language Processing**, gives you a broad idea about the book. As a reader, you will get the chance to learn about all the aspects of **natural language processing (NLP)** from scratch. In this book, I have specified NLP concepts in a very simple language, and there are some really cool practical examples that enhance your understanding of this domain. By implementing these examples, you can improve your NLP skills. Don't you think that sounds interesting?

Now let me answer some of the most common questions I have received from my friends and colleagues about the NLP domain. These questions really inspired me to write this book. For me, it's really important that all my readers understand why I am writing this book. Let's find out!

Here, I would like answer some of the questions that I feel are critical to my readers. So, I'll begin with some of the questions, followed by the answers. The first question I usually get asked is--what is NLP? The second one is--why is Python mainly used for developing NLP applications? And last but not least, the most critical question is--what are the resources I can use for learning NLP? Now let's look at the answers!

The answer to the first question is that NLP, simply put, is the language you speak, write, read, or understand as a human; natural language is, thus, a medium of communication. Using computer science algorithms, mathematical concepts, and statistical techniques, we try to process the language so machines can also understand language as humans do; this is called **NLP**.

Now let's answer the second question--why do people mainly use Python to develop NLP applications? So, there are some facts that I want to share with you. The very simple and straightforward thing is that Python has a lot of libraries that make your life easy when you develop NLP applications. The second reason is that if you are coming from a C or C++ coding background, you don't need to worry about memory leakage. The Python interpreter will handle this for you, so you can just focus on the main coding part. Besides, Python is a coder-friendly language. You can do much more by writing just a few lines of codes, compared to other object-oriented languages. So all these facts drive people to use Python for developing NLP and other data science-related applications for rapid prototyping.

The last question is critical to me because I used to explain the previous answers to my friends, but after hearing all these and other fascinating things, they would come to me and say that they want to learn NLP, so what are the resources available? I used to recommend books, blogs, YouTube videos, education platforms such as Udacity and Coursera, and a lot more, but after a few days, they would ask me if there is a single resource in the form of book, blog, or anything that they could use. Unfortunately, for them, my answer was no. At that stage, I really felt that juggling all these resources would always be difficult for them, and that painful realization became my inspiration to write this book.

So in this book, I have tried to cover most of the essential parts of NLP, which will be useful for everyone. The great news is that I have provided practical examples using Python so readers can understand all the concepts theoretically as well as practically. Reading, understanding, and coding are the three main processes that I have followed in this book to make readers lives easier.

What this book covers

Chapter 1, *Introduction*, provides an introduction to NLP and the various branches involved in the NLP domain. We will see the various stages of building NLP applications and discuss NLTK installation.

Chapter 2, *Practical Understanding of Corpus and Dataset*, shows all the aspects of corpus analysis. We will see the different types of corpus and data attributes present in corpuses. We will touch upon different corpus formats such as CSV, JSON, XML, LibSVM, and so on. We will see a web scraping example.

Chapter 3, *Understanding Structure of Sentences*, helps you understand the most essential aspect of natural language, which is linguistics. We will see the concepts of lexical analysis, syntactic analysis, semantic analysis, handling ambiguities, and so on. We will use NLTK to understand all the concepts practically.

Chapter 4, *Preprocessing*, helps you get to know the various types of preprocessing techniques and how you can customize them. We will see the stages of preprocessing such as data preparation, data processing, and data transformation. Apart from this, you will understand the practical aspects of preprocessing.

Chapter 5, *Feature Engineering and NLP Algorithms*, is the core part of an NLP application. We will see how different algorithms and tools are used to generate input for machine learning algorithms, which we will be using to develop NLP applications. We will also understand the statistical concepts used in feature engineering, and we will get into the customization of tools and algorithms.

Chapter 6, *Advance Feature Engineering and NLP Algorithms*, gives you an understanding of the most recent concepts in NLP, which are used to deal with semantic issues. We will see word2vec, doc2vec, GloVe, and so on, as well as some practical implementations of word2vec by generating vectors from a Game of Thrones dataset.

Chapter 7, *Rule-Based System for NLP*, details how we can build a rule-based system and all the aspects you need to keep in mind while developing the same for NLP. We will see the rule-making process and code the rules too. We will also see how we can develop a template-based chatbot.

Chapter 8, *Machine Learning for NLP Problems*, provides you fresh aspects of machine learning techniques. We will see the various algorithms used to develop NLP applications. We will also implement some great NLP applications using machine learning.

Chapter 9, *Deep Learning for NLU and NLG Problems*, introduces you to various aspects of artificial intelligence. We will look at the basic concepts of **artificial neural networks (ANNs)** and how you can build your own ANN. We will understand hardcore deep learning, develop the mathematical aspect of deep learning, and see how deep learning is used for **natural language understanding(NLU)** and **natural language generation (NLG)**. You can expect some cool practical examples here as well.

Appendix A, *Advance Tools*, gives you a brief introduction to various frameworks such as Apache Hadoop, Apache Spark, and Apache Flink.

Appendix B, *How to Improve Your NLP Skills*, is about suggestions from my end on how to keep your NLP skills up to date and how constant learning will help you acquire new NLP skills.

Appendix C, *Installation Guide*, has instructions for installations required.

What you need for this book

Let's discuss some prerequisites for this book. Don't worry, it's not math or statistics, just basic Python coding syntax is all you need to know. Apart from that, you need Python 2.7.X or Python 3.5.X installed on your computer; I recommend using any Linux operating system as well.

The list of Python dependencies can be found at GitHub repository at https://github.com/jalajthanaki/NLPython/blob/master/pip-requirements.txt.

Now let's look at the hardware required for this book. A computer with 4 GB RAM and at least a two-core CPU is good enough to execute the code, but for machine learning and deep learning examples, you may have more RAM, perhaps 8 GB or 16 GB, and computational power that uses GPU(s).

Who this book is for

This book is intended for Python developers who wish to start with NLP and want to make their applications smarter by implementing NLP in them.

Conventions

In this book, you will find a number of text styles that distinguish between different kinds of information. Here are some examples of these styles and an explanation of their meaning.

Code words in text, database table names, folder names, filenames, file extensions, path names, dummy URLs, user input, and Twitter handles are shown as follows: "The nltk library provides some inbuilt corpuses."

A block of code is set as follows:

```
import nltk
from nltk.corpus import brown as cb
from nltk.corpus import gutenberg as cg
```

Any command-line input or output is written as follows:

pip install nltk or **sudo pip install nltk**

New terms and **important words** are shown in bold. Words that you see on the screen, for example, in menus or dialog boxes, appear in the text like this: "This will open an additional dialog window, where you can choose specific libraries, but in our case, click on **All packages**, and you can choose the path where the packages reside. Wait till all the packages are downloaded."

Warnings or important notes appear like this.

 Tips and tricks appear like this.

Reader feedback

Feedback from our readers is always welcome. Let us know what you think about this book-what you liked or disliked. Reader feedback is important for us as it helps us develop titles that you will really get the most out of. To send us general feedback, simply e-mail feedback@packtpub.com, and mention the book's title in the subject of your message. If there is a topic that you have expertise in and you are interested in either writing or contributing to a book, see our author guide at www.packtpub.com/authors.

Customer support

Now that you are the proud owner of a Packt book, we have a number of things to help you to get the most from your purchase.

Downloading the example code

You can download the example code files for this book from your account at http://www.packtpub.com. If you purchased this book elsewhere, you can visit http://www.packtpub.com/support and register to have the files emailed directly to you. You can download the code files by following these steps:

1. Log in or register to our website using your e-mail address and password.
2. Hover the mouse pointer on the **SUPPORT** tab at the top.
3. Click on **Code Downloads & Errata**.
4. Enter the name of the book in the **Search** box.
5. Select the book for which you're looking to download the code files.
6. Choose from the drop-down menu where you purchased this book from.
7. Click on **Code Download**.

Once the file is downloaded, please make sure that you unzip or extract the folder using the latest version of:

- WinRAR / 7-Zip for Windows
- Zipeg / iZip / UnRarX for Mac
- 7-Zip / PeaZip for Linux

The code bundle for the book is also hosted on GitHub at `https://github.com/PacktPubl ishing/Python-Natural-Language-Processing`. We also have other code bundles from our rich catalog of books and videos available at `https://github.com/PacktPublishing/`. Check them out!

Downloading the color images of this book

We also provide you with a PDF file that has color images of the screenshots/diagrams used in this book. The color images will help you better understand the changes in the output. You can download this file from `https://www.packtpub.com/sites/default/files/downloads/PythonNaturalLanguagePro cessing_ColorImages.pdf`.

Errata

Although we have taken every care to ensure the accuracy of our content, mistakes do happen. If you find a mistake in one of our books-maybe a mistake in the text or the code-we would be grateful if you could report this to us. By doing so, you can save other readers from frustration and help us improve subsequent versions of this book. If you find any errata, please report them by visiting `http://www.packtpub.com/submit-errata`, selecting your book, clicking on the **Errata Submission Form** link, and entering the details of your errata. Once your errata are verified, your submission will be accepted and the errata will be uploaded to our website or added to any list of existing errata under the **Errata** section of that title. To view the previously submitted errata, go to `https://www.packtpub.com/book s/content/support` and enter the name of the book in the search field. The required information will appear under the **Errata** section.

Piracy

Piracy of copyrighted material on the Internet is an ongoing problem across all media. At Packt, we take the protection of our copyright and licenses very seriously. If you come across any illegal copies of our works in any form on the Internet, please provide us with the location address or website name immediately so that we can pursue a remedy. Please contact us at copyright@packtpub.com with a link to the suspected pirated material. We appreciate your help in protecting our authors and our ability to bring you valuable content.

Questions

If you have a problem with any aspect of this book, you can contact us at questions@packtpub.com, and we will do our best to address the problem.

1
Introduction

In this chapter, we'll have a gentle introduction to **natural language processing** (**NLP**) and how natural language processing concepts are used in real-life artificial intelligence applications. We will focus mainly on Python programming paradigms, which are used to develop NLP applications. Later on, the chapter has a tips section for readers. If you are really interested in finding out about the comparison of various programming paradigms for NLP and why Python is the best programming paradigm then, as a reader, you should go through the *Preface* of this book. As an industry professional, I have tried most of the programming paradigms for NLP. I have used Java, R, and Python for NLP applications. Trust me, guys, Python is quite easy and efficient for developing applications that use NLP concepts.

We will cover following topics in this chapter:

- Understanding NLP
- Understanding basic applications
- Understanding advance applications
- Advantages of the togetherness--NLP and Python
- Environment setup for NLTK
- Tips for readers

Understanding natural language processing

In the last few years, branches of **artificial intelligence** (**AI**) have created a lot of buzz, and those branches are data science, data analytics, predictive analysis, NLP, and so on.

As mentioned in the *Preface* of this book, we are focusing on Python and natural language processing. Let me ask you some questions--Do you really know what natural language is? What is natural language processing? What are the other branches involved in building expert systems using various concepts of natural language processing? How can we build intelligent systems using the concept of NLP?

Let's begin our roller coaster ride of understanding NLP.

What is natural language?

- As a human being, we express our thoughts or feelings via a language
- Whatever you speak, read, write, or listen to is mostly in the form of natural language, so it is commonly expressed as natural language
- For example:
    - The content of this book is a source of natural language
    - Whatever you speak, listen, and write in your daily life is also in the form of natural language
    - Movie dialogues are also a source of natural language
    - Your WhatsApp conversations are also considered a form of natural language

What is natural language processing?

- Now you have an understanding of what natural language is. NLP is a sub-branch of AI. Let's consider an example and understand the concept of NLP. Let's say you want to build a machine that interacts with humans in the form of natural language. This kind of an intelligent system needs computational technologies and computational linguistics to build it, and the system processes natural language like humans.
- You can relate the aforementioned concept of NLP to the existing NLP products from the world's top tech companies, such as Google Assistant from Google, Siri speech assistance from Apple, and so on.
- Now you will able to understand the definitions of NLP, which are as follows:
    - Natural language processing is the ability of computational technologies and/or computational linguistics to process human natural language
    - Natural language processing is a field of computer science, artificial intelligence, and computational linguistics concerned with the interactions between computers and human (natural) languages
    - Natural language processing can be defined as the automatic (or semi-automatic) processing of human natural language

What are the other branches involved in building expert systems using, various concepts of NLP? *Figure 1.1* is the best way to know how many other branches are involved when you are building an expert system using NLP concepts:

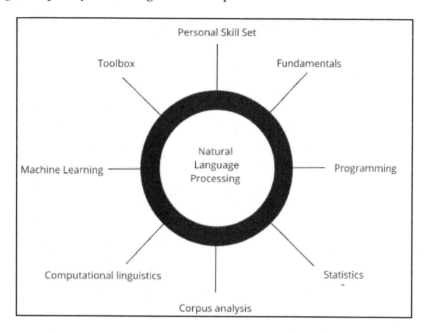

Figure 1.1: NLP concepts

Figures 1.2 and *1.3* convey all the subtopics that are included in every branch given in *Figure 1.1*:

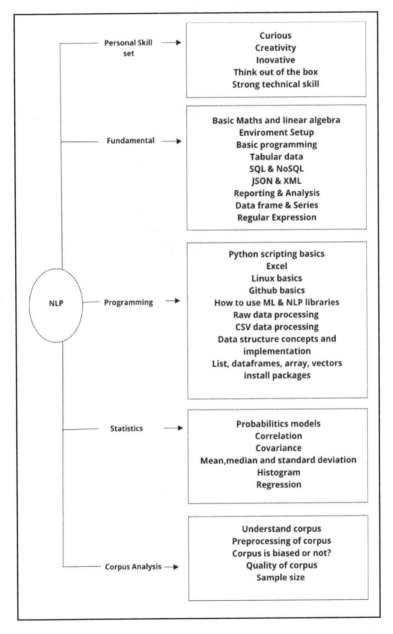

Figure 1.2: Sub-branches of NLP concepts

Figure 1.3 depicts the rest of the sub-branches:

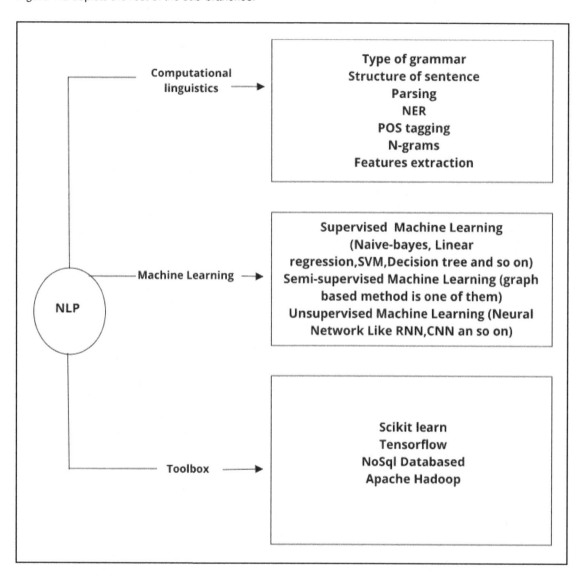

Figure 1.3: Sub-branches of NLP concepts

How can we build an intelligent system using concepts of NLP? *Figure 1.4* is the basic model, which indicates how an expert system can be built for NLP applications. The development life cycle is defined in the following figure:

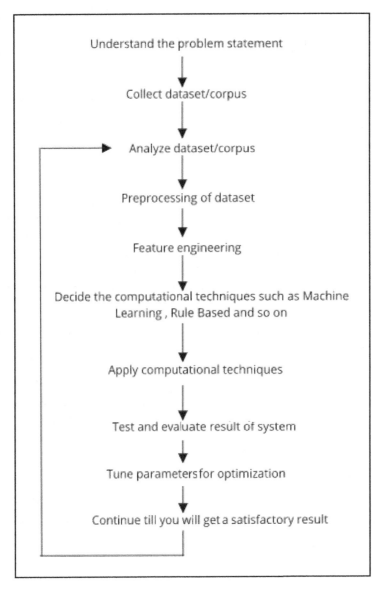

Figure 1.4: Development life cycle

Let's see some of the details of the development life cycle of NLP-related problems:

1. If you are solving an NLP problem, you first need to understand the problem statement.
2. Once you understand your problem statement, think about what kind of data or corpus you need to solve the problem. So, data collection is the basic activity toward solving the problem.
3. After you have collected a sufficient amount of data, you can start analyzing your data. What is the quality and quantity of our corpus? According to the quality of the data and your problem statement, you need to do preprocessing.
4. Once you are done with preprocessing, you need to start with the process of feature engineering. Feature engineering is the most important aspect of NLP and data science related applications. We will be covering feature engineering related aspects in much more detail in Chapter 5, *Feature Engineering and NLP Algorithms* and Chapter 6, *Advance Feature Engineering and NLP Algorithms.*
5. Having decided on and extracted features from the raw preprocessed data, you are to decide which computational technique is useful to solve your problem statement, for example, do you want to apply machine learning techniques or rule-based techniques?.
6. Now, depending on what techniques you are going to use, you should ready the feature files that you are going to provide as an input to your decided algorithm.
7. Run your logic, then generate the output.
8. Test and evaluate your system's output.
9. Tune the parameters for optimization, and continue till you get satisfactory results.

We will be covering a lot of information very quickly in this chapter, so if you see something that doesn't immediately make sense, please do not feel lost and bear with me. We will explore all the details and examples from the next chapter onward, and that will definitely help you connect the dots.

Understanding basic applications

NLP is a sub-branch of AI. Concepts from NLP are used in the following expert systems:

* Speech recognition system
* Question answering system

- Translation from one specific language to another specific language
- Text summarization
- Sentiment analysis
- Template-based chatbots
- Text classification
- Topic segmentation

We will learn about most of the NLP concepts that are used in the preceding applications in the further chapters.

Understanding advanced applications

Advanced applications include the following:

- Human robots who understand natural language commands and interact with humans in natural language.
- Building a universal machine translation system is the long-term goal in the NLP domain because you could easily build a machine translation system which can convert one specific language to another specific language, but that system may not help you to translate other languages. With the help of deep learning, we can develop a universal machine translation system and Google recently announced that they are very close to achieving this goal. We will build our own machine translation system using deep learning in Chapter 9, *Deep Learning for NLP and NLG Problems.*
- The NLP system, which generates the logical title for the given document is one of the advance applications. Also, with the help of deep learning, you can generate the title of document and perform summarization on top of that. This kind of application, you will see in Chapter 9, *Deep Learning for NLP and NLG Problems.*
- The NLP system, which generates text for specific topics or for an image is also considered an advanced NLP application.
- Advanced chatbots, which generate personalized text for humans and ignore mistakes in human writing is also a goal we are trying to achieve.
- There are many other NLP applications, which you can see in *Figure 1.5:*

More Deeper Application of NLP		
Group 1	**Group 2**	**Group 3**
Cleanup, Tokenization	Information Retrieval and Extraction (IR)	Machine Translation
Stemming	Relationship Extraction	Automatic Summarization/ Paraphracing
Lemmatization	Named Entity Recognation (NER)	Natural Language Generation
Part of Speech Tagging	Sentiment Analysis/Sentance Boundary Dismbiguation	Reasoning over Knowledge Based
Query Expansion	World sense and Dismbiguation	
Parsing	Text Similarity	Quation Answering System
Topic Segmentationand Recognation	Coreference Resolution	Dialog System
Morphological Degmentation (Word/Sentences)	Discourse Analysis	Image Captioning & other Multimodel Tasks

Figure 1.5: Applications In NLP domain

Advantages of togetherness - NLP and Python

The following points illustrate why Python is one of the best options to build an NLP-based expert system:

- Developing prototypes for the NLP-based expert system using Python is very easy and efficient
- A large variety of open source NLP libraries are available for Python programmers

- Community support is very strong
- Easy to use and less complex for beginners
- Rapid development: testing, and evaluation are easy and less complex
- Many of the new frameworks, such as Apache Spark, Apache Flink, TensorFlow, and so on, provide API for Python
- Optimization of the NLP-based system is less complex compared to other programming paradigms

Environment setup for NLTK

I would like to suggest to all my readers that they pull the NLPython repository on GitHub. The repository URL is https://github.com/jalajthanaki/NLPython

I'm using Linux (Ubuntu) as the operating system, so if you are not familiar with Linux, it's better for you to make yourself comfortable with it, because most of the advanced frameworks, such as Apache Hadoop, Apache Spark, Apache Flink, Google TensorFlow, and so on, require a Linux operating system.

The GitHub repository contains instructions on how to install Linux, as well as basic Linux commands which we will use throughout this book. On GitHub, you can also find basic commands for GitHub if you are new to Git as well. The URL is https://github.com/jalajthanaki/NLPython/tree/master/ch1/documentation

I'm providing an installation guide for readers to set up the environment for these chapters. The URL is https://github.com/jalajthanaki/NLPython/tree/master/ch1/installation_guide

Steps for installing nltk are as follows (or you can follow the URL: https://github.com/jalajthanaki/NLPython/blob/master/ch1/installation_guide/NLTK%2BSetup.md):

1. Install Python 2.7.x manually, but on Linux Ubuntu 14.04, it has already been installed; otherwise, you can check your Python version using the python -V command.
2. Configure pip for installing Python libraries (https://github.com/jalajthanaki/NLPython/blob/master/ch1/installation_guide/NLTK%2BSetup.md).
3. Open the terminal, and execute the following command:

```
pip install nltk or sudo pip install nltk
```

4. Open the terminal, and execute the `python` command.

5. Inside the Python shell, execute the `import nltk` command.

   If your `nltk` module is successfully installed on your system, the system will not throw any messages.

6. Inside the Python shell, execute the `nltk.download()` command.

7. This will open an additional dialog window, where you can choose specific libraries, but in our case, click on **All packages**, and you can choose the path where the packages reside. Wait till all the packages are downloaded. It may take a long time to download. After completion of the download, you can find the folder named `nltk_data` at the path specified by you earlier. Take a look at the NLTK Downloader in the following screenshot:

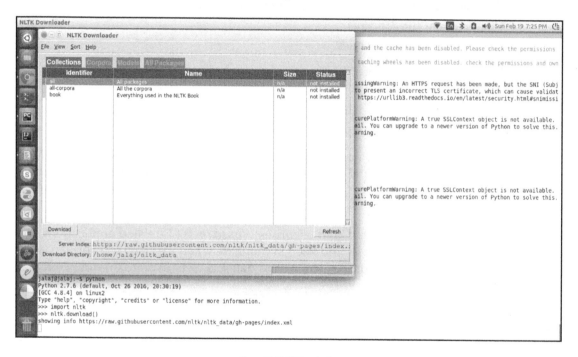

Figure 1.6: NLTK Downloader

This repository contains an installation guide, codes, wiki page, and so on. If readers have questions and queries, they can post their queries on the Gitter group. The Gitter group URL is `https://gitter.im/NLPython/Lobby?utm_source=share-link&utm_medium=link &utm_campaign=share-link`

Tips for readers

This book is a practical guide. As an industry professional, I strongly recommend all my readers replicate the code that is already available on GitHub and perform the exercises given in the book. This will improve your understanding of NLP concepts. Without performing the practicals, it will be nearly impossible for you to get all the NLP concepts thoroughly. By the way, I promise that it will be fun to implement them.

The flow of upcoming chapters is as follows:

- Explanation of the concepts
- Application of the concepts
- Needs of the concepts
- Possible ways to implement the concepts (code is on GitHub)
- Challenges of the concepts
- Tips to overcome challenges
- Exercises

Summary

This chapter gave you an introduction to NLP. You now have a brief idea about what kind of branches are involved in NLP and the various stages for building an expert system using NLP concepts. Lastly, we set up the environment for NLTK. All the installation guidelines and codes are available on GitHub.

In the next chapter, we will see what kind of corpus is used on NLP-related applications and what all the critical points we should keep in mind are when we analyze a corpus. We will deal with the different types of file formats and datasets. Let's explore this together!

2
Practical Understanding of a Corpus and Dataset

In this chapter, we'll explore the first building block of natural language processing. We are going to cover the following topics to get a practical understanding of a corpus or dataset:

- What is corpus?
- Why do we need corpus?
- Understanding corpus analysis
- Understanding types of data attributes
- Exploring different file formats of datasets
- Resources for access free corpus
- Preparing datasets for NLP applications
- Developing the web scrapping application

What is a corpus?

Natural language processing related applications are built using a huge amount of data. In layman's terms, you can say that a large collection of data is called **corpus**. So, more formally and technically, corpus can be defined as follows:

Corpus is a collection of written or spoken natural language material, stored on computer, and used to find out how language is used. So more precisely, a corpus is a systematic computerized collection of authentic language that is used for linguistic analysis as well as corpus analysis. If you have more than one corpus, it is called **corpora**.

In order to develop NLP applications, we need corpus that is written or spoken natural language material. We use this material or data as input data and try to find out the facts that can help us develop NLP applications. Sometimes, NLP applications use a single corpus as the input, and at other times, they use multiple corpora as input.

There are many reasons of using corpus for developing NLP applications, some of which are as follows:

- With the help of corpus, we can perform some statistical analysis such as frequency distribution, co-occurrences of words, and so on. Don't worry, we will see some basic statistical analysis for corpus later in this chapter.
- We can define and validate linguistics rules for various NLP applications. If you are building a grammar correction system, you will use the text corpus and try to find out the grammatically incorrect instances, and then you will define the grammar rules that help us to correct those instances.
- We can define some specific linguistic rules that depend on the usage of the language. With the help of the rule-based system, you can define the linguistic rules and validate the rules using corpus.

In a corpus, the large collection of data can be in the following formats:

- Text data, meaning written material
- Speech data, meaning spoken material

Let's see what exactly text data is and how can we collect the text data. Text data is a collection of written information. There are several resources that can be used for getting written information such as news articles, books, digital libraries, email messages, web pages, blogs, and so on. Right now, we all are living in a digital world, so the amount of text information is growing rapidly. So, we can use all the given resources to get the text data and then make our own corpus. Let's take an example: if you want to build a system that summarizes news articles, you will first gather various news articles present on the web and generate a collection of new articles so that the collection is your corpus for news articles and has text data. You can use web scraping tools to get information from raw HTML pages. In this chapter, we will develop one.

Now we will see how speech data is collected. A speech data corpus generally has two things: one is an audio file, and the other one is its text transcription. Generally, we can obtain speech data from audio recordings. This audio recording may have dialogues or conversations of people. Let me give you an example: in India, when you call a bank customer care department, if you pay attention, you get to know that each and every call is recorded. This is the way you can generate speech data or speech corpus. For this book, we are concentrating just on text data and not on speech data.

A corpus is also referred to as a dataset in some cases.

There are three types of corpus:

- **Monolingual corpus:** This type of corpus has one language
- **Bilingual corpus:** This type of corpus has two languages
- **Multilingual corpus:** This type of corpus has more than one language

A few examples of the available corpora are given as follows:

- Google Books Ngram corpus
- Brown corpus
- American National corpus

Why do we need a corpus?

In any NLP application, we need data or corpus to building NLP tools and applications. A corpus is the most critical and basic building block of any NLP-related application. It provides us with quantitative data that is used to build NLP applications. We can also use some part of the data to test and challenge our ideas and intuitions about the language. Corpus plays a very big role in NLP applications. Challenges regarding creating a corpus for NLP applications are as follows:

- Deciding the type of data we need in order to solve the problem statement
- Availability of data
- Quality of the data
- Adequacy of the data in terms of amount

Now you may want to know the details of all the preceding questions; for that, I will take an example that can help you to understand all the previous points easily. Consider that you want to make an NLP tool that understands the medical state of a particular patient and can help generate a diagnosis after proper medical analysis.

Here, our aspect is more biased toward the corpus level and generalized. If you look at the preceding example as an NLP learner, you should process the problem statement as stated here:

- What kind of data do I need if I want to solve the problem statement?
    - Clinical notes or patient history
    - Audio recording of the conversation between doctor and patient

- Do you have this kind of corpus or data with you?
  - If yes, great! You are in a good position, so you can proceed to the next question.
  - If not, OK! No worries. You need to process one more question, which is probably a difficult but interesting one.
- Is there an open source corpus available?
  - If yes, download it, and continue to the next question.
  - If not, think of how you can access the data and build the corpus. Think of web scraping tools and techniques. But you have to explore the ethical as well as legal aspects of your web scraping tool.
- What is the quality level of the corpus?
  - Go through the corpus, and try to figure out the following things:
    - If you can't understand the dataset at all, then what to do?
      - Spend more time with your dataset.
      - Think like a machine, and try to think of all the things you would process if you were fed with this kind of a dataset. Don't think that you will throw an error!
      - Find one thing that you feel you can begin with.
      - Suppose your NLP tool has diagnosed a human disease, think of what you would ask the patient if you were the doctor's machine. Now you can start understanding your dataset and then think about the preprocessing part. Do not rush to the it.
    - If you can understand the dataset, then what to do?
      - Do you need each and every thing that is in the corpus to build an NLP system?
        - If yes, then proceed to the next level, which we will look at in Chapter 5, *Feature Engineering and NLP Algorithms*.
        - If not, then proceed to the next level, which we will look at in Chapter 4, *Preprocessing*.

- Will the amount of data be sufficient for solving the problem statement on at least a **proof of concept (POC)** basis?
  - According to my experience, I would prefer to have at least 500 MB to 1 GB of data for a small POC.
  - For startups, to collect 500 MB to 1 GB data is also a challenge for the following reasons:
    - Startups are new in business.

- Sometimes they are very innovative, and there is no ready-made dataset available.
- Even if they manage to build a POC, to validate their product in real life is also challenging.

Refer to *Figure 2.1* for a description of the preceding process:

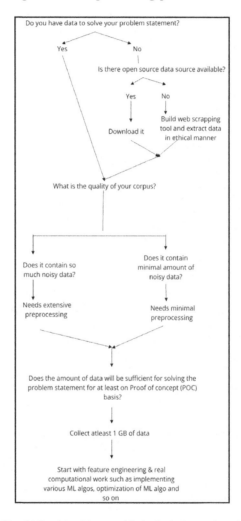

Figure 2.1: Description of the process defined under why do we need corpus?

Understanding corpus analysis

In this section, we will first understand what corpus analysis is. After this, we will briefly touch upon speech analysis. We will also understand how we can analyze text corpus for different NLP applications. At the end, we will do some practical corpus analysis for text corpus. Let's begin!

Corpus analysis can be defined as a methodology for pursuing in-depth investigations of linguistic concepts as grounded in the context of authentic and communicative situations. Here, we are talking about the digitally stored language corpora, which is made available for access, retrieval, and analysis via computer.

Corpus analysis for speech data needs the analysis of phonetic understanding of each of the data instances. Apart from phonetic analysis, we also need to do conversation analysis, which gives us an idea of how social interaction happens in day-to-day life in a specific language. Suppose in real life, if you are doing conversational analysis for casual English language, maybe you find a sentence such as *What's up, dude?* more frequently used in conversations compared to *How are you, sir (or madam)?*.

Corpus analysis for text data consists in statistically probing, manipulating, and generalizing the dataset. So for a text dataset, we generally perform analysis of how many different words are present in the corpus and what the frequency of certain words in the corpus is. If the corpus contains any noise, we try to remove that noise. In almost every NLP application, we need to do some basic corpus analysis so we can understand our corpus well. nltk provides us with some inbuilt corpus. So, we perform corpus analysis using this inbuilt corpus. Before jumping to the practical part, it is very important to know what type of corpora is present in nltk.

nltk has four types of corpora. Let's look at each of them:

- **Isolate corpus**: This type of corpus is a collection of text or natural language. Examples of this kind of corpus are gutenberg, webtext, and so on.

- **Categorized corpus**: This type of corpus is a collection of texts that are grouped into different types of categories.
  An example of this kind of corpus is the brown corpus, which contains data for different categories such as news, hobbies, humor, and so on.

- **Overlapping corpus**: This type of corpus is a collection of texts that are categorized, but the categories overlap with each other. An example of this kind of corpus is the reuters corpus, which contains data that is categorized, but the defined categories overlap with each other.

  More explicitly, I want to define the example of the reuters corpus. For example, if you consider different types of coconuts as one category, you can see subcategories of coconut-oil, and you also have cotton oil. So, in the reuters corpus, the various data categories are overlapped.

- **Temporal corpus**: This type of corpus is a collection of the usages of natural language over a period of time.

  An example of this kind of corpus is the inaugural address corpus.

  Suppose you recode the usage of a language in any city of India in 1950. Then you repeat the same activity to see the usage of the language in that particular city in 1980 and then again in 2017. You will have recorded the various data attributes regarding how people used the language and what the changes over a period of time were.

Now enough of theory, let's jump to the practical stuff. You can access the following links to see the codes:

This chapter code is on the GitHub directory URL at https://github.com/jalajthanaki /NLPython/tree/master/ch2.

Follow the Python code on this URL: https://nbviewer.jupyter.org/github/jalajthan aki/NLPython/blob/master/ch2/2_1_Basic_corpus_analysis.html

The Python code has basic commands of how to access corpus using the nltk API. We are using the brown and gutenberg corpora. We touch upon some of the basic corpus-related APIs.

A description of the basic API attributes is given in the following table:

API Attributes	Description
fileids()	This results in files of the corpus
fileids([categories])	This results in files of the corpus corresponding to these categories
categories()	This lists categories of the corpus
categories([fileids])	This shows categories of the corpus corresponding to these files

`raw()`	This shows the raw content of the corpus
`raw(fileids=[f1,f2,f3])`	This shows the raw content of the specified files
`raw(categories=[c1,c2])`	This shows the raw content of the specified categories
`words()`	This shows the words of the whole corpus
`words(fileids=[f1,f2,f3])`	This shows the words of specified `fileids`
`words(categories=[c1,c2])`	This shows the words of the specified categories
`sents()`	This shows the sentences of the whole corpus
`sents(fileids=[f1,f2,f3])`	This shows the sentences of specified `fileids`
`sents(categories=[c1,c2])`	This shows the sentences of the specified categories
`abspath(fileid)`	This shows the location of the given file on disk
`encoding(fileid)`	This shows the encoding of the file (if known)
`open(fileid)`	This basically opens a stream for reading the given corpus file
`root`	This shows a path, if it is the path to the root of the locally installed corpus
`readme()`	This shows the contents of the README file of the corpus

We have seen the code for loading your customized corpus using `nltk` as well as done the frequency distribution for the available corpus and our custom corpus.

The `FreqDist` class is used to encode frequency distributions, which count the number of times each word occurs in a corpus.

All `nltk` corpora are not that noisy. A basic kind of preprocessing is required for them to generate features out of them. Using a basic corpus-loading API of `nltk` helps you identify the extreme level of junk data. Suppose you have a bio-chemistry corpus, then you may have a lot of equations and other complex names of chemicals that cannot be parsed accurately using the existing parsers. You can then, according to your problem statement, make a decision as to whether you should remove them in the preprocessing stage or keep them and do some customization on parsing in the **part-of-speech tagging (POS)** level.

In real-life applications, corpora are very dirty. Using `FreqDist`, you can take a look at how words are distributed and what we should and shouldn't consider. At the time of preprocessing, you need to check many complex attributes such as whether the results of parsing, POS tagging, and sentence splitting are appropriate or not. We will look at all these in a detailed manner in `Chapter 4`, *Preprocessing*, and `Chapter 5`, *Feature Engineering and NLP Algorithms*.

Note here that the corpus analysis is in terms of the technical aspect. We are not focusing on corpus linguistics analysis, so guys, do not confuse the two.
If you want to read more on corpus linguistics analysis, refer to this URL: `https://en.wikipedia.org/wiki/Corpus_linguistics`
If you want to explore the `nltk` API more, the URL is `http://www.nltk.org/`.

Exercise

1. Calculate the number of words in the `brown` corpus with `fileID: fileidcc12`.
2. Create your own corpus file, load it using `nltk`, and then check the frequency distribution of that corpus.

Understanding types of data attributes

Now let's focus on what kind of data attributes can appear in the corpus. *Figure 2.3* provides you with details about the different types of data attributes:

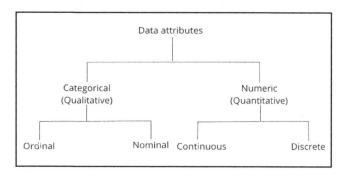

Figure 2.3: Types of data attributes

I want to give some examples of the different types of corpora. The examples are generalized, so you guys can understand the different type of data attributes.

Categorical or qualitative data attributes

Categorical or qualitative data attributes are as follows:

- These kinds of data attributes are more descriptive
- Examples are our written notes, corpora provided by `nltk`, a corpus that has recorded different types of breeds of dogs, such as collie, shepherd, and terrier

There are two sub-types of categorical data attributes:

- **Ordinal data**:
    - This type of data attribute is used to measure non-numeric concepts such as satisfaction level, happiness level, discomfort level, and so on.
    - Consider the following questions, for example, which you're to answer from the options given:
        - Question 1: How do you feel today?
        - Options for Question 1:
            - Very bad
            - Bad
            - Good
            - Happy
            - Very happy
        - Now you will choose any of the given options. Suppose you choose Good, nobody can convert how good you feel to a numeric value.
    - All the preceding options are non-numeric concepts. Hence, they lie under the category of ordinal data.
        - Question 2: How would you rate our hotel service?
        - Options for Question 2:
            - Bad
            - Average
            - Above average
            - Good
            - Great

- Now suppose you choose any of the given options. All the aforementioned options will measure your satisfaction level, and it is difficult to convert your answer to a numeric value because answers will vary from person to person.
- Because one person says Good and another person says Above average, there may be a chance that they both feel the same about the hotel service but give different responses. In simple words, you can say that the difference between one option and the other is unknown. So you can't precisely decide the numerical values for these kinds of data.

- **Nominal data**:
  - This type of data attribute is used to record data that doesn't overlap.
  - Example: What is your gender? The answer is either male or female, and the answers are not overlapping.
  - Take another example: What is the color of your eyes? The answer is either black, brown, blue, or gray. (By the way, we are not considering the color lenses available in the market!)

In NLP-related applications, we will mainly deal with categorical data attributes. So, to derive appropriate data points from a corpus that has categorical data attributes is part of feature engineering. We will see more on this in `Chapter 5`, *Feature Engineering and NLP Algorithms*.

Some corpora contain both sub-types of categorical data.

Numeric or quantitative data attributes

The following are numeric or quantitative data attributes:

- These kinds of data attributes are numeric and represent a measurable quantity
- Examples: Financial data, population of a city, weight of people, and so on

There are two sub-types of numeric data attributes:

- **Continuous data**:
  - These kinds of data attributes are continuous
  - Examples: If you are recording the weight of a student, from 10 to 12 years of age, whatever data you collect about the student's weight is continuous data; Iris flower corpus

- **Discrete data**:
  - Discrete data can only take certain values
  - Examples: If you are rolling two dice, you can only have the resultant values of 2, 3, 4, 5, 6, 7, 8, 9, 10, 11, and 12; you never get 1 or 1.5 as a result if you are rolling two dice
  - Take another example: If you toss a coin, you will get either heads or tails

These kinds of data attributes are a major part of analytics applications.

Exploring different file formats for corpora

Corpora can be in many different formats. In practice, we can use the following file formats. All these file formats are generally used to store features, which we will feed into our machine learning algorithms later. Practical stuff regarding dealing with the following file formats will be incorporated from Chapter 4, *Preprocessing* onward. Following are the aforementioned file formats:

- .txt: This format is basically given to us as a raw dataset. The gutenberg corpus is one of the example corpora. Some of the real-life applications have parallel corpora. Suppose you want to make Grammarly a kind of grammar correction software, then you will need a parallel corpus.
- .csv: This kind of file format is generally given to us if we are participating in some hackathons or on Kaggle. We use this file format to save our features, which we will derive from raw text, and the feature .csv file will be used to train our machines for NLP applications.
- .tsv: To understand this kind of file format usage, we will take an example. Suppose you want to make an NLP system that suggests where we should put a comma in a sentence. In this case, we cannot use the .csv file format to store our features because some of our feature attributes contain commas, and this will affect the performance when we start processing our feature file. You can also use any customized delimiter as well. You can put \t, ||, and so on for ease of further processing.
- .xml: Some well-known NLP parsers and tools provide results in the .xml format. For example, the Stanford CoreNLP toolkit provides parser results in the .xml format. This kind of file format is mainly used to store the results of NLP applications.
- .json: The Stanford CoreNLP toolkit provides its results in the .json format. This kind of file format is mainly used to store results of NLP applications, and it is easy to display and integrate with web applications.

- `LibSVM`: This is one of the special file formats. Refer to the following *Figure 2.4*:

```
-1 1:1 6:1 17:1 19:1 39:1 42:1 53:1 64:1 67:1 73:1 74:1 76:1 80:1 83:1
-1 2:1 6:1 18:1 20:1 37:1 42:1 48:1 64:1 71:1 73:1 74:1 76:1 81:1 83:1
+1 5:1 11:1 15:1 32:1 39:1 40:1 52:1 63:1 67:1 73:1 74:1 76:1 78:1 83:1
```

Figure 2.4: LibSVM file format example

- `LibSVM` allows for sparse training data. The non-zero values are the only ones that are included in the training dataset. Hence, the index specifies the column of the instance data (feature index). To convert from a conventional dataset, just iterate over the data, and if the value of `X(i,j)` is non-zero, print `j + 1`: `X(i,j)`.
- `X(i,j)`: This is a sparse matrix:
  - If the value of `X(i,j)` is equal to non-zero, include it in the `LibSVM` format
    - `j+1`: This is the value of `X(i,j)`, where `j` is the column index of the matrix starting with `0`, so we add `1`
  - Otherwise, do not include it in the `LibSVM` format
- Let's take the following example:
  - Example: 1 5:1 7:1 14:1 19:1
    - Here, *1* is the class or label
    - In the preceding example, let's focus on *5:1*, where *5* is the key, and *1* is the value; *5:1* is the key : value pair
    - *5* is the column number or data attribute number, which is the key and is in the `LibSVM` format; we are considering only those data columns that contain non-zero values, so here, *1* is the value
    - The values of parameters with indexes 1, 2, 3, 4, 6, and others unmentioned are 0s, so we are not including these in our example
- This kind of data format is used in Apache Spark to train your data, and you will learn how to convert text data to the `LibSVM` format from `Chapter 5`, *Feature Engineering and NLP Algorithms* onwards.

- **Customized format**: You can make your feature file using the customized file format. (Refer to the `CoNLL` dataset.) It is kind of a customized file format. There are many different `CoNLL` formats since `CoNLL` is a different shared task each year. *Figure 2.5* shows a data sample in the `CoNLL` format:

```
0              0        Both       DT (TOP(S(NP(NP*          -       -      -   speaker1        *     (ARG1*     (ARG2*        -
bc/msnbc/00/msnbc_0004   0     1  vehicles   NNS        *)         -       -      1  speaker1        *         *)          *       -
bc/msnbc/00/msnbc_0004   0     2     which   WDT (SBAR(WHNP*)      -       -      -   speaker1       *  (R-ARG1*)          *       -
bc/msnbc/00/msnbc_0004   0     3       are   VBP      (S(VP*      be      01      1  speaker1        *       (V*)          *       -
bc/msnbc/00/msnbc_0004   0     4   armored    JJ (ADJP*)))))       -       -      -  speaker1        *    (ARG2*)         *)       -
bc/msnbc/00/msnbc_0004   0     5       can    MD        (VP*       -       -      -  speaker1        *         * (ARGM-MOD*)       -
bc/msnbc/00/msnbc_0004   0     6     house    VB        (VP*   house      01      1  speaker1        *         *       (V*)       -
bc/msnbc/00/msnbc_0004   0     7        up    IN     (NP(QP*       -       -      -  speaker1 (CARDINAL*       *     (ARG1*       -
bc/msnbc/00/msnbc_0004   0     8        to    TO           *       -       -      -  speaker1        *         *          *       -
bc/msnbc/00/msnbc_0004   0     9    twenty    CD           *       -       -      -  speaker1        *         *          *       -
bc/msnbc/00/msnbc_0004   0    10      five    CD          *)       -       -      -  speaker1       *)         *          *       -
bc/msnbc/00/msnbc_0004   0    11   marines   NNS        *)))       -       -      -  speaker1        *         *         *)       -
bc/msnbc/00/msnbc_0004   0    12        /.     .         *))
```

Figure 2.5: Data sample in CoNLL format

Resources for accessing free corpora

Getting the corpus is a challenging task, but in this section, I will provide you with some of the links from which you can download a free corpus and use it to build NLP applications.

The `nltk` library provides some inbuilt `corpus`. To list down all the corpus names, execute the following commands:

```
import nltk.corpus
dir(nltk.corpus) # Python shell
print dir(nltk.corpus) # Pycharm IDE syntax
```

In *Figure 2.2*, you can see the output of the preceding code; the highlighted part indicates the name of the corpora that are already installed:

```
→  ~ python
Python 2.7.6 (default, Oct 26 2016, 20:30:19)
[GCC 4.8.4] on linux2
Type "help", "copyright", "credits" or "license" for more information.
>>> import nltk.corpus
>>> dir(nltk.corpus)
['AlignedCorpusReader', 'AlpinoCorpusReader', 'BNCCorpusReader', 'BracketParseCorpusReader', 'CHILDESCorpusReader', 'CMUDictCorpusReader', 'CategorizedBracket
ParseCorpusReader', 'CategorizedCorpusReader', 'CategorizedPlaintextCorpusReader', 'CategorizedSentencesCorpusReader', 'CategorizedTaggedCorpusReader', 'Chase
nCorpusReader', 'ChunkedCorpusReader', 'ComparativeSentencesCorpusReader', 'ConllChunkCorpusReader', 'ConllCorpusReader', 'CorpusReader', 'CrubadanCorpusReade
r', 'DependencyCorpusReader', 'EuroparlCorpusReader', 'FramenetCorpusReader', 'IEERCorpusReader', 'IPIPANCorpusReader', 'IndianCorpusReader', 'KNBCorpusReader
', 'LazyCorpusLoader', 'LinThesaurusCorpusReader', 'MTECorpusReader', 'MacMorphoCorpusReader', 'NKJPCorpusReader', 'NPSChatCorpusReader', 'NombankCorpusReader
', 'NonbreakingPrefixesCorpusReader', 'OpinionLexiconCorpusReader', 'PPAttachmentCorpusReader', 'PanLexLiteCorpusReader', 'Pl196xCorpusReader', 'PlaintextCorp
usReader', 'PortugueseCategorizedPlaintextCorpusReader', 'PropbankCorpusReader', 'ProsConsCorpusReader', 'RTECorpusReader', 'RegexpTokenizer', 'ReviewsCorpusR
eader', 'SemcorCorpusReader', 'SensevalCorpusReader', 'SentiSynset', 'SentiWordNetCorpusReader', 'SinicaTreebankCorpusReader', 'StringCategoryCorpusReader', '
SwadeshCorpusReader', 'SwitchboardCorpusReader', 'SyntaxCorpusReader', 'TEICorpusView', 'TaggedCorpusReader', 'TimitCorpusReader', 'TimitTaggedCorpusReader',
'ToolboxCorpusReader', 'TwitterCorpusReader', 'UdhrCorpusReader', 'UnicharsCorpusReader', 'VerbnetCorpusReader', 'WordListCorpusReader', 'WordNetCorpusReader'
, 'WordNetICCorpusReader', 'XMLCorpusReader', 'YCOECorpusReader', '_LazyModule__lazymodule_globals', '_LazyModule__lazymodule_import', '_LazyModule__lazymodul
e_init', '_LazyModule__lazymodule_loaded', '_LazyModule__lazymodule_locals', '_LazyModule__lazymodule_name', '__builtins__', '__doc__', '__file__', '__getattr
__', '__init__', '__lazymodule_loaded', '__module__', '__name__', '__package__', '__path__', '__repr__', '__setattr__', 'abc', 'alpino', 'brown', 'cess_cat',
'cess_esp', 'cmudict', 'comparative_sentences', 'comtrans', 'conll2000', 'conll2002', 'conll2007', 'crubadan', 'demo', 'dependency_treebank', 'find_corpus_fil
eids', 'floresta', 'framenet', 'framenet15', 'gazetteers', 'genesis', 'gutenberg', 'ieer', 'inaugural', 'indian', 'ipipan', 'jeita', 'knbc', 'lin_thesaurus',
'mac_morpho', 'machado', 'masc_tagged', 'movie_reviews', 'multext_east', 'names', 'nkjp', 'nombank', 'nombank_ptb', 'nonbreaking_prefixes', 'nps_chat', 'opini
on_lexicon', 'panlex_lite', 'perluniprops', 'pl196x', 'ppattach', 'product_reviews_1', 'product_reviews_2', 'propbank', 'propbank_ptb', 'pros_cons', 'ptb', 'q
c', 're', 'reader', 'reuters', 'rte', 'semcor', 'senseval', 'sentence_polarity', 'sentiwordnet', 'shakespeare', 'sinica_treebank', 'state_union', 'stopwords',
'subjectivity', 'swadesh', 'swadesh110', 'swadesh207', 'switchboard', 'tagged_treebank_para_block_reader', 'teardown_module', 'timit', 'timit_tagged', 'toolb
ox', 'treebank', 'treebank_chunk', 'treebank_raw', 'twitter_samples', 'udhr', 'udhr2', 'universal_treebanks', 'util', 'verbnet', 'webtext', 'wordnet', 'wordne
t_ic', 'words', 'ycoe']
>>>
```

Figure 2.2: List of all available corpora in nltk

If you guys want to use IDE to develop an NLP application using Python, you can use the PyCharm community version. You can follow its installation steps by clicking on the following URL: `https://github.com/jalajthanaki/NLPython/blob/master/ch2/Pycharm_installation_guide.md`

If you want to explore more corpus resources, take a look at *Big Data: 33 Brilliant and Free Data Sources for 2016*, Bernard Marr (`https://www.forbes.com/sites/bernardmarr/2016/02/12/big-data-35-brilliant-and-free-data-sources-for-2016/#53369cd5b54d`).

Until now, we have looked at a lot of basic stuff. Now let me give you an idea of how we can prepare a dataset for a natural language processing applications, which will be developed with the help of machine learning.

Preparing a dataset for NLP applications

In this section, we will look at the basic steps that can help you prepare a dataset for NLP or any data science applications. There are basically three steps for preparing your dataset, given as follows:

- Selecting data
- Preprocessing data
- Transforming data

Selecting data

Suppose you are working with world tech giants such as Google, Apple, Facebook, and so on. Then you could easily get a large amount of data, but if you are not working with giants and instead doing independent research or learning some NLP concepts, then how and from where can you get a dataset? First, decide what kind of dataset you need as per the NLP application that you want to develop. Also, consider the end result of the NLP application that you are trying to build. If you want to make a chatbot for the healthcare domain, you should not use a dialog dataset of banking customer care. So, understand your application or problem statement thoroughly.

You can use the following links to download free datasets:

`https://github.com/caesar0301/awesome-public-datasets.`

`https://www.kaggle.com/datasets.`

`https://www.reddit.com/r/datasets/.`

You can also use the Google Advanced Search feature, or you can use Python web scraping libraries such as `beautifulsoup` or `scrapy`.

After selecting the dataset as per the application, you can move on to the next step.

Preprocessing the dataset

In this step, we will do some basic data analysis, such as which attributes are available in the dataset. This stage has three sub-stages, and we will look at each of them. You will find more details about the preprocessing stage in `Chapter 4`, *Preprocessing*. Here, I'll give you just the basic information.

Formatting

In this step, generate the dataset format that you feel most comfortable working with. If you have a dataset in the JSON format and you feel that you are most comfortable working with CSV, then convert the dataset from JSON to CSV.

Cleaning

In this step, we clean the data. If the dataset has missing values, either delete that data record or replace it with the most appropriate nearest value. If you find any unnecessary data attributes, you can remove them as well. Suppose you are making a grammar correction system, then you can remove the mathematical equations from your dataset because your grammar correction application doesn't use equations.

Sampling

In this stage, you can actually try to figure out which of the available data attributes our present dataset has and which of the data attributes can be derived by us. We are also trying to figure out what the most important data attributes are as per our application. Suppose we are building a chatbot. We will then try to break down sentences into words so as to identify the keywords of the sentence. So, the word-level information can be derived from the sentence, and both word-level and sentence level information are important for the chatbot application. As such, we do not remove sentences, apart from junk sentences. Using sampling, we try to extract the best data attributes that represent the overall dataset very well.

Now we can look at the last stage, which is the transformation stage.

Transforming data

In this stage, we will apply some feature engineering techniques that help us convert the text data into numeric data so the machine can understand our dataset and try to find out the pattern in the dataset. So, this stage is basically a data manipulation stage. In the NLP domain, for the transformation stage, we can use some encoding and vectorization techniques. Don't get scared by the terminology. We will look at all the data manipulation techniques and feature extraction techniques in Chapter 5, *Feature Engineering and NLP Algorithms* and Chapter 6, *Advance Feature Engineering and NLP Algorithms*.

All the preceding stages are basic steps to prepare the dataset for any NLP or data science related applications. Now, let's see how you can generate data using web scraping.

Web scraping

To develop a web scraping tool, we can use libraries such as beautifulsoup and scrapy. Here, I'm giving some of the basic code for web scraping.

Take a look at the code snippet in *Figure 2.6,* which is used to develop a basic web scraper using beautifulsoup:

```
# Various ways to scrape the page here I'm using my own blog pages.

import requests
from bs4 import BeautifulSoup


def Get_the_page_by_beautibulsoup():
    page = requests.get("https://simplifydatascience.wordpress.com/about/")
    #print page.status_code
    #print page.content
    soup = BeautifulSoup(page.content, 'html.parser')
    #print soup()
    #print(soup.prettify()) #display source of the html page in readable format.
    soup = BeautifulSoup(page.content, 'html.parser')
    print soup.find_all('p')[0].get_text()
    print soup.find_all('p')[1].get_text()
    print soup.find_all('p')[2].get_text()
    print soup.find_all('p')[3].get_text()


if __name__ =="__main__":
    Get_the_page_by_beautibulsoup()
```

Figure 2.6: Basic web scraper tool using beautifulsoup

The following *Figure 2.7* demonstrates the output:

```
/usr/bin/python2.7 /home/jalaj/PycharmProjects/NLPython/NLPython/ch2/webscraping.py
/usr/local/lib/python2.7/dist-packages/requests/packages/urllib3/util/ssl_.py:334: SNIMissingWarning: An HTTPS request has been made, but the SNI (Subject Name Indication)
extension to TLS is not available on this platform. This may cause the server to present an incorrect TLS certificate, which can cause validation failures. You can upgrade to a
newer version of Python to solve this. For more information, see https://urllib3.readthedocs.io/en/latest/advanced-usage.html#ssl-warnings
  SNIMissingWarning

/usr/local/lib/python2.7/dist-packages/requests/packages/urllib3/util/ssl_.py:132: InsecurePlatformWarning: A true SSLContext object is not available. This prevents urllib3
from configuring SSL appropriately and may cause certain SSL connections to fail. You can upgrade to a newer version of Python to solve this. For more information, see https://
urllib3.readthedocs.io/en/latest/advanced-usage.html#ssl-warnings
  InsecurePlatformWarning

simplify data science
SDS
I'm data science researcher by practice and data scientist by profession. I like to deal with data science related problems. My research interest lies into Big Data Analytics ,
Natural Language Processing , Machine Learning  and Deep Learning.
I am still learning myself, but I found that writing posts and tutorials is the best way to deepen my own understanding and knowledge. On this platform, I'm sharing my
experiences and also coming up with tutorials for beginners and posting articles. I am happy to help in any way I can. So don't hesitate to get in touch!
```

Figure 2.7: Output of basic web scraper using beautifulsoup

You can find the installation guide for beautifulsoup and scrapy at this link:

```
https://github.com/jalajthanaki/NLPython/blob/master/ch2/Chapter_2_Installati
on_Commands.txt.
```

You can find the code at this link:

`https://github.com/jalajthanaki/NLPython/blob/master/ch2/2_2_Basic_webscrapin g_byusing_beautifulsuop.py`.

If you get any warning while running the script, it will be fine; don't worry about warnings.

Now, let's do some web scraping using `scrapy`. For that, we need to create a new scrapy project.

Follow the command to create the scrapy project. Execute the following command on your terminal:

```
$ scrapy startproject project_name
```

I'm creating a scrapy project with the `web_scraping_test` name; the command is as follows:

```
$ scrapy startproject web_scraping_test
```

Once you execute the preceding command, you can see the output as shown in *Figure 2.8*:

```
$ scrapy startproject web_scraping_test                                                    (master $) jalaj-System-Product-Name
New Scrapy project 'web_scraping_test', using template directory '/usr/local/lib/python2.7/dist-packages/scrapy/templates/project', created in:
    /home/jalaj/PycharmProjects/NLPython/NLPython/web_scraping_test

You can start your first spider with:
    cd web_scraping_test
    scrapy genspider example example.com
$                                                                                          (master $) jalaj-System-Product-Name
```

Figure 2.8: Output when you create a new scrapy project

After creating a project, perform the following steps:

1. Edit your `items.py` file, which has been created already.
2. Create the `WebScrapingTest spider` file inside the `spiders` directory.
3. Go to the website page that you want to scrape, and select `xpath` of the element. You can read more on the `xpath` selector by clicking at this link: `https://doc.scrapy.org/en/1.0/topics/selectors.html`

Take a look at the code snippet in *Figure 2.9*. Its code is available at the GitHub URL:

```
https://github.com/jalajthanaki/NLPython/tree/master/web_scraping_test
```

```python
# -*- coding: utf-8 -*-

# Define here the models for your scraped items
#
# See documentation in:
# http://doc.scrapy.org/en/latest/topics/items.html

import scrapy


class WebScrapingTestItem(scrapy.Item):
    title = scrapy.Field()
    url = scrapy.Field()
    pass
```

Figure 2.9: The items.py file where we have defined items we need to scrape

Figure 2.10 is used to develop a basic web scraper using `scrapy`:

```python
from scrapy import Spider
from scrapy.selector import Selector

class WebScrapingTestspider(Spider):
    name = "WebScrapingTestspider"
    allowed_domains = ["stackoverflow.com"]
    start_urls = [
        "http://stackoverflow.com/questions?pagesize=50&sort=newest",
    ]

    def parse(self, response):
        questions = Selector(response).xpath('//div[@class="summary"]/h3')

        for question in questions:
            item = dict()
            item['title'] = question.xpath(
                'a[@class="question-hyperlink"]/text()').extract()[0]
            item['url'] = question.xpath(
                'a[@class="question-hyperlink"]/@href').extract()[0]
            yield item

#Now you can run this by using following commands.
#$ cd web_scraping_test/web_scraping_test
#If you what to export data in csv format execute the following command
#$ scrapy crawl WebScrapingTestspider -o result.csv -t csv
```

Figure 2.10: Spider file containing actual code

Figure 2.11 demonstrates the output, which is in the form of a CSV file:

```
url,title
/questions/43223545/what-should-be-my-application-type-in-google-console-if-i-am-working-on-a-cordov,What should be my application type in google consol
/questions/43223543/drop-values-saved-comma-separated-in-a-cell-in-excel,Drop values saved comma separated in a cell in excel
/questions/43223541/android-using-incompatible-plugins-for-the-annotation-processing,Android Using incompatible plugins for the annotation processing
/questions/43223536/in-python3-what-is-called-when-a-number-is-referenced,"In python3, what is called when a number is referenced?"
/questions/43223535/how-to-send-message-to-skpe-user-from-chatbot,How to send message to skpe user from chatbot
/questions/43223534/how-to-use-session-to-avoid-some-user-to-view-some-pages,how to use session to avoid some user to view some pages?
/questions/43223533/how-to-do-auto-verify-otp-like-whatsup-in-recharge-app-in-ionic2,How to do auto verify OTP like Whats'up in Recharge App in IONIC2
/questions/43223531/how-can-i-install-librados-on-mac-osx,How can I install librados on mac osx?
/questions/43223528/how-do-i-retrieve-links-inside-a-href-from-a-page-and-show-on-rails-page,How do I retrieve links inside <a href> from a page and sho
/questions/43223526/rest-post-http-json-objects-400-error-android,REST POST HTTP JSON Objects 400 error Android
/questions/43223525/how-to-add-fixed-header-and-footer-to-each-pdf-page-using-jspdf,How to add fixed header and footer to each pdf page using jspdf ..?
/questions/43223521/how-to-design-email-template,How to design Email Template
/questions/43223520/how-to-manage-multiple-database-schema-from-simple-docker,How to manage multiple database schema from simple docker?
/questions/43223515/faceted-search-with-a-sample,Faceted search with a sample
```

Figure 2.11: Output of scraper is redirected to a CSV file

If you get any SSL-related warnings, refer to the answer at this link:

```
https://stackoverflow.com/questions/29134512/insecureplatformwarning-a-true-ssl
context-object-is-not-available-this-prevent
```

You can develop a web scraper that bypasses AJAX and scripts, but you need to be very careful when you do this because you need to keep in mind that you are not doing anything unethical. So, here, we are not going to cover the part on bypassing AJAX and scripts and scraping data. Out of curiosity, you can search on the web how people actually do this. You can use the `Selenium` library to do automatic clicking to perform web events.

Summary

In this chapter, we saw that a corpus is the basic building block for NLP applications. We also got an idea about the different types of corpora and their data attributes. We touched upon the practical analysis aspects of a corpus. We used the `nltk` API to make corpus analysis easy.

In the next chapter, we will address the basic and effective aspects of natural language using linguistic concepts such as parts of speech, lexical items, and tokenization, which will further help us in preprocessing and feature engineering.

3
Understanding the Structure of a Sentences

In this chapter, we'll explore the basic concepts of NLP. This chapter is the most important chapter, as it helps to make your foundation strong.

We are going to cover the following topics to improve your understanding of the basic NLP concepts, which will help understand the next chapter:

- Understanding the components of NLP
- What is context-free grammar?
- Morphological analysis
- Lexical analysis
- Syntactic analysis
- Semantic analysis
- Handling ambiguity
- Discourse integration
- Pragmatic analysis

Understanding components of NLP

There are two major components of NLP. We are going to understand both of them.

Natural language understanding

Let's learn about natural language understanding:

- **Natural language understanding** (**NLU**) is considered the first component of NLP
- NLU is considered an **Artificial Intelligence-Hard** (**AI-Hard**) problem or **Artificial Intelligence-Complete** (**AI-Complete**) problem
- NLU is considered an AI-Hard problem because we are trying to make a computer as intelligent as a human
- NLU is hard, but nowadays, tech giants and research communities are improvising traditional Machine Learning algorithms and applying various types of deep neural network that will help to achieve the goal (computers can also have the intelligence to process **natural language** (**NL**))
- NLU is defined as the process of converting NL input into useful a representation by using computational linguistics tools
- NLU requires the following analysis to convert NL into a useful representation:
  - Morphological analysis
  - Lexical analysis
  - Syntactic analysis
  - Semantic analysis
  - Handling ambiguity
  - Discourse integration
  - Pragmatic analysis

In this book, we will focus on NLU and develop an NLP-based system that uses NLU representation.

Natural language generation

Let's learn about **natural language generation** (**NLG**):

- NLG is considered the second component of NLP.
- NLG is defined as the process of generating NL by a machine as output.

- The output of the machine should be in a logical manner, meaning, whatever NL is generated by the machine should be logical.
- In order to generate logical output, many NLG systems use basic facts or knowledge-based representation.
- Let's take an example. You have a system that writes an essay on a particular topic. If I am instructing my machine to generate 100 words on the topic of **The Cows**, and my machine generates 100 words on the topic of cows, then the output (here, 100 words about cows) generated by the machine should be in form of valid sentences, all sentences should be logically correct, and the context should also make sense.

Differences between NLU and NLG

In this section, we are looking at the differences between NLU and NLG:

NLU	NLG
This component helps to explain the meaning behind the NL, whether it is written text or in speech format. We can analyze English, French, Spanish, Hindi, or any other human language.	This component helps to generate the NL using machines.
NLU generates facts from NL by using various tools and techniques, such as POS tagger, parsers, and so on, in order to develop NLP applications.	NLG start from facts like POS tags, parsing results, and so on to generate the NL.
It is the process of reading and interpreting language.	It is the process of writing or generating language.

Branches of NLP

NLP involves two major branches that help us to develop NLP applications. One is computational, the **Computer Science** branch, and the other one is the **Linguistics** branch.

Refer to *Figure 3.1*:

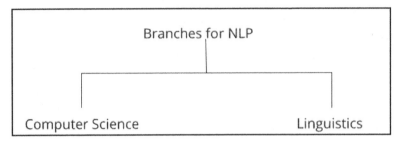

Figure 3.1: Branches of NLP

The **Linguistics** branch focuses on how NL can be analyzed using various scientific techniques. So, the **Linguistics** branch does scientific analysis of the form, meaning, and context.

All linguistics analysis can be implemented with the help of computer science techniques. We can use the analysis and feed elements of analysis in a machine learning algorithm to build an NLP application. Here, the machine learning algorithm is a part of **Computer Science**, and the analysis of language is **Linguistics**.

Computational linguistics is a field that helps you to understand both computer science and linguistics approaches together.

Here is a list of tools that are linguistics concepts and are implemented with the help of computer science techniques. These tools are often used for developing NLP applications:

- For POS tagging, POS taggers are used. Famous libraries are `nltk` and `pycorenlp`.
- Morph analyzers are used to generate word-level stemming. For this, the `nltk` and `polyglot` libraries are used.
- Parsers are used to identify the structure of the sentences. For this, we are using Stanford CoreNLP and `nltk` to generate a parsing tree. You can use Python package called `spaCy`.

Defining context-free grammar

Now let's focus on NLU, and to understand it, first we need to understand **context-free grammar** (**CFG**) and how it is used in NLU.

Context-free grammar is defined by its four main components. Those four components are shown in this symbolic representation of CFG:

- A set of non-terminal symbols, **N**
- A set of terminal symbols, **T**
- A start symbol, **S**, which is a non-terminal symbol
- A set of rules called **production rules P**, for generating sentences

Let's take an example to get better understanding of the context-free grammar terminology:

$X \rightarrow \propto$

Here, **X->** $\propto$ is called the **phrase structure rule** or **production rule**, **P**. $X \, \varepsilon \, N$ means X belongs to non-terminal symbol; $\propto \, \varepsilon \, \{N$ or $T\}$ means $\propto$ belongs to either terminal symbols or non-terminal symbols. X can be rewritten in the form of $\propto$. The rule tells you which element can be rewritten to generate a sentence, and what the order of the elements will be as well.

Now I will take a real NLP example. I'm going to generate a sentence using CFG rules. We are dealing with simple sentence structure to understand the concepts.

Let's think. What are the basic elements required to generate grammatically correct sentences in English? Can you remember them? Think!

I hope you remember that noun phrases and verb phrases are important elements of the sentences. So, start from there. I want to generate the following sentence:

He likes cricket.

In order to generate the preceding sentence, I'm proposing the following production rules:

- R1: S -> NP VP
- R2: NP -> N
- R3: NP -> Det N
- R4: VP -> V NP
- R5: VP -> V
- R6: N -> Person Name | He | She | Boy | Girl | It | cricket | song | book
- R7: V -> likes | reads | sings

See the parse tree of the sentence: **He likes cricket**, in *Figure 3.2*:

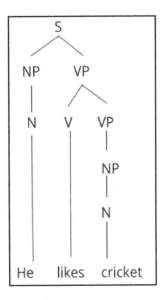

Figure 3.2: Parse tree for the sentence using the production rule

Now, let's know how we have generated a parse tree:

- According to the production rules, we can see **S** can be rewritten as a combination of a **noun phrase (NP)** and a **verb phrase (VP)**; see rule *R1*.
- **NP** can be further rewritten as either a **noun (NN)** or as a **determiner (Det)** followed by a noun; see rules *R2* and *R3*.
- Now you can rewrite the **VP** in form of a **verb (V)** followed by a **NP**, or a **VP** can be rewritten as just **V**; see rules *R4* and *R5*.
- Here, **N** can be rewritten in the form of **Person Name, He, She**, and so on. **N** is a terminal symbol; see the rule *R6*.
- **V** can be rewritten by using any of the options on the right-hand side in rule *R7*. **V** is also terminal symbol.

By using all the rules, we have generated the parse tree in *Figure 3.2*.

Don't worry if you cannot generate a parse tree. We will see the concept and implementation details in the `Chapter 5`, *Feature Engineering and NLP Algorithms*.

Here, we have seen a very basic and simple example of CFG. Context-free grammar is also called **phrase structure grammar**.

Exercise

1. Generate a parse tree by using the rule given previously in this section and generate the parse tree for the following sentence:
   She sings a song.
2. Generate production rules and make a parse tree for the following sentence:
   That boy is reading a book.

Morphological analysis

Here, we are going to explore the basic terminology used in field of morphological analysis. The terminology and concepts will help you when you are solving real-life problems.

What is morphology?

Morphology is branch of linguistics that studies how words can be structured and formed.

What are morphemes?

In linguistics, a morpheme is the smallest meaningful unit of a given language. The important part of morphology is morphemes, which are the basic unit of morphology.

Let's take an example. The word *boy* consists of single morpheme whereas *boys* consists of two morphemes; one is *boy* and the other morpheme *-s*

What is a stem?

The part of a word that an affix is attached to is called as **stem**. The word *tie* is **root** whereas *Untie* is **stem.**

Now, let's understand morphological analysis.

What is morphological analysis?

Morphological analysis is defined as grammatical analysis of how words are formed by using morphemes, which are the minimum unit of meaning.

Generally, morphemes are affixes. Those affixes can be divided into four types:

- Prefixes, which appear before a stem, such as **un**happy
- Suffixes, which appear after a stem, such as happ**iness**
- Infixes, which appear inside a stem, such as b**um**ili (this means buy in Tagalog, a language from the Philippines)
- Circumfixes surround a word. It is attached to the beginning and end of the stem. For example, **ka**baddang**an** (this means help in Tuwali Ifugao, another language from the Philippines)

Morphological analysis is used in word segmentation, and **Part Of Speech** (**POS**) tagging uses this analysis. I will explain about POS in the *Lexical analysis* section, so bear with me until we will connect the dots.

Let's take an example to practically explain the concepts that I have proposed. I would like to take the word **Unexpected**. Refer to *Figure 3.3*, which gives you an idea about the morphemes and how morphological analysis has taken place:

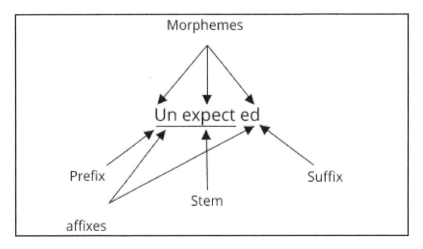

Figure 3.3: Morphemes and morphological analysis

In *Figure 3.3*, we have expressed **Unexpected** as morphemes and performed morphological analysis the morphemes. Here, **Un** is a **Prefix**, and **ed** is a **Suffix**. **Un** and **ed** can be considered as **affixes**, **Unexpect** is the **Stem**.

Let's refer to another important concept and try to relate it to the concept of morphemes. I'm talking about how you define a word. Let's see.

What is a word?

A word can be isolated from a sentence as the single smallest element of a sentence that carries meaning. This smallest single isolated part of a sentence is called a **word**.

Please refer to the morphemes definition again and try to relate it to the definition of word. The reason why I have told you to do this is that you may confuse words and morphemes, or maybe you are not sure what the difference is between them. It is completely fine that you have thought in this way. They are confusing if you do not understand them properly.

The definitions look similar, but there is a very small difference between words and morphemes. We can see the differences in the following table:

Morpheme	Word
Morphemes can or cannot stand alone. The word *cat* can stand alone but plural marker *-s* cannot stand alone. Here *cat* and *-s* both are morpheme.	A word can stand alone. So, words are basically free-standing units in sentences.
When a morpheme stands alone then that morpheme is called **root** because it conveys the meaning of its own, otherwise morpheme mostly takes affixes. The analysis of what kind of affixes morpheme will take is covered under morphological analysis.	A word can consist of a single morpheme.
For example, *cat* is a standalone morpheme, but when you consider *cats*, then the suffix *-s* is there, which conveys the information that *cat* is one morpheme and the suffix *-s* indicates the grammatical information that the given morpheme is the plural form of *cat*.	For example: *Cat* is a standalone word. *Cats* is also a standalone word.

Classification of morphemes

The classification of morphemes gives us lots of information about how the whole concept of morphological analysis works. Refer to *Figure 3.4*:

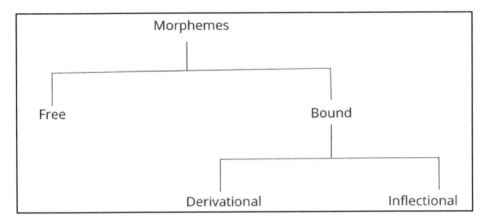

Figure 3.4: Classification of morphemes

There two major part of morphemes.

Free morphemes

Free morphemes can be explained as follows:

- Free morphemes can stand alone and act as a word. They are also called **unbound morphemes** or **free-standing morphemes**.
- Let's see some of examples:
    - Dog, cats, town, and house.
    - All the preceding words can be used with other words as well. Free morphemes can appear with other words as well. These kinds of words convey meaning that is different if you see the words individually.
        - Let's see examples of that:
            - Doghouse, town hall.
            - Here, the meaning of doghouse is different from the individual meanings of dog and house. The same applies to town hall.

Bound morphemes

Bound morphemes usually take affixes. They are further divided into two classes.

Derivational morphemes

Derivational morphemes are identified when infixes combine with the root and changes either the semantic meaning.

Now, let's look at some examples:

- Take the word **unkind**. In this word, **un** is a prefix and **kind** is the root. The prefix **un** acts as a derivational morpheme that changes the meaning of the word **kind** to its opposite meaning, unkind.
- Take the word **happiness**. In this word, -**ness** is a derivational morpheme and **happy** is the root word. So, -**ness** changes happy to happiness. Check the POS tag, **happy** is an adjective and **happiness** is a noun. Here, tags that indicate the class of word, such as adjective and noun, are called POS.

Inflectional morphemes

Inflection morphemes are suffixes that are added to a word to assign particular grammatical property to that word. Inflectional morphemes are considered to be grammatical markers that indicate tense, number, POS, and so on. So, in more simple language, we can say that inflectional morphemes are identified as types of morpheme that modify the verb tense, aspect, mood, person, number (singular and plural), gender, or case, without affecting the words meaning or POS.

Here's some examples:

- In the word **dogs**, -**s** changes the number of **dog**. -**s** converts **dog** from singular to plural form of it
- The word **expected** contains -**ed**, which is an inflectional morpheme that modifies the verb tense

Here is the code for generating the stem from morphemes. We are using the nltk and polyglot libraries. You can find the code on this link:
https://github.com/jalajthanaki/NLPython/blob/master/ch3/3_1_wordsteam.py

See the code snippets in *Figure 3.5* and *Figure 3.6*:

```python
from nltk.stem import PorterStemmer
from polyglot.text import Text, Word

word = "unexpected"
text = "disagreement"
text1 = "disagree"
text2 = "agreement"
text3 = "quirkiness"
text4 = "historical"
text5 = "canonical"
text6 = "happiness"
text7 = "unkind"
text8 = "dogs"
text9 = "expected"
words_derv = ["happiness", "unkind"]
word_infle = ["dogs", "expected"]
words = ["unexpected", "disagreement", "disagree", "agreement", "quirkiness", "canonical" "historical"]

def stemmer_porter():
    port = PorterStemmer()
    print "\nDerivational Morphemes"
    print " ".join([port.stem(i) for i in text6.split()])
    print " ".join([port.stem(i) for i in text7.split()])
    print "\nInflectional  Morphemes"
    print " ".join([port.stem(i) for i in text8.split()])
    print " ".join([port.stem(i) for i in text9.split()])
    print "\nSome examples"
    print " ".join([port.stem(i) for i in word.split()])
    print " ".join([port.stem(i) for i in text.split()])
    print " ".join([port.stem(i) for i in text1.split()])
    print " ".join([port.stem(i) for i in text2.split()])
    print " ".join([port.stem(i) for i in text3.split()])
    print " ".join([port.stem(i) for i in text4.split()])
    print " ".join([port.stem(i) for i in text5.split()])
```

Figure 3.5: Generating stems from morphemes using NLTK

Now, let's see how the `polyglot` library has been used refer to *Figure 3.6*:

```python
def polygolt_stem():
    print "\nDerivational Morphemes using polyglot library"
    for w in words_derv:
        w = Word(w, language="en")
        print("{:<20}{}".format(w, w.morphemes))
    print "\nInflectional Morphemes using polyglot library"
    for w in word_infle:
        w = Word(w, language="en")
        print("{:<20}{}".format(w, w.morphemes))
    print "\nSome Morphemes examples using polyglot library"
    for w in word_infle:
        w = Word(w, language="en")
        print("{:<20}{}".format(w, w.morphemes))


if __name__ == "__main__":
    stemmer_porter()
    polygolt_stem()
```

Figure 3.6: Generating stems from morphemes using the polyglot library

The output of the code snippet is displayed in *Figure 3.7*:

```
Derivational Morphemes
happi
unkind

Inflectional   Morphemes
dog
expect

Some examples
unexpect
disagr
disagre
agreement
quirki
histor
canon

Derivational Morphemes using polyglot library
happiness              ['happi', 'ness']
unkind                 ['un', 'kind']

Inflectional Morphemes using polyglot library
dogs                   ['dog', 's']
expected               ['expect', 'ed']

Some Morphemes examples using polyglot library
dogs                   ['dog', 's']
expected               ['expect', 'ed']
```

Figure 3.7: Output of code snippets in Figure 3.5 and Figure 3.6

What is the difference between a stem and a root?

This could be explained as follows:

Stem	Root
In order to generate a stem, we need to remove affixes from the word	A root cannot be further divided into smaller morphemes
From the stem, we can generate the root by further dividing it	A stem is generated by using a root plus derivational morphemes
The word **Untie** is stem	The word **tie** is root

Exercise

1. Do a morphological analysis like we did in *Figure 3.3* for the morphemes in redness, quickly, teacher, unhappy, and disagreement. Define prefixes, suffixes, verbs, and stems.
2. Generate the stems of the words redness, quickly, teacher, disagreement, reduce, construction, deconstruction, and deduce using the `nltk` and `polyglot` libraries.
3. Generate the stems and roots of disagree, disagreement, historical.

Lexical analysis

Lexical analysis is defined as the process of breaking down a text into words, phrases, and other meaningful elements. Lexical analysis is based on word-level analysis. In this kind of analysis, we also focus on the meaning of the words, phrases, and other elements, such as symbols.

Sometimes, lexical analysis is also loosely described as the **tokenization process**. So, before discussing tokenization, let's understand what a token is and what a POS tag is.

What is a token?

Tokens are defined as the meaningful elements that are generated by using techniques of lexical analysis.

What are part of speech tags?

A part of speech is a category of words or lexical items that have similar grammatical properties. Words belonging to the same **part of speech** (**POS**) category have similar behavior within the grammatical structure of sentences.

In English, POS categories are verb, noun, adjective, adverb, pronoun, preposition, conjunction, interjection, and sometimes numeral, article, or determiner.

Process of deriving tokens

Sentences are formed by stream of words and from a sentence we need to derive individual meaningful chunks which are called the **tokens** and process of deriving token is called **tokenization**:

- The process of deriving tokens from a stream of text has two stages. If you have a lot of paragraphs, then first you need to do sentence tokenization, then word tokenization, and generate the meaning of the tokens.
- Tokenization and lemmatization are processes that are helpful for lexical analysis. Using the `nltk` library, we can perform tokenization and lemmatization.
- Tokenization can be defined as identifying the boundary of sentences or words.
- Lemmatization can be defined as a process that identifies the correct intended POS and meaning of words that are present in sentences.
- Lemmatization also includes POS tagging to disambiguate the meaning of the tokens. In this process, the context window is either phrase level or sentence level.

You can find the code at the GitHub link:
`https://github.com/jalajthanaki/NLPython/tree/master/ch3`

The code snippet is shown in *Figure 3.8*:

```
from nltk.tokenize import word_tokenize
from nltk.stem.wordnet import WordNetLemmatizer

def wordtokenization():
    content = """Stemming is funnier than a bummer says the sushi loving computer scientist.
    She really wants to buy cars. She told me angrily. It is better for you.
    Man is walking. We are meeting tomorrow. You really don't know..!"""
    print word_tokenize(content)

def wordlemmatization():
    wordlemma = WordNetLemmatizer()
    print wordlemma.lemmatize('cars')
    print wordlemma.lemmatize('walking',pos='v')
    print wordlemma.lemmatize('meeting',pos='n')
    print wordlemma.lemmatize('meeting',pos='v')
    print wordlemma.lemmatize('better',pos='a')
    print wordlemma.lemmatize('is',pos='v')
    print wordlemma.lemmatize('funnier',pos='a')
    print wordlemma.lemmatize('expected',pos='v')
    print wordlemma.lemmatize('fantasized',pos='v')

if __name__ =="__main__":
    wordtokenization()
    print "\n"
    print "---------Word Lemmatization----------"
    wordlemmatization()
```

Figure 3.8: Code snippet for tokenization

The output of the code in *Figure 3.8* is shown in *Figure 3.9*:

```
['Stemming', 'is', 'funnier', 'than', 'a', 'bummer', 'says', 'the', 'sushi', 'loving', 'computer',
'scientist', '.', 'She', 'really', 'wants', 'to', 'buy', 'cars', '.', 'She', 'told', 'me', 'angrily', '.', 'It', 'is',
'better', 'for', 'you', '.', 'Man', 'is', 'walking', '.', 'We', 'are', 'meeting', 'tomorrow', '.', 'You',
'really', 'do', 'n't', 'know..', '!']
---------Word Lemmatization----------
car
walk
meeting
meet
good
be
funny
expect
fantasize
```

Figure 3.9: Output of tokenization and lemmatization

Difference between stemming and lemmatization

Stemming and lemmatization both of these concepts are used to normalized the given word by removing infixes and consider its meaning. The major difference between these is as shown:

Stemming	Lemmatization
Stemming usually operates on single word without knowledge of the context	Lemmatization usually considers words and the context of the word in the sentence
In stemming, we do not consider POS tags	In lemmatization, we consider POS tags
Stemming is used to group words with a similar basic meaning together	Lemmatization concept is used to make dictionary or WordNet kind of dictionary.

Applications

You must think how this lexical analysis has been used for developing NLP applications. So, here we have listed some of the NLP applications which uses lexical analysis concepts:

- Lexical analysis such as sentence tokenization and stop word identification is often used in preprocessing.
- Lexical analysis also used to develop a POS tagger. A POS tagger is a tool that generates POS tags for a stream of text.

Syntactic analysis

We have seen word-level analysis in lexical analysis. In this section, we will look at things from a higher level. We are going to focus on the grammar and structure of sentences by considering the phrases in the sentences.

Now, let's define syntactic analysis and see how it will be used in NLP applications.

What is syntactic analysis?

Syntactic analysis is defined as analysis that tells us the logical meaning of certain given sentences or parts of those sentences. We also need to consider rules of grammar in order to define the logical meaning as well as correctness of the sentences.

Let's take an example: If I'm considering English and I have a sentence such as **School go a boy**, this sentence does not logically convey its meaning, and its grammatical structure is not correct. So, syntactic analysis tells us whether the given sentence conveys its logical meaning and whether its grammatical structure is correct.

Syntactic analysis is a well-developed area of NLP that deals with the syntax of NL. In syntactic analysis, grammar rules have been used to determine which sentences are legitimate. The grammar has been applied in order to develop a parsing algorithm to produce a structure representation or a parse tree.

Here, I will generate the parse tree by using the `nltk` and Python wrapper libraries for Stanford CoreNLP called `pycorenlp`. Refer the following code snippet in *Figure 3.10* and in *Figure 3.11*. The output is given in *Figure 3.12*:

```python
# This script is for generating parsing tree by using NLTK.
# We are using python wrapper for stanford CoreNLP called-"pycorenlp" to generate Parsing result for us.
# NLTK gives us tree representation of stanford parser.
import nltk
from nltk import CFG
from nltk.tree import *
from pycorenlp import StanfordCoreNLP
from collections import defaultdict

# Part 1: Define a grammar and generate parse result using NLTK
def definegrammar_pasrereult():
    Grammar = nltk.CFG.fromstring("""
    S -> NP VP
    PP -> P NP
    NP -> Det N | Det N PP | 'I'
    VP -> V NP | VP PP
    Det -> 'an' | 'my'
    N -> 'elephant' | 'pajamas'
    V -> 'shot'
    P -> 'in'
    """)
    sent = "I shot an elephant".split()
    parser = nltk.ChartParser(Grammar)
    trees = parser.parse(sent)
    for tree in trees:
        print tree

# Part 2: Draw the parse tree
def draw_parser_tree():
    dp1 = Tree('dp', [Tree('d', ['the']), Tree('np', ['dog'])])
    dp2 = Tree('dp', [Tree('d', ['the']), Tree('np', ['cat'])])
    vp = Tree('vp', [Tree('v', ['chased']), dp2])
    tree = Tree('s', [dp1, vp])
    print(tree)
    print(tree.pformat_latex_qtree())
```

Figure 3.10: Code snippet for syntactic analysis

How you can use Stanford parser for syntactic analysis is demonstrated in next *Figure 3.11*:

```
# Part 3: Stanford parser wrapper library "pycorenlp"
# you need to install pycorenlp as well as you need to download stanford-corenlp-full-* from standford corenlp website.
def stanford_parsing_result():
    text ="""" I shot an elephant. The dog chased the cat. School go to boy. """
    nlp = StanfordCoreNLP('http://localhost:9000')
    res = nlp.annotate(text, properties={
        'annotators': 'tokenize,ssplit,pos,depparse,parse',
        'outputFormat': 'json'
    })
    print(res['sentences'][0]['parse'])
    print(res['sentences'][2]['parse'])


if __name__ == "__main__":
    print "\n--------Parsing result as per defined grammar-------"
    definegrammar_pasrereult()
    print "\n--------Drawing Parse Tree-------"
    draw_parser_tree()
    print "\n--------Stanford Parser result------"
    stanford_parsing_result()
```

Figure 3.11: Code snippet for syntactic analysis

You can see the output of the preceding two code snippet as follows. Refer to *Figure 3.12*:

```
--------Parsing result as per defined grammar-------
(S (NP I) (VP (V shot) (NP (Det an) (N elephant))))

--------Drawing Parse Tree-------
(s (dp (d the) (np dog)) (vp (v chased) (dp (d the) (np cat))))
\Tree [.s
        [.dp [.d the ] [.np dog ] ]
        [.vp [.v chased ] [.dp [.d the ] [.np cat ] ] ] ]
                    s
            _____|_____
            |            vp
            |        ____|___
            dp       |       dp
          __|__      |     __|__
          d    np    v     d    np
          |    |     |     |    |
         the  dog chased the  cat


--------Stanford Parser result------
(ROOT
  (S
    (NP (PRP I))
    (VP (VBD shot)
      (NP (DT an) (NN elephant)))
    (. .)))
(ROOT
  (S
    (NP (NNP School))
    (VP (VB go)
      (PP (TO to)
        (NP (NN boy))))
    (. .)))
```

Figure 3.12: Output of parsing as part of syntactic analysis

We will see the parsing tools and its development cycle related details in `Chapter 5`, *Feature Engineering and NLP Algorithms*.

Semantic analysis

Semantic analysis is basically focused on the meaning of the NL. Its definition, various elements of it, and its application are explored in this section.

Now let's begin our semantic journey, which is quite interesting if you want to do some cool research in this branch.

What is semantic analysis?

Semantic analysis is generating representation for meaning of the NL. You might think, if lexical analysis also focuses on the meaning of the words given in stream of text, then what is the difference between semantic analysis and lexical analysis? The answer is that lexical analysis is based on smaller tokens; its focus is on meaning of the words, but semantic analysis focuses on larger chunks. Semantic analysis can be performed at the phrase level, sentence level, paragraph level, and sometimes at the document level as well. Semantic analysis can be divided into two parts, as follows:

- The study of the meaning of the individual word is called **lexical semantics**
- The study of how individual words combine to provide meaning in sentences or paragraphs in the context of dealing with a larger unit of NL

I want to give an example. If you have a sentence such as the **white house is great**, this can mean the statement is in context of the White House in the USA, whereas it is also possible the statement is literally talking about a house nearby, whose color is white is great. So, getting the proper meaning of the sentence is the task of semantic analysis.

Lexical semantics

Lexical semantics includes words, sub-words, or sub-units such as affixes, and even compound words, and phrases. Here words, sub-words and so on called **lexical items**.

The study of lexical semantics includes the following points:

- Classification of lexical items
- Decomposition of lexical items
- Differences and similarities between various lexical semantic structures
- Lexical semantics is the relationship among lexical items, meaning of the sentences and syntax of the sentence

Let's see the various elements that are part of semantic analysis.

Hyponymy and hyponyms

Hyponymy describes the relationship between a generic term and instances of the specified generic term. Here, a generic term is called a **hypernym**, and instances of the generic term are called **hyponyms**.

So, color is a hypernym; red, green, yellow, and so on are hyponyms.

Homonymy

Homonyms are words that have a same syntax or same spelling or same form but their meaning are different and unrelated to each other.

The word bank is a classic example. It can mean a financial institution or a river bank, among other things.

Polysemy

In order to understand polysemy, we are focused on words of the sentences. Polysemy is a word or phrase which have different, but related senses. These kinds of words are also referred as lexically ambiguous words.

Take the word bank. There are several senses or meaning you can consider.

- Bank is financial institution
- Bank can be interpreted as river bank

What is the difference between polysemy and homonymy?

A word is called **polysemous** if it is used to express different meanings. The difference between the meanings of the word can be obvious.

Two or more words are called **homonyms** if they either have the same sound or have the same spelling but do not have related meanings.

Application of semantic analysis

Semantic analysis is one of the open research area so its basic concepts can be used by following applications:

- Word sense disambiguation is one of the major tasks in NLP where semantic analysis has been heavily used, and it's still an open research area for Indian languages
- We will see **word sense disambiguation (WSD)** usage in Chapter 7, *Rule-Based System for NLP*
- The word2vec concept has emerged to handle semantic similarity. We will see this in Chapter 6, *Advance Feature Engineering and NLP Algorithms*

Handling ambiguity

When we jump into semantic analysis, we may find there are many cases that are too ambiguous for an NLP system to handle. In these cases, we need to know what kinds of ambiguity exist and how we can handle them.

Ambiguity is one of the areas of NLP and cognitive sciences that doesn't have a well-defined solution. Sometimes, sentences are so complex and ambiguous that only the speaker can define the original or definite meaning of the sentence.

A word, phrase, or sentence is ambiguous if it has more than one meaning. If we consider word **light**, than it can mean not very heavy or not very dark. This is word level ambiguity. The phrase **porcelain egg container** is structure level ambiguity. So, here we will see different types of ambiguities in NLP .

First, let's see the types of ambiguity, and then see how to handle them by using the means that are available. Refer to *Figure 3.13* for the different types of ambiguity:

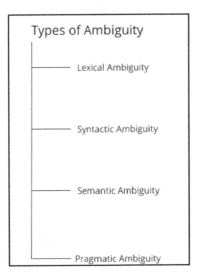

Figure 3.13: Types of ambiguity

Lexical ambiguity

Lexical ambiguity is word-level ambiguity. A single word can have ambiguous meaning in terms of its internal structure and its syntactic class. Let's look at some examples:

- Sentence 1: Look at the stars. Here, *look* is a verb.
- Sentence 2: The person gave him a warm look. Here, *look* is a noun.
- Sentence 3: She won three silver medals. Here, *silver* is a noun.
- Sentence 4: She made silver speech. Here, *silver* is a adjective.
- Sentence 5: His stress had silvered his hair. Here, *silvered* is a verb.

In the preceding examples, specific words change their POS tags according to their usage in sentence structure. This kind of ambiguity can been resolved by using two approaches:

- By using accurate POS tagger tools, this kind of ambiguity can be resolved
- WordNet sense has various scenes available for a word when the words take specific POS tag. This also helps to handle ambiguity

Many Indian languages have the same issue of lexical ambiguity.

Syntactic ambiguity

We have seen, in syntactic analysis, sequences of words are grammatically structured. There are different ways of interpreting sequences of words, and each structure has a different interpretation. In syntactic ambiguity, syntax is unclear, not the word-level meaning. Here is an example of structural ambiguity:

- The man saw the girl with the telescope. Here, the ambiguity is because it is not clear whether the man sees the girl, who has a telescope, or the man sees the girl by using telescope. This ambiguity is called **prepositional phrase (PP)** ambiguity.

Approach to handle syntactic ambiguity

To handle this ambiguity, we need to use statistical approaches and get the most likelihood ratio. We need to take co-occurrences between the verb and the preposition in one hand, and preposition and the noun on other hand, and then calculate the log-likelihood ratio by using following equation:

$$F(v,n,p) = log\frac{p(p/v)}{p(p/n)}$$

Figure 3.14: Log-likelihood ratio

Here, $p(p/v)$ is the probability of seeing a PP with preposition p and after verb v.

And $p(p/n)$ is the probability of seeing a PP with preposition p after noun n.

If $F(v,p,n) < 0$, then we need to attach the preposition to the noun, and if $F(v,p,n) > 0$, then we need to attach preposition to the verb. We will see the implementation in `Chapter 5`, *Feature Engineering and NLP Algorithms*.

Semantic ambiguity

Semantic ambiguity occurs when the meaning of the words themselves can be misinterpreted. Here's an example:

- ABC head seeks arms
- Here, the word head either means chief or body part, and in the same way, arms can be interpreted as weapons or as body parts
- This kind of ambiguity is considered in semantic ambiguity

Handling semantic ambiguity with high accuracy is an open research area. Nowadays, the word2vec representation technique is very useful for handling semantic ambiguity.

Pragmatic ambiguity

Pragmatics ambiguity occurs when the context of a phrase gives it multiple different interpretations. Let's take an example:

- Give it to that girl. This could mean any number of things.

Now let's take a large context:

- I have chocolate and a packet of biscuits. Give it to that girl. Here, it is not clear whether it refers to chocolate or the packet of biscuits.

Handling this kind of ambiguity is still an open area of research.

Discourse integration

Discourse integration is closely related to pragmatics. Discourse integration is considered as the larger context for any smaller part of NL structure. NL is so complex and, most of the time, sequences of text are dependent on prior discourse.

This concept occurs often in pragmatic ambiguity. This analysis deals with how the immediately preceding sentence can affect the meaning and interpretation of the next sentence. Here, context can be analyzed in a bigger context, such as paragraph level, document level, and so on.

Applications

Concepts of discourse integration have been used by following NLP applications:

- This concept often used in NLG applications.
- Chatbots, which are developed to deliver generalized AI. In this kind of application, deep learning has been used. We will see the NLG with deep learning in Chapter 9, *Deep Learning for NLP and NLG Problems*.

Pragmatic analysis

Pragmatic analysis deals with outside word knowledge, which means knowledge that is external to the documents and/or queries. Pragmatics analysis that focuses on what was described is reinterpreted by what it actually meant, deriving the various aspects of language that require real world knowledge.

Let's look at an example:

- Pruning a tree is a long process.
- Here, pruning a tree is one of the concepts of computer science algorithm techniques. So, the word **pruning** is not related to cutting the actual physical tree, we are talking about computer science algorithm. This is an ambiguous situation; how to deal with these kinds of ambiguous situations is also an open area of research. Big tech giants use deep learning techniques to do pragmatics analysis and try to generate the accurate context of the sentence in order to develop highly accurate NLP applications.

Summary

This chapter explored the basics of linguistics, which are often used to develop NLP applications. We have seen all kinds of analysis related to NL. We have seen word level analysis and larger context analysis. We have seen difference between some of the key concepts to resolve any confusion. After this chapter, you can identify which concepts of linguistics or tool is more interesting for you to use. Researchers can find the potential research area if they want to pursue research either in linguistics, computer linguistics or computer science with major in NLP.

In the next chapter, we will focus on practical and coding aspects and begin our journey to develop NLP applications. The next chapter is all about **preprocessing** the data, one of the basic but important steps in developing NLP applications. Preprocessing includes some of the concepts which we have described here. We will use them along with the standard ways of preprocessing.

4
Preprocessing

From here, all our chapters will mostly contain code. I want to remind all my readers to run and develop the code at their end. Let's start the coding ninja journey.

In this chapter, we will be learning how to do preprocessing according to the different NLP applications. We will learn the following topics:

- Handling corpus-raw text
- Handling corpus-raw sentences
- Basic preprocessing
- Practical and customized preprocessing

Handling corpus-raw text

In this section, we will see how to get the raw text and, in the following section, we will preprocess text and identify the sentences.

The process for this section is given in *Figure 4.1*:

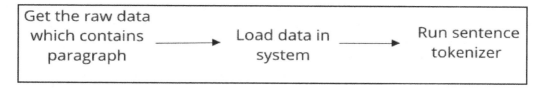

Figure 4.1: Process of handling corpus-raw text

Getting raw text

In this section, we will use three sources where we can get the raw text data.

The following are the data sources:

- Raw text file
- Define raw data text inside a script in the form of a local variable
- Use any of the available corpus from `nltk`

Let's begin:

- Raw text file access: I have a `.txt` file saved on my local computer which contains text data in the form of a paragraph. I want to read the content of that file and then load the content as the next step. I will run a sentence tokenizer to get the sentences out of it.
- Define raw data text inside a script in the form of a local variable: If we have a small amount of data, then we can assign the data to a local string variable. For example: **Text = This is the sentence, this is another example**.
- Use an available corpus from `nltk`: We can import an available corpus such as the `brown` corpus, `gutenberg` corpus, and so on from `nltk` and load the content.

I have defined three functions:

- `fileread()`: This reads the content of a file
- `localtextvalue()`: This loads locally defined text
- `readcorpus()`: This reads the `gutenberg` corpus content

Refer to the code snippet given in *Figure 4.2*, which describes all the three cases previously defined:

```python
import nltk
from nltk.corpus import gutenberg as cg
import re


# Get raw data form file
def fileread():
    file_contents = open("/home/jalaj/PycharmProjects/NLPython/NLPython/data/rawtextcorpus.txt", "r").read()
    # print file_contents
    return file_contents


# assign text data to local variable
def localtextvalue():
    text = """ one paragraph, of 100-250 words, which summarizes the purpose, methods, results and conclusions of the paper.
    It is not easy to include all this information in just a few words. Start by writing a summary that includes whatever you think is important.
    and then gradually prune it down to size by removing unnecessary words, while still retaini ng the necessary concepts.
    Don't use abbreviations or citations in the abstract. It should be able to stand alone without any footnotes. Fig 1.1.1 shows below."""
    # print text
    return text


# Use NLTK corpus which we seen in chapter 2 as well
def readcorpus():
    raw_content_cg = cg.raw("burgess-busterbrown.txt")
    # print raw_content_cg[0:1000]
    return raw_content_cg[0:1000]


if __name__ == "__main__":
    print ""
    print "----------Output from Raw Text file-----------"
    print ""
    filecontentdetails = fileread()
    print filecontentdetails

    print ""
    print "-------Output from assigned variable-------"
    print ""
    localveriabledata = localtextvalue()
    print localveriabledata

    print ""
    print "-------Output Corpus data--------------"
    print ""
    fromcorpusdata = readcorpus()
    print fromcorpusdata
```

Figure 4.2: Various ways to get the raw data

You can find the code by clicking on the GitHub link:
https://github.com/jalajthanaki/NLPython/blob/master/ch4/4_1_processrawtext.py

Lowercase conversion

Converting all your data to lowercase helps in the process of preprocessing and in later stages in the NLP application, when you are doing parsing.

So, converting the text to its lowercase format is quite easy. You can find the code on this GitHub link:
https://github.com/jalajthanaki/NLPython/blob/master/ch4/4_4_wordtokenization.py

You can find the code snippet in *Figure 4.3*:

```
def wordlowercase():
    text= "I am a person. Do you know what is time now?"
    print text.lower()
```

Figure 4.3: Converting data to lowercase

The output of the preceding code snippet is as follows:

```
----------converting data to lower case ----------
i am a person. do you know what is time now?
```

Sentence tokenization

In raw text data, data is in paragraph form. Now, if you want the sentences from the paragraph, then you need to tokenize at sentence level.

 Sentence tokenization is the process of identifying the boundary of the sentences. It is also called **sentence boundary detection** or **sentence segmentation** or **sentence boundary disambiguation**. This process identifies the sentences starting and ending points.

Some of the specialized cases need a customized rule for the sentence tokenizer as well.

The following open source tools are available for performing sentence tokenization:

- OpenNLP
- Stanford CoreNLP
- GATE
- nltk

Here we are using the nltk sentence tokenizer.

We are using sent_tokenize from nltk and will import it as st:

- sent_tokenize(rawtext): This takes a raw data string as an argument
- st(filecontentdetails): This is our customized raw data, which is provided as an input argument

You can find the code on this GitHub Link: `https://github.com/jalajthanaki/NLPython/blob/master/ch4/4_1_processrawtext.py`.

You can see the code in the following code snippet in *Figure 4.4*:

```
import nltk
from nltk.corpus import gutenberg as cg
from nltk.tokenize import sent_tokenize as st
import re


# Get raw data form file
def fileread():...
# assign text data to local variable
def localtextvalue():...

# Use NLTK corpus which we seen in chapter 2 as well
def readcorpus():...

if __name__ == "__main__":
    print ""
    print "----------Output from Raw Text file----------"
    print ""
    filecontentdetails = fileread()
    print filecontentdetails
    # sentence tokenizer
    st_list_rawfile = st(filecontentdetails)
    print len(st_list_rawfile)

    print ""
    print "-------Output from assigned variable-------"
    print ""
    localveriabledata = localtextvalue()
    print localveriabledata
    # sentence tokenizer
    st_list_local = st(localveriabledata)
    print len(st_list_local)
    print st_list_local

    print ""
    print "-------Output Corpus data-------------"
    print ""
    fromcorpusdata = readcorpus()
    print fromcorpusdata
    # sentence tokenizer
    st_list_corpus = st(fromcorpusdata)
    print len(st_list_corpus)
```

Figure 4.4: Code snippet for nltk sentence tokenizer

Challenges of sentence tokenization

At first glance, you would ask, what's the big deal about finding out the sentence boundary from the given raw text?

Sentence tokenization varies from language to language.

Things get complicated when you have the following scenarios to handle. We are using examples to explain the cases:

- If there is small letter after a dot, then the sentence should not split after the dot. The following is an example:
  - Sentence: He has completed his Ph.D. degree. He is happy.
  - In the preceding example, the sentence tokenizer should split the sentence after **degree**, not after **Ph.D.**
- If there is a small letter after the dot, then the sentence should be split after the dot. This is a common mistake. Let's take an example:
  - Sentence: This is an apple.an apple is good for health.
  - In the preceding example, the sentence tokenizer should split the sentence after **apple**.
- If there is an initial name in the sentence, then the sentence should not split after the initials:
  - Sentence: Harry Potter was written by J.K. Rowling. It is an entertaining one.
  - In the preceding example, the sentence should not split after **J.** It should ideally split after **Rowling**.

- Grammarly Inc., the grammar correction software, customized a rule for the identification of sentences and achieves high accuracy for sentence boundary detection. See the blog link:
  `https://tech.grammarly.com/blog/posts/How-to-Split-Sentences.html`.

To overcome the previous challenges, you can take the following approaches, but the accuracy of each approach depends on the implementation. The approaches are as follows:

- You can develop a rule-based system to increase the performance of the sentence tokenizer:
  - For the previous approach, you can use **name entity recognition** (**NER**) tools, POS taggers, or parsers, and then analyze the output of the described tools, as well as the sentence tokenizer output and rectify where the sentence tokenizer went wrong. With the help of NER tools, POS taggers, and parsers, can you fix the wrong output of the sentence tokenizer. In this case, write a rule, then code it, and check whether the output is as expected.
  - Test your code! You need to check for exceptional cases. Does your code perform well? If yes, great! And, if not, change it a bit:
    - You can improve the sentence tokenizer by using **machine learning** (**ML**) or deep learning techniques:
      - If you have enough data that is annotated by a human, then you can train the model using an annotated dataset. Based on that trained model, we can generate a new prediction from where the sentence boundary should end.
      - In this method, you need to check how the model will perform.

Stemming for raw text

As we saw in Chapter 3, *Understanding Structure of Sentences*, stemming is the process of converting each word of the sentence to its root form by deleting or replacing suffixes.

In this section, we will apply the Stemmer concept on the raw text.

Here, we have code where we are using the PorterStemmer available in nltk. Refer to *Figure 4.5*:

```
from nltk.stem import PorterStemmer

text = """Stemming is funnier than a bummer says the sushi loving computer scientist. She really wants to buy cars. She told me angrily."""

def stemmer_porter():
    port = PorterStemmer()
    return " ".join([port.stem(i) for i in text.split()])

if __name__ == "__main__":
    print stemmer_porter()
```

Figure 4.5: PorterStemmer code for raw text

The output of the preceding code is:

```
stem is funnier than a bummer say the sushi love comput scientist. she
realli want to buy cars. she told me angrily.
```

When you compare the preceding output with the original text, then we can see the following changes:

Stemming is funnier than a bummer says the sushi **loving computer** scientist. **She really** wants to buy cars. **She** told me angrily.

If you want to see the difference, then you can refer to the highlighted words to see the difference.

Challenges of stemming for raw text

Initially, stemming tools were made for the English language. The accuracy of stemming tools for the English language is high, but for languages such as Urdu and Hebrew, stemming tools do not perform well. So, to develop stemming tools for other languages is quite challenging. It is still an open research area.

Lemmatization of raw text

Lemmatization is the process that identifies the correct intended **part-of-speech** (**POS**) and the meaning of words that are present in sentences.

In lemmatization, we remove the inflection endings and convert the word into its base form, present in a dictionary or in the vocabulary. If we use vocabulary and morphological analysis of all the words present in the raw text properly, then we can get high accuracy for lemmatization.

Lemmatization transforms words present in the raw text to its lemma by using a tagged dictionary such as WordNet.

Lemmatization is closely related to stemming.

 In lemmatization, we consider POS tags, and in stemming we do not consider POS tags and the context of words.

Let's take some examples to make the concepts clear. The following are the sentences:

- Sentence 1: It is better for you.
    - There is a word **better** present in sentence 1. So, the lemma of word **better** is as **good** as a lemma. But stemming is missing as it requires a dictionary lookup.
- Sentence 2: Man is walking.
    - The word **walking** is derived from the base word walk and here, stemming and lemmatization are both the same.
- Sentence 3: We are meeting tomorrow.
    - Here, to meet is the base form. The word **meeting** is derived from the base form. The base form meet can be a noun or it can be a verb. So it depends on the context it will use. So, lemmatization attempts to select the right lemma based on their POS tags.
- Refer to the code snippet in *Figure 4.6* for the lemmatization of raw text:

```python
from nltk.stem import PorterStemmer
from nltk.stem import WordNetLemmatizer
text = """Stemming is funnier than a bummer says the sushi loving computer scientist.
She really wants to buy cars. She told me angrily.
It is better for you. Man is walking. We are meeting tomorrow."""


def stemmer_porter():
    port = PorterStemmer()
    print "\nStemmer"
    return " ".join([port.stem(i) for i in text.split()])

def lammatizer():
    wordnet_lemmatizer = WordNetLemmatizer()
    ADJ, ADJ_SAT, ADV, NOUN, VERB = 'a', 's', 'r', 'n', 'v'
    # Pos = verb
    print "\nVerb lemma"
    print " ".join([wordnet_lemmatizer.lemmatize(i,pos="v") for i in text.split()])
    # Pos = noun
    print "\nNoun lemma"
    print " ".join([wordnet_lemmatizer.lemmatize(i,pos="n") for i in text.split()])
    # Pos = Adjective
    print "\nAdjective lemma"
    print " ".join([wordnet_lemmatizer.lemmatize(i, pos="a") for i in text.split()])
    # Pos = satellite adjectives
    print "\nSatellite adjectives lemma"
    print " ".join([wordnet_lemmatizer.lemmatize(i, pos="s") for i in text.split()])
    print "\nAdverb lemma"
    # POS = Adverb
    print " ".join([wordnet_lemmatizer.lemmatize(i, pos="r") for i in text.split()])

if __name__ == "__main__":
    print stemmer_porter()
    lammatizer()
```

Figure 4.6: Stemming and lemmatization of raw text

The output of the preceding code is given as follows:

The given input is:

```
text = """Stemming is funnier than a bummer says the sushi loving computer
scientist.She really wants to buy cars. She told me angrily.It is better
for you. Man is walking. We are meeting tomorrow."""
```

The output is given as:

```
Stemmer
stem is funnier than a bummer say the sushi love comput scientist. she
realli want to buy cars. she told me angrily. It is better for you. man is
walking. We are meet tomorrow.
Verb lemma
Stemming be funnier than a bummer say the sushi love computer scientist.
She really want to buy cars. She tell me angrily. It be better for you. Man
be walking. We be meet tomorrow.
Noun lemma
Stemming is funnier than a bummer say the sushi loving computer scientist.
She really want to buy cars. She told me angrily. It is better for you. Man
is walking. We are meeting tomorrow.
Adjective lemma
Stemming is funny than a bummer says the sushi loving computer scientist.
She really wants to buy cars. She told me angrily. It is good for you. Man
is walking. We are meeting tomorrow.
Satellite adjectives lemma
Stemming is funny than a bummer says the sushi loving computer scientist.
She really wants to buy cars. She told me angrily. It is good for you. Man
is walking. We are meeting tomorrow.
Adverb lemma
Stemming is funnier than a bummer says the sushi loving computer scientist.
She really wants to buy cars. She told me angrily. It is well for you. Man
is walking. We are meeting tomorrow.
```

In lemmatization, we use different POS tags. The abbreviation description is as follows:

- v stands for verbs
- n stands for nouns
- a stands for adjectives
- s stands for satellite adjectives
- r stands for adverbs

You can see that, inside the `lemmatizer()` function, I have used all the described POS tags.

You can download the code from the GitHub link at: `https://github.com/jalajthanaki /NLPython/blob/master/ch4/4_2_rawtext_Stemmers.py`.

Challenges of lemmatization of raw text

Lemmatization uses a tagged dictionary such as WordNet. Mostly, it's a human-tagged dictionary. So human efforts and the time it takes to make WordNet for different languages is challenging.

Stop word removal

Stop word removal is an important preprocessing step for some NLP applications, such as sentiment analysis, text summarization, and so on.

Removing stop words, as well as removing commonly occurring words, is a basic but important step. The following is a list of stop words which are going to be removed. This list has been generated from `nltk`. Refer to the following code snippet in Figure 4.7:

```python
from nltk.corpus import stopwords


def stopwordlist():
    stopwordlist = stopwords.words('english')
    for s in stopwordlist:
        print s


if __name__ == "__main__":
    stopwordlist()
```

Figure 4.7: Code to see the list of stop words for the English language

The output of the preceding code is a list of stop words available in nltk, refer to *Figure 4.8*:

i	me	my	myself	we	our	ours	ourselves	you	your	yours	yourself	yourselves	he	him
his	himself	she	her	hers	herself	it	its	itself	they	them	their	theirs	themselves	what
which	who	whom	this	that	these	those	am	is	are	was	were	be	been	being
have	has	had	having	do	does	did	doing	a	an	the	and	but	if	or
because	as	until	while	of	at	by	for	with	about	against	between	into	through	during
before	after	above	below	to	from	up	down	in	out	on	off	over	under	again
further	then	once	here	there	when	where	why	how	all	any	both	each	few	more
most	other	some	such	no	nor	not	only	own	same	so	than	too	very	s
t	can	will	just	don	should	now	d	ll	m	o	re	ve	y	ain
aren	couldn	didn	doesn	hadn	hasn	haven	isn	ma	mightn	mustn	needn	shan	shouldn	wasn
weren	won	wouldn												

Figure 4.8: Output of nltk stop words list for the English language

The nltk has a readily available list of stop words for the English language. You can also customize which words you want to remove according to the NLP application that you are developing.

You can see the code snippet for removing customized stop words in *Figure 4.9*:

```python
from nltk.corpus import stopwords


def customizedstopwordremove():
    stop_words = set(["hi", "bye"])
    line = """hi this is foo. bye"""
    print " ".join(word for word in line.split() if word not in stop_words)


def stopwordlist():...


def stopwordremove():...


def fileloadandremovestopwords():...


if __name__ == "__main__":
    #stopwordlist()
    customizedstopwordremove()
```

Figure 4.9: Removing customized stop words

The output of the code given in *Figure 4.9* is as follows:

```
this is foo.
```

The code snippet in *Figure 4.10* performs actual stop word removal from raw text and this raw text is in the English language:

```
def stopwordremove():
    stop = set(stopwords.words('english'))
    sentence = "this is a test sentence. I am very happy today."
    print ""
    print "--------Stop word removal from raw text---------"
    print " ".join([i for i in sentence.lower().split() if i not in stop])


...


if __name__ == "__main__":
    stopwordlist()
    customizedstopwordremove()
    stopwordremove()
```

Figure 4.10: Stop words removal from raw text

The output of the preceding code snippet is as follows:

```
Input raw sentence: ""this is a test sentence. I am very happy today.""
--------Stop word removal from raw text---------
test sentence. happy today.
```

Exercise

Take a file which is placed in the data folder with the name `rawtextcorpus.txt`, open the file in read mode, load the content, and then remove the stop words by using the nltk stop word list. Please analyze the output to get a better idea of how things are working out.

Up until this section, we have analyzed raw text. In the next section, we will do preprocessing on sentence levels and word levels.

Handling corpus-raw sentences

In the previous section, we were processing on raw text and looked at concepts at the sentence level. In this section, we are going to look at the concepts of tokenization, lemmatization, and so on at the word level.

Word tokenization

Word tokenization is defined as the process of chopping a stream of text up into words, phrases, and meaningful strings. This process is called **word tokenization**. The output of the process are words that we will get as an output after tokenization. This is called a **token**.

Let's see the code snippet given in *Figure 4.11* of tokenized words:

```
from nltk.tokenize import word_tokenize


def wordtokenization():
    content = """Stemming is funnier than a bummer says the sushi loving computer scientist.
    She really wants to buy cars. She told me angrily. It is better for you.
    Man is walking. We are meeting tomorrow. You really don't know..!"""
    print word_tokenize(content)


if __name__ =="__main__":
    wordtokenization()
```

Figure 4.11: Word tokenized code snippet

The output of the code given in *Figure 4.11* is as follows:

The input for word tokenization is:

```
Stemming is funnier than a bummer says the sushi loving computer
scientist.She really wants to buy cars. She told me angrily. It is better
for you.Man is walking. We are meeting tomorrow. You really don''t know..!
```

The output for word tokenization is:

```
[''Stemming'', ''is'', ''funnier'', ''than'', ''a'', ''bummer'', ''says'',
''the'', ''sushi'', ''loving'', ''computer'', ''scientist'', ''.'',
''She'', ''really'', ''wants'', ''to'', ''buy'', ''cars'', ''.'', ''She'',
''told'', ''me'', ''angrily'', ''.'', ''It'', ''is'', ''better'', ''for'',
''you'', ''.'', ''Man'', ''is'', ''walking'', ''.'', ''We'', ''are'',
''meeting'', ''tomorrow'', ''.'', ''You'', ''really'', ''do'', ""n''t"",
''know..'', ''!'']
```

Challenges for word tokenization

If you analyze the preceding output, then you can observe that the word `don't` is tokenized as `do, n't know`. Tokenizing these kinds of words is pretty painful using the `word_tokenize` of `nltk`.

To solve the preceding problem, you can write exception codes and improvise the accuracy. You need to write pattern matching rules, which solve the defined challenge, but are so customized and vary from application to application.

Another challenge involves some languages such as Urdu, Hebrew, Arabic, and so on. They are quite difficult in terms of deciding on the word boundary and find out meaningful tokens from the sentences.

Word lemmatization

Word lemmatization is the same concept that we defined in the first section. We will just do a quick revision of it and then we will implement lemmatization on the word level.

Word lemmatization is converting a word from its inflected form to its base form. In word lemmatization, we consider the POS tags and, according to the POS tags, we can derive the base form which is available to the lexical WordNet.

You can find the code snippet in *Figure 4.12*:

```
from nltk.tokenize import word_tokenize
from nltk.stem.wordnet import WordNetLemmatizer

def wordtokenization():
    content = """Stemming is funnier than a bummer says the sushi loving computer scientist.
    She really wants to buy cars. She told me angrily. It is better for you.
    Man is walking. We are meeting tomorrow. You really don't know..!"""
    print word_tokenize(content)

def wordlemmatization():
    wordlemma = WordNetLemmatizer()
    print wordlemma.lemmatize('cars')
    print wordlemma.lemmatize('walking',pos='v')
    print wordlemma.lemmatize('meeting',pos='n')
    print wordlemma.lemmatize('meeting',pos='v')
    print wordlemma.lemmatize('better',pos='a')

if __name__ =="__main__":
    wordtokenization()
    print "\n"
    print "----------Word Lemmatization----------"
    wordlemmatization()
```

Figure 4.12: Word lemmatization code snippet

The output of the word lemmatization is as follows:

```
Input is: wordlemma.lemmatize(''cars'')   Output is: car
Input is: wordlemma.lemmatize(''walking'',pos=''v'') Output is: walk
Input is: wordlemma.lemmatize(''meeting'',pos=''n'') Output is: meeting
Input is: wordlemma.lemmatize(''meeting'',pos=''v'') Output is: meet
Input is: wordlemma.lemmatize(''better'',pos=''a'') Output is: good
```

Challenges for word lemmatization

It is time consuming to build a lexical dictionary. If you want to build a lemmatization tool that can consider a larger context, taking into account the context of preceding sentences, it is still an open area in research.

Basic preprocessing

In basic preprocessing, we include things that are simple and easy to code but seek our attention when we are doing preprocessing for NLP applications.

Regular expressions

Now we will begin some of the interesting concepts of preprocessing, which are the most useful. We will look at some of the advanced levels of regular expression.

For those who are new to regular expression, I want to explain the basic concept of **regular expression (regex)**.

Regular expression is helpful to find or find-replace specific patterns from a sequence of characters. There is particular syntax which you need to follow when you are making regex.

There are many online tools available which can give you the facility to develop and test your regex. One of my favorite online regex development tool links is given here: https://regex101.com/

You can also refer to the Python regex library documentation at: https://docs.python.org /2/library/re.html

Basic level regular expression

Regex is a powerful tool when you want to do customized preprocessing or when you have noisy data with you.

Here, I'm presenting some of the basic syntax and then we will see the actual implementation on Python. In Python, the re library is available and by using this library we can implement regex. You can find the code on this GitHub link: https://github.com/jalajthanaki/NLPython/blob/master/ch4/4_5_regualrexpression. py

Basic flags

The basic flags are I, L, M, S, U, X:

- re.I: This flag is used for ignoring casing
- re.M: This flag is useful if you want to find patterns throughout multiple lines
- re.L: This flag is used to find a local dependent
- re.S: This flag is used to find dot matches
- re.U: This flag is used to work for unicode data
- re.X: This flag is used for writing regex in a more readable format

We have mainly used `re.I`, `re.M`, `re.L`, and `re.U` flags.

We are using the `re.match()` and `re.search()` functions. Both are used to find the patterns and then you can process them according to the requirements of your application.

Let's look at the differences between `re.match()` and `re.search()`:

- `re.match()`: This checks for a match of the string only at the beginning of the string. So, if it finds the pattern at the beginning of the input string then it returns the matched pattern, otherwise; it returns a noun.
- `re.search()`: This checks for a match of the string anywhere in the string. It finds all the occurrences of the pattern in the given input string or data.

Refer to the code snippet given in *Figure 4.13*:

```python
import re

def searchvsmatch():
    line = "I love animals.";

    matchObj = re.match(r'animals', line, re.M | re.I)
    if matchObj:
        print "match: ", matchObj.group()
    else:
        print "No match!!"

    searchObj = re.search(r'animals', line, re.M | re.I)
    if searchObj:
        print "search: ", searchObj.group()
    else:
        print "Nothing found!!"

if __name__ == "__main__":
    searchvsmatch()
```

Figure 4.13: Code snippet to see the difference between re.match() versus re.search()

The output of the code snippet of *Figure 4.13* is given in *Figure 4.14*:

```
No match!!
search:  animals
```

Figure 4.14: Output of the re.match() versus re.search()

The syntax is as follows:

Find the single occurrence of character a and b:

```
Regex: [ab]
```

Find characters except a and b:

```
Regex: [^ab]
```

Find the character range of a to z:

```
Regex: [a-z]
```

Find range except to z:

```
Regex: [^a-z]
```

Find all the characters a to z as well as A to Z:

```
Regex: [a-zA-Z]
```

Any single character:

```
Regex: .
```

Any whitespace character:

```
Regex: \s
```

Any non-whitespace character:

```
Regex: \S
```

Any digit:

```
Regex: \d
```

Any non-digit:

```
Regex: \D
```

Any non-words:

```
Regex: \W
```

Any words:

```
Regex: \w
```

Either match a or b:

```
Regex: (a|b)
```

Occurrence of a is either zero or one:

```
Regex: a? ; ? Matches  zero or one occurrence not more than 1 occurrence
```

Occurrence of a is zero time or more than that:

```
Regex: a* ; * matches zero or more than that
```

Occurrence of a is one time or more than that:

```
Regex: a+ ; + matches occurrences one or more that one time
```

Exactly match three occurrences of a:

```
Regex: a{3}
```

Match simultaneous occurrences of a with 3 or more than 3:

```
Regex: a{3,}
```

Match simultaneous occurrences of a between 3 to 6:

```
Regex: a{3,6}
```

Starting of the string:

```
Regex: ^
```

Ending of the string:

```
Regex: $
```

Match word boundary:

```
Regex: \b
```

Non-word boundary:

```
Regex: \B
```

The basic code snippet is given in *Figure 4.15*:

```python
import re

def searchvsmatch():...


def basicregex():
    line = "This is test sentence and test sentence is also a sentence."
    contactInfo = 'Doe, John: 1111-1212'
    print "-----------Output of re.findall()--------"
    # re.findall() finds all occurences of sentence from line variable.
    findallobj = re.findall(r'sentence', line)
    print findallobj

    # re.search() and group wise extraction
    groupwiseobj = re.search(r'(\w+), (\w+): (\S+)', contactInfo)
    print "\n"
    print "-----------Output of Groups--------"
    print "1st group ------- " + groupwiseobj.group(1)
    print "2nd group ------- " + groupwiseobj.group(2)
    print "3rd group ------- " + groupwiseobj.group(3)

    # re.sub() replace string
    phone = "1111-2222-3333 # This is Phone Number"

    # Delete Python-style comments
    num = re.sub(r'#.*$', "", phone)
    print "\n"
    print "-----------Output of re.sub()--------"
    print "Phone Num : ", num

    # Replace John to Peter  in contactInfo
    contactInforevised = re.sub(r'John', "Peter", contactInfo)
    print "Revised contactINFO : ", contactInforevised



if __name__ == "__main__":
    print "\n"
    print "---------re.match() vs re.search()"
    searchvsmatch()
    print "\n"
    basicregex()
```

Figure 4.15: Basic regex functions code snippet

The output of the code snippet of *Figure 4.15* is given in *Figure 4.16*:

```
----------Output of re.findall()--------
['sentence', 'sentence', 'sentence']


----------Output of Groups--------
1st group ------- Doe
2nd group ------- John
3rd group ------- 1111-1212


----------Output of re.sub()--------
Phone Num :  1111-2222-3333
Revised contactINFO :  Doe, Peter: 1111-1212
```

Figure 4.16: Output of the basic regex function code snippet

Advanced level regular expression

There are advanced concepts of regex which will be very useful.

The **lookahead** and **lookbehind** are used to find out substring patterns from your data. Let's begin. We will understand the concepts in the basic language. Then we will look at the implementation of them.

Positive lookahead

Positive lookahead matches the substring from a string if the defined pattern is followed by the substring. If you don't understand, then let's look at the following example:

- Consider a sentence: I play on the playground.
- Now, you want to extract *play* as a pattern but only if it follows *ground*. In this situation, you can use positive lookahead.

The syntax of positive lookahead is `(?=pattern)`

The regex `rplay(?=ground)` matches *play*, but only if it is followed by *ground*. Thus, the first *play* in the text string won't be matched.

Positive lookbehind

Positive lookbehind matches the substring from a string if the defined pattern is preceded by the substring. Refer to the following example:

- Consider the sentence: I play on the playground. It is the best ground.
- Now you want to extract *ground*, if it is preceded by the string *play*. In this case, you can use positive lookbehind.

The syntax of positive lookbehind is `(?<=pattern)`

The regex `r(?<=play)ground` matches *ground*, but only if it is preceded by *play*.

Negative lookahead

Negative lookahead matches the string which is definitely not followed by the pattern which we have defined in the regex pattern part.

Let's give an example to understand the negative lookahead:

- Consider the sentence: I play on the playground. It is the best ground.
- Now you want to extract *play* only if it is not followed by the string *ground*. In this case, you can use negative lookahead.

The syntax of negative lookahead is `(?!pattern)`

The regex `r play(?!ground)` matches *play*, but only if it is not followed by *ground*. Thus the *play* just before *on* is matched.

Negative lookbehind

Negative lookbehind matches the string which is definitely not preceded by the pattern which we have defined in the regex pattern part.

Let's see an example to understand the negative lookbehind:

- Consider the sentence: I play on the playground. It is the best ground.
- Now you want to extract *ground* only if it is not preceded by the string *play*. In this case, you can use negative lookbehind.

The syntax of negative lookbehind is `(?<!pattern)`

The regex r(?<!play)ground matches *ground*, but only if it is not preceded by *play*.

You can see the code snippet which is an implementation of advanceregex() in *Figure 4.17*:

```python
def advanceregex():
    text = "I play on playground. It is the best ground."

    positivelookaheadobjpattern = re.findall(r'play(?=ground)',text,re.M | re.I)
    print "Positive lookahead: " + str(positivelookaheadobjpattern)
    positivelookaheadobj = re.search(r'play(?=ground)',text,re.M | re.I)
    print "Positive lookahead character index: "+ str(positivelookaheadobj.span())

    possitivelookbehindobjpattern = re.findall(r'(?<=play)ground',text,re.M | re.I)
    print "Positive lookbehind: " + str(possitivelookbehindobjpattern)
    possitivelookbehindobj = re.search(r'(?<=play)ground',text,re.M | re.I)
    print "Positive lookbehind character index: " + str(possitivelookbehindobj.span())

    negativelookaheadobjpattern = re.findall(r'play(?!ground)', text, re.M | re.I)
    print "Negative lookahead: " + str(negativelookaheadobjpattern)
    negativelookaheadobj = re.search(r'play(?!ground)', text, re.M | re.I)
    print "Negative lookahead character index: " + str(negativelookaheadobj.span())

    negativelookbehindobjpattern = re.findall(r'(?<!play)ground', text, re.M | re.I)
    print "negative lookbehind: " + str(negativelookbehindobjpattern)
    negativelookbehindobj = re.search(r'(?<!play)ground', text, re.M | re.I)
    print "Negative lookbehind character index: " + str(negativelookbehindobj.span())

if __name__ == "__main__":
    print "\n"
    print "---------re.match() vs re.search()"
    searchvsmatch()
    print "\n"
    basicregex()
    print "\n"
    advanceregex()
```

Figure 4.17: Advanced regex code snippet

The output of the code snippet of *Figure 4.17* is given in *Figure 4.18*:

```
Positive lookahead: ['play']
Positive lookahead character index: (10, 14)
Positive lookbehind: ['ground']
Positive lookbehind character index: (14, 20)
Negative lookahead: ['play']
Negative lookahead character index: (2, 6)
negative lookbehind: ['ground']
Negative lookbehind character index: (37, 43)
```

Figure 4.18: Output of code snippet of advanced regex

Practical and customized preprocessing

When we start preprocessing for NLP applications, sometimes you need to do some customization according to your NLP application. At that time, it might be possible that you need to think about some of the points which I have described as follows.

Decide by yourself

This section is a discussion of how to approach preprocessing when you don't know what kind of preprocessing is required for developing an NLP application. In this kind of situation, what you can do is simply ask the following questions to yourself and make a decision.

What is your NLP application and what kind of data do you need to build the NLP application?

- Once you have understood the problem statement, as well as having clarity on what your output should be, then you are in a good situation.
- Once you know about the problem statement and the expected output, now think what all the data points are that you need from your raw data set.
- To understand the previous two points, let's take an example. If you want to make a text summarization application, suppose you are using a news articles that are on the web, which you want to use for building news text summarization application. Now, you have built a scraper that scrapes news articles from the web. This raw news article dataset may contain HTML tags, long texts, and so on.

For news text summarization, how will we do preprocessing? In order to answer that, we need to ask ourselves a few questions. So, let's jump to a few questions about preprocessing.

Is preprocessing required?

- Now you have raw-data for text summarization and your dataset contains HTML tags, repeated text, and so on.
- If your raw-data has all the content that I described in the first point, then preprocessing is required and, in this case, we need to remove HTML tags and repeated sentences; otherwise, preprocessing is not required.
- You also need to apply lowercase convention.
- After that, you need to apply sentence tokenizer on your text summarization dataset.
- Finally, you need to apply word tokenizer on your text summarization dataset.
- Whether your dataset needs preprocessing depends on your problem statement and what data your raw dataset contains.

You can see the flowchart in *Figure 4.19:*

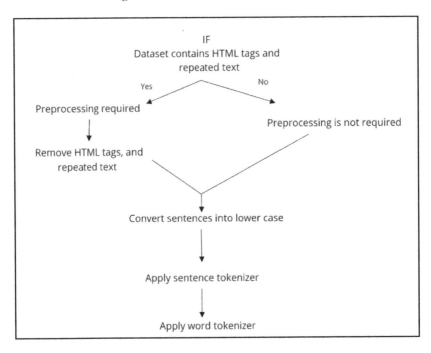

Figure 4.19: Basic flowchart for performing preprocessing of text-summarization

What kind of preprocessing is required?

In our example of text summarization, if a raw dataset contains HTML tags, long text, repeated text, then during the process of developing your application, as well as in your output, you don't need the following data:

- You don't need HTML tags, so you can remove them
- You don't need repeated sentences, so you can remove them as well
- If there is long text content then if you can find stop words and high frequency small words, you should remove them

Understanding case studies of preprocessing

Whatever I have explained here regarding customized preprocessing will make more sense to you when you have some real life case studies explained.

Grammar correction system

- You are making a grammar correction system. Now, think of the sub-task of it. You want to build a system which predicts the placement of articles a, an, and the in a particular sentence.
- For this kind of system, if you are thinking I need to remove stop words every time, then, OOPs, you are wrong because this time we really can't remove all the stop words blindly. In the end, we need to predict the articles a, an, and the.
- You can remove words which are not meaningful at all, such as when your dataset contains math symbols, then you can remove them. But this time, you need to do a detailed analysis as to whether you can remove the small length words, such as abbreviations, because your system also needs to predict which abbreviations don't take an article and which do.

Now, let's look at a system where you can apply all the preprocessing techniques that we have described here. Let's follow the points inside sentiment analysis.

Sentiment analysis

Sentiment analysis is all about evaluating the reviews of your customers and categorizing them into positive, negative, and neutral categories:

- For this kind of system, your dataset contains user reviews so user writing generally contains casual language.
- The data contains informal language so we need to remove stop words such as Hi, Hey, Hello, and so on. We do not use Hi, Hey, How are u? to conclude whether the user review is positive, negative, or neutral.
- Apart from that, you can remove the repeated reviews.
- You can also preprocess data by using word tokenization and lemmatization.

Machine translation

Machine translation is also one of the widely used NLP applications. In machine translation, our goal is to translate one language to another language in a logical manner. So, if we want to translate the English language to the German language, then you may the apply the following preprocessing steps:

1. We can apply convert to the whole dataset to be converted into lowercase.
2. Apply sentence splitter on the dataset so you can get the boundary for each of the sentences.
3. Now, suppose you have corpus where all English sentences are in `English_Sentence_File` and all German sentence are in `German_Sentence_File`. Now, you know for each English sentence there is a corresponding German sentence present in `German_Sentence_File`. This kind of corpus is called **parallel** corpus. So in this case, you also need to check that all sentences in both files are aligned appropriately.
4. You can also apply stemming for each of the words of the sentences.

Spelling correction

Spelling correction can be a very useful tool for preprocessing as well, as it helps to improve your NLP application.

Approach

The concept of spelling correction came from the concept of how much similarity is contained by two strings. This concept is used to compare two strings. The same concept has been used everywhere nowadays. We will consider some examples to better understand how this concept of checking the similarity of two strings can be helpful to us.

When you search on Google, if you make a typing mistake in your search query, then you get a suggestion on the browser, **Did you mean:** with your corrected query with the right spelling. This mechanism rectifies your spelling mistake and Google has its own way of providing almost perfect results every time. Google does not just do a spelling correction, but is also indexes on your submitted query and displays the best result for you. So, the concept behind the spelling correction is the similarity between two strings.

Take another example: If you are developing a machine translation system, then when you see the string translated by the machine, your next step is probably to validate your output. So now you will compare the output of the machine with a human translator and situation, which may not be perfectly similar to the output of the machine.

If the machine translated string is: **She said could she help me?**, the human string translated would say: **She asked could she help me?** When you are checking the similarity between a system string and a human string, you may find that *said* is replace by asked.

So, this concept of the similarity of two strings can be used in many applications, including speech recognition, NLP applications, and so on.

There are three major operations when we are talking about measuring the similarity of two strings. The operations are insertion, deletion, and substitution. These operations are used for the implementation of the spelling correction operation. Right now, to avoid complexity, we are not considering transpose and long string editing operations.

Let's start with the operations and then we will look at the algorithm specifically for the spelling correction.

Insertion operation

If you have an incorrect string, now after inserting one or more characters, you will get the correct string or expected string.

Let's see an example.

If I have entered a string `aple`, then after inserting `p` we will get `apple`, which is right. If you have entered a string `staemnt` then after inserting `t` and `e` you will get `statement`, which is right.

Deletion operation

You may have an incorrect string which can be converted into a correct string after deleting one or more characters of the string.

An example is as follows:

If I have entered `caroot`, then to get the correct string we need to delete one o. After that, we will get the correct string `carrot`.

Substitution operation

If you get the correct string by substituting one or more characters, then it is called a **substitution operation**.

Suppose you have a string `implemantation`. To make it correct, you need to substitute the first a to e and you will get the correct string `implementation`.

Algorithms for spelling corrections

We are using the minimum edit distance algorithm to understand spelling corrections.

Minimum edit distance

This algorithm is for converting one string X into another string Y and we need to find out what the minimum edit cost is to convert string X to string Y. So, here you can either do insertion, deletion, or substitution operations to convert string X to Y with the minimum possible sequences of the character edits.

Suppose you have a string X with a length of n,and string Y with a length of m.

Follow the steps of the algorithm:

```
Input: Two String, X and Y
Output: cheapest possible sequences of the character edits for converting
string from X to Y. D( i , j ) = minimum distance cost for converting X
string to Y
```

Let's look at the following steps:

1. Set n to a length of P.
   Set m to a length of Q.
2. If n = 0, return m and exit.
   If m = 0, return n and exit.
3. Create a matrix containing 0..*m* rows and 0..*n* columns.

4. Initialize the first row to 0..*n*.
   Initialize first column to 0..*m*.
5. Iterate each character of P (i from 1 to *n*).
   Iterate each character of Q (j from 1 to *m*).
6. If P[i] equals Q[j], the cost is 0.
   If Q[i] doesn't equal Q[j], the cost is 1.

   Set the value at cell `v[i,j]` of the matrix equal to the minimum of all three of the following points:

7. The cell immediately previous plus 1: `v[i-1,j] + 1`
8. The cell immediately to the left plus 1: `v[i,j-1] + 1`
9. The cell diagonally previous and to the left plus the cost: `v[i-1,j-1] +1` for minimum edit distance. If you are using the Levenshtein distance then `v[i-1,j-1] + cost` should be considered
10. After the iteration in *step 7* to *step 9* has been completed, the distance is found in cell `v[n,m]`.

The previous steps are the basic algorithm to develop the logic of spelling corrections but we can use probability distribution of words and take a consideration of that as well. This kind of algorithmic approach is based on dynamic programing.

Let's convert the string `tutour` to `tutor` by understanding that we need to delete `u`. The edit distance is therefore **1**. The table which is developed by using the defined algorithm is shown in *Figure 4.20* for computing the minimum edit distance:

	#	t	u	t	o	u	r
#	0	1	2	3	4	5	6
t	1	0	1	2	3	4	5
u	2	1	0	1	2	3	4
t	3	2	1	1	2	3	4
o	4	3	2	2	1	2	3
r	5	4	3	3	2	2	2

Figure 4.20: Computing minimum edit distance

Implementation

Now, for the spelling correction, we need to add a dictionary or extract the words from the large documents. So, in the implementation, we have used a big document from where we have extracted words. Apart from that, we have used the probability of occurring words in the document to get an idea about the distribution. You can see more details regarding the implementation part by clicking on this link: `http://norvig.com/spell-correct.html`

We have implemented the spelling correction for the minimum edit distance **2**.

See the implementation of the spelling correction in *Figure 4.21*:

```python
import re
from collections import Counter
def words(text):
    return re.findall(r'\w+', text.lower())

WORDS = Counter(words(open('/home/jalaj/PycharmProjects/NLPython/NLPython/data/big.txt').read()))

def P(word, N=sum(WORDS.values())):
    "Probability of 'word'."
    return WORDS[word] / N

def correction(word):
    "Most probable spelling correction for word."
    return max(candidates(word), key=P)

def candidates(word):
    "Generate possible spelling corrections for word."
    return (known([word]) or known(edits1(word)) or known(edits2(word)) or [word])

def known(words):
    "The subset of 'words' that appear in the dictionary of WORDS."
    return set(w for w in words if w in WORDS)

def edits1(word):
    "All edits that are one edit away from 'word'."
    letters    = 'abcdefghijklmnopqrstuvwxyz'
    splits     = [(word[:i], word[i:])    for i in range(len(word) + 1)]
    deletes    = [L + R[1:]               for L, R in splits if R]
    transposes = [L + R[1] + R[0] + R[2:] for L, R in splits if len(R) > 1]
    replaces   = [L + c + R[1:]           for L, R in splits if R for c in letters]
    inserts    = [L + c + R               for L, R in splits for c in letters]
    return set(deletes + transposes + replaces + inserts)

def edits2(word):
    "All edits that are two edits away from 'word'."
    return (e2 for e1 in edits1(word) for e2 in edits1(e1))


if __name__ == "__main__":
    print correction('aple')
    print correction('correcton')
    print correction('statament')
    print correction('tutpore')
```

Figure 4.21: Implementation of spelling correction

See the output of the spelling correction in *Figure 4.22*.

We are providing the string `aple`, which is converted to `apple` successfully:

```
apple
correction
statement
tutors
```

Figure 4.22: Output of spelling correction

Summary

In this chapter, we have looked at all kinds of preprocessing techniques which will be useful to you when you are developing an NLP system or an NLP application. We have also touched upon a spelling correction system which you can consider as part of the preprocessing technique because it will be useful for many of the NLP applications that you develop in the future. By the way, you can access the code on GitHub by clicking the following link: `https://github.com/jalajthanaki/NLPython/tree/master/ch4`

In the next chapter, we will look at the most important part for any NLP system: feature engineering. The performance of an NLP system mainly depends on what kind of data we provide to the NLP system. Feature engineering is an art and skill which you are going to adopt from the next chapter onwards and, trust me, it is the most important ingredient in developing the NLP systems, so read it and definitely implement it to enrich your skills.

5
Feature Engineering and NLP Algorithms

Feature engineering is the most important part of developing NLP applications. Features are the input parameters for **machine learning** (**ML**) algorithms. These ML algorithms generate output based on the input features. Feature engineering is a kind of art and skill because it generates the best possible features, and choosing the best algorithm to develop NLP application requires a lot of effort and understanding about feature engineering as well as NLP and ML algorithms. In Chapter 2, *Practical Understanding of Corpus and Dataset*, we saw how data is gathered and what the different formats of data or corpus are. In Chapter 3, *Understanding Structure of Sentences*, we touched on some of the basic but important aspects of NLP and linguistics. We will use these concepts to derive features in this chapter. In Chapter 4, *Preprocessing*, we looked preprocessing techniques. Now, we will work on the corpus that we preprocessed and will generate features from that corpus.

Refer to *Figure 5.1*, which will help you understand all the stages that we have covered so far, as well as all the focus points of this chapter:

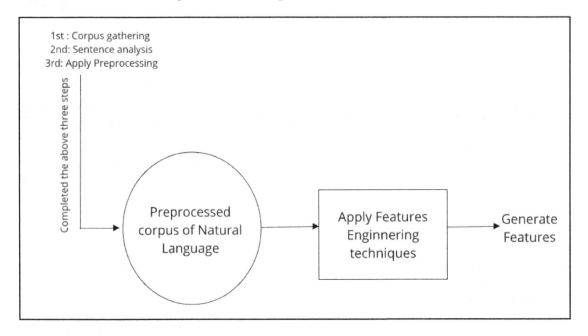

Figure 5.1: An overview of the features generation process

You can refer to *Figure 1.4* in Chapter 1, *Introduction*. We covered the first four stages in the preceding three chapters.

In this chapter, we will mostly focus on the practical aspect of NLP applications. We will cover the following topics:

- What is feature engineering?
- Understanding basic features of NLP
- Basic statistical features of NLP

As well as this, we will explore topics such as how various tools or libraries are developed to generate features, what the various libraries that we can use are, and how you can tweak open source libraries or open source tools as and when needed.

We will also look at the challenges for each concept. Here, we will not develop tools from scratch as it is out of the scope of this book, but we will walk you through the procedure and algorithms that are used to develop the tools. So if you want to try and build customized tools, this will help you, and will give you an idea of how to approach those kind of problem statements.

Understanding feature engineering

Before jumping into the feature generation techniques, we need to understand feature engineering and its purpose.

What is feature engineering?

Feature engineering is the process of generating or deriving features (attributes or an individual measurable property of a phenomenon) from raw data or corpus that will help us develop NLP applications or solve NLP-related problems.

A feature can be defined as a piece of information or measurable property that is useful when building NLP applications or predicting the output of NLP applications.

We will use ML techniques to process the natural language and develop models that will give us the final output. This model is called the **machine learning model** (**ML model**). We will feed features for machine learning algorithms as input and to generate the machine learning model. After this, we will use the generated machine learning model to produce an appropriate output for an NLP application.

If you're wondering what information can be a feature, then the answer is that any attribute can be a feature as long as it is useful in order to generate a good ML model that will produce the output for NLP applications accurately and efficiently. Here, your input features are totally dependent on your dataset and the NLP application.

Features are derived using domain knowledge for NLP applications. This is the reason we have explored the basic linguistics aspect of natural language, so that we can use these concepts in feature engineering.

What is the purpose of feature engineering?

In this section, we will look at the major features that will help us to understand feature engineering:

- We have raw data in natural language that the computer can't understand, and algorithms don't have the ability to accept the raw natural language and generate the expected output for an NLP application. Features play an important role when you are developing NLP applications using machine learning techniques.
- We need to generate the attributes that are representative for our corpus as well as those attributes that can be understood by machine learning algorithms. ML algorithms can understand only the language of feature for communication, and coming up with appropriate attributes or features is a big deal. This is the whole purpose of feature engineering.
- Once we have generated the feature, we then need to feed them to the machine learning algorithm as input, and after processing these input features, we will get the ML model. This ML model will be used to predict or generate the output for new features. The ML models, accuracy and efficiency is majorly dependent on features, which is why we say that features engineering is a kind of art and skill.

Challenges

The following are the challenges involved in feature engineering:

- Coming up with good features is difficult and sometimes complex.
- After generating features, we need to decide which features we should select this selection of features also plays a major role when we perform machine learning techniques on top of that. The process of selecting appropriate feature is called **feature selection**.
- Sometimes, during the feature selection, we need to eliminate some of the less important features, and this elimination of features is also a critical part of the feature engineering.
- Manual feature engineering is time-consuming.
- Feature engineering requires domain expertise or, at least, basic knowledge about domains.

Basic feature of NLP

Apart from the challenges, NLP applications heavily rely on feature that are manually crafted based on various NLP concepts. From this point onwards, we will explore the basic features that are available in the NLP world. Let's dive in!

Parsers and parsing

By parsing sentences, you can derive some of the most important features that can be helpful for almost every NLP application.

We will explore the concept of parser and parsing. Later, we will understand **context-free grammar (CFG)** and **probabilistic context-free grammar (PCFG)**. We will see how statistical parsers are developed. If you want to make your own parser, then we will explain the procedure to do so, or if you want to tweak the existing parser, then what steps you should follow. We will also do practical work using the available parser tools. We will look at the challenges later in this same section.

Understanding the basics of parsers

Here, I'm going to explain parser in terms of the NLP domain. The parser concept is also present in other computer science domains, but let's focus on the NLP domain and start understanding parser and what it can do for us.

In the NLP domain, a parser is the program or, more specifically, tool that takes natural language in the form of a sentence or sequence of tokens. It breaks the input stream into smaller chunks. This will help us understand the syntactic role of each element present in the stream and the basic syntax-level meaning of the sentence. In NLP, a parser actually analyzes the sentences using the rules of context-free grammar or probabilistic context-free grammar. We have seen CFG in Chapter 3, *Understanding Structure of Sentences*.

A parser usually generates output in the form of a parser tree or abstract syntax tree. Let's see some of the example parser trees here. There are certain grammar rules that parsers use to generate the parse tree with single words or lexicon items.

See the grammar rules in *Figure 5.2*:

```
Grammar Rules

  S  →  NP VP
 NP  →  NAME
 VP  →  V NP
 NP  →  ART N


Lexical Entries

NAME  →  John
V     →  is
ART   →  a
N     →  student
```

Figure 5.2: Grammar rules for parser

Let's discuss the symbols first:

- **S** stands for sentence
- **NP** stands for noun phrase
- **VP** stands for verb phrase
- **V** stands for verb
- **N** stand for noun
- **ART** stands for article a, an, or the

See a parse tree generated using the grammar rules in *Figure 5.3*:

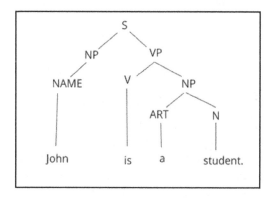

Figure 5.3: A parse tree as per the grammar rules defined in Figure 5.2

Here in *Figure 5.3*, we converted our sentence into the parse tree format, and as you can see, each word of the sentence is expressed by the symbols of the grammar that we already defined in *Figure 5.2*.

There are two major types of parsers. We are not going to get into the technicality of each type of parser here because it's more about the compiler designing aspect. Instead, we will explore the different types of parsers, so you can get some clarity on which type of parser we generally use in NLP. Refer to *Figure 5.4*:

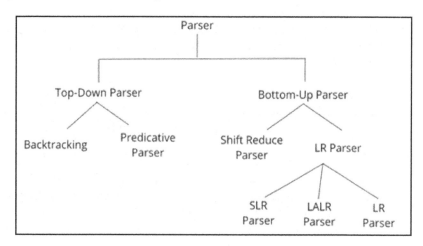

Figure 5.4: Types of parser

We will also look at the differences between top-down parsers and bottom-up parsers in the next section, as the difference is related to the process; this will be followed by each of the parsers so that we understand the difference.

Let's jump into the concept of parsing.

Understanding the concept of parsing

First of all, let's discuss what parsing is. Let's define the term parsing. Parsing is a formal analysis or a process that uses a sentence or the stream of tokens, and with the help of defined formal grammar rules, we can understand the sentence structure and meaning. So, parsing uses each of the words in the sentence and determines its structure using a constituent structure. What is a consistent structure? A constituent structure is based on the observation of which words combine with other words to form a sensible sentence unit. So, in the English language, the subject mostly comes first in the sentence; the sentence **He is Tom** makes sense to us, whereas the sentence **is Tom he** doesn't make sense. By parsing, we actually check as well as try to obtain a sensible constituent structure. These are the following points that will explain what parser and parsing does for us:

- The parser tool performs the process of parsing as per the grammar rules and generates a parse tree. This parse tree structure is used to verify the syntactical structure of the sentence. If a parse tree of the sentence follows the grammar rules as well as generates a meaningful sentence, then we say that the grammar as well as the sentence generated using that grammar is valid.
- At the end of the parsing, a parse tree is generated as output that will help you to detect ambiguity in the sentence because. Ambiguous sentences often result in multiple parse trees.

Let's see the difference between a top-down parser and a bottom-up parser:

Top-down parsing	Bottom-up parsing
Top-down parsing is hypothesis-driven.	Bottom-up parsing is data-driven.
At each stage of parsing, the parser assumes a structure and takes a word sequentially from the sentence and tests whether the taken word or token fulfills the hypothesis or not.	In this type of parsing, the first words are taken from the input string, then the parser checks whether any predefined categories are there in order to generate a valid sentence structure, and lastly, it tries to combine them into acceptable structures in the grammar.

It scans a sentence in a left-to-right manner. When grammar production rules derive lexical items, the parser usually checks with the input to see whether the right sentence is being derived or not.	This kind of parsing starts with the input string of terminals. This type of parsing searches for substrings of the working string because if any string or substring matches the right-hand side production rule of grammar, then it substitutes the left-hand side non-terminal for the matching right-hand side rule.
It includes a backtracking mechanism. When it is determined that the wrong rule has been used, it backs up and tries another rule.	It usually doesn't include a backtracking mechanism.

You will get to know how this parser has been built in the following section.

Developing a parser from scratch

In this section, we will try to understand the procedure of the most famous Stanford parser, and which algorithm has been used to develop the most successful statistical parser.

In order to get an idea about the final procedure, we need to first understand some building blocks and concepts. Then, we will combine all the concepts to understand the overall procedure of building a statistical parser such as the Stanford parser.

Types of grammar

In this section, we will see two types of grammar that will help us understand the concept of how a parser works. As a prerequisite, we will simply explain them and avoid getting too deep into the subject. We will make them as simple as possible and we will explore the basic intuition of the concepts that will be used to understand the procedure to develop the parser. Here we go!

There are two types of grammar. You can refer to *Figure 5.5*:

- Context-free grammar
- Probabilistic context-free grammar

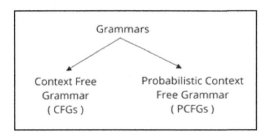

Figure 5.5: Types of grammar

Context-free grammar

We have seen the basic concept of context-free grammar in `Chapter 3`, *Understanding Structure of Sentences*. We have already seen the formal definition of the CFG to find a moment and recall it. Now we will see how the rules of grammar are important when we build a parser.

CFG is also referred to as phrase structure grammar. So, CFG and phrase structure grammar are two terms but refer to one concept. Now, let's see some examples related to this type of grammar and then talk about the conventions that are followed in order to generate a more natural form of grammar rules. Refer to the grammar rules, lexicons, and sentences in *Figure 5.6*:

```
S   → NP VP        N → People
VP  → V NP         N → fish            Sentences: people fish tank
VP  → V NP PP      N → tank                       People fish tank with rods
NP  → NP NP        N → rods
NP  → NP PP        V → people
NP  → N            V → fish
NP  → e            V → tanks
PP  → P NP         P → with
```

Figure 5.6: CFG rules, lexicon, and sentences

Here, **S** is the starting point of grammar. **NP** stands for noun phrase and **VP** stands for verb phrase. Now we will apply top-down parsing and try to generate the given sentence by starting from the rule with the right-hand side non-terminal **S** and substitute **S** with **NP** and **VP**. Now substitute **NP** with **N** and **VP** with **V** and **NP**, and then substitute **N** with people. Substitute **V** with **fish**, **NP** with **N**, and **N** with **tank**. You can see the pictorial representation of the given process in *Figure 5.7*:

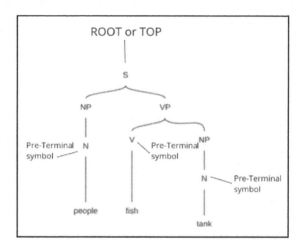

Figure 5.7: A parse tree representation of one of the sentences generated by the given grammar

Now try to generate a parse tree for the second sentence on your own. If you play around with this grammar rule for a while, then you will soon discover that it is a very ambiguous one. As well as this we will also discuss the more practical aspect of CFG that is used by linguists in order to derive the sentence structure. This is a more natural form of CFG and is very similar to the formal definition of CFG with one minor change, that is, we define the preterminal symbols in this grammar. If you refer to *Figure 5.7*, you will see that symbols such as **N, V** are called **preterminal symbols**. Now look at the definition of the natural form of CFG in *Figure 5.8*:

G = (T, C, N, S, L, R)
T are the lexical symbols
C are the preterminal symbols
N are the non-terminal symbols
S is the start symbol which belongs to the nonterminal N. (S ε N)
L is the lexical terminals, set of items which follows rule X → x, Here X → P and x → T
R is the grammar, set of items which follows rule X → y, here X ε N and y ε (N U C)*.

Figure 5.8: A formal representation of a more natural form of CFG

Here, the * symbol includes the existence of an empty sequence. We are starting from the **S** symbol, but in a statistical parser we add one more stage, which is TOP or ROOT. Therefore, when we generate the parse tree, the main top most node is indicated by **S.** Please refer to *Figure 5.7* for more information. Now we will put an extra node with the symbol ROOT or TOP before **S.**

You may have noticed one weird rule in *Figure 5.6*. **NP** can be substituted using **e**, which stands for an empty string, so let's see what the use of that empty string rule is. We will first look at see an example to get a detailed idea about this type of grammar as well as the empty string rule. We will begin with the concept of a preterminal because it may be new to you. Take a noun phrase in the English language--any phrase containing a determiner such as a, an, or the, along with the noun itself. When you substitute **NP** with the symbol **DT** and **NN**, you enter actual lexical terminals; where we substitute **NP** with **DT** and **NN**, it is called the preterminal symbol. Now let's talk about the empty string rule. We have included this rule because, in real life, you will find various instances where there are missing parts to a sentence. To handle these kinds of instances, we put this empty string rule in grammar. We will now give you an example that will help you.

We have seen the word sequence, **people fish tank**. From this, you can extract two phrases: one is **fish tank** and the second is **people fish**. In both examples, there are missing nouns. We will represent these phrases as **e fish tank** and **people fish e**. Here, **e** stands for empty string. You will notice that in the first phrase, there is a missing noun at the start of the phrase; more technically, there is a missing subject. In the second case, there is a missing noun at the end of the phrase; more technically, there is a missing object. These kinds of situations are very common when dealing with real **natural language** (**NL**) data.

There is one last thing we need to describe, which we will use in the topic on **grammar transformation**. Refer to *Figure 5.6*, where you will find the rules. Keep referring to these grammar rules as you go. The rule that has only an empty string on its right-hand side is called an **empty rule**. You can see that there are some rules that have just one symbol on their right side as well as on their left side; they are called **unary rules** because you can rewrite one category into another category, for example, **NP -> N**. There are also some other rules that have two symbols on their right side, such as **VP -> V NP**. These kinds of rules are called **binary rules.** There are also some rules that have three symbols on their right-hand side; we certain apply some techniques to get rid of the kind of rules that have more than two symbols on the right-hand side. We will look at these shortly.

Now we have looked at CFG, as well as the concepts needed to understand it. You will be able to connect those dots in the following sections. It's now time to move on to the next section, which will give you an idea about probabilistic CFG.

Probabilistic context-free grammar

In probabilistic grammar, we add the concept of probability. Don't worry - it's one of the most simple extensions of CFG that we've seen so far. We will now look at **probabilistic context-free grammar (PCFG)**.

Let's define PCFG formally and then explore a different aspect of it. Refer to *Figure 5.9*:

$$G = (T, N, S, R, P)$$

T is a set of terminal symbols

N is a set of nonterminal symbols

S is the start symbol ($S \in N$)

R is a set of rules/productions of the form $X \to \gamma$

P is the probability function

$$P \text{ is } | R \to [0,1]$$

$$\forall X \in N, \sum_{X \to \gamma \in R} P(X \to \gamma) = 1$$

Figure 5.9: PCFGs formal definition

Here, *T*, *N*, *S*, and *R* are similar to CFG; the only new thing here is the probability function, so let's look at that here, the probability function takes each grammar rule and gives us the probability value of each rule. This probability maps to a real number, *R*. The range for *R* is [0,1]. We are not blindly taking any probability value. We enter one constraint where we have defined that the sum of the probability for any non-terminal should add up to 1. Let's look at an example to understand things. You can see the grammar rules with probability in *Figure 5.10*:

S → NP VP	1.0
VP → V NP	0.6
VP → V NP PP	0.4
NP → NP NP	0.1
NP → NP PP	0.2
NP → N	0.7
PP → P NP	1.0

Figure 5.10: Probabilities for grammar rules

You can see the lexical grammar rules with probability in *Figure 5.11*:

N → *people*	0.5
N → *fish*	0.2
N → *tanks*	0.2
N → *rods*	0.1
V → *people*	0.1
V → *fish*	0.6
V → *tanks*	0.3
P → *with*	1.0

Figure 5.11: Probabilities for lexical rules

As you can see, *Figure 5.10* has three NP rules, and if you look at the probability distribution, you will notice the following:

- Its probability adds up to 1 (0.1 + 0.2 + 0.7 = 1.0)
- It is likely that NP is further rewritten as a noun as its probability is 0.7

In the same way, you can see that the first rule at the start of the sentence has a value of 1.0 because of a certain event that occurred first. If you look carefully, you'll notice that we have removed the empty string rule to make our grammar less ambiguous.

So, how are we going to use these probability values? This question leads us to the description of calculating the probability of trees and strings.

Calculating the probability of a tree

If we want to calculate the probability of a tree, it is quite easy because you need to multiply the probability values of lexicons and grammar rules. This will give us the probability of a tree.

Let's look at an example to understand this calculation. Here, we will take two trees and the sentence for which we have generated trees, **people fish tank with rods**.

Refer to *Figure 5.12* and *Figure 5.13* for tree structures with their respective probability values before we calculate the probability of each tree:

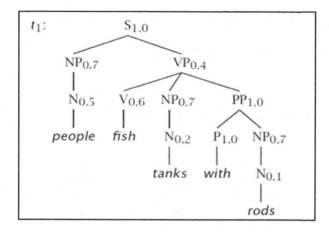

Figure 5.12: Parse Tree

If we want calculate the probability for the parse tree given in *Figure 5.12*, then the steps of obtaining the probability is given as follows. We start scanning the tree from the top, so our string point is **S**, the top most node of the parse tree. Here, the preposition modifies the verb:

$P(t1) = 1.0 * 0.7 * 0.4 * 0.5 * 0.6 * 0.7 * 1.0 * 0.2 * 1.0 * 0.7 * 0.1 = 0.0008232$

The value 0.0008232 is the probability of the tree. Now you can calculate the same for another parse tree given in *Figure 5.13*. In this parse tree, the preposition modifies the noun. Calculate the tree probability for this parse tree:

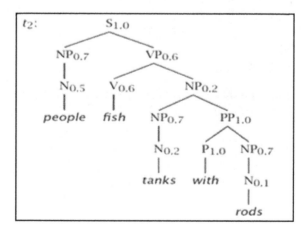

Figure 5.13: Second parse tree

If you calculate the parse tree probability, the value should be 0.00024696.

Now let's look at the calculation of the probability of string that uses the concept of the probability of a tree.

Calculating the probability of a string

Calculating the probability of a string is more complex compared to calculating the probability of a tree. Here, we want to calculate the probability of strings of words, and for that we need to consider all the possible tree structures that generate the string for which we want to calculate the probability. We first need to consider all the trees that have the string as part of the tree and then calculate the final probability by adding the different probabilities to generate the final probability value.

Let's revisit *Figure 5.12* and *Figure 5.13*, which we used to calculate the tree probability. Now, in order to calculate the probability of the string, we need to consider both the tree and the tree probability and then add those. Calculate the probability of the string as follows:

P(S) = P(t1) +P(t2)

= 0.0008232 + 0.00024696

= 0.00107016

Here, *t1* tree has a high probability, so a **VP**-attached sentence structure is more likely to be generated compared to *t2*, which has **NP** attached to it. The reason behind this is that *t1* has a **VP** node with *0.4*, whereas *t2* has two nodes, **VP** with a probability of *0.6* and **NP** with a probability of *0.2* probability. When you multiply this, you will get *0.12*, which is less than *0.4*. So, the *t1* parse tree is the most likely structure.

You should now understand the different types of grammar. Now, it's time to explore the concept of grammar transformation for efficient parsing.

Grammar transformation

Grammar transformation is a technique used to make grammar more restrictive, which makes the parsing process more efficient. We will use **Chomsky Normal Form (CNF)** to transform grammar rules. Let's explore CNF before looking at an example.

Let's see CNF first. It states that all rules should follow the following rules:

X-> Y Z or X-> w where X, Y, Z ε N and w ε T

The meaning of the rule is very simple. You should not have more than two non-terminals on the right-hand side of any grammar rule; you can include the rules where the right-hand side of the rule has a single terminal. To transform the existing grammar into CNF, there is a basic procedure that you can follow:

- Empty rules and unary rules can be removed using recursive functions.
- *N*-ary rules are divided by introducing new non-terminals in the grammar rules. This applies to rules that have more than two non-terminals on the right-hand side. When you use CNF, you can get the same string using new transform rules, but its parse structure may differ. The newly generated grammar after applying CNF is also CFG.

Let's look at the intuitive example. We take the grammar rules that we defined earlier in *Figure 5.6* and apply CNF to transform those grammar rules. Let's begin. See the following steps:

1. We first remove the empty rules. When you have **NP** on the right-hand side, you can have two rules such as **S -> NP VP**, and when you put an empty value for **NP**, you will get **S -> VP**. By applying this method recursively, you will get rid of the empty rule in the grammar.

2. Then, we must try to remove unary rules. So, in this case, if you try to remove the first unary rule **S -> VP**, then you need to consider all the rules that have **VP** on their left-hand side. When you do this, you need to introduce new rules because **S** will immediately go to **VP**. We will introduce the rule, **S -> V NP**. You need to keep doing this until you get rid of the unary rules. When you remove all the unary rules, such as **S -> V**, then you also need to change your lexical entries.

Refer to *Figure 5.14* for the CNF process:

Step 1	Step 2	Step 3		Step 4	Step 5
S → NP VP	S → NP VP	S → NP VP	N → *people*	S → NP VP	S → NP VP
S → VP	VP → V NP	VP → V NP	N → *fish*	VP → V NP	VP → V NP
VP → V NP	S → V NP	S → V NP	N → *tanks*	S → V NP	S → V NP
VP → V	VP → V	VP → V		VP → V NP PP	VP → V NP PP
VP → V NP PP	S → V	VP → V NP PP	N → *rods*	S → V NP PP	S → V NP PP
VP → V PP	VP → V NP PP	S → V NP PP	V → *people*	VP → V PP	VP → V PP
NP → NP NP	S → V NP PP	VP → V PP	S → *people*	S → V PP	S → V PP
NP → NP	VP → V PP	S → V PP	V → *fish*	NP → NP NP	NP → NP NP
NP → NP PP	S → V PP	NP → NP NP	S → *fish*	NP → NP	NP → NP PP
NP → PP	NP → NP NP	NP → NP	S → *fish*	NP → NP PP	NP → P NP
NP → N	NP → NP	NP → NP PP	V → *tanks*	NP → PP	PP → P NP
PP → P NP	NP → NP PP	NP → PP	S → *tanks*	NP → N	
PP → P	NP → PP	NP → N	P → *with*	PP → P NP	
	NP → N	PP → P NP		PP → P	
	PP → P NP	PP → P			
	PP → P				

Figure 5.14: CNF steps 1 to 5

You can see the final result of the CNF process in *Figure 5.15*:

S → NP VP	NP → *people*
VP → V NP	NP → *fish*
S → V NP	NP → *tanks*
VP → V @VP_V	NP → *rods*
@VP_V → NP PP	V → *people*
S → V @S_V	S → *people*
@S_V → NP PP	VP → *people*
VP → V PP	V → *fish*
S → V PP	S → *fish*
NP → NP NP	VP → *fish*
NP → NP PP	V → *tanks*
NP → P NP	S → *tanks*
PP → P NP	VP → *tanks*
	P → *with*
	PP → *with*

Figure 5.15: Step 6 - Final grammar rules after applying CNF

In real life, it is not necessary to apply full CNF, and it can often be quite painful to do so. It just makes parsing more efficient and your grammar rules cleaner. In real-life applications, we keep unary rules as our grammar rules because they tell us whether a word is treated as a verb or noun, as well as the non-terminal symbol information, which means that we have the information of the POS tag.

That's enough of the boring conceptual part. Now it's time to combine all the basic concepts of parsers and parsing to learn the algorithm that is used to develop a parser.

Developing a parser with the Cocke-Kasami-Younger Algorithm

For the English language, there are plenty of parsers that you can use, CNF if you want to build a parser for any other language, you can use the **Cocke-Kasami-Younger (CKY)** algorithm. Here, we will look at some information that will be useful to you in terms of making a parser. We will also look at the main logic of the CKY algorithm.

We need to look at the assumption that we are considering before we start with the algorithm. Our technical assumption is that, here, each of the parser subtrees is independent. This means that if we have a tree node NP, then we just focus on this NP node and not on the node its, derived from; each of the subtrees act independently. The CKY algorithm can give us the result in cubic time.

Now let's look at the logic of the CKY algorithm. This algorithm takes words from the sentences and tries to generate a parse tree using bottom-up parsing. Here, we will define a data structure that is called a **parse triangle** or **chart**. Refer to *Figure 5.16*:

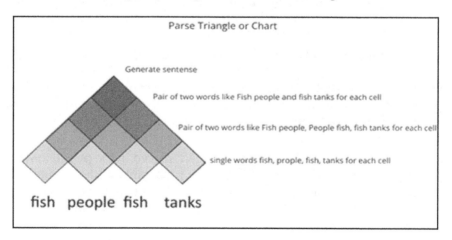

Figure 5.16: Parse triangle for the CKY algorithm

Its bottom cells represent single words such as **fish, people, fish,** and **tanks**. The cells in the middle row represent the overlapped word pairs such as **Fish people, People fish,** and **fish tanks.** Its third row represents the pair of two words without overlapping such as **Fish people** and **fish tanks**. The last row represents the top or root of the sentence. To understand the algorithm, we first need the grammar rules of rule probability. To understand the algorithm, we should refer to *Figure 5.17*:

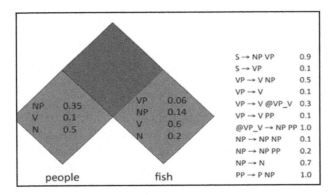

Figure 5.17: To understand the CKY algorithm (Image credit: http://spark-public.s3.amazonaws.com/nlp/slides/Parsing-Probabilistic.pdf page no: 36)

As shown in *Figure 5.17*, to explain the algorithm logic, we have entered the basic probability values in the bottom-most cells. Here, we need to find all the combinations that the fulfill grammar rules. Follow the given steps:

1. We will first take **NP** from the **people** cell and **VP** from the **fish** cell. In the grammar rules, check whether there is any grammar rule present that takes the sequence, **NP VP**, which you will need to find on the right-hand side of the grammar rule. Here, we found that the rule is **S -> NP VP** with a probability of 0.9.

2. Now, calculate the probability value, and to find this, you need to multiply the probability value of **NP** given in the people cell, the probability value of **VP** in the **fish** cell, and the probability value of the grammar rule itself. So here, the probability value of **NP** placed in the **people** cell = 0.35, the probability value of **VP** placed in the **fish** cell =*0.06* and the probability of the grammar rule **S -> NP VP** = 0.9.

3. We then multiply 0.35 (the probability of **NP** placed in the **people** cell) * 0.06 (the probability of **VP** in the **fish** cell) * 0.9 (the probability of the grammar rule **S -> NP VP**). Therefore, the final multiplication value = *0.35 * 0.06 * 0.9 = 0.0189. 0.0189* is the final probability for the grammar rule if we expand **S** into the **NP VP** grammar rule.

4. In the same way, you can calculate other combinations, such as **NP** from the **people** cell and **NP** from the **fish** cell, and find the grammar rule, that is, **NP NP** on the right-hand side. Here, the **NP - NP NP** rule exists. So we calculate the probability value, *0.35 * 0.14 * 0.2 = 0.0098*. We continue with this process until we generate the probability value for all the combinations, and then we will see for which combination we have generated the maximum probability. The process of finding the maximum probability is called **Viterbi max score**.

5. For the combination **S -> NP VP**, we will get the maximum probability when the cells generate the left-hand side non-terminal on its upward cell. So, those two cells generate **S**, which is a sentence.

This is the core logic of the CKY algorithm. Let's look at one concrete example for this concept. For writing purposes, we will rotate the parse triangle 90 degrees clockwise. Refer to *Figure 5.18*:

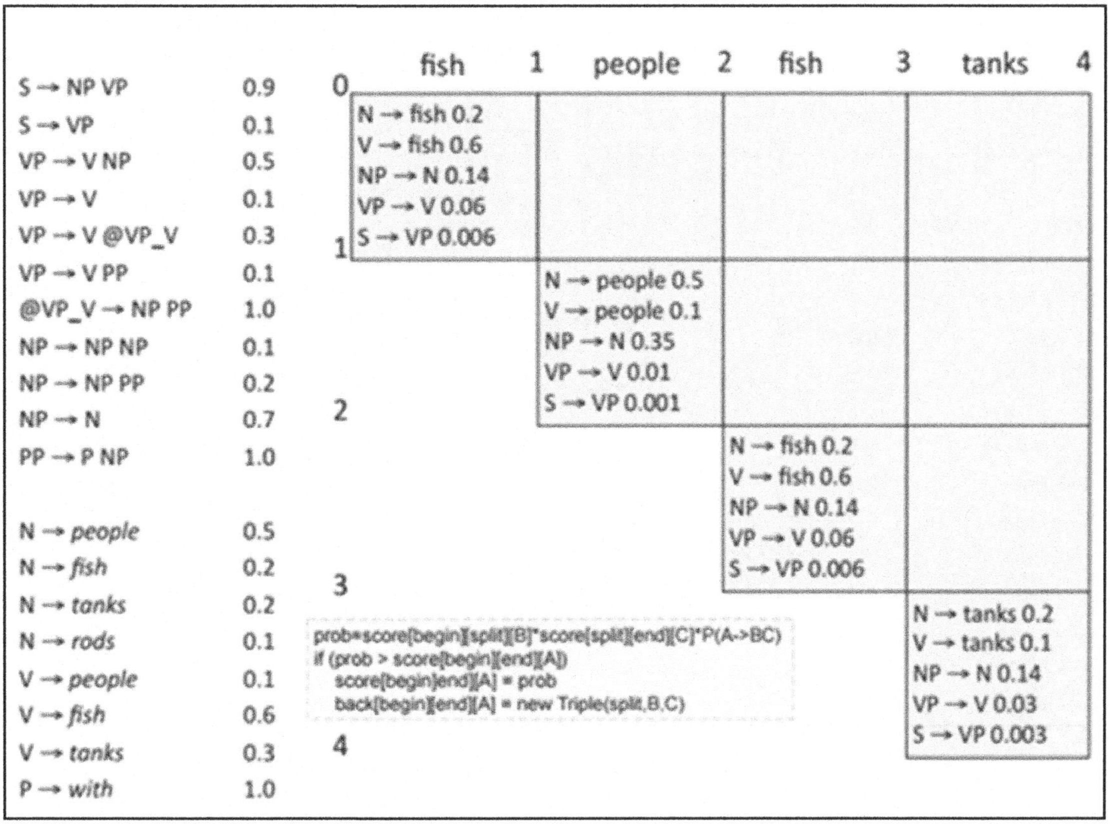

Figure 5.18: Step 1 for the CKY algorithm (Image credit: http://spark-public.s3.amazonaws.com)

Here, *cell (0,1)* is for **fish** and it fills using lexical rules. We have put **N -> fish** with *0.2* probability because this is defined in our grammar rule. We have put **V -> fish** with *0.6* probability. Now we focus on some unary rules that have **N** or **V** only on the right-hand side. We have the rules that we need to calculate the probability by considering the grammar rules probability and lexical probability. So, for rule **NP -> N**, the probability is *0.7* and **N -> fish** has the probability value *0.2*. We need to multiply this value and generate the probability of the grammar rule **NP -> N** = *0.14*. In the same way, we generate the probability for the rule **VP -> V**, and its value is *0.1 * 0.6 = 0.6*. This way, you need to fill up all the four cells.

In the next stage, we follow the same procedure to get the probability for each combination generated from the grammar rules. Refer to *Figure 5.19*:

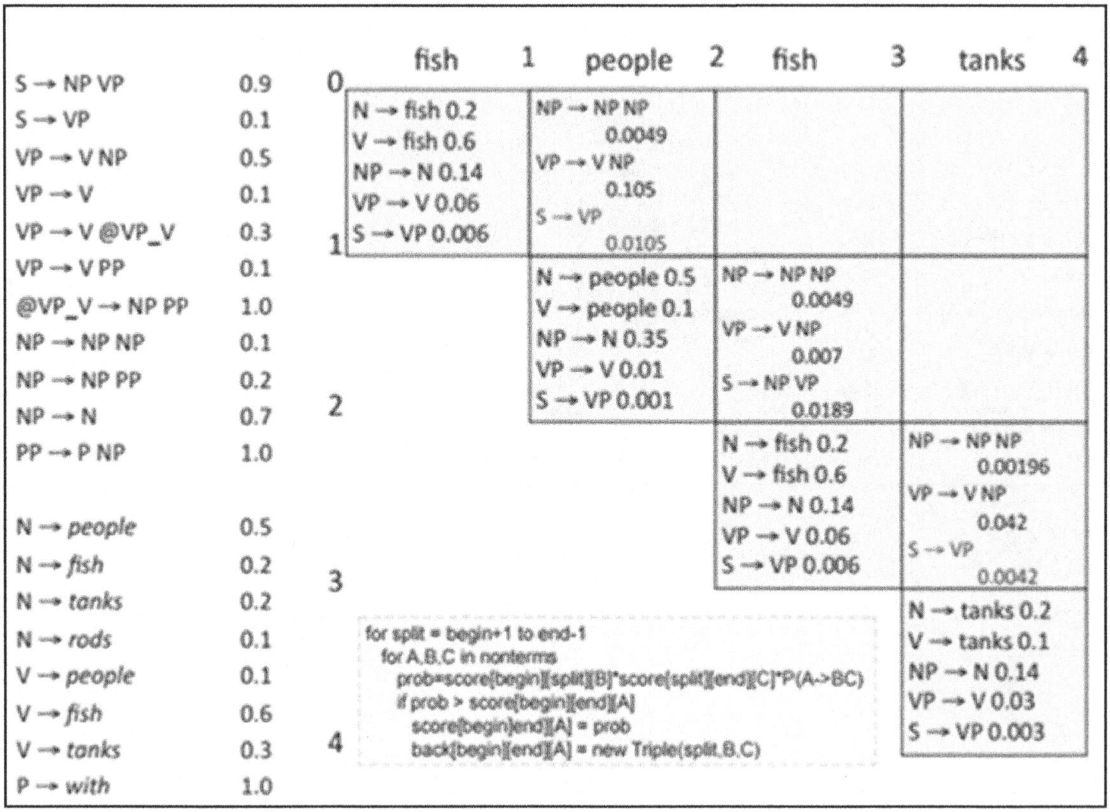

Figure 5.19 : Stage 2 of the CKY algorithm (Image credit: http://spark-public.s3.amazonaws.com)

In *Figure 5.20*, you can see the final probability values, using which you can decide the best parse tree for the given data:

Grammar rules:

Rule	Prob
S → NP VP	0.9
S → VP	0.1
VP → V NP	0.5
VP → V	0.1
VP → V @VP_V	0.3
VP → V PP	0.1
@VP_V → NP PP	1.0
NP → NP NP	0.1
NP → NP PP	0.2
NP → N	0.7
PP → P NP	1.0
N → people	0.5
N → fish	0.2
N → tanks	0.2
N → rods	0.1
V → people	0.1
V → fish	0.6
V → tanks	0.3
P → with	1.0

CKY chart (words: 0 fish 1 people 2 fish 3 tanks 4):

	fish (0–1)	people (1–2)	fish (2–3)	tanks (3–4)
1	N → fish 0.2 V → fish 0.6 NP → N 0.14 VP → V 0.06 S → VP 0.006	NP → NP NP 0.0049 VP → V NP 0.105 S → VP 0.0105	NP → NP NP 0.0000686 VP → V NP 0.00147 S → NP VP 0.000882	NP → NP NP 0.0000009604 VP → V NP 0.00002058 S → NP VP 0.00018522
2		N → people 0.5 V → people 0.1 NP → N 0.35 VP → V 0.01 S → VP 0.001	NP → NP NP 0.0049 VP → V NP 0.007 S → NP VP 0.0189	NP → NP NP 0.0000686 VP → V NP 0.000098 S → NP VP 0.01323
3			N → fish 0.2 V → fish 0.6 NP → N 0.14 VP → V 0.06 S → VP 0.006	NP → NP NP 0.00196 VP → V NP 0.042 S → VP 0.0042
4				N → tanks 0.2 V → tanks 0.1 NP → N 0.14 VP → V 0.03 S → VP 0.003

Call buildTree(score, back) to get the best parse

Figure 5.20: The final stage of the CKY algorithm (Image credit: http://spark-public.s3.amazonaws.com)

Now you know how the parse tree has been generated we want to share with you some important facts regarding the Stanford parser. It is built based on this CKY algorithm. There are a couple of technical assumptions and improvisations applied to the Stanford parser, but the following are the core techniques used to build the parser.

Developing parsers step-by-step

Here, we will look at the steps required to build your own parser with the help of the CKY algorithm. Let's begin summarizing:

1. You should have tagged the corpus that has a human-annotated parse tree: if it is tagged as per the Penn Treebank annotation format, then you are good to go.
2. With this tagged parse corpus, you can derive the grammar rules and generate the probability for each of the grammar rules.
3. You should apply CNF for grammar transformation.

4. Use the grammar rules with probability and apply them to the large corpus; use the CKY algorithm with the Viterbi max score to get the most likely parse structure. If you are providing a large amount of data, then you can use the ML learning technique and tackle this problem as a multiclass classifier problem. The last stage is where you get the best parse tree for the given data as per the probability value.

That's enough theory; let's now use some of the famous existing parser tools practically and also check what kind of features you can generate from the parse tree.

Existing parser tools

In this section, we will look at some of the existing parsers and how you can generate some cool features that can be used for ML algorithms or in rule-based systems.

Here, we will see two parsers:

- The Stanford parser
- The spaCy parser

The Stanford parser

Let's begin with the Stanford parser. You can download it from `https://stanfordnlp.github.io/CoreNLP/`. After downloading it, you just need to extract it to any location you like. The prerequisite of running the Stanford parser is that you should have a Java-run environment installed in your system. Now you need to execute the following command in order to start the Stanford parser service:

```
$ cd stanford-corenlp-full-2016-10-31/
$ java -mx4g -cp "*"
edu.stanford.nlp.pipeline.StanfordCoreNLPServer
```

Here, you can change the memory from -mx4g to -mx3g.

Let's look at the concept of dependency in the parser before can fully concentrating on the coding part.

The dependency structure in the parser shows which words depend on other words in the sentence. In the sentence, some words modify the meaning of other words; on the other hand, some act as an argument for other words. All of these kinds of relationships are described using dependencies. There are several dependencies in the Stanford parser. We will go through some of them. Let's take an example and we will explain things as we go.

The sentence is: The boy put the tortoise on the rug.

For this given sentence, the **head** of the sentence is *put* and it modifies three sections: *boy*, *tortoise*, and *on the rug*. How do you find the head word of the sentence? Find out by asking the following questions:

- Who put it down? You get the answer: *boy*
- Then, what thing did he put down? You get the answer: *tortoise*
- Where is it put? You get the answer: *on the rug*

So, the word **put** modifies three things. Now look at the word *boy*, and check whether there is any modifier for it. Yes, it has a modifier: **the**. Then, check whether there is any modifier for *tortoise*. Yes, it has a modifier: **the**. For the phrase *on the rug on* complements *rug* and *rug* acts as the head for this phrase, taking a modifier, *the*. Refer to *Figure 5.21*:

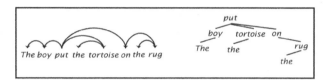

Figure 5.21: Dependency structure of the sentence

The Stanford parser has dependencies like `nsubjpass` (passive nominal subject), `auxpass` (passive auxiliary), `prep` (prepositional modifier), `pobj` (object of preposition), `conj` (conjunct), and so on. We won't go into more detail regarding this, but is worth mentioning that dependency parsing also follows the tree structure and it's linked by binary asymmetric relations called **dependencies**. You can find more details about each of the dependencies by accessing the Stanford parser document here:

`https://nlp.stanford.edu/software/dependencies_manual.pdf`.

You can see the basic example in *Figure 5.22*:

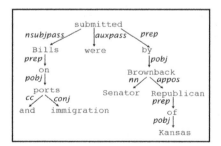

Figure 5.22: Dependency parsing of the sentence

Now if you want to use the Stanford parser in Python, you have to use the dependency named `pycorenlp`. We will use it to generate the output from the Stanford parser.

You can see the sample code in which we have used the Stanford parser to parse the sentence. You can parse multiple sentences as well. You can find the code at the following GitHub link:

`https://github.com/jalajthanaki/NLPython/tree/master/ch5/parserexample`.

You can see the code snippet in *Figure 5.23*:

```python
nlp = StanfordCoreNLP('http://localhost:9000')
def stanfordparserdemo(sentnece):
    text = (sentnece)

    output = nlp.annotate(text, properties={
        'annotators': 'tokenize,ssplit,pos,depparse,parse',
        'outputFormat': 'json'
    })

    print "\n------------Stanford Parser Parseing Result------------"
    parsetree = output['sentences'][0]['parse']
    print "\n------parsing------\n"
    print parsetree
    print "\n------ Words inside NP ------\n"
    for i in Tree.fromstring(parsetree).subtrees():
        if i.label() == 'NP':
            print i.leaves(),i.label()
    print "\n------ Words inside NP with POS tags ------\n"
    for i in Tree.fromstring(parsetree).subtrees():
        if i.label() == 'NP':
            print i

def NLTKparserfordependancies(sentnece):

    path_to_jar = '/home/jalaj/stanford-corenlp-full-2016-10-31/stanford-corenlp-3.7.0.jar'
    path_to_models_jar = '/home/jalaj/stanford-corenlp-full-2016-10-31/stanford-corenlp-3.7.0-models.jar'
    dependency_parser = StanfordDependencyParser(path_to_jar=path_to_jar, path_to_models_jar=path_to_models_jar)
    result = dependency_parser.raw_parse(sentnece)
    dep = result.next()
    print "\n------Dependencies------\n"
    print list(dep.triples())

if __name__ == "__main__":
    stanfordparserdemo('The boy put tortoise on the rug.')
    NLTKparserfordependancies('The boy put tortoise on the rug.')
```

Figure 5.23: Code snippet for the Stanford parser demo

You can see the output of this code in *Figure 5.24*:

```
-----------Stanford Parser Parseing Result-----------

------parsing------

(ROOT
  (S
    (NP (DT The) (NN boy))
    (VP (VBD put)
      (NP (NN tortoise))
      (PP (IN on)
        (NP (DT the) (NN rug))))
    (. .)))

------ Words inside NP ------

[u'The', u'boy'] NP
[u'tortoise'] NP
[u'the', u'rug'] NP

------ Words inside NP with POS tags ------

(NP (DT The) (NN boy))
(NP (NN tortoise))
(NP (DT the) (NN rug))

------Dependencies------

[((u'put', u'VBD'), u'nsubj', (u'boy', u'NN')), ((u'boy', u'NN'),
u'det', (u'The', u'DT')), ((u'put', u'VBD'), u'dobj', (u'tortoise', u'NN')),
((u'put', u'VBD'), u'nmod', (u'rug', u'NN')), ((u'rug', u'NN'), u'case', (u'on', u'IN')),
((u'rug', u'NN'), u'det', (u'the', u'DT'))]
```

Figure 5.24: Output of the Stanford parser

The spaCy parser

This parser helps you generate the parsing for the sentence. This is a dependency parser. You can find the code at the following GitHub link:

https://github.com/jalajthanaki/NLPython/blob/master/ch5/parserexample/scpacy parserdemo.py.

You can find the code snippet of this parser in *Figure 5.25*:

```
import spacy
from spacy.en import English
parser = English()
nlp = spacy.load('en')

def spacyparserdemo():
        example = u"The boy with the spotted dog quickly ran after the firetruck."
        parsedEx = parser(example)
        # shown as: original token, dependency tag, head word, left dependents, right dependents
        print "\n----------original token, dependency tag, head word, left dependents, right dependents-------\n"
        for token in parsedEx:
            print(
                token.orth_, token.dep_, token.head.orth_, [t.orth_ for t in token.lefts], [t.orth_ for t in token.rights])

if __name__ == "__main__":
    spacyparserdemo()
```

Figure 5.25: spaCy dependency parser code

You can see the output of the spaCy parser in *Figure 5.26*:

```
----------original token, dependency tag, head word, left dependents, right dependents-------

(u'The', u'det', u'boy', [], [])
(u'boy', u'nsubj', u'ran', [u'The'], [u'with'])
(u'with', u'prep', u'boy', [], [])
(u'the', u'det', u'dog', [], [])
(u'spotted', u'amod', u'dog', [], [])
(u'dog', u'nsubj', u'ran', [u'the', u'spotted'], [])
(u'quickly', u'advmod', u'ran', [], [])
(u'ran', u'ROOT', u'ran', [u'boy', u'dog', u'quickly'], [u'after', u'.'])
(u'after', u'prep', u'ran', [], [u'firetruck'])
(u'the', u'det', u'firetruck', [], [])
(u'firetruck', u'pobj', u'after', [u'the'], [])
(u'.', u'punct', u'ran', [], [])
```

Figure 5.26: The spaCy parser output

People used the Stanford parser because it provides good accuracy as well as a lot of flexibility in terms of generating output. Using the Stanford parser, you can generate the output in a JSON format, XML format, or text format. You may think that we get the parse tree using the preceding code, but the kind of features that we can derive from the parsing result will be discussed in the next section.

Extracting and understanding the features

Generally, using the parse result, you can derive many features such as generating noun phrases and POS tags inside the noun phrase; you can also derive the head word from phrases. You can use each word and its tag. You can use the dependency relationships as features. You can see the code snippet in *Figure 5.27*:

```
print   "\n------------Stanford Parser Parseing Result------------"
parsetree = output['sentences'][0]['parse']
print "\n------parsing------\n"
print parsetree
print   "\n------ Words inside NP ------\n"
for i in Tree.fromstring(parsetree).subtrees():
    if i.label() == 'NP':
        print i.leaves(),i.label()
print   "\n------ Words inside NP with POS tags ------\n"|
for i in Tree.fromstring(parsetree).subtrees():
    if i.label() == 'NP':
        print i
```

Figure 5.27: Code to get NP from sentences

The output snippet is in *Figure 5.28*:

```
------ Words inside NP with POS tags ------

(NP (DT The) (NN boy))
(NP (NN tortoise))
(NP (DT the) (NN rug))
```

Figure 5.28: Output all NP from sentences

You can generate the stem as well as lemma from each word, as we saw in `Chapter 3`, *Understanding Structure of Sentences*.

In real life, you can generate the features easily using libraries, but which features you need to use is critical and depends on your NLP application. Let's assume that you are making a grammar correction system; in that case, you need to consider all the phrases of the sentence as well as the POS tags of each word present in the phrase. If you are developing a question-answer system, then noun phases and verb phrases are the important features that you can select.

Features selection is a bit tricky and you will need to do some iteration to get an idea of which features are good for your NLP application. Try to dump your features in a `.csv` file so you can use the `.csv` file later on in your processing. Each and every feature can be a single column of the `.csv` file. For example, you have NP words stored in one column, lemma in the other column for all words in NP, and so on. Now, suppose you have more than 100 columns; in that case, you would need to find out which are the important columns (features) and which are not. Based on the problem statement and features, you can decide what the most important features are that help us to solve our problem. In `Chapter 8`, *Machine Learning for NLP Problems*, we will look at features selection in more detail.

Customizing parser tools

In real life, datasets are quite complex and messy. In that case, it may be that the parser is unable to give you a perfect or accurate result. Let's take an example.

Let's assume that you want to parse a dataset that has text content of research papers, and these research papers belong to the chemistry domain. If you are using the Stanford parser in order to generate a parse tree for this dataset, then sentences that contain chemical symbols and equations may not get parsed properly. This is because the Stanford parser has been trained on the Penn TreeBank corpus, so it's accuracy for the generation of a parse tree for chemical symbols and equation is low. In this case, you have two options - either you search for a parser that can generate parsing for symbols and equations accurately or if you have a corpus that has been tagged, you have the flexibility of retraining the Stanford parser using your tagged data.

You can follow the same tagging notation given in the Penn TreeBank data for your dataset, then use the following command to retrain the Stanford parser on your dataset, save the trained model, and use it later on. You can use the following command to retrain the Stanford Parser:

```
$ java —mx1500m —cp "stanford-parser.jar"
edu.stanford.nlp.parser.lexparser.LexicalizedParser —sentences newline —
tokenized —tagSeparator / —outputFormat "penn" englishPCFG.ser.gz
/home/xyz/PROJECT/COMPARING_PARSER_NOTES/data/483_18.taggedsents >
/home/xyz/PROJECT/COMPARING_PARSER_NOTES/data/483_18.stanford.parsed
```

Challenges

Here are some of the challenges related to parsers:

- To generate a parser for languages such as Hebrew, Gujarati, and so on is difficult and the reason is that we don't have a tagged corpus.
- Developing parsers for fusion languages is difficult. A fusion language means that you are using another language alongside the English language, with a sentence including more than one language. Processing these kinds of sentences is difficult.

Now that we have understood some features of the parser, we can move on to our next concept, which is POS tagging. This is one of the essential concepts of NLP.

POS tagging and POS taggers

In this section, we will discuss the long-awaited topic of POS tags.

Understanding the concept of POS tagging and POS taggers

POS tagging is defined as the process of marking words in the corpus corresponding to their particular part of speech. The POS of the word is dependent on both its definition and its context. It is also called **grammatical tagging** or **word-category disambiguation**. POS tags of words are also dependent on their relationship with adjacent and related words in the given phrase, sentence, and paragraph.

POS tagger is the tool that is used to assign POS tags for the given data. Assigning the POS tags is not an easy task because POS of words is changed as per the sentence structure and meaning. Let's take an example. Let's take the word dogs; generally, we all know that dogs is a plural noun, but in some sentences it acts as a verb. See the sentence: **The sailor dogs the hatch**. Here, the correct POS for *dogs* is the verb and not the plural noun. Generally, many POS taggers use the POS tags that are generated by the University of Pennsylvania. You can find word-level POS tags and definitions at the following link:

`https://www.ling.upenn.edu/courses/Fall_2003/ling001/penn_treebank_pos.html`.

We will now touch on some of the POS tags. There are 36 POS tags in the Penn Treebank POS list, such as **NN** indicates noun, **DT** for determiner words, and **FW** for foreign words. The word that is new to POS tags is generally assigned the **FW** tag. Latin names and symbols often get the **FW** tag by POS tagger. So, if you have a (lambda) symbol then POS may tagger suggest the **FW** POS tag for it. You can see some word-level POS tags in *Figure 5.29*:

```
SYM - Symbol
TO - to
UH - Interjection
VB - Verb, base form
VBD - Verb, past tense
VBG - Verb, gerund or present participle
VBN - Verb, past participle
VBP - Verb, non-3rd person singular present
VBZ - Verb, 3rd person singular present
WDT - Wh-determiner
WP - Wh-pronoun
WP$ - Possessive wh-pronoun (prolog version WP-S)
WRB - Wh-adverb
```

Figure 5.29: Some word-level POS tags

There are POS tags available at the phrase-level as well as the clause-level. All of these tags can be found at the following GitHub link:

https://github.com/jalajthanaki/NLPython/blob/master/ch5/POStagdemo/POS_tags.txt.

See each of the tags given in the file that we have specified as they are really useful when you evaluating your parse tree result. POS tags and their definitions are very straightforward, so if you know basic English grammar, then you can easily understand them.

You must be curious to know how POS taggers are built. Let's find out the procedure of making your own POS tagger.

Developing POS taggers step-by-step

To build your own POS tagger, you need to perform the following steps:

1. You need a tagged corpus.
2. Select features.
3. Perform training using a decision tree classifier available in the Python library, scikit-learn.
4. Check your accuracy.
5. Try to predict the POS tags using your own trained model.

A great part of this section is that we will code our own POS tagger in Python, so you guys will get an idea of how each of the preceding stages are performed in reality. If you don't know what a decision tree algorithm is, do not worry - we will cover this topic in more detail in Chapter 8, *Machine Learning for NLP Applications*.

Here, we will see a practical example that will help you understand the process of developing POS taggers. You can find the code snippet for each stage and you can access the code at the following GitHub link:

https://github.com/jalajthanaki/NLPython/tree/master/ch5/CustomPOStagger.

See the code snippet of getting the Pann TreeBank corpus in *Figure 5.30*:

```
tagged_sentences = nltk.corpus.treebank.tagged_sents()
print tagged_sentences[0]
```

Figure 5.30: Load the Penn TreeBank data from NLTK

You can see the feature selection code snippet in *Figure 5.31*:

```python
def features(sentence, index):
    " sentence: [w1, w2, ...], index: the index of the word "
    return {
    'word': sentence[index],
    'is_first': index == 0,
    'is_last': index == len(sentence) - 1,
    'is_capitalized': sentence[index][0].upper() == sentence[index][0],
    'is_all_caps': sentence[index].upper() == sentence[index],
    'is_all_lower': sentence[index].lower() == sentence[index],
    'prefix-1': sentence[index][0],
    'prefix-2': sentence[index][:2],
    'prefix-3': sentence[index][:3],
    'suffix-1': sentence[index][-1],
    'suffix-2': sentence[index][-2:],
    'suffix-3': sentence[index][-3:],
    'prev_word': '' if index == 0 else sentence[index - 1],
    'next_word': '' if index == len(sentence) - 1 else sentence[index + 1],
    'has_hyphen': '-' in sentence[index],
    'is_numeric': sentence[index].isdigit(),
    'capitals_inside': sentence[index][1:].lower() != sentence[index][1:]
    }

pprint.pprint(features(['This', 'is', 'a', 'sentence'], 2))

def untag(tagged_sentence):
    return [w for w, t in tagged_sentence]

def transform_to_dataset(tagged_sentences):
    X, y = [], []
    for tagged in tagged_sentences:
        for index in range(len(tagged)):
            X.append(features(untag(tagged), index))
            y.append(tagged[index][1])
            #print "index:"+str(index)+"original word:"+str(tagged)+"Word:"+str(untag(tagged))+"  Y:"+y[index]
    return X, y
```

Figure 5.31: Extracting features of each word

We have to extract the features for each word. You can see the code snippet for some basic transformation such as splitting the dataset into training and testing. Refer to *Figure 5.32*:

```python
cutoff = int(.75 * len(tagged_sentences))
training_sentences = tagged_sentences[:cutoff]
test_sentences = tagged_sentences[cutoff:]
```

Figure 5.32: Splitting the data into training and testing

See the code to train the model using a decision tree algorithm in *Figure 5.33*:

```python
X, y = transform_to_dataset(training_sentences)
clf = Pipeline([
    ('vectorizer', DictVectorizer(sparse=False)),
    ('classifier', DecisionTreeClassifier(criterion='entropy'))
])

clf.fit(X[:10000],
        y[:10000])   # Use only the first 10K samples if you're running it multiple times. It takes a fair bit :)

print 'Training completed'

X_test, y_test = transform_to_dataset(test_sentences)

print "Accuracy:", clf.score(X_test, y_test)


def pos_tag(sentence):
    tagged_sentence = []
    tags = clf.predict([features(sentence, index) for index in range(len(sentence))])
    return zip(sentence, tags)


print pos_tag(word_tokenize('This is my friend, John.'))
```

Figure 5.33: Actual training using a decision tree algorithm

See the output prediction of POS tags for the sentence that you provided in *Figure 5.34*:

```
[(u'Pierre', u'NNP'), (u'Vinken', u'NNP'), (u',', u','), (u'61', u'CD'),
(u'years', u'NNS'),(u'old', u'JJ'), (u',', u','), (u'will', u'MD'), (u'join', u'VB'),
(u'the', u'DT'),(u'board', u'NN'), (u'as', u'IN'), (u'a', u'DT'),
(u'nonexecutive', u'JJ'),(u'director', u'NN'), (u'Nov.', u'NNP'),
(u'29', u'CD'), (u'.', u'.')]

{'capitals_inside': False,
 'has_hyphen': False,
 'is_all_caps': False,
 'is_all_lower': True,
 'is_capitalized': False,
 'is_first': False,
 'is_last': False,
 'is_numeric': False,
 'next_word': 'sentence',
 'prefix-1': 'a',
 'prefix-2': 'a',
 'prefix-3': 'a',
 'prev_word': 'is',
 'suffix-1': 'a',
 'suffix-2': 'a',
 'suffix-3': 'a',
 'word': 'a'}
Training completed
Accuracy: 0.896271894585

[('This', u'DT'), ('is', u'VBZ'), ('my', u'NN'), ('friend', u'NN'), (',', u','), ('John', u'NNP'), ('.', u'.')]
```

Figure 5.34: Output of a custom POS tagger

You should have now understood the practical aspect of making your own POS tags, but you can still also use some of the cool POS taggers.

Plug and play with existing POS taggers

There are many POS taggers available nowadays. Here, we will use the POS tagger available in the Stanford CoreNLP and polyglot library. There are others such as the Tree tagger; NLTK also has a POS tagger that you can use. You can find the code at the following GitHub link:

```
https://github.com/jalajthanaki/NLPython/blob/master/ch5/POStagdemo.
```

A Stanford POS tagger example

You can see the code snippet for the Stanford POS tagger in *Figure 5.35*:

```python
from pycorenlp import StanfordCoreNLP
nlp = StanfordCoreNLP('http://localhost:9000')


def stnfordpostagdemofunction(text):
    output = nlp.annotate(text, properties={
        'annotators': 'pos',
        'outputFormat': 'json'
    })
    for s in output["sentences"]:
        for t in s["tokens"]:
            print str(t["word"])+ " --- postag --"+ str(t["pos"])


if __name__ == "__main__":
    stnfordpostagdemofunction("This is a car.")
```

Figure 5.35: Stanford POS tagger code

The output from the Stanford POS tagger can be found in *Figure 5.36*:

```
This --- postag --DT
is --- postag --VBZ
a --- postag --DT
car --- postag --NN
. --- postag --.
```

Figure 5.36: POS tags generated by the Stanford POS tagger

Using polyglot to generate POS tagging

You can see the code snippet for the `polyglot` POS tagger in *Figure 5.37*:

```
import polyglot
from polyglot.text import Text, Word
# EXECUTE THIS COMMAND ON YOUR TERMINAL
# polyglot download embeddings2.en pos2.en
text = Text("Bonjour, Mesdames.")
print("Language Detected: Code={}, Name={}\n".format(text.language.code, text.language.name))

zen = Text("Beautiful is better than ugly. "
           "Explicit is better than implicit. "
           "Simple is better than complex.")
print(zen.words)
text = Text("This is a car")

print("{:<16}{}".format("Word", "POS Tag")+"\n"+"-"*30)
for word, tag in text.pos_tags:
    print(u"{:<16}{:>2}".format(word, tag))
```

Figure 5.37: Polyglot POS tagger

The output from the `polyglot` POS tagger can be found in *Figure 5.38*:

```
Language Detected: Code=fr, Name=French

[u'Beautiful', u'is', u'better', u'than', u'ugly',
u'.', u'Explicit', u'is', u'better', u'than',
u'implicit', u'.', u'Simple', u'is', u'better',
u'than', u'complex', u'.']

Word            POS Tag
- - - - - - - - - - - - - - - - - - - - - - - - - -
This            DET
is              VERB
a               DET
car             NOUN
```

Figure 5.38:The polyglot POS tagger output

Exercise

Try using the TreeTagger library to generate POS tagging. You can find the installation details at this link:

`http://www.cis.uni-muenchen.de/~schmid/tools/TreeTagger/.`

Using POS tags as features

Now that we have generated POS tags for our text data using the POS tagger, where can we use them? We will now look at NLP applications that can use these POS tags as features.

POS tags are really important when you are building a chatbot with machine learning algorithms. POS tag sequences are quite useful when a machine has to understand various sentence structures. It is also useful if you are building a system that identifies **multiword express** (**MWE**). Some examples of MWE phrases are be able to, a little bit about, you know what, and so on.

If you have a sentence: **He backed off from the tour plan of Paris**. Here, *backed off* is the MWE. To identify these kinds of MWEs in sentences, you can use POS tags and POS tag sequences as features. You can use a POS tag in sentiment analysis, and there are other applications as well.

Challenges

The following are some challenges for POS tags:

- Identifying the right POS tag for certain words in an ambiguous syntax structure is difficult, and if the word carries a very different contextual meaning, then the POS tagger may generate the wrong POS tags.
- Developing a POS tagger for Indian languages is a bit difficult because, for some languages, you cannot find the tagged dataset.

Now let's move on to the next section, where we will learn how to find the different entities in sentences.

Name entity recognition

In this section, we will look at a tool called **name entity recognition** (**NER**). The use of this tool is as follows. If you have a sentence, such as **Bank of America announced its earning today**, we as humans can understand that the *Bank of America* is the name of a financial institution and should be referred to as a single entity. However, for machine to handle and recognize that entity is quite challenging. There is where NER tools come into the picture to rescue us.

With the NER tool, you can find out entities like person name, organization name, location, and so on. NER tools have certain classes in which they classify the entities. Here, we are considering the words of the sentence to find out the entities, and if there are any entities present in the sentence. Let's get some more details about what kind of entities we can find in our sentence using some of the available NER tools.

Classes of NER

NER tools generally segregate the entities into some predefined classes. Different NER tools have different types of classes. The Stanford NER tool has three different versions based on the NER classes:

- The first version is the three-class NER tool that can identify the entities - whether it's Location, Person, or Organization.
- The second version is the four-class NER tool that can identify the Location, person, Organization, and Misc. Misc is referred to as a miscellaneous entity type. If an entity doesn't belong to Location, Person, or Organization and is still an entity, then you can tag it as Misc.
- The third version is a seven-class tool that can identify Person, Location, Organization, Money, Percent, Date, and Time.

The spaCy parser also has an NER package available with the following classes.

- PERSON class identifies the name of a person
- NORP class meaning Nationality, Religious or Political groups
- FACILITY class including buildings, airports, highways, and so on
- ORG class for organization, institution and so on
- GPE class for cities, countries and so on
- LOC class for non-GPE locations such as mountain ranges and bodies of water
- PRODUCT that includes objects, vehicles, food, and so on, but not services
- EVENT class for sports events, wars, named hurricanes, and so on
- WORK_OF_ART class for titles of books, songs, and so on
- LANGUAGE that tags any named language
- Apart from this, spaCy's NER package has classes such as date, time, percent, money, quantity, ordinal, and cardinal

Now it's time to do some practical work. We will use the Stanford NER tool and spaCy NER in our next section.

Plug and play with existing NER tools

In this section, we will look at the coding part as well as information on how to practically use these NER tools. We will begin with the Stanford NER tool and then the Spacy NER. You can find the code at the following GitHub link:

```
https://github.com/jalajthanaki/NLPython/tree/master/ch5/NERtooldemo.
```

A Stanford NER example

You can find the code and output snippet as follows. You need to download the Stanford NER tool at `https://nlp.stanford.edu/software/CRF-NER.shtml#Download`.

You can see the code snippet in *Figure 5.39*:

```python
from nltk.tag import StanfordNERTagger
from nltk.tokenize import word_tokenize

st = StanfordNERTagger('/home/jalaj/stanford-ner-2016-10-31/classifiers'
                       '/english.muc.7class.distsim.crf.ser.gz',
                       '/home/jalaj/stanford-ner-2016-10-31/stanford-ner-3.7.0.jar',
                       encoding='utf-8')

text = 'While in France, Christine Lagarde discussed short-term ' \
       'stimulus efforts in a recent interview at 5:00 P.M with the Wall Street Journal.'

tokenized_text = word_tokenize(text)
classified_text = st.tag(tokenized_text)
print(classified_text)
```

Figure 5.39: Stanford NER tool code

You can see the output snippet in *Figure 5.40*:

```
[(u'While', u'O'), (u'in', u'O'), (u'France', u'LOCATION'),
(u',', u'O'), (u'Christine', u'PERSON'), (u'Lagarde', u'PERSON'),
(u'discussed', u'O'), (u'short-term', u'O'), (u'stimulus', u'O'),
(u'efforts', u'O'), (u'in', u'O'), (u'a', u'O'), (u'recent', u'O'),
(u'interview', u'O'), (u'at', u'O'), (u'5:00', u'O'), (u'P.M', u'O'),
(u'with', u'O'), (u'the', u'O'), (u'Wall', u'O'), (u'Street', u'O'),
(u'Journal', u'O'), (u'.', u'O')]
```

Figure 5.40: Output of Stanford NER

A Spacy NER example

You can find the code and output snippet as follows. You can see the code snippet in *Figure 5.41*:

```
import spacy
nlp = spacy.load('en')
doc = nlp(u'London is a big city in the United Kingdom.')
print "\n-------Example 1 ------\n"
for ent in doc.ents:
    print(ent.label_, ent.text)
    # GPE London
    # GPE United Kingdom
doc1 = nlp(u'While in France, Christine Lagarde discussed short-term stimulus efforts in a '
          u'recent interview on 5:00 P.M. with the Wall Street Journal')
print "\n-------Example 2 ------\n"
for ent1 in doc1.ents:
    print(ent1.label_, ent1.text)
```

Figure 5.41: spaCy NER tool code snippet

You can see the output snippet in *Figure 5.42*:

```
-------Example 1 ------

(u'GPE', u'London')
(u'GPE', u'the United Kingdom')

-------Example 2 ------

(u'GPE', u'France')
(u'PERSON', u'Christine Lagarde')
(u'TIME', u'5:00')
(u'ORG', u'Wall Street Journal')
```

Figure 5.42: Output of the spaCy tool

Extracting and understanding the features

NER tags are really important because they help you to understand sentence structure and help machines or NLP systems to understand the meaning of certain words in a sentence.

Let's take an example. If you are building a proofreading tool, then this NER tool is very useful because NER tools can find a person's name, an organizations' name, currency-related symbols, numerical formats, and so on that will help your proofreading tool identify exceptional cases present in text. Then, according to the NER tag, the system can suggest the necessary changes. Take the sentence, **Bank of America announced its earning today morning**. In this case, the NER tool gives the tag organization for *Bank of America*, which helps our system better understand the meaning of the sentence and the structure of the sentence.

NER tags are also very important if you are building a question-answer system as it is very crucial to extract entities in this system. Once you have generated the entities, you can use a syntactic relationship in order to understand questions. After this stage, you can process the question and generate the answer.

Challenges

There are certain challenges for the NER system, which are as follows:

- NER tools train on a closed domain dataset. So, an NER system developed for one domain does not typically perform well on an other domain. This requires a universal NER tool that can work for all domains, and after training it should able to generalize enough to deal with unseen situations.
- Sometimes you will find words which are the names of locations as well as the name of a person. The NER tool can't handle a case where one word can be expressed as the location name, person name, and organization name. This is a very challenging case for all NER tools. Suppose you have word TATA hospital; the single the words TATA can be the name of a person as well as the name of an organization. In this case, the NER tool can't decide whether TATA is the name of a person or the name of an organization.
- To build an NER tool specifically for microblogging web platforms is also a challenging task.

Let's move on to the next section, which is about n-gram algorithms. You will get to learn some very interesting stuff.

n-grams

n-gram is a very popular and widely used technique in the NLP domain. If you are dealing with text data or speech data, you can use this concept.

Let's look at the formal definition of n-grams. An n-gram is a continuous sequence of n items from the given sequence of text data or speech data. Here, items can be phonemes, syllables, letters, words, or base pairs according to the application that you are trying to solve.

There are some versions of n-grams that you will find very useful. If we put n=1, then that particular n-gram is referred to as a unigram. If we put n=2, then we get the bigram. If we put n=3, then that particular n-gram is referred to as a trigram, and if you put n=4 or n=5, then these versions of n-grams are referred to as four gram and five gram, respectively. Now let's take some examples from different domains to get a more detailed picture of n-grams. See examples from NLP and computational biology to understand a unigram in *Figure 5.43*:

Name of domain	items	Sample sequence of the data	1-gram unigram
Computational biology (DNA sequence)	base pair	...AGCTTCGA...	..., A,G,C,T,T,C,G,A ,...
Computational biology (Protine sequence)	Amino acid	...Cys-Gly-Leu-Ser-Trp ...	..., Cys, Gly, Leu, Ser, Trp, ...
NLP	character	...this_is_a_pen...	..., t,h,i,s,_,i,s,_,a,p,e,n ,...
NLP	words	...This is a pen...	..., this,is,a,pen ,...

Figure 5.43: Unigram example sequence

You have seen unigrams. Now we will look at the bigram. With bigrams, we are considering overlapped pairs, as you can see in the following example. We have taken the same NLP and computational biology sequences to understand bigrams. See *Figure 5.44*:

Name of domain	items	Sample sequence of the data	2-gram bigram
Computational biology (DNA sequence)	base pair	...AGCTTCGA...	..., AG,GC,CT,TC,CG,GA ,...
Computational biology (Protine sequence)	Amino acid	...Cys-Gly-Leu-Ser-Trp ...	..., Cys-Gly, Gly-Leu, Leu-Ser, Ser-Trp, ...
NLP	character	...this_is_a_pen...	..., th,hi,is,s_,_i,is,s_,_a,a_,_p,pe,en ,...
NLP	words	...This is a pen...	..., this is, is a, a pen ,...

Figure 5.44: Bigram example sequence

If you understood the bigram overlapped pairing concept from the example, then a trigram will be easier for you to understand. A trigram is just an extension of the bigram, but if you are still confused, then let's explain it for you in laymans' terms. In the first three rows of *Figure 5.44*, we generated a character-based bigram and the fourth row is a word-based bigram. We will start from the first character and consider the very next character because we are considering n=2 and the same is applicable to words as well. See the first row where we are considering a bigram such as *AG* as the first bigram. Now, in the next iteration, we are considering *G* again and generate *GC*. In the next iteration, we are considering *C* again and so on. For generating a trigram, see the same examples that we have looked at previously for. Refer to *Figure 5.45*:

Name of domain	items	Sample sequence of the data	3-gram trigram
Computational biology (DNA sequence)	base pair	...AGCTTCGA...	..., AGC,GCT,CTT,TTC,TCG,CGA ,...
Computational biology (Protine sequence)	Amino acid	...Cys-Gly-Leu-Ser-Trp ...	..., Cys-Gly-Leu, Gly-Leu-Ser, Leu-Ser-Trp ,...
NLP	character	...this_is_a_pen...	..., thi,his,is_,s_i,_is,is_,s_a,_a_,a_p,_pe,pen ,...
NLP	words	...This is a pen...	..., this is a, is a pen ,...

Figure 5.45: Trigram example sequence

The preceding examples are very much self-explanatory. You can figure out how we are taking up the sequencing from the number of n. Here, we are taking the overlapped sequences, which means that if you are taking a trigram and taking the words **this**, **is**, and **a** as a single pair, then next time, you are considering **is**, **a**, and **pen**. Here, the word *is* overlaps, but these kind of overlapped sequences help store context. If we are using large values for n-five-gram or six-gram, we can store large contexts but we still need more space and more time to process the dataset.

Understanding n-gram using a practice example

Now we are going to implement n-gram using the `nltk` library. You can see the code at this GitHub link:

`https://github.com/jalajthanaki/NLPython/tree/master/ch5/n_gram`.

You can see the code snippet in *Figure 5.46*:

```
from nltk import ngrams
sentence = 'this is a foo bar sentences and i want to ngramize it'
n = 4 # you can give 4, 5, 1 or any number less than sentences length
ngramsres = ngrams(sentence.split(), n)
for grams in ngramsres:
  print grams
```

Figure 5.46: NLTK n-gram code

You can see the output code snippet in *Figure 5.47*:

```
('this', 'is', 'a', 'foo')
('is', 'a', 'foo', 'bar')
('a', 'foo', 'bar', 'sentences')
('foo', 'bar', 'sentences', 'and')
('bar', 'sentences', 'and', 'i')
('sentences', 'and', 'i', 'want')
('and', 'i', 'want', 'to')
('i', 'want', 'to', 'ngramize')
('want', 'to', 'ngramize', 'it')
```

Figure 5.47: Output of the n-gram

Application

In this section, we will see what kinds of applications n-gram has been used in:

- If you are making a plagiarism tool, you can use n-gram to extract the patterns that are copied, because that's what other plagiarism tools do to provide basic features
- Computational biology has been using n-grams to identify various DNA patterns in order to recognize any unusual DNA pattern; based on this, biologists decide what kind of genetic disease a person may have

Now let's move on to the next concept, which is an easy but very useful concept for NLP applications: Bag of words.

Bag of words

Bag of words (**BOW**) is the technique that is used in the NLP domain.

Understanding BOW

This BOW model makes our life easier because it simplifies the representation used in NLP. In this model, the data is in the form of text and is represented as the bag or multiset of its words, disregarding grammar and word order and just keeping words. Here, text is either a sentence or document. Let's an example to give you a better understanding of BOW.

Let's take the following sample set of documents:

Text document 1: John likes to watch cricket. Chris likes cricket too.

Text document 2: John also likes to watch movies.

Based on these two text documents, you can generate the following list:

```
List  of words= ["John", "likes", "to", "watch", "cricket", "Chris", "too",
"also", "movies"]
```

This list is called **BOW**. Here, we are not considering the grammar of the sentences. We are also not bothered about the order of the words. Now it's time to see the practical implementation of BOW. BOW is often used to generate features; after generating BOW, we can derive the term-frequency of each word in the document, which can later be fed to a machine learning algorithm. For the preceding documents, you can generate the following frequency list:

Frequency count for Document 1: [1, 2, 1, 1, 2, 1, 1, 0, 0]

Frequency count for Document 2: [1, 1, 1, 1, 0, 0, 0, 1, 1]

So, how did we generate the list of frequency counts? In order to generate the frequency count of Document 1, consider the list of words and check how many times each of the listed words appear in Document 1. Here, we will first take the word, *John*, which appears in Document 1 once; the frequency count for Document 1 is 1. **Frequency count for Document 1: [1]**. For the second entry, the word *like* appears twice in Document 1, so the frequency count is 2. **Frequency count for Document 1: [1, 2]**. Now, we will take the third word from our list and the word is *to*. This word appears in Document 1 once, so we make the third entry in the frequency count as 1. **Frequency count for Document 1: [1, 2, 1]**. We have generated the frequency count for Document 1 and Document 2 in the same way. We will learn more about frequency in the upcoming section, TF-IDF, in this chapter.

Understanding BOW using a practical example

In this section, we will look at the practical implementation of BOW using `scikit-learn`. You can find the code at this GitHub link:

`https://github.com/jalajthanaki/NLPython/blob/master/ch5/bagofwordsdemo/BOWdemo.py`.

See the code snippet in *Figure 5.48*:

```
from sklearn.feature_extraction.text import CountVectorizer
import numpy as np

ngram_vectorizer = CountVectorizer(analyzer='char_wb', ngram_range=(2, 2), min_df=1)
# List is noumber of document here there are two document and each has only one word
# we are considering n_gram = 2 on chapracter unit leve
counts = ngram_vectorizer.fit_transform(['words', 'wprds'])
# this check weather the given word character is present in the above teo word which are documents here.
ngram_vectorizer.get_feature_names() == ([' w', 'ds', 'or', 'pr', 'rd', 's ', 'wo', 'wp'])
print counts.toarray().astype(int)
```

Figure 5.48: BOW scikit-learn implementation

The first row of the output belongs to the first document with the word, `words`, and the second row belongs to the document with the word, `wprds`. You can see the output in *Figure 5.49*:

```
[[1 1 1 0 1 1 1 0]
 [1 1 0 1 1 1 0 1]]
```

Figure 5.49: BOW vector representation

Comparing n-grams and BOW

We have looked at the concepts of n-grams and BOW. So, let's now see how n-grams and BOW are different or related to each other.

Let's first discuss the differences. Here, the difference is in terms of their usage in NLP applications. In n-grams, word order is important, whereas in BOW it is not important to maintain word order. During the NLP application, n-gram is used to consider words in their real order so we can get an idea about the context of the particular word; BOW is used to build vocabulary for your text dataset.

Now let's look at some meaningful relationships between n-grams and BOW that will give you an idea of how n-grams and BOW are related to each other. If you are considering n-gram as a feature, then BOW is the text representation derived using a unigram. So, in that case, an n-gram is equal to a feature and BOW is equal to a representation of text using a unigram (one-gram) contained within.

Now, let's check out an application of BOW.

Applications

In this section, we will look at which applications use BOW as features in the NLP domain:

- If you want to make an NLP application that classifies documents in different categories, then you can use BOW.
- BOW is also used to generate frequency count and vocabulary from a dataset. These derived attributes are then used in NLP applications such as sentiment analysis, Word2vec, and so on.

Now it's time to look at some of the semantic tools that we can use if we want to include semantic-level information in our NLP applications.

Semantic tools and resources

Trying to get the accurate meaning of a natural language is still a challenging task in the NLP domain, although we do have some techniques that have been recently developed and resources that we can use to get semantics from natural language. In this section, we will try to understand these techniques and resources.

The latent semantic analysis algorithm uses **term frequency - inverse document Frequency (tf-idf)** and the concept of linear algebra, such as cosine similarity and Euclidean distance, to find words with similar meanings. These techniques are a part of distributional semantics. The other one is word2vec. This is a recent algorithm that has been developed by Google and can help us find the semantics of words and words that have similar meanings. We will explore word2vec and other techniques in Chapter 6, *Advance Features Engineering and NLP Algorithms.*

Apart from Word2vec, another powerful resource is WordNet, which is the largest corpus available to us and it's tagged by humans. It also contains sense tags for each word. These databases are really helpful for finding out the semantics of a particular word.

 You can have a look at WordNet at the following link:
https://wordnet.princeton.edu/
Here, we have listed some of the most useful resources and tools for generating semantics. There is a lot of room for improvement in this area.

We have seen most of the NLP domain-related concepts and we have also seen how we can derive features using these concepts and available tools. Now it's time to jump into the next section, which will give us information about statistical features.

Basic statistical features for NLP

In the last section, we looked at most of the NLP concepts, tools, and algorithms that can be used to derive features. Now it's time to learn about some statistical features as well. Here, we will explore the statistical aspect. You will learn how statistical concepts help us derive some of the most useful features.

Before we jump into statistical features, as a prerequisite, you need to understand basic mathematical concepts, linear algebra concepts, and probabilistic concepts. So here, we will seek to understand these concepts first and then understand the statistical features.

Basic mathematics

We will begin with the basics of linear algebra and probability; this is because we want you to recall and memorize the necessary concepts so it will help you in this chapter as well as the upcoming chapters. We will explain the necessary math concepts as and when needed.

Basic concepts of linear algebra for NLP

In this section, we will not look at all the linear algebra concepts in great detail. The purpose of this section is to get familiar with the basic concepts. Apart from the given concepts, there are many other concepts that can be used in NLP applications. Here, we will cover only the much needed concepts. We will give you all the necessary details about algorithms and their mathematical aspects in upcoming chapters. Let's get started with the basics.

There are four main terms that you will find consistently in NLP and ML:

- **Scalars**: They are just single, the real number
- **Vectors**: They are a one-dimensional array of the numbers
- **Matrices**: They are two-dimensional arrays of the numbers
- **Tensors**: They are n-dimensional arrays of the numbers

The pictorial representation is given in *Figure 5.50*:

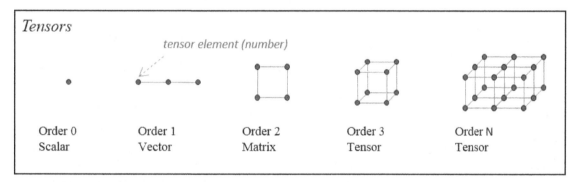

Figure 5.50: A pictorial representation of scalar, vector, matrix, and tensor (Image credit: http://hpe-cct.github.io/programmingGuide/img/diagram1.png)

Matrix manipulation operations are available in the NumPy library. You can perform vector-related operations using the SciPy and scikit-learn libraries. We will suggest certain libraries because their sources are written to give you optimal solutions and provide you with a high-level API so that you don't need to worry about what's going on behind the scenes. However, if you want to develop a customized application, then you need to know the math aspect of each manipulation. We will also look at the concept of linear regression, gradient descent, and linear algebra. If you really want to explore math that is related to machine learning and deep learning, then the following learning materials can help you.

Part one of this book will really help you:
`http://www.deeplearningbook.org/`

A cheat sheet of statistics, linear algebra, and calculus can be found at this link:
`https://github.com/jalajthanaki/NLPython/tree/master/Appendix2/C heatsheets/11_Math.`

If you are new to math, we recommend that you check out these videos:
`https://www.khanacademy.org/math/linear-algebra`
`https://www.khanacademy.org/math/probability`
`https://www.khanacademy.org/math/calculus-home`
`https://www.khanacademy.org/math/calculus-home/multivariable-cal culus`
`https://www.khanacademy.org/math`
`If you want to see the various vector similarity concepts, then this article will help you:`
`http://dataaspirant.com/2015/04/11/five-most-popular-similarity-measures-implementation-in-python/`

Now let's jump into the next section, which is all about probability. This is one of the core concepts of probabilistic theory.

Basic concepts of the probabilistic theory for NLP

In this section, we will look at some of the concepts of probabilistic theory. We will also look at some examples of them so that you can understand what is going on. We will start with probability, then the concept of an independent event, and then conditional probability. At the end, we will look at the Bayes rule.

Probability

Probability is a measure of the likelihood that a particular event will occur. Probability is quantified as a number and the range of probability is between 0 and 1. 0 means that the particular event will never occur and 1 indicates that the particular event will definitely occur. Machine learning techniques use the concept of probability widely. Let's look at an example just to refresh the concept. Refer to *Figure 5. 51*:

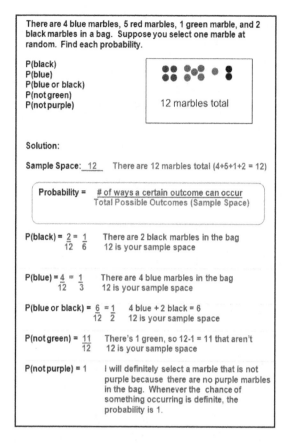

There are 4 blue marbles, 5 red marbles, 1 green marble, and 2 black marbles in a bag. Suppose you select one marble at random. Find each probability.

P(black)
P(blue)
P(blue or black)
P(not green)
P(not purple)

12 marbles total

Solution:

Sample Space: __12__   There are 12 marbles total (4+5+1+2 = 12)

Probability = # of ways a certain outcome can occur
Total Possible Outcomes (Sample Space)

P(black) = 2/12 = 1/6   There are 2 black marbles in the bag
12 is your sample space

P(blue) = 4/12 = 1/3   There are 4 blue marbles in the bag
12 is your sample space

P(blue or black) = 6/12 = 1/2   4 blue + 2 black = 6
12 is your sample space

P(not green) = 11/12   There's 1 green, so 12-1 = 11 that aren't
12 is your sample space

P(not purple) = 1   I will definitely select a marble that is not purple because there are no purple marbles in the bag. Whenever the chance of something occurring is definite, the probability is 1.

Figure 5.51: Probability example (Image credit: http://www.algebra-class.com/image-files/examples-of-probability-3.gif)

Now let's see what dependent and independent events are.

Independent event and dependent event

In this section, we will look at what dependent events and independent events are. After that, we will see how to decide if an event is dependent or not. First, let's begin with definitions.

If the probability of one event doesn't affect the probability of the other event, then this kind of event is called an independent event. So technically, if you take two events, A and B, and if the fact that A occurs does not affect the probability of B occurring, then it's called an independent event. Flipping a fair coin is an independent event because it doesn't depend on any other previous events.

Sometimes, some events affect other events. Two events are said to be dependent when the probability of one event occurring influences the other event's occurrence.

For example, if you were to draw two cards from a deck of 52 cards, and on your first draw you had an ace, the probability of drawing another ace on the second draw has changed because you drew an ace the first time. Let's calculate these different probabilities to see what's going on.

There are four aces in a deck of 52 cards. See *Figure 5.52*:

$$P(Ace) = \frac{\text{number of Aces in a deck of cards}}{\text{number of cards in a deck}}$$

Figure 5.52: Equation of probability

On your first draw, the probability of getting an ace is in *Figure 5.53*:

$$P(Ace) = \frac{4}{52} = \frac{1}{13}$$

Figure 5.53: Calculation step (Image credit: https://dj1hlxw0wr920.cloudfront.net/userfiles/wyzfiles/02cec729-378c-4293-8a5c-3873e0b06942.gif)

Now if you don't return this drawn card to the deck, the probability of drawing an ace on the second round is given in the following equation. See *Figure 5.54*:

$$P(Ace) = \frac{\text{number of Aces remaining in the deck of cards}}{\text{number of cards remaining in a deck}}$$

Figure 5.54: Dependent event probability equation (Image credit: https://dj1hlxw0wr920.cloudfront.net/userfiles/wyzfiles/7a45b393-0275-47ac-93e1-9669f5c31caa.gif)

See the calculation step in *Figure 5.55*:

$$P(Ace) = \frac{4 - 1}{52 - 1}$$

Figure 5.55: Calculation step (Image credit: https://dj1hlxw0wr920.cloudfront.net/userfiles/wyzfiles/11221e29-96ea-44fb-b7b5-af614f1bec96.gif)

See the final answer in *Figure 5.56*:

$$P(Ace) = \frac{3}{51}$$

Figure 5.56: Final answer of the example (Image credit: https://dj1hlxw0wr920.cloudfront.net/userfiles/wyzfiles/78fdf71e-fc1c-41d2-8fb8-bc2baeb25c25.gif)

As you can see, the preceding two probability values are different, so we say that the two events are dependent because the second event depends on the first event.

The mathematical condition to check whether the events are dependent or independent is given as: events A and B are independent events if, and only if, the following condition will be satisfied:

$P(A \cap B) = P(A) * P(B)$

Otherwise, *A* and *B* are called dependent events.

Now let's take an example to understand the defined condition.

Example: A poll finds that 72% of the population of Mumbai consider themselves football fans. If you randomly pick two people from the population, what is the probability that the first person is a football fan and the second is as well? That the first one is and the second one isn't?

Solution: The first person being a football fan doesn't have any impact on whether the second randomly selected person is a football fan or not. Therefore, the events are independent.

The probability can be calculated by multiplying the individual probabilities of the given events together. If the first person and second person both are football fans, then P(A∩B) = P(A) P(B) = .72 * .72 = .5184.

For the second question: The first one is a football fan, the second one isn't:

$P(A \cap not\ B) = P(A) P(B') = .72 * (1 - 0.72) = 0.202.$

In this part of the calculation, we multiplied by the complement.

Here, events *A* and *B* are independent because the equation *P(A∩B) = P(A) P(B)* holds true.

Now it's time to move on to the next concept called conditional probability.

Conditional probability

In this section, we will look at a concept called conditional probability. We will use the concept of a dependent event and independent event to understand the concept of conditional probability.

The conditional probability of an event B is the probability that the event will occur given the knowledge that an event, A, has already occurred. This probability is written as $P(B|A)$, the notation for the probability of B given A. Now let's see how this conditional probability turns out when events are independent. Where events A and B are independent, the conditional probability of event B given event A is simply the probability of event B, that is, $P(B)$. What if events A and B are not independent? Then, the probability of the intersection of A and B means that the probability that both events occur is defined by the following equation:

$P(A \text{ and } B) = P(A) * P(B|A)$

Now we will look at an example.

Example: Jalaj's two favorite food items are tea and pizza. Event A represents the event that I drink tea for my breakfast. B represents the event that I eat pizza for lunch. On randomly selected days, the probability that I drink tea for breakfast, P(A), is 0.6. The probability that I eat pizza for lunch, P(B), is 0.5 and the conditional probability that I drink tea for breakfast, given that I eat pizza for lunch, P(A|B) is 0.7. Based on this, please calculate the conditional probability of P(B|A). P(B|A) will indicate the probability that I eat pizza for lunch, given that I drink tea for breakfast. In layman's terms, find out the probability of having pizza for lunch when drinking tea for breakfast.

Solution

$P(A) = 0.6$, $P(B) = 0.5$, $P(A|B) = 0.7$

Here, two events are dependent because the probability of B being true has changed the probability of A being true. Now we need to calculate P(B|A).

See the equation $P(A \text{ and } B) = P(A) * P(B|A)$. To find out P(B|A), we first need to calculate P(A and B):

$P(A \text{ and } B) = P(B) * P(A|B) = P(A) * P(B|A)$

Here, we know that *P(B) = 0.5 and P(A|B) =0.7*

*P(A and B) = 0.5 * 0.7 = 0.35*

P(B|A) = P(A and B) / P(A) = 0.35 / 0.6 = 0.5833

So, we have found the conditional probability for dependent events.

Now we have seen the basics of probability that we will use in upcoming chapters to understand ML algorithms. We will define additional concepts as we go. The scikit-learn, TensorFlow, SparkML, and other libraries already implement major probability calculation, provide us with high-level APIs, and have options that can change the predefined parameter and set values according to your application. These parameters are often called **hyperparameters**. To come up with the best suited values for each of the parameters is called **hyperparameter tuning**. This process helps us optimize our system. We will look at hyperparameter tuning and other major concepts in Chapter 8, *Machine Learning for NLP Applications*.

This is the end of our prerequisite section. From this section onwards, we look at see some statistical concepts that help us extract features from the text. Many NLP applications also use them.

TF-IDF

The concept TF-IDF stands for **term frequency-inverse document frequency**. This is in the field of numerical statistics. With this concept, we will be able to decide how important a word is to a given document in the present dataset or corpus.

Understanding TF-IDF

This is a very simple but useful concept. It actually indicates how many times a particular word appears in the dataset and what the importance of the word is in order to understand the document or dataset. Let's give you an example. Suppose you have a dataset where students write an essay on the topic, My Car. In this dataset, the word **a** appears many times; it's a high frequency word compared to other words in the dataset. The dataset contains other words like **car**, **shopping**, and so on that appear less often, so their frequency are lower and they carry more information compared to the word, **a**. This is the intuition behind TF-IDF.

Let's explain this concept in detail. Let's also look at its mathematical aspect. TF-IDF has two parts: Term Frequency and Inverse Document Frequency. Let's begin with the term frequency. The term is self-explanatory but we will walk through the concept. The term frequency indicates the frequency of each of the words present in the document or dataset. So, its equation is given as follows:

TF(t) = (Number of times term t appears in a document) / (Total number of terms in the document)

Now let's look at the second part - inverse document frequency. IDF actually tells us how important the word is to the document. This is because when we calculate TF, we give equal importance to every single word. Now, if the word appears in the dataset more frequently, then its term frequency (TF) value is high while not being that important to the document. So, if the word **the** appears in the document 100 times, then it's not carrying that much information compared to words that are less frequent in the dataset. Thus, we need to define some weighing down of the frequent terms while scaling up the rare ones, which decides the importance of each word. We will achieve this with the following equation:

IDF(t) = log_{10}(Total number of documents / Number of documents with term t in it).

So, our equation is calculate TF-IDF is as follows.

*TF * IDF = [(Number of times term t appears in a document) / (Total number of terms in the document)] * log10(Total number of documents / Number of documents with term t in it).*

Note that in TF-IDF, - is hyphen, not the minus symbol. In reality, TF-IDF is the multiplication of TF and IDF, such as *TF * IDF*.

Now, let's take an example where you have two sentences and are considering those sentences as different documents in order to understand the concept of TF-IDF:

Document 1: This is a sample.

Document 2: This is another example.

Now to calculate TF-IDF, we will follow these steps:

1. We first calculate the frequency of each word for each document.
2. We calculate IDF.
3. We multiply TF and IDF.

Refer to *Figure 5.57*:

Step 1 : Calculate TF

Step 1.1 : Term Count for each document

Document 1			Document 2	
Term	**Term Count**		**Term**	**Term Count**
this	1		this	1
is	1		is	1
a	2		another	2
sample	1		example	3

Step 1.2 : Now calculate total nuber of words in each document

Document 1 : Total words are = 5
Document 2 : Total words are = 7

Step 1.3 : Now calculate TF

TF(t) = (Number of times term t appears in a document) / (Total number of terms in the document)

$$\text{tf}(''\text{this}'', d_1) = \frac{1}{5} = 0.2$$

$$\text{tf}(''\text{this}'', d_2) = \frac{1}{7} \approx 0.14$$

Figure 5.57: TF-IDF example

Now, let's see the calculation of IDF and TF * IDF in *Figure 5.58*:

Step 2 : Calculate IDF

Step 2.1 : IDF calculation

IDF(t) = log(Total number of documents / Number of documents with term t in it)

So here there are 2 document and term "this" appears in both of them
So IDF is given below.

$$\text{idf}(''\text{this}'', D) = \log\left(\frac{2}{2}\right) = 0$$

Step 3 : TF x IDF calculation

$$\text{tfidf}(''\text{this}'', d_1) = 0.2 \times 0 = 0$$
$$\text{tfidf}(''\text{this}'', d_2) = 0.14 \times 0 = 0$$

zero implies that the word is not very informative
For other words is given below

$$\text{tf}(''\text{example}'', d_1) = \frac{0}{5} = 0$$

$$\text{tf}(''\text{example}'', d_2) = \frac{3}{7} \approx 0.429$$

$$\text{idf}(''\text{example}'', D) = \log\left(\frac{2}{1}\right) = 0.301$$

Step 4: TF X IDF for word example

$$\text{tfidf}(''\text{example}'', d_1) = \text{tf}(''\text{example}'', d_1) \times \text{idf}(''\text{example}'', D) = 0 \times 0.301 = 0$$
$$\text{tfidf}(''\text{example}'', d_2) = \text{tf}(''\text{example}'', d_2) \times \text{idf}(''\text{example}'', D) = 0.429 \times 0.301 \approx 0.13$$

Figure 5.58: TF-IDF example

Understanding TF-IDF with a practical example

Here, we will use two libraries to calculate TF-IDF - textblob and scikit-learn. You can see the code at this GitHub link:

```
https://github.com/jalajthanaki/NLPython/tree/master/ch5/TFIDFdemo.
```

Using textblob

You can see the code snippet in *Figure 5.59*:

```python
from __future__ import division
from textblob import TextBlob
import math

def tf(word, blob):
        return blob.words.count(word) / len(blob.words)

def n_containing(word, bloblist):
    return 1 + sum(1 for blob in bloblist if word in blob)

def idf(word, bloblist):
    x = n_containing(word, bloblist)
    return math.log(len(bloblist) / (x if x else 1))

def tfidf(word, blob, bloblist):
    return tf(word, blob) * idf(word, bloblist)

text = 'tf idf, short form of term frequency, inverse document frequency'
text2 = 'is a numerical statistic that is intended to reflect how important'
text3 = 'a word is to a document in a collection or corpus'

blob = TextBlob(text)
blob2 = TextBlob(text2)
blob3 = TextBlob(text3)
bloblist = [blob, blob2, blob3]
tf_score = tf('short', blob)
idf_score = idf('short', bloblist)
tfidf_score = tfidf('short', blob, bloblist)
print "tf score for word short--- "+ str(tf_score)+"\n"
print "idf score for word short--- "+ str(idf_score)+"\n"
print "tf x idf score of word short--- "+str(tfidf_score)
```

Figure 5.59: TF-IDF using textblob

The output of the code is in *Figure 5.60*:

```
tf score for word short--- 0.1

idf score for word short--- 0.405465108108

tf x idf score of word short--- 0.0405465108108
```

Figure 5.60: Output of TF-IDF for the word short

Using scikit-learn

We will try to generate the TF-IDF model using a small Shakespeare dataset. For a new given document with a TF-IDF score model, we will suggest the top three keywords for the document. You can see the code snippet in *Figure 5.61*:

```python
for subdir, dirs, files in os.walk(path):...

# this can take some time
tfidf = TfidfVectorizer(tokenizer=tokenize, stop_words='english')
tfs = tfidf.fit_transform(token_dict.values())

str = 'this sentence has unseen text such as computer but also king lord juliet'
response = tfidf.transform([str])
#print response


feature_names = tfidf.get_feature_names()
for col in response.nonzero()[1]:
    print feature_names[col], ' - ', response[0, col]


feature_array = np.array(tfidf.get_feature_names())
tfidf_sorting = np.argsort(response.toarray()).flatten()[::-1]
n = 3
top_n = feature_array[tfidf_sorting][:n]
print top_n

n = 4
top_n = feature_array[tfidf_sorting][:n]
print top_n
```

Figure 5.61: Using scikit-learn to generate a TF-IDF model

You can see the output in *Figure 5.62*:

```
thi  -  0.346181611599
lord  -  0.663384613852
king  -  0.663384613852
[u'king' u'lord' u'thi']
[u'king' u'lord' u'thi' u'youth']
```

Figure 5.62: Output of the TF-IDF model

Now it's time to see where we can use this TF-IDF concept, so let's look at some applications.

Application

In this section, we will look at some cool applications that use TF-IDF:

- In general, text data analysis can be performed by TF-IDF easily. You can get information about the most accurate keywords for your dataset.
- If you are developing a text summarization application where you have a selected statistical approach, then TF-IDF is the most important feature for generating a summary for the document.
- Variations of the TF-IDF weighting scheme are often used by search engines to find out the scoring and ranking of a document's relevance for a given user query.
- Document classification applications use this technique along with BOW.

Now let's look at the concept of vectorization for an NLP application.

Vectorization

Vectorization is an important aspect of feature extraction in the NLP domain. Transforming the text into a vector format is a major task.

Vectorization techniques try to map every possible word to a specific integer. There are many available APIs that make your life easier. `scikit-learn` has `DictVectorizer` to convert text to a one-hot encoding form. The other API is the `CountVectorizer`, which converts the collection of text documents to a matrix of token counts. Last but not least, there are a couple of other APIs out there. We can also use word2vec to convert text data to the vector form. Refer to this link's *From text* section for more details:

`http://scikit-learn.org/stable/modules/classes.html#module-sklearn.feature_extraction.text`.

Now let's look at the concept of one-hot encoding for an NLP application. This one-hot encoding is considered as part of vectorization.

Encoders and decoders

The concept of encoding in NLP is quite old as well as useful. As we mentioned earlier, it is not easy to handle categorical data attributes present in our dataset. Here, we will explore the encoding technique named one-hot encoding, which helps us convert our categorical features in to a numerical format.

One-hot encoding

In an NLP application, you always get categorical data. The categorical data is mostly in the form of words. There are words that form the vocabulary. The words from this vocabulary cannot turn into vectors easily.

Consider that you have a vocabulary with the size N. The way to approximate the state of the language is by representing the words in the form of one-hot encoding. This technique is used to map the words to the vectors of length n, where the nth digit is an indicator of the presence of the particular word. If you are converting words to the one-hot encoding format, then you will see vectors such as 0000...001, 0000...100, 0000...010, and so on. Every word in the vocabulary is represented by one of the combinations of a binary vector. Here, the nth bit of each vector indicates the presence of the nth word in the vocabulary. So, how are these individual vectors related to sentences or other words in the corpus? Let's look at an example that will help you understand this concept.

For example, you have one sentence, *Jalaj likes NLP*. Suppose after applying one-hot encoding, this sentence becomes 00010 00001 10000. This vector is made based on the vocabulary size and encoding schema. Once we have this vector representation, then we can perform the numerical operation on it. Here, we are turning words into vectors and sentences into matrices.

Understanding a practical example for one-hot encoding

In this section, we will use `scikit-learn` to generate one-hot encoding for a small dataset. You can find the code at this GitHub link:

`https://github.com/jalajthanaki/NLPython/tree/master/ch5/onehotencodingdemo.`

You can see the code snippet in *Figure 5.63*:

```
import pandas as pd
from sklearn.feature_extraction import DictVectorizer


df = pd.DataFrame([['rick','young'],['phil','old']],columns=['name','age-group'])
print df
print "\n----By using Panda ----\n"
print pd.get_dummies(df)

X = pd.DataFrame({'income': [100000,110000,90000,30000,14000,50000],
                  'country':['US', 'CAN', 'US', 'CAN', 'MEX', 'US'],
                  'race':['White', 'Black', 'Latino', 'White', 'White', 'Black']})



print "\n----By using Sikit-learn ----\n"
v = DictVectorizer()
qualitative_features = ['country']
X_qual = v.fit_transform(X[qualitative_features].to_dict('records'))
print v.vocabulary_
print X_qual.toarray()
```

Figure 5.63: Pandas and scikit-learn to generate one-hot encoding

You can see the output in *Figure 5.64*:

```
    name age-group
0   rick     young
1   phil       old

----By using Panda ----

    name_phil  name_rick  age-group_old  age-group_young
0           0          1              0                1
1           1          0              1                0

----By using Sikit-learn ----

{'country=US': 2, 'country=CAN': 0, 'country=MEX': 1}
[[ 0.  0.  1.]
 [ 1.  0.  0.]
 [ 0.  0.  1.]
 [ 1.  0.  0.]
 [ 0.  1.  0.]
 [ 0.  0.  1.]]
```

Figure 5.64: Output of one-hot encoding

Application

These techniques are very useful. Let's see some of the basic applications for this mapping technique:

- Many artificial neural networks accept input data in the one-hot encoding format and generate output vectors that carry the sematic representation as well
- The word2vec algorithm accepts input data in the form of words and these words are in the form of vectors that are generated by one-hot encoding

Now it's time to look at the decoding concept. Decoding concepts are mostly used in deep learning nowadays. So here, we will define the decoder in terms of deep learning because we will use this encoding and decoding architecture in Chapter 9, *Deep Learning for NLU and NLG Problems*, to develop a translation system.

An encoder maps input data to a different feature representation; we are using one-hot encoding for the NLP domain. A decoder maps the feature representation back to the input data space. In deep learning, a decoder knows which vector represents which words, so it can decode words as per the given input schema. We will see the detailed concept of encoder-decoder when we cover the sequence-to-sequence model.

Now, let's look at the next concept called **normalization**.

Normalization

Here, we will explain normalization in terms of linguistics as well as statistics. Even though they are different, the word normalization can create a lot of confusion. Let's resolve this confusion.

The linguistics aspect of normalization

The linguistics aspect of normalization includes the concept text normalization. Text normalization is the process of transforming the given text into a single canonical form. Let's take an example to understand text normalization properly. If you are making a search application and you want the user to enter **John**, then John becomes a search string and all the strings that contain the word **John** should also pop up. If you are preparing data to search, then people prefer to take the stemmed format; even if you search **flying** or **flew**, ultimately these are forms that are derived from the word **fly**. So, the search system uses the stemmed form and other derived forms are removed. If you recall Chapter 3, *Understanding Structure of Sentences*, then you will remember that we have already discussed how to derive lemma, stem, and root.

The statistical aspect of normalization

The statistical aspect of normalization is used to do features scaling. If you have a dataset where one data attribute's ranges are too high and the other data attributes' ranges are too small, then generally we need to apply statistical techniques to bring all the data attributes or features into one common numerical range. There are many ways to perform this transformation, but here we will illustrate the most common and easy method of doing this called **min-max scaling**. Let's look at equation and mathematical examples to understand the concept.

Min-max scaling brings the features in the range of [0,1]. The general formula is given in *Figure 5.65*:

$$z = \frac{x - \min(x)}{\max(x) - \min(x)}$$

Figure 5.65: The min-max normalization equation

Suppose you have features values such as *[1, 8, 22, 25]*; i you apply the preceding formula and calculate the value for each of the elements, then you will get the feature with a range of [0,1]. For the first element, $z = 1 - 1/25 - 1 = 0$, for the second element, $z = 8 - 1/25 - 1 = 0.2917$, and so on. The `scikit-learn` library has an API that you can use for min-max scaling on the dataset.

In the next section, we will cover the language model.

Probabilistic models

We will discuss one of the most famous probabilistic models in NLP, which has been used for a variety of applications - the language model. We will look at the basic idea of the language model. We are not going to dive deep into this, but we will get an intuitive idea on how the language model works and where we can use it.

Understanding probabilistic language modeling

There are two basic goals of the **language model (LM)**:

- The goal of LM is to assign probability to a sentence or sequence of words
- LM also tells us about the probability of the upcoming word, which means that it indicates which is the next most likely word by observing the previous word sequence

If any model can compute either of the preceding tasks, it is called a language model. LM uses the conditional probability chain rule. The chain rule of conditional probability is just an extension of conditional probability. We have already seen the equation:

P(A | B) = P(A and B) / P(B)

P(A and B) = P(A,B) = P(A | B) P(B)

Here, P(A,B) is called **joint probability**. Suppose you have multiple events that are dependent, then the equation to compute joint probability becomes more general:

P(A,B,C,D) = P(A) P(B | A)P(C | A,B)P(D | A,B,C)

P(x1,x2,x3,...,xn) =P(x1)P(x2 | x1)P(x3 | x1,x2)...P(xn | x1,x2,x3,...xn-1)

The preceding equation is called chain rule for conditional probability. LM uses this to predict the probability of upcoming words. We often calculate probability by counting the number of times a particular event occurs and dividing it by the total number of possible combinations, but we can't apply this to language because, with certain words, you can generate millions of sentences. So, we are not going to use the probability equation; we are using an assumption called **Markov Assumption** to calculate probability instead. Let's understand the concept intuitively before looking at a technical definition of it. If you have very a long sentence and you are trying to predict what the next word in the sentence sequence will be, then you actually need to consider all the words that are already present in the sentence to calculate the probability for the upcoming word. This calculation is very tedious, so we consider only the last one, two or three words to compute the probability for the upcoming word; this is called the Markov assumption. The assumption is that you can calculate the probability of the next word that comes in a sequence of the sentence by looking at the last word two. Let's take an example to understand this. If you want to calculate the probability of a given word, then it is only dependent on the last word. You can see the equation here:

P(the | its water is so transparent that) = P(the | that) or you can consider last two words P(the | its water is so transparent that) = P(the | transparent that)

A simple LM uses a unigram, which means that we are just considering the word itself and calculating the probability of an individual word; you simply take the probability of individual words and generate a random word sequence. If you take a bigram model, then you consider that one previous word will decide the next word in the sequence. You can see the result of the bigram model in *Figure 5.66*:

$$P(w_i \mid w_1 w_2 \ldots w_{i-1}) \approx P(w_i \mid w_{i-1})$$

```
texaco, rose, one, in, this, issue, is, pursuing, growth, in,
a, boiler, house, said, mr., gurria, mexico, 's, motion,
control, proposal, without, permission, from, five, hundred,
fifty, five, yen

outside, new, car, parking, lot, of, the, agreement, reached

this, would, be, a, record, november
```

Figure 5.66: Output using a bigram LM

How can we count the n-gram probability that is a core part of LM? Let's look at the bigram model. We will see the equation and then go through the example. See the equation in *Figure 5.67*:

The Maximum Likelihood Estimate

$$P(w_i \mid w_{i-1}) = \frac{count(w_{i-1}, w_i)}{count(w_{i-1})}$$

Figure 5.67: Equation to find out the next most likely word in the sequence

The equation is easy to understand. We need to calculate how many times the words *wi-1* and *wi* occurred together, and we also need to count how many times the word *wi-1* occurred. See the example in *Figure 5.68*:

$$P(w_i \mid w_{i-1}) = \frac{c(w_{i-1}, w_i)}{c(w_{i-1})}$$

<s> I am Sam </s>

<s> Sam I am </s>

<s> I do not like green eggs and ham </s>

$$P(\text{I} \mid \text{<s>}) = \frac{2}{3} = .67 \qquad P(\text{Sam} \mid \text{<s>}) = \frac{1}{3} = .33 \qquad P(\text{am} \mid \text{I}) = \frac{2}{3} = .67$$

$$P(\text{</s>} \mid \text{Sam}) = \frac{1}{2} = 0.5 \qquad P(\text{Sam} \mid \text{am}) = \frac{1}{2} = .5 \qquad P(\text{do} \mid \text{I}) = \frac{1}{3} = .33$$

Figure 5.68: Example to find out the most likely word using LM

As you can see, we is followed by <s> twice in three given sentences, so we have *P(I|<s>)* =2/3, and for every word, we will calculate the probability. Using LM, we can come to know how the word pairs are described in the corpus as well as what the more popular word pairs that occur in the corpus are. If we use a four-gram or five-gram model, it will give us a good result for LM because some sentences have a long-dependency relationship in their syntax structure with subject and verbs. So, with a four-gram and five-gram model, you can build a really good LM.

Application of LM

LM has a lot of great applications in the NLP domain. Most NLP applications use LM at some point. Let's see them:

- Machine translation systems use LM to find out the probability for each of the translated sentences in order to decide which translated sentence is the best possible translation for the given input sentence
- To spell the correct application, we can use a bigram LM to provide the most likely word suggestion
- We can use LM for text summarization
- We can use LM in a question answering system to rank the answers as per their probability

Indexing

Indexing is quite a useful technique. This is used to convert the categorical data to its numerical format. In an NLP application, you may find that the data attributes are categorical and you want to convert them to a certain numerical value. In such cases, this indexing concept can help you. We can use the SparkML library, which has a variety of APIs to generate indexes. SparkML has an API named StringIndexer that uses the frequency of the categorical data and assigns the index as per the frequency count. So, the most frequent category gets an index value of 0. This can sometimes be a naïve way of generating indexing, but in some analytical applications, you may find this technique useful. You can see the example at this link:

`https://spark.apache.org/docs/latest/ml-features.html#stringindexer.`

SparkML has the API, IndexToString, which you can use when you need to convert your numerical values back to categorical values. You can find the example at this link:

`https://spark.apache.org/docs/latest/ml-features.html#indextostring.`

Application

Here are some applications which use indexing for extracting features:

- When we are dealing with a multiclass classifier and our target classes are in the text format and we want to convert our target class labels to a numerical format, we can use StingIndexer
- We can also generate the text of the `target` class using the IndexToString API

Now it's time to learn about a concept called ranking.

Ranking

In many applications, ranking plays a key role. The concept of **ranking** is used when you search anything on the web. Basically, the ranking algorithm is used to find the relevance of the given input and generated output.

Let's look at an example. When you search the web, the search engine takes your query, processes it, and generates some result. It uses the ranking algorithm to find the most relevant link according to your query and displays the most relevant link or content at the top and least relevant at the end. The same thing happens when you visit any online e-commerce website; when you search for a product, they display the relevant product list to you. To make their customer experience enjoyable, they display those products that are relevant to your query, whose reviews are good, and that have affordable prices. These all are the parameters given to the ranking algorithm in order to generate the most relevant products.

 The implementation of the ranking algorithm is not a part of this book. You can find more information that will be useful here: https://medium.com/towards-data-science/learning-to-rank-with-py thon-scikit-learn-327a5cfd81f.

Indexing and ranking are not frequently used in the NLP domain, but they are much more important when you are trying to build an application related to analytics using machine learning. It is mostly used to learn the user's preferences. If you are making a Google News kind of NLP application, where you need to rank certain news events, then ranking and indexing plays a major role. In a question answering system, generating ranks for the answers is the most critical task, and you can use indexing and ranking along with a language model to get the best possible result Applications such as grammar correction, proofreading, summarization systems, and so on don't use this concept.

We have seen most of the basic features that we can use in NLP applications. We will be using most of them in Chapter 8, *Machine Learning for NLP Application*, where we will build some real-life NLP applications with ML algorithms. In the upcoming section, we will explain the advantages and challenges of features engineering.

Advantages of features engineering

Features engineering is the most important aspect of the NLP domain when you are trying to apply ML algorithms to solve your NLP problems. If you are able to derive good features, then you can have many advantages, which are as follows:

- Better features give you a lot of flexibility. Even if you choose a less optimal ML algorithm, you will get a good result. Good features provide you with the flexibility of choosing an algorithm; even if you choose a less complex model, you get good accuracy.
- If you choose good features, then even simple ML algorithms do well.
- Better features will lead you to better accuracy. You should spend more time on features engineering to generate the appropriate features for your dataset. If you derive the best and appropriate features, you have won most of the battle.

Challenges of features engineering

Here, we will discuss the challenges of features engineering for NLP applications. You must be thinking that we have a lot of options available in terms of tools and algorithms, so what is the most challenging part? Let's find out:

- In the NLP domain, you can easily derive the features that are categorical features or basic NLP features. We have to convert these features into a numerical format. This is the most challenging part.
- An effective way of converting text data into a numerical format is quite challenging. Here, the trial and error method may help you.
- Although there are a couple of techniques that you can use, such as TF-IDF, one-hot encoding, ranking, co-occurrence matrix, word embedding, Word2Vec, and so on to convert your text data into a numerical format, there are not many ways, so people find this part challenging.

Summary

In this chapter, we have seen many concepts and tools that are widely used in the NLP domain. All of these concepts are the basic building blocks of features engineering. You can use any of these techniques when you want to generate features in order to generate NLP applications. We have looked at how parse, POS taggers, NER, n-grams, and bag-of-words generate Natural Language-related features. We have also explored the how they are built and what the different ways to tweak some of the existing tools are in case you need custom features to develop NLP applications. Further, we have seen basic concepts of linear algebra, statistics, and probability. We have also seen the basic concepts of probability that will be used in ML algorithms in the future. We have looked at some cool concepts such as TF-IDF, indexing, ranking, and so on, as well as the language model as part of the probabilistic model.

In the next chapter, we will look at advanced features such as word2vec, Doc2vec, Glove, and so on. All of these algorithms are part of word embedding techniques. These techniques will help us convert our text features into a numerical format efficiently; especially when we need to use semantics. The next chapter will provide you with much more detailed information about the word2Vec algorithm. We will cover each and every technicality behind the word2vec model. We will also understand how an **artificial neural network (ANN)** is used to generate the semantic relationship between words, and then we will explore an extension of this concept from word level, sentence level, document level, and so on. We will build an application that includes some awesome visualization for word2vec. We will also discuss the importance of vectorization, so keep reading!

6
Advanced Feature Engineering and NLP Algorithms

In this chapter, we will look at an amazing and simple concept called **word to vector** (**word2vec**). This concept was developed by a team of researchers led by Tomas Mikolov at Google. As we all know, Google provides us with a lot of great products and concepts. Word2vec is one of them. In NLP, developing tools or techniques that can deal with the semantics of words, phrases, sentences, and so on are quite a big deal, and the word2vec model does a great job of figuring out the semantics of words, phrases, sentences, paragraphs, and documents. We are going to jump into this vectorization world and live our life in it for a while. Don't you think this is quite amazing? We will be starting from the concepts and we will end with some fun and practical examples. So, let's begin.

Recall word embedding

We have already covered word embedding in Chapter 5, *Feature Engineering and NLP Algorithms*. We have looked at language models and feature engineering techniques in NLP, where words or phrases from the vocabulary are mapped to vectors of real numbers. The techniques used to convert words into real numbers are called **word embedding**. We have been using vectorization, as well as **term frequency-inverse document frequency** (**tf-idf**) based vectorization. So, let's just jump into the world of word2vec.

Understanding the basics of word2vec

Here, we will try to handle semantics at word level by using word2vec. Then, we will expand our concepts to paragraph level and document level. By looking at *Figure 6.1*, you will see the different kinds of semantics that we are going to cover in this book:

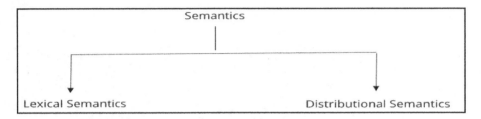

Figure 6.1: Different kinds of semantics

Semantics is a branch that deals with meaning in the area of NLP. We have already covered lexical semantic in `Chapter 3`, *Understanding Structure of Sentences*. So, here we will discuss more about distributional semantics. There are also other techniques or types in semantics, such as formal semantics compositional semantics; but right now, in this book, we are not going to cover these types or techniques.

Distributional semantics

Distributional semantics is a research area that focuses on developing techniques or theories that quantify and categorize semantic similarities between linguistic items based on their distributional properties in large samples of text data.

I want to give an example here that gives you an idea of what I mean by distributional semantics. Suppose you have text data of travelling blogs. Now, you as a person know that pasta, noodles, burgers, and so on are edible food items, whereas juice, tea, coffee, and so on are drinkable items. As a human, we can easily classify drinkable and edible food items because we have a certain context related with each of them, but machines cannot really know these kind of semantics. There is a higher chance that all described food items come along with certain words in the dataset. So, here we are focusing on the distribution of words in corpus and, let's say, that linguistic items or words with similar distributions have similar meanings. This is called the **distributional hypothesis**.

I will give you another example. Suppose you have a dataset of research papers. Some of the research papers in the dataset belong to the engineering category, and others belong to the legal category. Documents with words such as engineering, equation, methods, and so on are related to engineering, so they should be part of one group, and words such as legal, lawyer, law institutes, and so on are related to research papers of the legal domain, so they should be grouped together. By using distributional semantics techniques such as word2vec, we can segregate the different domain words by using their vector values. All words with a similar meaning are grouped together because they have a similar distribution on the corpus. You can refer to *Figure 6.2*, which shows a pictorial representation of a vector space of our given distributional semantics example where similar contextual words come together:

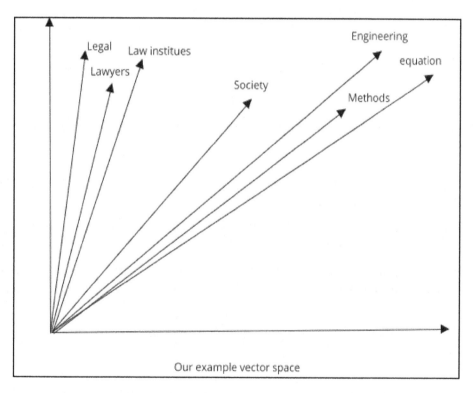

Figure 6.2: Pictorial representation of vector space of our distributional semantics example

Figure 6.3, gives you an idea about from which branch the word2vec model was derived:

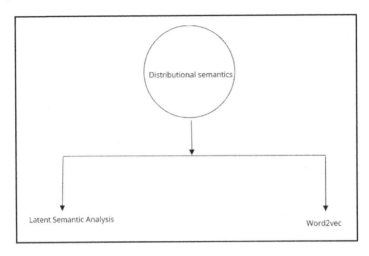

Figure 6.3: Major models derived from distributional semantics

Our main concentration in this chapter is the distributional semantics technique called **word2vec**.

Defining word2vec

Word2vec is developed by using two-layer neural networks. It takes a large amount of text data or text corpus as input and generates a set of vectors from the given text.

In other words, we can say that it generates high-dimensional vector space. This vector space has several hundred dimensions.

 Please don't be afraid of the high dimensionality. I make the whole concept of word2vec simple for you during this chapter.

You will really want to know what I mean here when I say that the word2vec model generates a set of vectors or vector space from text. Here, we are using a two-layer neural network, which right now a black box that performs some kind of logic and generates vectors in the vector space for us. In the vector space, each unique word in the corpus is assigned a corresponding vector. So, the vector space is just a vector representation of all words present in the large text corpus.

So, I think you get it, right? On the basics of what we have learnt, you are able to say that word2vec is one of the models that generates word embedding. Please recall the vectorization section of `Chapter 5`, *Feature Engineering and NLP Algorithms*. I also want to make a point here, by saying that word2vec is a powerful, unsupervised word embedding technique.

Necessity of unsupervised distribution semantic model - word2vec

This section gives us an idea of the numerous challenges that word2vec solves for us. The solution of those challenges leads us to the real need for word2vec. So, first we will look at some challenges, and then take a look at how the word2vec model solves those challenges.

Challenges

There are a couple of challenges that are listed here that we are trying to solve:

- When we are developing an NLP application, there is one fundamental problem--we know that the machine can't understand our text and we need to convert the text data into a numerical format.
- There are certain ways to convert text data into a numerical format, but we apply some naive techniques, and one of them is one-hot encoding, but the problems with this techniques are given as follows:
    - Suppose you have a sentence: I like apple juice. Now, suppose that you apply one-hot encoding for each of the words in the sentence. If you have thousands of sentences in your corpus, then vector dimension is equal to the entire vocabulary of your corpus, and if these kind of high dimensional columns have been used to develop an NLP application, then we need high computation power and matrix operation on these high-dimension columns as they take too much time.
    - For speech recognition vocabulary, size is on average 20,000 words. If we are developing a machine translation system then perhaps we will use more vocabulary, like 500,000 words. To deal with these kinds of gigantic vectors is a big challenge.

- Another problem is that when you apply one-hot encoding on a particular word in a sentence, then the whole entry has zero values, except the one that actually represents the word, and that value is **1**. Suppose, for simplicity, we take the sentence: *I like apple juice*. For a while consider that there is only one sentence in our corpus. Now, if I try to apply one hot encoding on the word **apple** then one-hot representation of **apple**, is given as follows. Refer to *Figure 6.4*:

Sentence : I like apple juice.

Apple =
```
0
0
1
0
```
juice =
```
0
0
0
1
```

Figure 6.4:One-hot encoding representation of the words apple and juice

- One-hot encoding doesn't reveal the facts about context similarity between words. To understand this, I want to give an example, if your corpus has words cat and cats then one-hot encoding does not reveal the fact that word cat and cats are very similar words.
- If I apply an AND operation on the one-hot encoded vectors, then it will not express any contextual similarity. Take an example, if I apply an AND operation means a dot product on the one-hot vectors of **Apple** and **juice**,then the answer is **0**. In reality, these words can appear together and have a strong contextual relationship as well, but one-hot encoding alone does not express anything significant about word similarity.
- If you want to find accurate word similarities, then WordNet will not help you enough. WordNet is made by experts and whatever WordNet contains is more subjective because human users created it.
- Using WordNet takes a lot of time and effort.
- Some new words, such as Coding Ninja, Wizard, and so on are new words for WordNet and may not be present on the website. Because of the absence of these kinds of words, we cannot derive the other semantic relationships from WordNet.

Each of the preceding challenges has played a major role in the development of the techniques to solve them. In the last two decades, there has been a lot of effort put into developing an efficient, concise, and relevant numerical representation of words. Finally, in 2013, Tomas Mikolov and his research team at Google came up with the word2vec model, which solves many of the previous challenges in an efficient way.

Word2vec is very good at finding out word similarity, as well as preserving the semantic relationship between words that couldn't be handled by previous techniques, such as one-hot encoding or by using WordNet.

I have given so much background on word2vec now, so let's start understanding the representation, components, and other parameters of the word2vec model.

Let's begin our magical journey!

Converting the word2vec model from black box to white box

From this section onwards, we are going to get an understanding of each of the components of the word2vec model, as well as the model's working process. So, in short, we are converting the black box part of word2vec into a white box.

We will focus on the following procedures in order to understand the word2vec model:

- Distributional similarity based representation
- Understanding the components of the word2vec model
- Understanding the logic of the word2vec model
- Understanding the algorithms and math behind the word2vec model
- Some of the facts regarding the word2vec model
- Application of the word2vec model

Let's begin!

Distributional similarity based representation

This is quite an old and powerful idea in NLP. The notion of distributional similarity is that you can get a lot of value for representing the meaning of a word by considering the context in which that particular word appears, and it is highly related with that context. There is a very famous quote by a famous linguist John Firth:

> *"You shall know the word by the company it keeps."*

Let's take an example: if I want to find the meaning of the word banking, I am going to collect thousands of sentences in which the word banking is included, and then I will start looking at the other words with the word banking and try to understand the context in which the word banking is used. So, look at these examples and understand the distributional similarity:

- Sentence 1: The banking sector is regulated by the government
- Sentence 2: Banking institutions need some technology to change their traditional operations.

In the previous sentences, the word banking is included more frequently with words such as government, department, operations, and so on. All these words are very useful to understand the context and meaning of the word banking.

These other words are really helpful to represent the meaning of the word banking. You can also use the word banking to predict the most common frequently occurring words or phrases when the word banking is present in a sentence.

To understand how we can better represent the meaning of a particular word, as well as performing predictions about other words appearing in the context of this given word, we need to understand the distributional representation of the word in question.

The distributional representation of a word is a vector form in which the word can be represented. Words are expressed in the form of a dense vector, and the dense vector has to be chosen so that it will be good at predicting other words that appear in the context of this word. Now, each of those other words that we are making predictions about also have other words attached to them, so we use a similarity measure, such as the vector dot product. This is a kind of recursive approach, where each word will predict the other words that can appear in the same context, and other predicted words also perform the same operation by predicting some other words. So, we need a clever algorithm to perform this kind of recursive operation.

Here, please do not get confused between the terminology of distributional similarity and distribution representation. Distributional similarity based representation is actually used as part of the theory of semantics, which helps us to understand the meaning of the word in regular life usage; whereas the distributional representation of a word is the representation of a word in a vector form. To generate the vector form of a word, we can use one hot encoding or any other techniques, but the major point here is to generate the vector for a word that also carries the significance of similarity measure so that you can understand the contextual meaning of the word. Word2vec comes into the picture when we talk about distributional similarity.

Understanding the components of the word2vec model

In this section, we will get an understanding of the main three components of the word2vec model, which are given as follows:

- Input of word2vec
- Output of word2vec
- Construction components of the word2vec model

Input of the word2vec

First of all, we should be aware of our input for developing the word2vec model, because that is a fundamental thing, from which you can start building word2vec.

So, I want to state that we will use a raw text corpus as an input for developing the word2vec model.

In real-life applications, we use large corpora as input. For simplicity, we will use a fairly small corpus to understand the concepts in this chapter. In later parts of this chapter, we will use a big corpus to develop some cool stuff by using word2vec model concepts.

Output of word2vec

This section is very important for your understanding because, after this point, whatever you understand will be just to achieve the output that you have set here. So, so far, we know that we want to develop the vector representation of a word that carries the meaning of the word, as well as to express the distribution similarity measure.

Now, I will jump towards defining our goal and output. We want to define a model that aims to predict a central word and words that appear in its context. So, we can say that we want to predict the probability of the context given the word. Here, we are setting up the simple prediction objective. You can understand this goal by referring to the following figure:

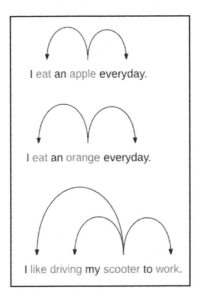

Figure 6.5: Help to understand our goal

As you can see, there are some simple example sentences given in the preceding figure. If we take the word **apple** from the first sentence and, as per our goal, convert the word **apple** into a vector form such that, by using that vector form of **apple**, we can predict the probability of the word **eat** appearing in the context of the word **apple**. The same logic applies to the other sentences. For example, in the third sentence, where we try to find out the vector of the word **scooter**, which helps us to predict the probability of words such as **driving** and **work** in the context of the given word **scooter**.

So, in general, our straightforward goal is that we need to convert every word into vector format, such that they are good at predicting the words that appear in their context, and by giving the context, we can predict the probability of the word that is best suited for the given context.

Construction components of the word2vec model

We know our input and output so far, so now you're probably thinking: how can we achieve our goal by using our input. As I mentioned, we need a clever algorithm that will help us to achieve our goal. Researchers have done the work for us and concluded that we can use neural network techniques. I would like to give you just a brief idea of why we are going to use neural network, but if you want a deep insight of it, then I would encourage you to read some of these papers.

http://wwwold.ece.utep.edu/research/webfuzzy/docs/kk-thesis/kk-thesis-html/node12.html.

http://s3.amazonaws.com/academia.edu.documents/44666285/jhbs.pdf?AWSAccessKeyId=AKIAIWOWYYGZ2Y53UL3A&Expires=1497377031&Signature=CtXl5qOa4OpzF%2BAcergNU%2F6dUAU%3D&response-content-disposition=inline%3B%20filename%3DPhysio_logical_circuits_The_intellectua.pdf.

http://blogs.umass.edu/brain-wars/files/2016/03/rosenblatt-1957.pdf.

The reason why we are using a neural network technique is because neural networks are good algorithms when we are trying to learn from a large amount of data. If you want to build a simple, scalable, and easy to train model then a neural network is one of the best approaches. If you read the modern research papers that I have listed as follows, they will tell you the same truth. Links to the papers mentioned are as follows:

http://web2.cs.columbia.edu/~blei/seminar/2016_discrete_data/readings/MikolovSutskeverChenCorradoDean2013.pdf.

https://arxiv.org/abs/1301.3781.

This kind of neural network creates magic in terms of generating distributional similarity. Google generated the word2vec model by using the large corpus of Wikipedia. Refer to *Figure 6.6*, which gives you an overview of the input, and some famous output from the Google word2vec model. For us, the word2vec model is still a powerful black box that generates some great results. See the black box representation of word2vec in the following figure:

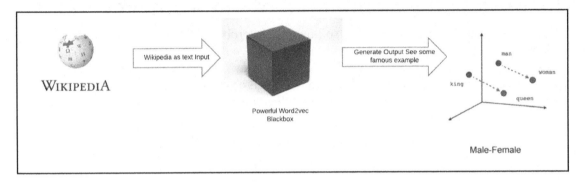

Figure 6.6: Google word2vec model takes Wikipedia text as input and generates output

The preceding image shows that we have provided text data as input to the word2vec model. The word2vec model converts our text data to the vector form so that we can perform mathematical operations on this vector representation of words. The most famous example of word2vec is: if you have the vectors of king, man, and woman. Then, if you apply the mathematical operation subtracting the vector value of man from the king vector and add the vector value of the word woman to it, then we will get a resultant vector that represents the same vector value of the word queen. Here's the mathematical representation of this example: *king - man + woman = queen*.

Now we need to focus on the overview of the architectural component for word2vec.

Architectural component

Let's look at the architectural components involved in building a word2vec model.

The major architectural component for the word2vec model is its neural network. The neural network for a word2vec model has two layers, and in that sense, it is not a deep neural network. The fact is that word2vec doesn't use deep neural networks to generate vector forms of words.

This is one of the critical and main components of the word2vec model and we need to decode its functionality to get a clear idea about how word2vec works. Now it's time to decode the magical logic of the word2vec model.

Understanding the logic of the word2vec model

We will start decomposing the word2vec model and try to understand the logic of it. word2vec is a piece of software and it uses a bunch of algorithms. Refer to *Figure 6.7*:

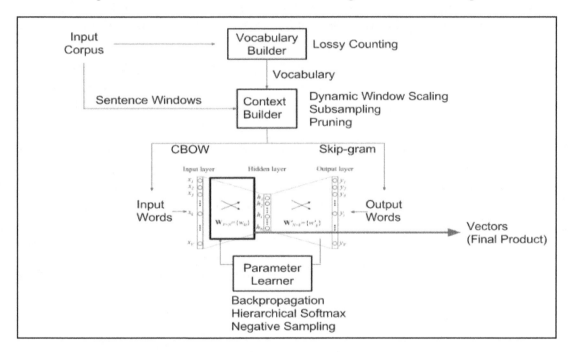

Figure 6.7: Word2vec building block (Image credit: Xin Rong)

As you can see in *Figure 6.7*, there are three main building blocks. We will examine each of them in detail:

- Vocabulary builder
- Context builder
- Neural network with two layers

Vocabulary builder

The vocabulary builder is the first building block of the word2vec model. It takes raw text data, mostly in the form of sentences. The vocabulary builder is used to build vocabulary from your given text corpus. It will collect all the unique words from your corpus and build the vocabulary.

In Python, there is a library called `gensim`. We will use `gensim` to generate word2vec for our corpus. There are some parameters available in `gensim` that we can use to build vocabulary from our corpus as per your application needs. The parameter list is given as follows:

- `min_count`: This parameter is used as a threshold value. This ignores all words with a total frequency of lower than the specified value. So, for example, if you set `min_count` = 5, then the output of the vocabulary builder doesn't contain words that occur less than five times. The vocabulary builder output contains only words that appeared in the corpus more than or equal to five times.
- `build_vocab(sentences, keep_raw_vocab=False, trim_rule=None, progress_per=10000, update=False)`: This syntax is used to build vocabulary from a sequence of sentences (can be a once-only generator stream). Each sentence must be a list of unicode strings.

> There are other parameters that you can read about by clicking on this link: `https://radimrehurek.com/gensim/models/Word2vec.html`.

Each word present in the vocabulary has an association with the vocabulary object, which contains an index and a count. That is the output of the vocabulary builder. So you can refer to *Figure 6.8*, which helps you to understand the input and output of the vocabulary builder:

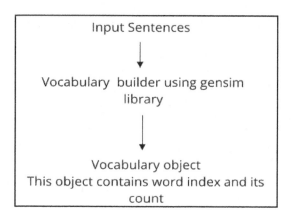

Figure 6.8: Input and output flow of vocabulary builder

Context builder

The context builder uses output of the vocabulary builder, as well as words that are part of the context window, as input and generates the output.

First of all, let's understand the concept of a context window. This context window is kind of a sliding window. You can define the window size as per the NLP application in which you will use word2vec. Generally, NLP applications use the context window size of five to ten words. If you decide to go with a window size of five, then we need to consider the five words on the left side from the center word and the five words on the right side of the center word. In this way, we capture the information about what all the surrounding words are for our center word.

Here, I want to state an example, and for this, the context window's size is equal to one, as we have a one-sentence corpus. I have the sentence: **I like deep learning,** and **deep** is the center word. So then, you should consider the surrounding words as per our window size. So here, I need to consider the words **like** and **learning**. In the next iteration our center word will be **learning,** its surrounding words are **deep**, and at the end of the sentence is a **period** (.).

I hope the context window concept is clear in your head. Now, we need to link this concept and see how the context builder uses this concept and the output of the vocabulary builder. The vocabulary builder object has word indexes and the frequency of the word in the corpus. By using the index of the word, the context builder has an idea of which word we are looking at and, according to the context window size, it considers the other surrounding words. These center words and the other surrounding words are input to the context builder.

Now you have a clear idea about what the inputs to the context builder are. Let's try to understand the output of the context builder. This context builder generates the word pairing. Refer to *Figure 6.9*, to get an idea about word paring:

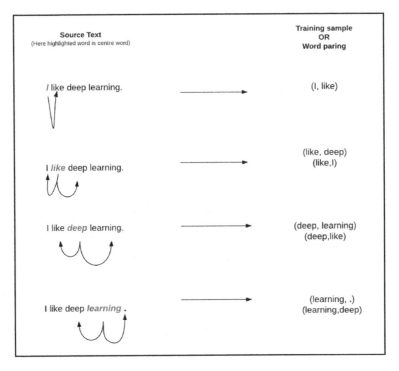

Figure 6.9: Understanding word paring

These word pairings will be given to the neural network. The network is going to learn the basic statistics from the number of times each word pairing shows up. So, for example, the neural network is probably going to get many more training examples of (deep, learning) than it is of (deep, communication). When the training is finished, if you give it the word **deep** as input, then it will output a much higher probability for learning or network than it will for communication.

So this word pair is the output of the context builder and it will pass to the next component, which is a two layer neural network. Refer to *Figure 6.10*, to see the summary of the flow of context builder:

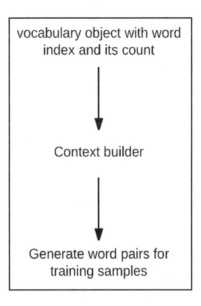

Figure 6.10: Input and output flow of context builder

So far, we have seen two major components of the word2vec building blocks. Now, our next focus will be on the final component, which is the neural network.

Neural network with two layers

In this section, we will look at the input and output of the neural network. Apart from that, we will also focus on the structural part of the neural network, which will give us an idea of how a single neuron looks, how many neurons there should be, what an activation function is, and so on. So, now, let's get started!

Structural details of a word2vec neural network

Word2vec uses the neural network for training. So, for us, it is very important to understand the basic structure of the neural network. The structural details of a neural network are given as follows:

- There is one input layer
- The second layer is the hidden layer
- The third and final layer is the output layer

Word2vec neural network layer's details

As we know, there are two layers in the neural network for generating word vectors. We will start to look at each of the layers and their input and output in detail. Here, we are not including the math behind the word2vec model in this section. Later in this chapter, we will also look at the math behind word2vec, and I will let you know at that point of time to map your dots for better interpretation.

Let's understand the task of each layer in brief:

- **Input layer**: An input layer has as many neurons as there are words in the vocabulary for training
- **Hidden layer**: The hidden layer size in terms of neurons is the dimensionality of the resulting word vectors
- **Output layer**: The output layer has the same number of neurons as the input layer

The input for the first input layer is the word with one-hot encoding. Assume that our vocabulary size for learning word vectors is **V**, which means there are **V** numbers of different words in the corpus. In that case, the position of the word that represents itself is encoded as **1** and all others positions are encoded as **0**. Refer to *Figure 6.4* again to recall the concept of one-hot encoding. Suppose the dimension of these words is **N**. So, the input to the hidden layer connections can be represented by our input matrix **WI** (input matrix symbol) of size $V * N$, with each row of the matrix **WI** representing a vocabulary word. Similarly, the connections from the hidden layer to the output layer means the output from the hidden layer can be described by the hidden layer output matrix **WO** (hidden layer matrix symbol). The **WO** matrix is of size $N * V$. In this case, each column of the **WO** matrix represents a word from the given vocabulary. Refer to *Figure 6.11* to get a crystal clear picture of the input and output. As well as this, we will also look at one short example to understand the concept:

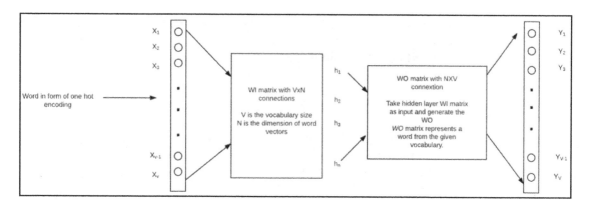

Figure 6.11: two layer neural network input and output structural representation

Now let's talk in terms of examples. I will take a very small set of the corpus. See the sentences from our small corpus given as follows:

- the dog saw a cat
- the dog chased a cat
- the cat climbed a tree

The preceding three sentences have eight (8) unique words. We need to order them in alphabetical order, and if we want to access them, then we will refer to the index of each word. Refer to the following table:

Words	Index
a	1
cat	2
chased	3
climbed	4
dog	5
saw	6
the	7
tree	8

So, here our value for **V** is equal to **8**. In our neural network, we need eight input neurons and eight output neurons. Now let's assume we will have three (3) neurons in the hidden layer. So in this case, our **WI** and **WO** values are defined as follows:

- $WI = [V * N] = [8 * 3]$
- $WO = [N * V] = [3 * 8]$

Before training begins, these matrices, **WI** and **WO** , are initialized by using small random values, as is very common in neural network training. Just for illustration purposes, let us assume that **WI** and **WO** are to be initialized to the following values:

$WI =$

```
-0.094491   -0.443977    0.313917
-0.490796   -0.229903    0.065460
 0.072921    0.172246   -0.357751
 0.104514   -0.463000    0.079367
-0.226080   -0.154659   -0.038422
 0.406115   -0.192794   -0.441992
 0.181755    0.088268    0.277574
-0.055334    0.491792    0.263102
```

$WO =$

```
 0.023074    0.479901    0.432148    0.375480   -0.364732   -0.119840    0.266070   -0.351000
-0.368008    0.424778   -0.257104   -0.148817    0.033922    0.353874   -0.144942    0.130904
 0.422434    0.364503    0.467865   -0.020302   -0.423890   -0.438777    0.268529   -0.446787
```

Image source: https://iksinc.wordpress.com

We are targeting it so that our neural network can learn the relationship between the words **cat** and **climbed**. So, in other words, we can explain that the neural network should give high probability for the word **climbed** when the word **cat** is fed into the neural network as an input. So, in word embedding, the word **cat** is referred to as a context word and the word **climbed** is referred to as a target word.

The input vector X stands for the word **cat** and it will be *[0 1 0 0 0 0 0 0]t*. Notice that only the second component of the vector is *1*. The reason behind this is that the input word **cat**, holds the second position in a sorted list of the corpus. In the same way, the target word is **climbed** and the target vector for **climbed** will look like *[0 0 0 1 0 0 0 0]t*.

The input for the first layer is *[0 1 0 0 0 0 0 0]t*.

The hidden layer output *Ht* is calculated by using the following formula:

Ht = XtWI = [-0.490796 -0.229903 0.065460]

From the preceding calculation, we can figure out that, here, the output of the hidden neurons mimics the weights of the second row of the **WI** matrix because of one-hot encoding representation. Now we need to check a similar calculation for the hidden layer and output layer. The calculation for the hidden layer and output layer is defined as follows:

HtWO = [0.100934 -0.309331 -0.122361 -0.151399 0.143463 -0.051262 -0.079686 0.112928]

Here, our final goal is to obtain probabilities for words in the output layer. From the output layer, we are generating probability that reflects the next word relationship with the context word at input. So, the mathematical representation is given as follows:

Probability (wordk | wordcontext) for k = 1...V

Here, we are talking in terms of probability, but our output is in the form of a set of vectors, so we need to convert our output into probability. We need to take care that the sum of the neuron output from the final output layer should be added to one. In word2vec, we are converting activation values of the output layer neurons to probabilities by using the softmax function.

Softmax function

In this section, we will look at the softmax function. The softmax function is used for converting output vectors into a probability form. We are using the softmax function because we want to convert out last layer output in terms of probability and softmax function can easily convert vector values into probability values. Here, the output of the kth neuron will be computed by the following equation, where activation(n) represents the activation value of the nth output layer neuron:

$$y_k = \Pr(word_k \mid word_{context}) = \frac{\exp(activation(k))}{\sum_{n=1}^{V} \exp(activation(n))}$$

By using this equation, we can calculate the probabilities for eight words in the corpus and the probability values are given as follows:

[0.143073 0.094925 0.114441 0.111166 0.149289 0.122874 0.119431 0.144800]

You must be wondering how I got these probability values. I used the previous softmax probability equation and generated the final probability vector. You can find the Python code for the softmax function in the following code snippet:

```
import numpy as np
def stablesoftmax(x):
"""Compute the softmax of vector x in a numerically stable way."""
shiftx = x - np.max(x)
exps = np.exp(shiftx)
return exps / np.sum(exps)
print stablesoftmax([0.100934,-0.309331,-0.122361,-0.151399,
0.143463,-0.051262,-0.079686, 0.112928])
```

The given code will generate the following output vector:

```
[ 0.143073    0.094925    0.114441    0.111166    0.149289    0.122874
0.119431    0.144800 ]
```

As you can see, the probability *0.111166* is for the chosen target word climbed. As we know, the target vector is *[0 0 0 1 0 0 0 0]t*, so we can compute the error by prediction. To generate a prediction error or error vector, we need to subtract the probability vector from the target vector, and once we know the error vector or error values, we can adjust the weight according to that. Here, we need to adjust the weight values of the matrices *WI* and *WO*. The technique of propagating errors in the network and readjusting the weight values of *WI* and *WO* is called **backpropagation**.

Thus, the training can continue by taking different context-target word pairs from the corpus. This is the way word2vec learns relationships between words in order to develop a vector representation of words in the corpus.

Main processing algorithms

Word2vec has two different versions. These versions are the main algorithms for word2vec. Refer to *Figure 6.12*:

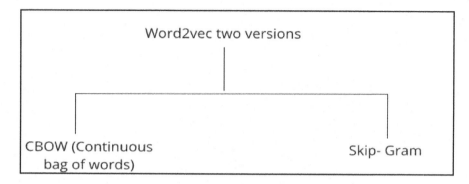

Figure 6.12: Versions of word2vec

In this section, we will look at the main two processing algorithms. Those algorithms names are given as follows:

- Continuous bag of words
- Skip-gram

Continuous bag of words

In the **continuous bag of words** (CBOW) algorithm, context is represented by multiple words for given target words. Just recall our example that we stated in an earlier section, where our context word was **cat** and our target word was **climbed.** For example, we can use **cat** as well as **tree** as context words to predict the word **climbed** as the target word. In this case, we need to change the architecture of the neural network, especially the input layer. Now, our input layer may not represent the single-word one-hot encode vector, but we need to put another input layer that represents the word **tree**.

If you increase the context words, then you need to put an additional input layer to represent each of the words, and all these input layers are connected to the hidden layer. Refer to *Figure 6.13*:

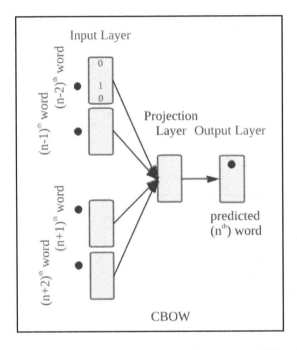

Figure 6.13: CBOW neural network architecture (Image credit: https://www.semanticscholar.org)

Here, the good part is that the computation formula remains the same; we just need to compute the *Ht* for other context words as well.

Skip-gram

The **skip-gram (SG)** model reverses the usage of target words and context words. Here, the target word is given as input to the input layer in the form of a one-hot encoded vector. The hidden layer remains the same. The output layer of the neural network is repeated multiple times to generate the chosen number of context words.

Let's take an example of the words **cat** and **tree** as context words and the word **climbed** as a target word. The input vector in the SG model will be the one-hot encoded word vector of the word **climbed** *[0 0 0 1 0 0 0 0]t* and this time, our output vectors should be vectors for the word **cat** and the word **tree**. So, the output vector should be *[0 1 0 0 0 0 0 0]* for **cat** and *[0 0 0 0 0 0 0 1]* for **tree**. Refer to the structure of the skip-gram algorithm in *Figure 6.14*:

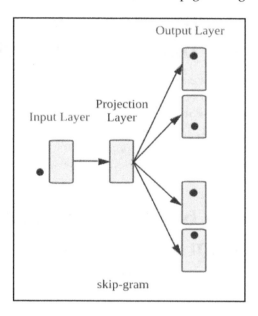

Figure 6.14: Skip gram neural network architecture (Image credit: https://www.semanticscholar.org)

This time the output will not be a single vector of probability, but two different vectors of probability, as we have two words as the context word. Here, error vector will be calculated in the same manner as we defined earlier. The small change in skip-gram is that the error vectors from all the output layers are summed up to adjust the weights via backpropagation. This means we need to ensure that the weight of matrix *WO* for each output layer should remain identical through the training.

Some of the algorithmic techniques and math behind word2vec and other techniques will be explained in the next section. So, let's get ready to deal with some cool mathematical stuff!

Understanding algorithmic techniques and the mathematics behind the word2vec model

This section is very important, as we are going to discuss here the core algorithms that have been used in word2vec. By the end of this section, there won't be any secrets left in order for you to understand the concept of word2vec. Thus, this section is converting word2vec black box into word2vec white box. Here, I'm going to include the math part as well, so readers can understand the core concepts in a better manner. Don't worry if you don't know the math, because I will provide you with some resources that you may find really useful.

Understanding the basic mathematics for the word2vec algorithm

To begin with, we need some of the basic mathematics concepts in place for a better understanding of the algorithm. The topics from mathematics that we need are listed as follows:

- **Vectors**: Vectors have magnitude and direction. So, when we draw a vector in vector space it carries some magnitude as well as direction. You can perform basic math operations on vectors.
- **Matrices**: A matrix is a grid of numbers or frequency count of words. It has rows and columns. We can define the dimensions of the matrix by counting the number of rows and columns it contains. You can refer to this link for more information on matrices.
- **Partial derivative**: If there is a function that contains more than one variable and we perform a derivative for this kind of function with respect to one of these variables and hold others constant, this is how we perform partial derivative. Partial derivatives are used in vector calculus.
- **Partial derivative chain rule**: The chain rule is defined as a formula that is used for computing the derivative of the composition of two or more functions.

Now let's jump to the understanding of the techniques. I have segregated all concepts broadly into three sections according to the stages where each and every technique has been used.

I have listed some of the reference links from where you get an in-depth idea about each of the given concepts. You can follow this link:

```
https://www.khanacademy.org/math.
```

You can refer to the following links for vectors:

```
http://emweb.unl.edu/math/mathweb/vectors/vectors.html.
```

```
https://www.mathsisfun.com/algebra/vectors.html.
```

You can refer to this link for more information on matrix:

```
https://medium.com/towards-data-science/linear-algebra-cheat-s
heet-for-deep-learning-cd67aba4526c.
```

You can see some basic examples by using this link:

```
http://mathinsight.org/partial_derivative_examples.
```

```
http://www.analyzemath.com/calculus/multivariable/partial_deri
vatives.html.
```

You can refer to the following links for the partial derivative chain rule:

```
https://math.oregonstate.edu/home/programs/undergrad/CalculusQ
uestStudyGuides/vcalc/chain/chain.html.
```

```
https://www.youtube.com/watch?v=HOYA0-pOHsg.
```

```
https://www.youtube.com/watch?v=aZcw1kN6B8Y.
```

The preceding list is more than enough for this chapter to understand the mathematics behind the algorithms.

Techniques used at the vocabulary building stage

While generating vocabulary from the dataset, you may use an optimization technique, and lossy counting is the one that is used the most for the word2vec model.

Lossy counting

The lossy count algorithm is used to identify elements in a dataset whose frequency count exceeds a user-given threshold. This algorithm takes data streams as an input instead of the finite set of a dataset.

With lossy counting, you periodically remove very low-count elements from the frequency table. The most frequently accessed words would almost never have low counts anyway, and if they did, they wouldn't be likely to stay there for long.

Here, the frequency threshold is usually defined by the user. When we give a parameter of `min_count = 4`, we remove the words that appear in the dataset less than four times and we will not consider them.

Using it at the stage of vocabulary building

Lossy counting is very useful; especially when you have a large corpus and you don't want to consider the words that appear very rarely.

At this time, lossy counting is very useful because the user can set the minimum word frequency count as a threshold, so words that occur less than the threshold frequency count won't be included in our vocabulary.

So, if you have a large corpus and you want to optimize the speed of training, then we can use this algorithm.

In other words, you can say that by using this algorithm you narrow down your vocabulary size, thus, you can speed up the training process.

Applications

Apart from word2vec, the lossy counting algorithm is used in network traffic measurements and analysis of web server logs.

Techniques used at the context building stage

While generating word context pairs, the context builder uses the following techniques:

- Dynamic window scaling or dynamic context window
- Subsampling
- Pruning

Dynamic window scaling

As you can see, dynamic window scaling is a part of the context builder. We will see how it can be useful and what kind of impact it generates when we use it. Dynamic window scaling is also known as **dynamic context window**.

Understanding dynamic context window techniques

In the word2vec implementation, dynamic context window is an optional technique that may be applied to generate more accurate output. You can also consider these techniques as hyperparameters.

Dynamic context window techniques use weight schema for context words with respect to target words.

So the intuition here is that words that are near to the target word are more important than other words that are far away from the target word.

Let us see how it will be useful when we are building word pairs. Dynamic context window considers that nearby context words hold more importance to predicting the target word. Here, we are applying the weighting scheme by using uniform sampling on the actual window size between 1 and L. For example, suppose the context window size is 5 and now the weight of context words are distributed in a uniform manner, so the weight of most nearby words is 5/5, the very next context word weight is 4/5, and so on. So, the final weight for context words will be 5/5, 4/5, 3/5, 2/5, 1/5. Thus, by providing weight, you can fine-tune the final result.

Subsampling

Subsampling is also one of the techniques that we use when we are building word pairs, and as we know, these word pairs are sample training data.

Subsampling is the method that removes the most frequent words. This technique is very useful for removing stop words.

These techniques also remove words randomly, and these randomly chosen words occur in the corpus more frequently. So, words that are removed are more frequent than some threshold t with a probability of p, where f marks the words corpus frequency and we use $t = 10-5$ in our experiments. Refer to the following equation given in *Figure 6.15*:

$$p = 1 - \sqrt{\frac{t}{f}}$$

Figure 6.15: Subsampling probability equation

This also acts as one of the useful hyperparameters, and it is very useful because we are removing the most frequent and unnecessary words from the corpus, as well as from the context window, and that way, we are improving the quality of our training sample set.

Pruning

Pruning is also used when we are building our word pairs for training purposes using context builder. When you have a large amount of vocabulary to deal with, if you have included less frequent words, then you need to remove them. You can also restrict the size of the total vocabulary by using the `max_vocab_size` parameter given in the Python `gensim` library.

Let's see how useful pruning is for us in order to generate word2vec. Pruning is used to prune the training sample size, as well as make the quality of it better. If you don't prune the rarely occurred words from the dataset, then the model accuracy may degrade. This is a kind of hack to improve the accuracy.

Algorithms used by neural networks

Here, we will look at the structure of individual neurons. We will also look into the details about the two algorithms, thus, we will understand how word2vec generates vectors from words.

Structure of the neurons

We have seen the overall neural network structure, but we haven't yet seen what each neuron is made of and what the structure of the neurons is. So, in this section, we will look at the structure of each single input neuron.

We will look at the following structures:

- Basic neuron structure
- Training a single neuron
- Single neuron application
- Multi-layer neural network
- Backpropagation
- Mathematics behind the word2vec model

In this, we will heavily include the mathematical formulas. If you are not from a mathematical background, then don't worry. I will give you explanations in simple words so you know what is going on in each section.

Basic neuron structure

Refer to *Figure 6.16*; it shows the basic neuron structure:

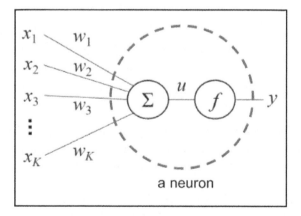

Figure 6.16: Basic neuron structure (Image credits: Xin Rong)

Figure 6.16 shows a basic neuron structure. This structure is not new. This structure takes an input, and there are weights also as input, and they calculate the weighted sum. Here, *x1* to *xk* is the input value and *w1* to *wk* is the corresponding weights. So, the weighted sum is expressed by the following equation given in *Figure 6.17*:

$$u = \sum_{i=0}^{K} w_i x_i$$

Figure 6.17: Weighted sum equation

Let's take an example to understand the usage of the equation. So, if you have input *x=[1 5 6]* and *w=[0.5 0.2 0.1]*, the weighted sum *u* is equal to *[1 * 0.5 + 5 * 0.2 + 6 * 0.1]*, so our final answer is *u = [0.5 + 1 + 0.6] = 2.1*. This is just a simple example to give you some concrete practical intuition about the real workings of the given equation. This is all about our input. Now we will talk about the output.

In order to generate output, we can say from our basic neuron structure that our output is the function of weighted sum *u*. Here, *y* is the output and *f(u)* is the function of the weighted sum. You can see the equation given in *Figure 6.18*:

$$y = f(u)$$

Figure 6.18: Output y is function of weighted sum u

In neural networks, we can use different available functions and these functions are called **activation functions**. These functions are listed as follows:

- Step function
- Sigmoid function

Some great scientists have stated that the given functions are a good choice as activation functions. For this chapter, we are not getting into the details of activation functions, but we will look at all the details regarding the activation functions in Chapter 9, *Deep Learning for NLP and NLG Problems*. So, we will consider the given two functions as activation functions for word2vec. We will use either the step function or sigmoid function, not both at the same time, to develop word2vec. Refer to the equation of both of the functions in *Figure 6.19*:

$$f(u) = \begin{cases} 1 & \text{if } u > 0 \\ 0 & \text{otherwise} \end{cases}$$

$$f(u) = \frac{1}{1 + e^{-u}}$$

Figure 6.19: Activation functions, the first is the step function and the second is the sigmoid function

Here, *f(u)* is the step function and *f(u)* is the sigmoid function.

When we draw a circle to represent the neuron similar to the one drawn in *Figure 6.11*, this circle contains the weighted sum and activation function, which is the reason we have indicated the dotted circle in *Figure 6.16*.

In the next section, we will see how these activation functions can be used and how we can calculate the errors in predicted output by using the error function. We will see this in detail about the usage of the activation function and error function. So let's begin!

Training a simple neuron

Now it is time to see how we can use a single neuron for training by using the activation function, and let's understand the loss function to calculate the error in predicted output.

The main idea is defined as the error function, which actually tells us the degree of error in our prediction; we will actually try to make our error value as low as possible. So, in other words, we are actually trying to improve our prediction. During training, we use input and calculate the error by using the error function and update the weight of neurons and repeat our training process. We will continue this process until we get the minimum error rate of maximum, best, and accurate output.

The two most important concepts that we are going to look at are listed as follows:

- Define error function (loss function)
- Understanding of gradient descent in word2vec

Define error function

Here, our input is vector X with vocabulary x1 to *xk* and our output y is the output vector. So, to calculate the error E , we need to define the error function or loss function, and we are using the L2 loss function. Let's begin with understanding the basic concept of the L2 loss function, and then we will see how it will be useful in word2vec.

There are two type of loss functions that are mostly used across **machine learning** (**ML**) and **deep learning** (**DL**). By the way, we will look at ML and DL in upcoming chapters, which are Chapter 8, *Machine Learning (ML) for NLP Problems* and Chapter 9, *Deep Learning for NLP and NLG Problems*. There are two standard types of loss functions, but here we will only look at **least square error** (**L2**), and in upcoming chapters, which are Chapter 8, *Machine Learning for NLP Problems* and Chapter 9, *Deep Learning for NLP and NLG Problems* we will look at various error functions in detail and compare those error functions as well. The two standard types of loss functions are:

- Least absolute deviation (L1)
- Least square error (L2)

Least square error is also called **L2 loss** function. In general, loss functions want to achieve their minimized value while learning from a dataset and L2 loss functions also want to achieve their value where the error value will be minimal. So, precisely, the L2 function wants to minimize the squared differences between the estimated and existing target values.

The structure of a single neuron at the time of training is given in *Figure 6.20*:

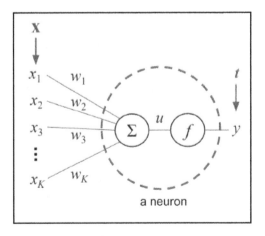

Figure 6.20: Single neuron at the time of training

So, when we are trying to calculate an L2 loss function of a single neuron, we will use the following equation given in *Figure 6.21*:

$$E = \frac{1}{2}(t - y)^2$$

Figure 6.21: L2 loss function equation (Least Squared error function)

Here, t is the target vector value, y is the estimated vector value or predicted vector value, and E is the error function. We have defined our L2 error function. I know you must be very keen to know what we will be doing with this L2 error function to get a least error value, and that is where we need to understand the concept of gradient descent.

Understanding gradient descent in word2vec

Now, let's understand what we are going to do with the L2 function and how it will be useful in achieving an accurate output.

As we said earlier, we want to minimize this function value so, we can accurately predict the target value, and to achieve this we will take partial derivative of the L2 function equation given in *Figure 6.21* with respect to y. The procedure of deriving derivation and then by using this derivation trying to minimize error values, is called **gradient descent**.

In that case, the result is given in *Figure 6.22*:

$$\frac{\partial E}{\partial y} = y - t$$

Figure 6.22: Result of Partial derivatives of L2 loss function with respect to y

We know that output y is dependent on $f(u)$ and $f(u)$ is dependent on input weight values wi. So we need to apply chain rules and generate the error function value. If we use partial derivative chain rules, then we will get the following equation, which will be useful in word2vec. *Figure 6.23* shows the result of the partial derivative chain rule:

$$\frac{\partial E}{\partial u} = \frac{\partial E}{\partial y} \cdot \frac{\partial y}{\partial u}$$
$$= (y - t)y(1 - y)$$

$$\frac{\partial E}{\partial w_i} = \frac{\partial E}{\partial y} \cdot \frac{\partial y}{\partial u} \cdot \frac{\partial u}{\partial w_i}$$
$$= (y - t) \cdot y(1 - y) \cdot x_i$$

Figure 6.23: Partial derivative chain rule result for L2 error function

After calculating the L2 loss function as per the value of the error, the neural network input weight will be updated and this kind of iteration will continue until we achieve the minimum error value or error rate.

So far, we have been deriving equations for a single neuron, so it will be important to know what this single neuron can do for us. That is our next point of discussion.

Single neuron application

We have learnt a lot of technical and mathematical stuff about single neurons, so I really want to walk you through the application on single neurons with respect to the word2vec model. So let's begin!

If you want to build a model that identifies the words that are edible and that are not, then we can use a single neuron to build the model. This kind of application, where we are segregating words either into edible classes or non-edible classes is called a **binary classification task**. For this kind of task, neurons are used to take one-hot encoded vectors as input and a single neuron will learn which words are related to edible items and which are not related to edible items. So, it will generate a look up table, which you can see in *Figure 6.24*:

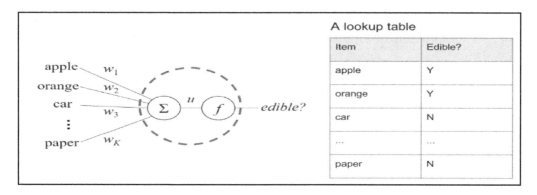

Figure 6.24: Single neuron can classify words into edible and non edible categories

The reason why this kind of application can be built with such ease is that when you are continuously providing the one-hot word vector and use the sigmoid or step functions as the activation function, then it becomes a standard classification problem, and this kind of problem can be solved easily by using mathematics. We have defined this in previous sections because for edible items, the output vector have the same kind of values, and for non-edible items generated vectors, they represent the same kind of output vector. In the end, we will be able to build the lookup table. This kind of standard classification problem reminds us of logistic regression, and we are applying the same logistic regression concepts, but here we are using a single neuron structure.

We have seen enough about the single neuron structure, now it is time to explore the multi-layer neural network. Our next section will provide you with information about multilayer neural networks.

Multi-layer neural networks

A multi-layer neural network is the structure that we are using for word2vec. This function takes input as a one-hot encoded word vector and this vector, as well as a weighted sum is passed to a hidden layer. By using the activation function, which is the sigmoid function in this case, output is generated from the hidden layer and this output is passed to the next layer, which is the output layer. We have already seen an example in this chapter, in the section entitled *Neural network with two layers*. In that section, we did not look at the mathematical aspect, so here I will walk you through the mathematical aspect of neural networks.

So, let's represent what I told you in the preceding paragraph through a mathematical equation. See the structure of a multi-layer neural network in *Figure 6.25*:

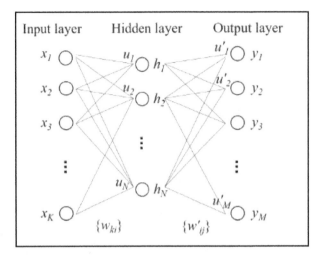

Figure 6.25: Multi-layer neural network

Now, let's see the mathematical equations for the given neural network. Here, I'm going to provide you with high-level intuition, which will help you to understand the flow and you will get an idea about the input and output functions. Refer to *Figure 6.26*:

$$u_i = \sum_{k=1}^{K} w_{ki} x_k$$

$$h_i = f(u_i)$$

$$u'_j = \sum_{i=1}^{N} w'_{ij} h_i$$

$$y_j = f(u'_j)$$

Figure 6.26: Mathematical equation for multilayer neural networks

The flow of the input and output is given as follows:

- The first equation of *Figure 6.24* is a weighted sum the of input layer and the result of the input layer will be passed on to the hidden layer. *ui* is the weighted sum of the input layer. The activation function of the hidden layer is given in the second equation. The activation function *hi* uses the sigmoid function and generates the intermediate output.
- The weighted sum of the hidden layer will be passed to the output layer and the third equation shows the calculation of the hidden layer weighted sum. *u'j* is the weighted sum from the hidden layer and it will be passed to the output layer. *yj* uses the weighted sum from the hidden layer, which is *u'j* as well, as here also the activation function is sigmoid.

We have seen the flow of input and output by using a basic mathematical representation.

Now, a major concern is how this structure is used to get trained for the word2vec model, and the answer to that is, we use backpropagation to train the model, which we will see in the next section.

Backpropagation

We have already seen how errors have been calculated using the L2 loss function, and the L2 loss function wants to minimize the squared differences between the estimated and existing target values. We will apply the same concepts to the multi-layer neural network. So, we need to define the loss function as well as we to take the gradient of the function and update the weight of the neural network in order to generate a minimum error value. Here, our input and output is vectors.

Refer to *Figure 6.27* to see the neural network structure, and *Figure 6.28* shows what equations we need to apply to calculate error functions in a multi-layer neural network:

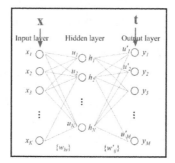

Figure 6.27: Multi-layer neural network for calculating error functions

Now let's see the derivation and mathematical calculation performed by neural networks. You can see the equations are given as follows, refer to *Figure 6.28*:

$$E = \frac{1}{2} \sum_{j=1}^{M} (y_j - t_j)^2$$

$$\frac{\partial E}{\partial y_j} = y_j - t_j$$

$$\frac{\partial E}{\partial u'_j} = \frac{\partial E}{\partial y_j} \cdot \frac{\partial y_j}{\partial u'_j}$$

$$\frac{\partial E}{\partial w'_{ij}} = \frac{\partial E}{\partial u'_j} \cdot \frac{\partial u'_j}{\partial w'_{ij}}$$

$$\frac{\partial E}{\partial h_i} = \sum_{j=1}^{M} \frac{\partial E}{\partial u'_j} \frac{\partial u'_j}{\partial h_i}$$

$$\frac{\partial E}{\partial u_i} = \frac{\partial E}{\partial h_i} \cdot \frac{\partial h_i}{\partial u_i}$$

$$\frac{\partial E}{\partial w_{ki}} = \frac{\partial E}{\partial u_i} \cdot \frac{\partial u_i}{\partial w_{ki}}$$

Figure 6.28: Equations for calculating error function for multi-layer neural networks

When you are calculating error function for multi-layer neural networks, you need to be very careful about the indexes, as well as which layer you are calculating an error function value for. As you can see in *Figure 6.28*, we will start with the output index, backpropagate the error to the hidden layer, and update the weight. In the fifth equation, you can see that we need to calculate the error function for the output layer so that backpropagate the error and we can update the weight of the input layer. To deal with indexes is a kind of a challenging task in multi-layer neural networks. But coding it up is quite easy because you just need to write a `for` loop to calculate each of the layer gradients.

Now, we will put all the mathematical equations and concepts of word2vec together and understand the final mathematical piece of word2vec neural networks.

Mathematics behind the word2vec model

In this section, we will look at the final piece of mathematics by combining all the previous equations and concepts, and we will derive the final equation in the form of probability. We have already seen the concept and basic intuition, calculation, and example in the previous section, *Word2vec neural network layers details*.

The word2vec neural network is using a one-hot encoded word vector as input and then it passes this vector value to the next layer, which is the hidden layer, and this is nothing but the weighted sum values that feed into the hidden layer as input. The last output layer generates the vector value, but to make sense of the output, we will convert the vector into probability format, and with the help of softmax techniques, we will also convert the output word vector into probability format. We will see all the different techniques that are used to generate probability from the output vector in the upcoming section, until then, just use softmax as a magic function.

Refer to *Figure 6.29* to understand the mathematics behind word2vec neural networks:

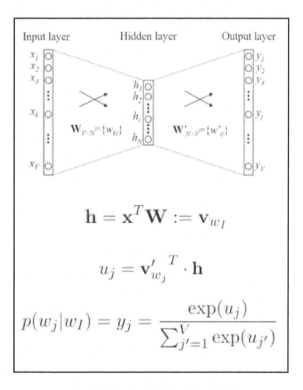

Figure 6.29: Mathematics behind word2vec model

In the first equation, we can see the weighted sum of the input word vector and weights and get *h* in the second equation. We multiply *h* and the weighted sum of word vectors of the hidden layer *v'wj*. Here, weight and index has been changed. This multiplication is *uj* . Here, *uj* is the activation function. We will then generate probability by using the value of *uj* . So, the final equation is the softmax function. Let's simplify the equation by replacing *uj* in the third equation with the input and output word vector format, then you will get the final equation. Refer to *Figure 6.30*:

$$p(w_j|w_I) = \frac{\exp\left(\mathbf{v'}_{w_O}{}^T \mathbf{v}_{w_I}\right)}{\sum_{j'=1}^{V} \exp\left(\mathbf{v'}_{w_j'}{}^T \mathbf{v}_{w_I}\right)}$$

Figure 6.30: Final probability equation of the word2vec model

This time, our output is a softmax function, so for updating weight using backpropagation, we need to define the loss function. So, here, we will define the loss function in the form of the softmax function, so we will use minus log probability of the softmax function and then we will perform gradient descent. See *Figure 6.31*:

$$E = -\log \frac{\exp\left(\mathbf{v'}_{w_O}{}^T \mathbf{v}_{w_I}\right)}{\sum_{j'=1}^{V} \exp\left(\mathbf{v'}_{w_j'}{}^T \mathbf{v}_{w_I}\right)}$$

$$\frac{\partial E}{\partial u_j} = y_j - t_j := e_j$$

$$\frac{\partial E}{\partial w'_{ii}} = \frac{\partial E}{\partial u_j} \cdot \frac{u_j}{\partial w'_{ii}}$$

$$\frac{\partial E}{\partial h_i} = \sum_{j=1}^{V} \frac{\partial E}{\partial u_j} \cdot \frac{\partial u_j}{\partial h_i}$$

$$\frac{\partial E}{\partial w_{ki}} = \frac{\partial E}{\partial h_i} \cdot \frac{\partial h_i}{\partial w_{ki}}$$

Figure 6.31: Error function gradient descent in form of minus log probability of the softmax function

Here, I want to give some idea of how the output vector value has been updated. So, it is an updating rule for an output layer. You can find the equation given as follows. Refer to *Figure 6.32*:

$$\mathbf{v}'_{w_j}{}^{(\text{new})} = \mathbf{v}'_{w_j}{}^{(\text{old})} - \eta \cdot e_j \cdot \mathbf{h}$$

Figure 6.32: Rule for updating the output vector

In this equation, we are taking the original output vector and subtracting the prediction error *ej* of the output node and *h* is the value of the hidden layer. So, the meaning of this equation is that, if we have the word **climbed** as input, and we want to predict the word **cat** as output, then how we can update the vector value of the word **climbed** so that it will be more similar to the vector of the word **cat**? So in simple language we can say we will add some part of the vector of **climbed** to the vector of the word **cat** and apart from this, we also need to update the output vector of other words because all other words that are not our target words should update their output vector so that they will be less similar to the target words.

The rule for updating the input vector is also useful; the equation of updating an input vector is given as follows. Refer to *Figure 6.33*:

$$\text{EH}_i := \frac{\partial E}{\partial h_i} = \sum_{j=1}^{V} e_j \cdot w'_{ij}$$

$$\mathbf{v}_{w_I}^{(\text{new})} = \mathbf{v}_{w_I}^{(\text{old})} - \eta \cdot \text{EH}$$

Figure 6.33: Rule for updating input vector

This equation is a bit complex. So, here, intuition is the input vector, which will be subtracted from the weighted sum of the prediction errors. The meaning of this is that, this time, we are going to update the input vector **cat**. We will update the vector value of the word cat in such a manner that it will come close to the vector of the word **climbed**. Here, co-occurrence of the words play a major role.

We are almost done with the math portion of the word2vec model. We have seen a lot of mathematical equations that are used in the word2vec model. Now we will talk about the techniques that are used to generate the final vectors and probability of the prediction.

Techniques used to generate final vectors and probability prediction stage

In this section, we will see how we will generate the final vector. We will also use some heuristics to generate output efficiently. So, we will talk about those heuristics as well.

As we have already seen, to generate the word vector we need to update input as well as the output vector. Suppose we have a million words in our vocabulary, so the process of updating the input and output vectors will take a lot of time and it will be inefficient. We have to solve this challenge. So we use some of the optimized ways to perform the same operations and those techniques are given as follows:

- Hierarchical softmax
- Negative sampling

So, let's start to understand these techniques.

Hierarchical softmax

In hierarchical softmax, instead of mapping each output vector to its corresponding word, we consider the output vector as a form of binary tree. Refer to the structure of hierarchical softmax in *Figure 6.34*:

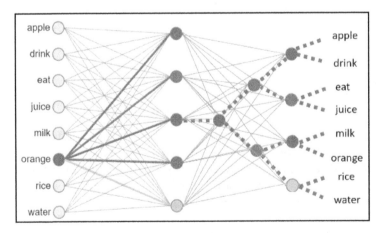

Figure 6.34: Hierarchical Softmax structure

So, here, the output vector is not making a prediction about how probable the word is, but it is making a prediction about which way you want to go in the binary tree. So, either you want to visit this branch or you want to visit the other branch. Refer to *Figure 6.35*:

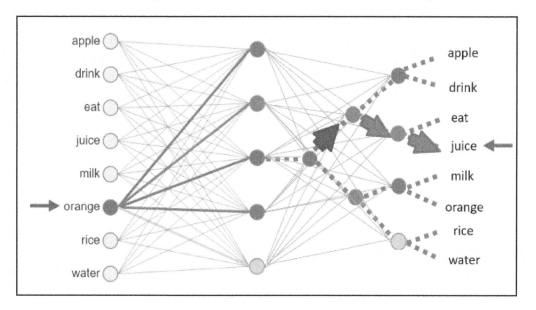

Figure 6.35: Prediction path using hierarchical softmax mantle representation

In this case, consider the red activated dot going up (light grey here) and the blue activated dot going downwards (dark grey here), so you can see that, here, we can predict the word **juice** with high probability.

Here, the advantage is, if you want to backpropagate an error, then you just need to update one output vector and the error will propagate to only three nodes that are activated at the time of prediction. We use the Huffman binary tree construction to generate the binary tree.

Negative sampling

Negative sampling is also a kind of optimization method. In this method, we are going to update the vector of the output word, but we are not going to update all the vectors of other words. We just take the sample from the words other than the output vector. So, we are selecting a sample from the negative sample set of words, hence the name of this technique is negative sampling.

Some of the facts related to word2vec

Here are some of the facts about the word2vec models that you should keep in mind when you are actually using it:

- So far, you will have realized that word2vec uses neural networks and this neural network is not a deep neural network. It only has two layers, but it works very well to find out the words similarity.
- Word2vec neural network uses a simple logistic activation function that does not use non-linear functions.
- The activation function of the hidden layer is simply linear because it directly passes its weighted sum of inputs to the next layer.

Now, we have seen almost all the major aspects of word2vec, so in the next section, we will look at the application of word2vec.

Applications of word2vec

Allow me to introduce some real-life applications in which word2vec has been used. They are:

- Dependency parser uses word2vec to generate better and accurate dependency relationship between words at the time of parsing.
- Name entity recognition can also use word2vec, as word2vec is very good at finding out similarity in **named entity recognition** (**NER**). All similar entities can come together and you will have better results.
- Sentiment analysis uses it to preserve semantic similarity in order to generate better sentiment results. Semantic similarity helps us to know which kind of phrases or words people use to express their opinions, and you can generate good insights and accuracy by using word2vec concepts in sentiment analysis.
- We can also build an application that predicts a person's name by using their writing style.
- If you want to do document classification with high accuracy and using simple statistics, then word2vec is for you. You can use the concept and categorize the documents without any human labels.
- Word clustering is the fundamental product of word2vec. All words carrying a similar meaning are clustered together.
- Google uses word2vec and deep learning to improve their machine translation product.

There are so many use cases where you could use word2vec concepts. Here, we are going to implement some fun examples. We are going to build fun applications, as well as doing some visualization on them so you can understand the concept in a far better manner.

Implementation of simple examples

In this section, we are going to implement the famous word2vec example, which is adding woman and king and subtracting man, and then the resultant vector shows the vector value of queen.

We are not going to train the word2vec model, on our data and then build our own word2vec model because there is a huge amount of data on which Google has already trained their word2vec model and provided us with pre-trained models. Now, if you want to replicate the training process on that much data, then we need a lot of computational resources, so we will use pre-trained word2vec models from Google. You can download the pre-trained model from this link: https://code.google.com/archive/p/Word2vec/.

After clicking on this link, you need to go to the section entitled pre-trained word and phrase vectors, download the model named GoogleNews-vectors-negative300.bin.gz, and extract it.

We will use the genism library to build our famous example.

Famous example (king - man + woman)

We are going to load the binary model by using the gensim library and replicate the example. If you are running it on your computer, then it will take a few minutes, so don't worry and keep the script running. Refer to *Figure 6.36*, for the code snippet:

```
from gensim import models
w = models.Word2Vec.load_word2vec_format('/home/jalaj/Downloads/GoogleNews-vectors-negative300.bin', binary=True)
print('King - man + woman:')
print('')
print w.wv.most_similar(positive=['woman', 'king'], negative=['man'])
print('Similarity between man and woman:')
print(w.similarity('woman', 'man'))
```

Figure 6.36: Code snippet for example King - man + woman = queen

You can see the code by clicking on this GitHub link:
`https://github.com/jalajthanaki/NLPython/blob/master/ch6/kingque`
`enexample.py`

You can refer to *Figure 6.37* for the output we are generating:

```
King - man + woman:

[
(u'queen', 0.7118192315101624),
(u'monarch', 0.6189674139022827),
(u'princess', 0.5902431607246399),
(u'crown_prince', 0.5499460697174072),
(u'prince', 0.5377321243286133),
(u'kings', 0.5236844420433044),
(u'Queen_Consort', 0.5235946178436279),
(u'queens', 0.5181134343147278),
(u'sultan', 0.5098593235015869),
(u'monarchy', 0.5087411999702454)
]

Similarity between man and woman:
0.7664012231
```

Figure 6.37: Output of the example King - man + woman = queen

Now, if you want to train the model from scratch by using data that is provided by Google, then download the training dataset by using the following link: `https://code.google.com/archive/p/Word2vec/`. Go to the section entitled *Where to obtain the training data* and download all training datasets, then, by taking a reference from the given GitHub link `https://github.com/LasseRegin/gensim-Word2vec-model`, you can replicate the whole training process, but it will take a lot of time because this kind of training needs a lot of computational power.

Advantages of word2vec

As we have seen, word2vec is a very good technique for generating distributional similarity. There are other advantages of it as well, which I've listed here:

- Word2vec concepts are really easy to understand. They are not so complex that you really don't know what is happening behind the scenes.
- Using word2vec is simple and it has very powerful architecture. It is fast to train compared to other techniques.
- Human effort for training is really minimal because, here, human tagged data is not needed.
- This technique works for both a small amount of datasets and a large amount of datasets. So it is an easy-to-scale model.
- Once you understand the concept and algorithms, then you can replicate the whole concept and algorithms on your dataset as well.
- It does exceptionally well on capturing semantic similarity.
- As this is a kind of unsupervised approach, human effort is very minimal, so it is a time-saving method.

Challenges of word2vec

Although the word2vec concept is very efficient, there are some points that you may find complex or challenging. Here, I will propose the most common challenges. Those points are listed as follows:

- The word2vec model is easy to develop, but difficult to debug, so debug ability is one of the major challenges when you are developing a word2vec model for your dataset.
- It does not handle ambiguities. So, if a word has multiple meanings, and in the real world we can find many of these kinds of words, then in that case, embedding will reflect the average of these senses in vector space.

How is word2vec used in real-life applications?

This section will give you an idea of which kinds of NLP applications use word2vec and how NLP applications use this concept. Apart from that, I will also discuss some of the most frequently-asked questions across the community in order for you to have a clear insight of word2vec when you try it out in real life.

NLP applications such as document classification, sentiment analysis, and so on can use word2vec techniques. Especially in document classification, word2vec implementation gives you more good results, as it preserves semantic similarity.

For sentiment analysis, we can apply word2vec, which gives you an idea about how words are spread across the dataset, and then you can use customized parameters such as context window size, subsampling, and so on. You should first generate **bag of words** (**BOW**) and then start to train word2vec on that BOW and generate word vectors. These vectors can be fed as input features for the ML algorithm, then generate sentiment analysis output.

Now, it's time to discuss some of the questions that people usually ask when they are trying to understand and use word2vec techniques on their own dataset.

Now, let's fire up the questions!

- **What kind of corpus do we need?**: Word2vec techniques can be applied on text datasets. As such, there is not any specific kind of text data that you cannot use. So, as per my view, you can apply word2vec on any dataset.
- **Should I always remove stop words?**: In original models of word2vec that were from Google, remove some of the stop words, such as **a** has been removed in word2vec, but the word **the** has not been removed. So it is not mandatory that you remove the words:
  - It is totally dependent on your NLP application. If you are developing a sentiment analysis application, then you can remove all stop words, but if you are developing machine translation applications, then you should remove some of the stop words; not all. If you are using word2vec for developing word clusters to understand the grammar of the language, then you should not remove any of the words.
- **Should I remove all stop words?**: This question is related to the previous question. The straightforward answer to this question is no. It is not compulsory that you should remove all stop words blindly for every NLP application. Each and every NLP application is different, so you should take a decision based on the NLP application that you are trying to build:
  - If you look at the Google original word2vec model, then you will see that in

that model the word **a** is not there, which means a vector that represents the word **a** is not present, but a vector for the word **the** is there.

- We will load the original Google word2vec model and, using simple lines of code, we will look at some of the facts regarding stop words.
  Refer to the code snippet in *Figure 6.38*:

```python
from gensim import models
w = models.Word2Vec.load_word2vec_format('/home/jalaj/Downloads/GoogleNews-vectors-negative300.bin', binary=True)
if 'the' in w.wv.vocab:
    print "Vector for word 'the' \n"
    print w.wv['the']
else:
    print "Vocabulary doesn't include word 'the'\n"
if 'a' in w.wv.vocab:
    print "Vector for word 'a' \n"
    print w.wv['a']
else:
    print "Vocabulary doesn't include word 'a'\n"
```

Figure 6.38: Code snippet that shows the fact of stop words

For the output that is the vector value of `the`, refer to *Figure 6.39*:

```
Vector for word 'the'

[ 0.08007812  0.10498047  0.04980469  0.0534668  -0.06738281 -0.12060547
  0.03515625 -0.11865234  0.04394531  0.03015137 -0.05688477 -0.07617188
  0.01287842  0.04980469 -0.08496094 -0.06347656  0.00628662 -0.04321289
  0.02026367  0.01330566 -0.01953125  0.09277344 -0.171875   -0.00131989
  0.06542969  0.05834961 -0.08251953  0.0859375  -0.00318909  0.05859375
 -0.03491211 -0.0123291  -0.0480957  -0.00302124  0.05639648  0.01495361
 -0.07226562 -0.05224609  0.09667969  0.04296875 -0.03540039 -0.07324219
  0.03271484 -0.06176758  0.00787354  0.0035553  -0.00878906  0.0390625
  0.03833008  0.04443359  0.06982422  0.01263428 -0.00445557 -0.03320312
 -0.04272461  0.09765625 -0.02160645 -0.0378418   0.01190186 -0.01391602
 -0.11328125  0.09326172 -0.03930664 -0.11621094  0.02331543 -0.01599121
  0.02636719  0.10742188 -0.00466919  0.09619141  0.0279541  -0.05395508
  0.08544922 -0.03686523 -0.02026367 -0.08544922  0.125       0.14453125
  0.0267334   0.15039062  0.05273438 -0.18652344  0.08154297 -0.01062012
 -0.03735352 -0.07324219 -0.07519531  0.03613281 -0.13183594  0.00616455
  0.05078125  0.04516602  0.0100708  -0.15039062 -0.06005859  0.05761719
 -0.00692749  0.01586914 -0.0213623   0.10351562 -0.00029182 -0.046875
```

Figure 6.39: Sample values of word vector for the word the

See the output, where you can see that word2vec doesn't contain a in its vocabulary in *Figure 6.40*:

```
 0.11474609  0.03173828  0.02209473  0.07226562  0.03686523  0.02563477
 0.01367188 -0.02734375  0.00592041 -0.06738281  0.05053711 -0.02832031
-0.04516602 -0.01733398  0.02111816  0.03515625 -0.04296875  0.06640625
 0.12207031  0.12353516  0.0039978   0.04516602 -0.01855469  0.04833984
 0.04516602  0.08691406  0.02941895  0.03759766  0.03442383 -0.07373047
-0.0402832  -0.14648438 -0.02441406 -0.01953125  0.0065918  -0.0018158
-0.01092529  0.09326172  0.06542969  0.01843262 -0.09326172 -0.01574707
-0.07128906 -0.08935547 -0.07128906 -0.03015137 -0.01300049  0.01635742
-0.01831055  0.01483154  0.00500488  0.00366211  0.04760742 -0.06884766]
Vocabulary doesn't include word 'a'
```

Figure 6.40: Word2vec doesn't contain the word a

- **Don't you think that, here, we have generated two vectors for each word?**: I would like to let you know that we have generated two vectors for each word. The reason behind this is that word in a sentence is coming on a target word as well as a context word, so when a word appears as a target word, we will generate vectors, and when a word appears as a context word, then we also generate vectors. We consider the target word vector in our final output, but yes, you can use both vectors. How to use the two vectors and generate making sense out of that is kind of a million dollar question!

When should you use word2vec?

Word2vec captures semantic similarity; this is the most important point that we need to keep in mind when we are processing the answer to the preceding question.

If you have an NLP application in which you want to use the distributional semantic, then word2vec is for you! Some NLP applications will use this concept to generate the features and the output vector from the word2vec model, or similarly, vectors will be used as input features for the ML algorithm.

You should know which NLP applications can use word2vec. If you know the list of applications, it becomes easy for you to decide whether you should use it or not. Suppose you can use k-mean clustering for document classification; if you want document classification to carry some of the attributes of semantics, then you can use word2vec as well. If you want to build a question-answer system, then you will need techniques that differentiate questions on a semantic level. As we need some semantic level information, we can use word2vec.

Now, we have seen enough about the concepts and theories, so we will begin our favorite part, which is coding, and this time it is really fun.

Developing something interesting

Here, we are going to train our word2vec model. The dataset that I'm going to use is text data of *Game of Thrones*. So, our formal goal is to develop word2vec to explore semantic similarities between the entities of *A Song of Ice and Fire (from the show Game of Thrones)*. The good part is we are also doing visualization on top of that, to get a better understanding of the concept practically. The original code credit goes to Yuriy Guts. I have just created a code wrapper for better understanding.

I have used IPython notebook. Basic dependencies are `gensim`, `scikit-learn`, and `nltk` to train the word2vec model on the text data of Game of Thrones. You can find the code on this GitHub link:

https://github.com/jalajthanaki/NLPython/blob/master/ch6/gameo
fthrones2vec/gameofthrones2vec.ipynb.

The code contains inline comments and you can see the snippet of the output. We have used the t-SNE technique to reduce the dimensions of the word vector, so we can use the two-dimensional vector for visualization. The t-SNE technique takes a lot of time if you want to run on a normal computer with 2 to 4 GB RAM. So, you need more RAM to run t-SNE code successfully at your end and you can skip the visualization part if you have memory constraints. You can see the visualization images. Once you have saved the model on to disk, you can use it and generate output easily. I have given sample output in *Figures 6.41* to *Figure 6.45*.

You may observe the output for the word `Stark` here:

```
thrones2vec.wv.most_similar("Stark")

2017-05-22 12:53:41,884 : INFO : precomputing L2-norms of word weight vectors

[(u'Eddard', 0.7480276226997375),
 (u'Winterfell', 0.6750659346580505),
 (u'direwolf', 0.6425904035568237),
 (u'Hornwood', 0.6366876363754272),
 (u'Lyanna', 0.6365906000137329),
 (u'beheaded', 0.6254189014434814),
 (u'Karstark', 0.6238248348236084),
 (u'executed', 0.6236813068389893),
 (u'Brandon', 0.6221044659614563),
 (u'Robb', 0.620850682258606)]
```

Figure 6.41: Word similarity output for the word stark

Here is the output for the nearest words:

```
def nearest_similarity_cosmul(start1, end1, end2):
    similarities = thrones2vec.most_similar_cosmul(
        positive=[end2, start1],
        negative=[end1]
    )
    start2 = similarities[0][0]
    print("{start1} is related to {end1}, as {start2} is related to {end2}".format(**locals()))
    return start2

nearest_similarity_cosmul("Stark", "Winterfell", "Riverrun")
nearest_similarity_cosmul("Jaime", "sword", "wine")
nearest_similarity_cosmul("Arya", "Nymeria", "dragons")

Stark is related to Winterfell, as Tully is related to Riverrun
Jaime is related to sword, as drank is related to wine
Arya is related to Nymeria, as Dany is related to dragons

u'Dany'
```

Figure 6.42: Output for the nearest words

Now we will see the following figures for output of visualization:

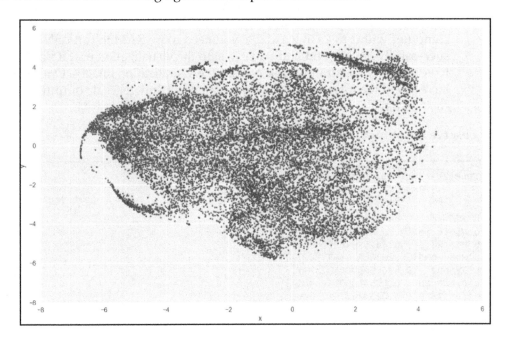

Figure 6.43: After using t-SNE you can visualize vectors in 2-D space

Now we will zoom in and try to see which words have ended up together.

See the following figure, which shows people related to Kingsguard ending up together:

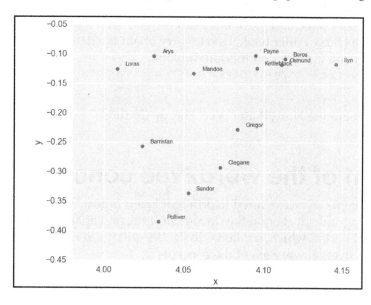

Figure 6.44: People names grouped together

See the following figure, which shows food products grouped together nicely:

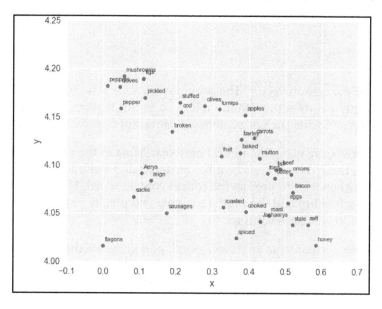

Figure 6.45: Name of food items grouped together

Exercise

I'm a big fan of Harry Potter, and so, in this exercise, you need to generate Word2vec from the text data from a Harry Potter book. Don't worry about the dataset; I have already provided it for you and it resides on this GitHub link:
`https://github.com/jalajthanaki/NLPython/tree/master/ch6/Harrypotter2vec/HPdataset`

Good luck with generating HarryPotter2Vec! Happy Coding!

Extension of the word2vec concept

The word2vec concept can be extended to different levels of text. This concept can be applied on the paragraph level or on the document level, and apart from this, you can also generate the global vector, which is called **GloVe**. We will try to understand them. Here, we are going to get an overview of each of the concepts.

Here are the following extended concepts built by using the word2vec concept:

- Para2vec
- Doc2vec
- GloVe

Para2Vec

Para2vec stands for paragraph vector. The paragraph vector is an unsupervised algorithm that uses fixed-length feature representation. It derives this feature representation from variable-length pieces of texts such as sentences, paragraphs, and documents.

Para2vec can be derived by using the neural network. Most of the aspects are the same as Word2vec. Usually, three context words are considered and fed into the neural network. The neural network then tries to predict the fourth context word. Here, we are trying to maximize the log probability and the prediction task is typically performed via a multi-class classifier. The function we use is softmax.

Please note that, here, the contexts are fixed-length and generate the context words by using a sliding window over the paragraph. The paragraph vector is shared with all contexts generated from the same paragraph, but not across paragraphs.

The advantage of Para2vec is to learn to predict the words from unlabeled data so that you can use these techniques when you don't have enough labeled datasets.

Doc2Vec

Doc2vec (Document vectors) is an extension of word2vec. It learns to correlate document labels and words, rather than words with other words. Here, you need document tags. You are able to represent an entire sentence using a fixed-length vector. This is also using word2vec concepts. If you feed the sentences with labels into the neural network, then it performs classification on a given dataset. So, in short, you tag your text and then use this tagged dataset as input and apply the Doc2vec technique on that given dataset. This algorithm will generate tag vectors for the given text. You can find the code at this GitHub link: `https://github.com/jalajthanaki/NLPython/blob/master/ch6/doc2vecexample.py`

 I have used very small datasets to just give you intuition on how you can develop Doc2vec, so I'm ignoring the accuracy factor of the developed model. You can refer to the code given at this reference link: `https://github.com/jhlau/doc2vec`

Let's see the intuitive code in *Figure 6.46* and see the output snippet in *Figure 6.47*:

```
vector_size = 300
window_size = 15
min_count = 1
sampling_threshold = 1e-5
negative_size = 5
train_epoch = 100
dm = 0   # 0 = dbow; 1 = dmpv
worker_count = 1   # number of parallel processes

# pretrained word embeddings
pretrained_emb = "/home/jalaj/PycharmProjects/NLPython/NLPython/ch6/doc2vecdata/pretrained_word_embeddings.txt"

# None if use without pretrained embeddings

# input corpus
train_corpus = "/home/jalaj/PycharmProjects/NLPython/NLPython/ch6/doc2vecdata/train_docs.txt"

# output model
saved_path = "/home/jalaj/PycharmProjects/NLPython/NLPython/ch6/doc2vecdata/model.bin"

# enable logging
logging.basicConfig(format='%(asctime)s : %(levelname)s : %(message)s', level=logging.INFO)

# train doc2vec model
docs = g.doc2vec.TaggedLineDocument(train_corpus)
model = g.Doc2Vec(docs, size=vector_size, window=window_size, min_count=min_count, sample=sampling_threshold,
                  workers=worker_count, hs=0, dm=dm, negative=negative_size, dbow_words=1, dm_concat=1,
                  iter=train_epoch)
```

Figure 6.47: Code snippet of doc2vec

You may see the following output:

```
[(u'plum', 0.7604337930679321)
,(u'bag', 0.7604188919067383)
,(u'tow', 0.7603976726531982)
,(u'clingstone', 0.7594519853591919)
,(u'peach', 0.7581210136413574)
,(u'andirons', 0.7574816942214966)
,(u'harmonica', 0.7570903301239014)
,(u'dragonfly', 0.7570433616638184)
,(u'burlap', 0.7561445236206055)
,(u'harp', 0.7559112906455994)
]
```

Figure 6.48: Sample output

Applications of Doc2vec

Let's see the applications that can use Doc2vec:

- Document clustering can be easily implemented by using Doc2vec
- We can perform sentiment analysis on larger chunks of text data, and I suppose you could consider a very big chunk of text and generate the sentiment output for that large chunk
- It is also used in product recommendation

GloVe

GloVe stands for global vector. GloVe is an unsupervised learning algorithm. This algorithm generates vector representations for words. Here, training is performed by using an aggregated global word-word co-occurrence matrix and other statistics from a corpus, and the resulting representations give you interesting linear substructures of the word vector space. So the co-occurrence matrix is the input of GloVe.

GloVe uses cosine similarity or the Euclidean distance to get an idea of similar words. Glove gives you fresh aspects and proves that if you take the nearest neighbor, then you can see such kinds of words that are very rare in terms of their frequent usage. GloVe can still capture those rare words in similar clusters. Let's look at the a famous example:

For example, here are the closest words when we have the target word frog:

- Frog
- Frogs
- Toad
- Litoria
- Leptodactylidae
- Rana
- Lizard
- Eleutherodactylus

Another example is the words related to the comparative-superlative form clustered together, and you can see the following output if you use the visualization tool. See *Figure 6.48*:

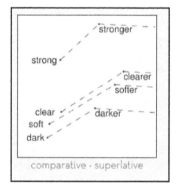

Figure 6.48: Result of GloVe famous example

 I'm using the `GloVe` Python library to give you an intuitive practical example of GloVe. See the code given at the following GitHub link: `https://github.com/jalajthanaki/NLPython/blob/master/ch6/gloveexample.py`

Before we start, we need to download the dataset, so execute the following command:

```
wget http://mattmahoney.net/dc/text8.zip -P /tmp
unzip text8.zip
cd /tmp
sudo chmod 777 ./text8
sudo chown yoursystemusername:yoursystemusername ./text8
```

You can see the snippet of code in *Figure 6.49* and see the output in *Figure 6.50*:

```
import itertools
from gensim.models.word2vec import Text8Corpus
from glove import Corpus, Glove

sentences = list(itertools.islice(Text8Corpus('/tmp/text8'), None))
corpus = Corpus()
corpus.fit(sentences, window=10)
glove = Glove(no_components=100, learning_rate=0.05)
glove.fit(corpus.matrix, epochs=30, no_threads=4, verbose=True)
glove.add_dictionary(corpus.dictionary)

print glove.most_similar('frog', number=10)
print glove.most_similar('girl', number=10)
print glove.most_similar('car', number=10)
```

Figure 6.49: GloVe code snippet

Following is the output of the preceding code snippet:

```
[
(u'stampede', 0.68898890286508008),
(u'dome', 0.6877015439616696),
(u'dodo', 0.66880217191693259)
,(u'coffin', 0.66225539108457376)
,(u'cerebral', 0.66159020499848764)
,(u'mysterious', 0.65478733848138226)
,(u'giant', 0.65038313074580578)
,(u'triangle', 0.64855186344301308)
,(u'vicious', 0.64641885680231859)
]


[
(u'man', 0.75136637433681674)
,(u'young', 0.7469214969113348)
,(u'baby', 0.73720725663573894)
,(u'woman', 0.72547071513284545)
,(u'wise', 0.68475484060033442)
,(u'girls', 0.67454497245994827)
,(u'boys', 0.67019967099320665)
,(u'teenage', 0.66537740499008224)
,(u'sick', 0.65327444225489562)
]
```

Figure 6.50: Sample output of GloVe

Exercise

This exercise is more of a reading exercise for you. You should read the research papers on Para2vec, Doc2vec, and GloVe. Apart from this, you can also check whether there is any way that you can find vector representation for continuous strings, such as a DNA pattern. The main purpose of this exercise is to give you an idea of how research work has been done. You can also think of some other aspects of vector representation and try to solve the challenges.

Importance of vectorization in deep learning

This is more of a discussion with you from my end. As we all know, computers can't understand NL directly, so we need to convert our NL output into numerical format. We have various word embedding techniques, as well as some basic statistical techniques such as indexing, tf-idf, one-hot encoding, and so on. By using all these techniques, or some of these techniques, you can convert your text input into numerical format. Which techniques you choose totally depends on the NLP applications. So, there are two major points behind why we convert NL input to numerical format. It is basically done because the computer can only understand numerical data, so we have to convert text data to numerical data and computers are very good at performing computation on given numerical data. These are two major points that come to my mind when we are converting text data.

Let's understand what deep learning is. Here, I want to give you just a brief idea about it. Don't worry; we will see more detail in `Chapter 9`, *Deep Learning for NLU and NLG Problems.* When a neural network is many layers deep, it is called **deep neural network**. When we use many-layered deep neural networks and use them to develop NLP applications using lots of data and lots of computation power, it is called **deep learning**.

Now let's talk about vectorization. Vectorization is a solid mathematical concept and it is easy to understand and deal with. Nowadays, Python has a lot of good libraries that make our life easier when we want to deal with high dimensional vector forms of data. The deep learning paradigm heavily relies on the vectorization and matrices concepts, so in order to get a good grip on deep learning, you should have knowledge of vectors and matrices. Deep learning applications that deal with input data such as video or audio also use vectors. Videos and images are converted into the dense vector format, and when talk about text input, word2vec is its basic building block for generating vectors from words. Google TensorFlow uses word2vec as their basic building block and it uses these concepts and improvises the results of Google Machine translation, Google Speech recognition, and Google Vision applications. So, vectors and matrices give us a lot of freedom in terms of their processing and making sense out of it.

Apart from this, I also need to give you some thoughts. I want you to focus on how we can improvise the way we deal with text. No doubt word2vec is one of the most simple and efficient approaches for converting words into vector form, but I would definitely encourage my readers who are interested in research work to extend this concept for their native languages or become creative and contribute to building very innovative techniques that will help the NLP community to overcome challenges such as word ambiguities. Well, these are all my thoughts for you!

Summary

In this chapter, we have seen how word2vec can be used to find semantics. The simple vectorization techniques help us a lot. We have seen some of the applications of it. We have touched upon the technicalities of the word2vec model. I have introduced lots of new mathematical, as well as statistical, terms to you in order to give you a better understanding of the model. We have converted the word2vec black box into the word2vec white box. I have also implemented basic as well as extended examples for better understanding. We have used a ton of libraries and APIs to develop word2vec models. We have also seen the advantages of having vectorization in deep learning. Then, we extended our word2vec understanding and developed the concepts of para2vec, doc2vec, and GloVe.

The next chapter will basically give you an in-depth idea of how rule-based techniques are used in order to develop NLP applications and how various NLP applications use a very simple, but yet very effective, technique called rules or logic for developing basic and effective prototypes for NLP applications. Google use the rule-based techniques for their machine translation projects, Apple also use this technique, and last but not least, Google used the rule-based system to make an early prototype of their self-driving car. We will discuss the rule-based system and its architecture. We will also see what the architecture of rule-based NLP applications is. I will provide you with a thought process, and by using that thought process, you can also make rules for your NLP application. We will implement the basic grammar rules and pattern-based rules. We will also develop a basic template-based chatbot from scratch.

7

Rule-Based System for NLP

We learned to derive various features by using the concepts of linguistics and statistics in Chapter 5, *Feature Engineering and NLP Algorithms* and Chapter 6, *Advanced Feature Engineering and NLP Algorithms*. For developing an NLP application, these features are going to be fed into the algorithms. These algorithms take features as input. As you know, we are referring to algorithms as black boxes that perform some kind of magic and gives us the appropriate output. Refer to *Figure 7.1*, which demonstrates our journey so far:

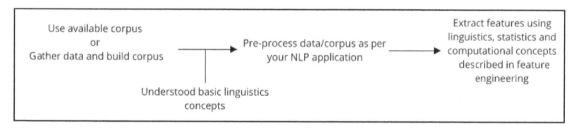

Figure 7.1: Stages we have learned so far

Congratulations, you have learned a lot about NLP, and specifically about the NLU!

Now, it is high time for us to explore the algorithms which we use to develop NLP applications. We refer to these algorithms, techniques, or approaches as our black boxes and their logic is works as some magic for us. Now, it's time to dive deep into these black boxes and understand the magic.

Algorithms (implementation techniques or approaches) for NLP applications can be divided into two parts. Refer to *Figure 7.2*:

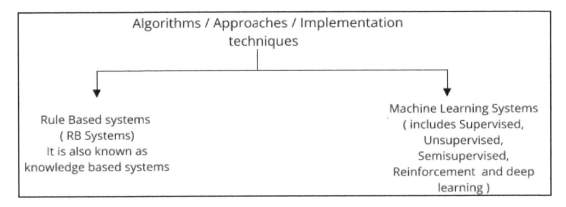

Figure 7.2: Algorithms or approaches or implementation techniques for black boxes

We will look at the **rule-based (RB)** system in this chapter and machine learning approaches in Chapter 8, *Machine Learning for NLP Problems* and Chapter 9, *Deep Learning for NLP and NLG Problems*.

In this chapter, we are going to focus on the rule-based system. We are going to touch upon the following topics:

- Understanding of the RB system
- Purpose of having the RB system
- Architecture of the RB system
- Understanding the RB system development life cycle
- Applications
- Developing NLP applications using the RB system
- Comparing the RB approach with other approaches
- Advantages
- Disadvantages
- Challenges
- Recent trends for the RB system

So, let's get started!

Understanding of the rule-based system

RB systems are also known as **knowledge-based systems**. But first, we will see what the RB system means and what it does for us? What kind of NLP applications can be implemented by using this approach? For a better understanding, I will explain the concepts with the help of the applications.

What does the RB system mean?

The rule-based system is defined as by using available knowledge or rules, we develop such a system which uses the rules, apply the available system rules on a corpus and try to generate or inference the results. Refer *Figure 7.3*, which will give you an idea about the RB system:

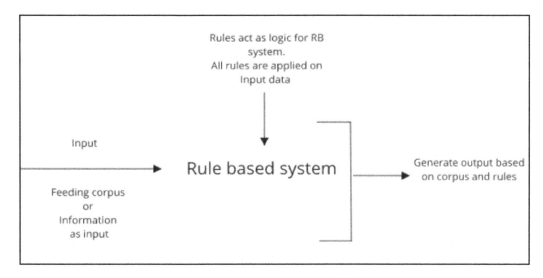

Figure 7.3: Rule based system input/output flow

 In short, you can say that the RB system is all about applying real-life rules or experiences to a available corpus, manipulating information as per the rules, and deriving certain decisions or results. Here, rules are generated or created by humans.

The RB system is used for interpreting available corpus (information) in a useful manner. Here, rules act as core logic for the RB system. The corpus is interpreted based on rules or knowledge, so our end result is dependent on these two factors, one is rules and the second is our corpus.

Now I will explain one of the **AI (Artificial Intelligence)** applications for getting the core essence of the RB system.

As humans, we all do very complicated work every day to perform some tasks. To perform tasks, we use our prior experiences or follow rules to successfully complete the task.

Take an example: If you are driving a car, you are following some rules. You have prior knowledge of these rules. Now, if you think about the self-driving car, then that car should react or perform the entire task that a human was doing previously. But cars don't understand how to drive automatically without a driver. To develop this kind of driver less car is quite complicated, as well as challenging.

Anyhow, you want to create a self-driving car. You know there are so many rules that the car needs to learn in order to perform as well as a human driver. Here you have a few major challenges:

- This is a kind of complicated application
- Lots of rules as well as situations need to be learned by the car
- The accuracy of the self-driving car should be high enough to launch it on the market for the consumer

So, to solve the challenges, we follow various steps:

1. We first try to reduce the problem statement to small chunks of a problem which is a subset of our original problem statement.
2. We try to solve small chunks of the problem first.
3. To solve it, we are trying to come up with generalized rules that help us to solve our problem as well as help us to achieve our end goal.

For our version of the driver less (self-driving) car, we need to think from the software perspective. So, what is the first step the car should learn? Think!

The car should learn to see and identify objects on the road. This is the first step for our car and we define some generalized rules which the car will use to learn and decide whether there is any object on the road?, then drive based on that. What should the speed of the car when it sees road conditions? And so on, (think right now using the rule-based system, and for some time don't think about the deep learning aspect to solve this step).

For every small part of our task, we try to define rules and feed that rule logic into the RB system. Then, we check whether that rule worked out properly on the given input data. We will also measure the performance of the system after getting the output.

Now, you must be thinking this is a book about NLP, so why am I giving an example of a generalized AI application? The reason behind it is that the self-driving car example is easy to relate to and can be understood by everyone. I want to highlight some of the points that also help us to understand the purpose of having a rule-based system.

Let's take one general example and understand the purpose:

- This self-driving car example helps you in identifying that sometimes a task that is very easy for a human to perform is so much more complicated for machines to do by themselves
- These kinds of complicated tasks need high accuracy! I mean very high!
- We don't expect our system to cover and learn about all situations, but whatever rules we feed into the system, it should learn about those situations in the best manner
- In the RB system, the coverage of various scenarios is less but accuracy of the system should be high. That is what we need
- Our rules are derived from real-life human experience or by using knowledge of humans.
- Development and implementation of rules is done by humans

All these points help us to decide when and where to use a rule-based system. This leads us to define our purpose of having a rule-based system. So let's jump into the next section where we define a rule of thumb for using the rule-based approach for any NLP or AI-related application.

Purpose of having the rule-based system

Generally, the rule-based system is used for developing NLP applications and generalized AI applications. There are bunch of questions that we need to answer to generate a clear picture about the rule-based system.

Why do we need the rule-based system?

The rule-based system tries to mimic human expert knowledge for the NLP applications. Here, we are going to address the factors that will help you to understand the purpose of the RB system:

- Available corpus size is small
- Output is too subjective

- Easy for humans of a specific domain to generate some specialized rules
- Difficult for machines to generate specialized rules by just observing small amounts of data
- System output should be highly accurate

All the preceding factors are very much critical if you want to develop NLP application using the RB system. How do the preceding factors help you to decide whether you should choose the RB approach or not?

You need to ask the following questions:

- Do you have a large amount of data or a small amount of data?
    - If you have a small amount of data, then ask the next question and if you have a large amount of data, then you have many other options
- Regarding the NLP application that you want to develop, is its output subjective or generalized?
    - If you have a small amount of data and the output of the application which you want to develop is too subjective and you know, with a small amount of data, the machine cannot generalize the patterns, then choose the RB system
- The NLP application that you want to develop should have very high accuracy:
    - If the application that you want to develop should have high accuracy, almost the same as a human by using a small dataset, then choose the RB system
    - Here, you should also keep in mind that human experts create rules for the system. According to that system, generate the output, so the RB system is highly accurate but does not cover all scenarios

The preceding questions define why and in what kind of situations we can use the RB system. If I needed to summarize the preceding questions, I would describe it like this: If you have small amount of data and you know you need a highly accurate system where it is easy for a human expert to identify various scenarios for making rules and its output but it is very difficult for machines to identify generalized rules by themselves accurately, then the RB system is for you! The output of the RB system should mimic the experiences of the human expert. This is the thumb rule for choosing the RB system.

We will see in Chapter 9, *Deep Learning for NLP and NLG Problems*, that there is a better approach when you have very large amount of data. For this chapter, the RB approach helps us to generate very accurate NLP applications.

Which kind of applications can use the RB approach over the other approaches?

As we defined earlier, the RB system is developed with the help of human domain experts. Let's take some examples in this section which can help to prove our rule of thumb:

- Say, we want to build the machine translation system from English to available Indian corpora and they are too small. The translation system should be accurate enough in order to develop it. We need human experts who know English as well as Gujarati. We don't want to address all the different levels of translation at a time, so we need to cover small chunks of the problem first and then on top of the developed prototype, we will build other chunks. So, here also, I would like to choose the RB system. What do you think?

- Say we want to develop a grammar correction system for the English language. Suppose we have a small amount of parallel corpora (documents with grammatical mistakes and the same documents without grammatical mistakes), and by using the available corpus we need to make an accurate grammar correction application which identifies, as well as corrects, the grammatical mistakes. So, in this kind of application, which approach would you take? Think for a minute and then come up with your answers! Here, I would like to go with the RB system as per our rule of thumb.

Exercise

- If you wanted to develop a basic chatbot system, which approach would you take?
    - RB approach
    - ML approach

- If you want to predict the sentiment of given sentences, which approach would you take?
    - RB approach
    - ML approach
    - Hybrid approach
    - None of them

What kind of resources do you need if you want to develop a rule-based system?

Now you have understood why we are using the RB system and for which kinds of application we use it. The third important aspect is what do we need if we want to develop the RB system for any NLP or AI applications?

There are three main resources that we need to consider at this point. Refer to *Figure 7.4*:

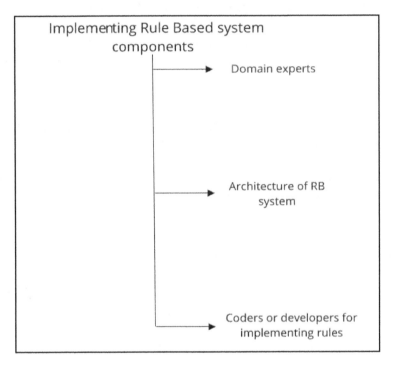

Figure 7.4: Resources for implementing RB system

Now, let's see the details of each resource that helps us to define RB system components:

- Domain expert (human expert/knowledge expert): For developing applications using the RB system, first and foremost, we need a domain expert, a person who knows almost everything about the domain.
  Suppose you want to build a machine translation system, then your domain expert could be a person who has deep knowledge of linguistics for the source and target languages. He can come up with rules by using his expertise and experience.

- System architect (system engineer) of RB system: For defining the architecture of the RB system, you need a team or person who has the following expertise:
  - Basic knowledge of the domain
  - Deep knowledge or high experience in designing system architectures

 Architecture is the most important part of the RB system because your architecture is one of the components which decide how efficient your whole system will be. Good architecture design for the RB system will provide good user experience, accurate and efficient output, and apart from that, it will make life easy for coders and other technical teams such as support or testing teams who will be able to work on the system easily. The system architecture is the responsibility of the system engineer or system architect.

- Coders (developers or knowledge engineers) for implementing rules: Once rules are developed by domain experts and the system architecture has been designed properly, then coders or developers come into the picture. Coders are our real ninjas! They implement the rules by using programming languages and help to complete the application. Their coding skills are a much needed part of the RB system. Programming can be done using any of the programming or scripting languages such as C, C++, Java, Python, Perl, shell scripts, and so on. You can use any of them as per the architecture, but not all of them in a single system without a streamlined architecture.

We will look at more technical stuff regarding the architecture part a little later in this chapter.

Architecture of the RB system

I will explain the architecture of the RB system by segregating it into three sections:

- General architecture of RB system as an expert system
- Practical architecture of the RB system for NLP applications
- Custom architecture - RB system for NLP applications
- Apache **UIMA (Unstructured Information Management Architecture)** the RB system for NLP applications

General architecture of the rule-based system as an expert system

If we described our rule-based system as an expert system, then the architecture of this kind of rule-based system would be the same as in *Figure 7.5*:

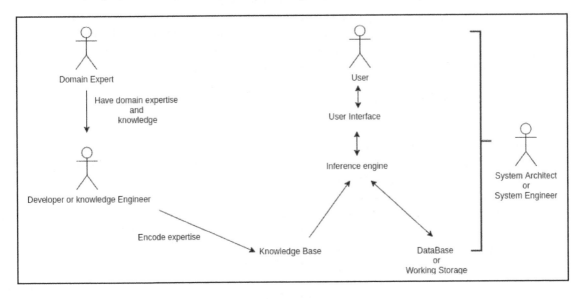

Figure 7.5: Architecture of the RB system, considering it as an expert system

Let's look at each of the components of the architecture in detail:

- **Domain expert**:
    - As we saw in the previous section, domain experts are the ones who have expertise for a specific domain and they can help us to generate the rules to solve our problems
- **Developers or knowledge engineer:**
    - Developers use the rules which are created by the domain expert and convert them into a machine-understandable format using their coding skills
    - Developers encode the rules created by experts
    - Mostly, this encoding is in the form of pseudo codes

- **Knowledge base:**
  - The knowledge base is where all the rules can be put by experts
  - The domain expert can add, update, or delete the rules

- **Database or working storage:**
  - All meta information-related rules can be put in the working storage
  - Here, we can store rules as well as special scenarios, some lists if available, examples, and so on
  - We also save data on which we want to apply rules

- **Inference engine:**
  - The inference engine is the core part of the system
  - Here, we put in actual codes for our rules
  - Rules will be triggered when predefined rules and conditions meet with a user query or on a dataset which we have given to the system as input

- **User inference:**
  - Sometimes, our end users also provide some conditions to narrow down their results, so all these user inference will also be considered when our system generates the output

- **User interface:**
  - The user interface helps our user to submit their input and in return they will get the output
  - This provides an interactive environment for our end users

- **System architect:**
  - The system architect takes care of the whole architecture of the system
  - The system architect also decides what is the most efficient architecture for the RB system

We have seen the traditional architecture of the RB system. Now it is time to see what will be the real-life practical architecture of the RB system for NLP applications.

Practical architecture of the rule-based system for NLP applications

I have already described the general architecture, now we will see the practical architecture of the RB system for NLP applications. Refer to *Figure 7.6*:

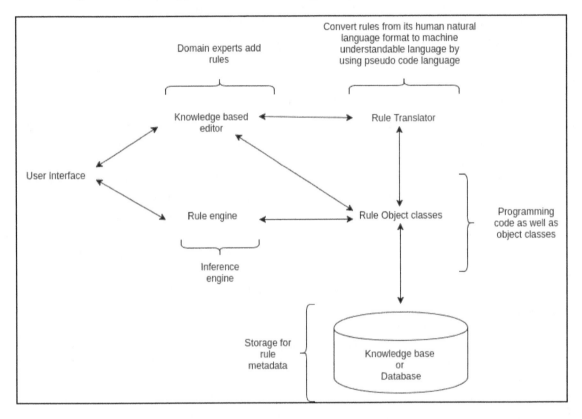

Figure 7.6: Real life architecture of RB system for NLP application

Let's look at each of the components of the architecture in detail.

Some of the parts, such as domain experts, user interfaces, and system engineer, we have seen in the previous section. So, here, we are focusing on new components:

- **Knowledge-based editor:**
    - The domain experts may not know how to code
    - So we are providing them a knowledge-based editor where they can write or create the rules by using human language
    - Suppose we are developing a grammar correction system for the English language and we have a linguist who knows how to create rules but doesn't know how to code them
    - In this case, they can add, update, or delete rules by using the knowledge-based editor
    - All the created rules are specified in the form of normal human language
- **Rule translator:**
    - As we know, all rules are in the form of the human language, so we need to translate or convert them into machine-understandable form
    - So, the rule translator is the section where pseudo logic for the rules has been defined with examples
    - Let's consider our grammar correction system example. Here our expert defines a rule if there is a singular subject and plural verb in the sentence, and then changes the verb to the singular verb format
    - In the rule translator, the defined rule has been converted as if there is a sentence **S** which has a singular subject with the POS tag **PRP\$**, **NP** with POS tag of verbs **VBP,** then change the verb to the **VBZ** format. Some examples have also been specified to understand the rules
- **Rule object classes:**
    - This rule object class act, as the container for supporting libraries
    - It contains various prerequisite libraries
    - It also sometimes contains an optional object class for libraries to optimize the entire system
    - For the grammar correction system, we can put tools such as parsers, POS taggers, **named entity recognition (NER)**, and so on in the container to be used by the rule engine
- **Database or knowledge base:** A database has metadata for rules, such as:
    - Which supporting libraries have been used from the rule object classes?
    - What is the category of the rule?
    - What is priority of the rule?

- **Rule engine:**
    - This is the core part, which is the brain of the RB system
    - By using the rule translator, rule object classes, and knowledge base we need to develop the core code which actually runs on the user query or on the input dataset and generates the output
    - You can code by using any programming language which is the best fit for your application and its architectures
    - For our grammar correction system, we will code the rule in this stage and the final code will be put into the rule engine repository

These are all the components that are useful if you are developing an RB system for NLP. Now you must have questions. Can we change the architecture of the system as per our needs? Is it fine? To get answers to these questions, you need to follow the next section.

Custom architecture - the RB system for NLP applications

According to the needs of different NLP applications, you can change the architecture or components. Customization is possible in this approach. There are some points that need to be taken care of if you are designing a customized RB system architecture. Ask the following questions:

- Did you analyze and study the problem and the already existing architectures?
    - Before doing customization, you need to do analysis of your application. If any existing system is there, then study its architecture and take the bad and good out of it
    - Take enough time for analysis
- Do you really need custom architecture?
    - If after the study, you feel that your application architecture needs to be customized, then write down the reasons why you you really need it
    - State the reasons that you have listed down and can help your system to make it better by asking a series of questions. If yes, then you are on the right track
- Does it help to streamline the development process?
    - Does the new architecture actually help your development process better? If it does, then you can consider that architecture

- Most of the time, defining a streamline process for developing the RB system is challenging but if your new customized architecture can help you, then it is really a good thing
- Does this streamline process actually stabilize your RB system?

- Is it maintainable?
  - A customized architecture can help you to maintain the system easily as well as efficiently
  - If you can add this feature to your customized architecture, then thumbs up!
- Is it modular?
  - If it will provide modularity in the RB system then it will be useful because then you can add, remove, or update certain modules easily
- Is it scalable?
  - With the help of the new architecture, you can scale up the system. You should also consider this
- Is it easy to migrate?
  - If it is with the defined architecture, it should be easy for the team to migrate the system from one platform to another
  - If we want to migrate a module from one system to another, it should be easy for the technical as well the infrastructure team
- Is it secure?
  - System security is a major concern. New architecture should definitely have this feature of security and user privacy if needed
- Is it easy to deploy?
  - If you want to deploy some changes in the future, then deployment should be easy
  - If you want to sell your end product, then the deployment process should be easy enough, which will reduce your efforts and time
- Is it time saving in terms of development time?
  - Implementation as well as the development of the RB system by using the architecture should be time saving
  - The architecture itself should not take too much time to implement
- Is it easy for our users to use?
  - The architecture can be complex but for end users it must be user-friendly and easy to use

If you can take all of the preceding points or most of them, then try to implement a small set of problems using the architecture that you think best for the system, then, at the end, ask all the previous questions again and evaluate the output.

If you still get positive answers, then you are good to go! Here, the design is neither right nor wrong; it's all about the best fit for your NLP application.

A **Question-Answering (Q/A)** system can use the architecture which is shown in the *Figure 7.7*:

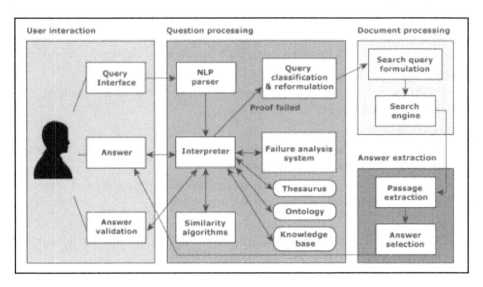

Figure 7.7: Architecture for Question-Answering RB system

You can see a very different kind of architecture. The approach of the Q/A system is an ontology based RB system. Question processing and document processing is the main rule engine for us. Here, we are not thinking of a high-level question answering system. We want to develop a Q/A system for small children who can ask questions about stories and the system will send back the answers as per the rules and available story data.

Let's see each of the components in details:

- When the user submits the question, the parser parses the question.
- Parse the question matching the parsing result with the knowledge base, ontology, and keywords thesaurus using the interpreter.
- Here, we apply the reasoning and facts as well.
- We derive some facts from the questions and categorized user questions using query classification and reformulation.

- After, the already-generated facts and categorized queries are sent to the document processing part where the facts are given to the search engine.

- Answer extraction is the core RB engine for the Q/A system because it uses facts and applies reasoning techniques such as forward chaining or backward chaining to extract all possible answers. Now you will want to know about backward chaining and forward chaining. So, here, I'm giving you just a brief overview. In forward chaining, we start with available data and use inference rules to extract more facts from data until a goal is achieved. This technique is used in expert system to understand what can happen next. And in backward chaining, we start with a list of goals and work backwards to find out which conditions could have happened in the past for the current result. These techniques help us to understand why this happened.

- Once all possible answers have been generated, then it will be sent back to the user.

I have one question in my mind that I would like to ask you.

What kind of database do you want to select if you develop a Q/A system? Think before you go ahead!

I would like to choose the NoSQL database over the SQL DBs, and there are a couple of reasons behind it. The system should be available for the user 24\7. Here, we care about our user. The user can access the system anytime, and availability is a critical part. So, I would like to choose the NoSQL database.If, in the future, we want to perform some analytics on the users' questions and answers, then we need to save the users' questions and the system's answers in the database . Read further to understand them:

You can choose your data warehouse or NoSQL DB. If you are new to NoSQL, then you can refer to NoSQL using this link: `https://en.wikiped ia.org/wiki/NoSQL`, and if you are new to the word data warehouse, then you can refer to this link:
`https://en.wikipedia.org/wiki/Data_warehouse`.

This will help us categorize our users, and we can make some creative changes that really matter to the user. We can also provide customized feed or suggestions to each of the users.

Exercise

Suppose you are developing a grammar correction system, what kind of system architecture do you design? Try to design it on paper! Let your thoughts come out.

Apache UIMA - the RB system for NLP applications

In this section, we will look at one of the famous frameworks for the RB system for NLP applications.

Apache UIMA is basically developed by IBM to process unstructured data. You can explore more details by clicking on this link: `https://uima.apache.org/index.html`

Here, I want to highlight some points from this framework, which will help you to make your own NLP application using the RB approach.

The following are the features of UIMA:

- UIMA will provide us with the infrastructure, components, and framework
- UMIA has an inbuilt RB engine and GATE library for performing preprocessing of text data
- The following tools are available as part of the components. I have listed down a few of them:
    - Language identification tool
    - Sentence segmentation tool
    - NER tool
- We can code in Java, Ruta, and C++
- It is a flexible, modular, and easy-to-use framework
- C/C++ annotators also supports Python and Perl

Applications/uses of UIMA include:

- IBM Watson uses UIMA to analyze unstructured data
- The **clinical Text Analysis and Knowledge Extraction System (Apache cTAKES)** uses the UIMA-based system for information extraction from medical records

The challenges of using UIMA include:

- You need to code rules in either Java, Ruta, or C++. Although, for optimization, many RB systems use C++; getting the best human resources for Ruta is a challenging task
- If you are new to UIMA, you need some time to become familiar with it

Understanding the RB system development life cycle

In this section, we will look at the development life cycle for the RB system, which will help you in the future if you want to develop your own. *Figure 7.8* describes the development life cycle of the RB system. This figure is quite self-explanatory, so there is no need for an extra description.

If we follow the stages of the RB development life cycle, then life will be easy for us:

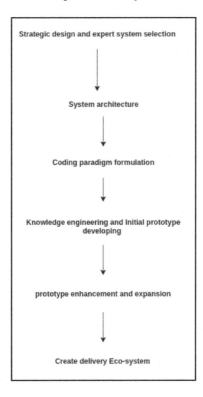

Figure 7.8: RB system development life cycle

Applications

In this section, I have divided the applications into two sections; one is the NLP application and the other one is the generalized AI application.

NLP applications using the rule-based system

Here, we mention some of the NLP applications that use the RB system:

- Sentence boundary detection:
    - Sentence boundary detection is easy for general English writing but it will be complicated when you are dealing with research papers or other scientific documents
    - So, handcrafted post-processing rules will help us to identify the sentence boundary accurately
    - This approach has been used by Grammarly Inc. for the grammar correction system
- Machine translation:
    - When we think of a machine translation system, in our mind, we think of the **Google Neural Machine Translation (GNMT)** system
    - For many Indian languages, Google used to use a complex rule-based system with a statistical prediction system, so they have an hybrid system
    - In 2016, Google launched the neural network based MT system
    - Many research projects still use the RB system for MT and the majority of them try tapping out the languages which are untapped
- Template based chatbots:
    - Nowadays, chatbots are the new trend and craze in the market
    - A basic version of them is a template-based approach where we have a defined set of questions or keywords and we have mapped the answers to each of the keywords
    - The good part of this system is matching the keywords. So if you are using any other language but if your chat messages contain keywords which we have defined, then the system is able to send you a proper message as a response
    - The bad part is, if you make any spelling mistakes then the system will not be able to respond in a proper manner
    - We will develop this application from scratch. I will explain the coding part in the next section, so keep reading and start your computer!

- Grammar correction system:
  - A grammar correction system is also implemented by using rules
  - In this application, we can define some of the simple rules to very complicated rules as well
  - In the next section, we will see some of the basic grammar correction rules which we are going to implement using Python
- Question answering systems:
  - A question answering system also uses the RB system, but here, there is one different thing going on
  - The Q/A system uses semantics to get the answer of the submitted question
  - For putting semantics into the picture, we are using the ontology-based RB approach

Generalized AI applications using the rule-based system

You have seen the NLP applications which use the RB approach. Now, move into the generalized AI applications, which use the RB approach along with other techniques:

- Self-driving cars or driver less cars:
  - At the start of the chapter, I gave the example of the self-driving car to highlight the purpose of having the RB system
  - The self-driving car also uses a hybrid approach. Many of the big companies, from Google to Tesla, are trying to build self-driving cars, and their experiments are in order to develop the most trustworthy self-driving cars
  - This application has been developed by using complex RB systems during its initial days
  - Then, the experiment turned into the direction of ML techniques
  - Nowadays, companies are implementing deep learning techniques to make the system better
- Robotics applications:
  - It has been a long-term goal of the AI community to develop robots which complement human skills
  - We have a goal where we want to develop robots which help humans to do their work, tasks which are basically time consuming

- Suppose there is a robot that helps you with household work. This kind of task can be performed by the robot with the help of defined rules for all possible situations
- Expert system of NASA:
  - NASA made the expert system by using the general purpose programming language, **CLIPS (C Language Integrated Production System)**

Now, I think that's enough of theories. Now we should try to develop some of the RB applications from scratch. Get ready for coding. We will begin our coding journey in the next section.

Developing NLP applications using the RB system

In this section, we will see how to develop NLP applications using the RB system. We are developing applications from the beginning. So, first you need the following dependencies.

You can run the following command to install all the dependencies:

```
pip install -r pip-requirements.txt
```

The list of dependencies can be found by clicking on this link:
https://github.com/jalajthanaki/NLPython/blob/master/pip-requirements.txt

Thinking process for making rules

We are talking a lot about rules, but how can these rules actually can be derived? What is the thinking process of a linguist when they are deriving rules for an NLP application? Then, let's begin with this thinking process.

You need to think like a linguist for a while. Remember all the concepts that you have learned so far in this book and be a linguist.

Suppose you are developing rules for a grammar correction system, especially for the English language. So, I'm describing the thought process of a linguist and this thought process helps you when you are developing rules:

- What should I need to know?
    - You should know about grammatical rules of the language for which you are creating rules, here that language is English
    - You should know the structure, word order, and other language related concepts
    - The preceding two points are prerequisites
- From where should I start?
    - If you know all the language-related things, then you need to observe and study incorrect sentences
    - Now, when you study incorrect sentences, you need to know what mistakes there are in the sentences
    - After that you need to think about the categories of the mistakes, whether the mistakes are syntax related, or whether they are because of semantic ambiguity
    - After all this, you can map your language-related knowledge to the mistakes in the sentences
- How can rules be derived?
    - Once you find the mistakes in the sentence, then at that moment focus on your thinking process. What does your brain think when you're capturing the mistakes?
    - Think about how your brain reacts to each of the mistakes that you have identified
    - You can capture the mistake because you know the grammatical facts of the language or other language related technical stuff (sentence syntax structures, semantics knowledge, and so on). Your brain actually helps you
    - Your brain knows the right way to interpret the given text using the given language
    - That is the reason you are able to catch the mistakes. At the same time, you have some solid reason; based on that, you have identified the mistakes
    - Once you have identified the mistakes, as per the different categories of the mistakes, you can correct the mistakes by changing some parts of the sentences using certain logical rules
    - You can change the word order, or you can change the subject verb agreement, or you can change some phrases or all of them together
    - Bingo! At this point, you will get your rule. You know what the mistakes are and you also know what are these steps are for converting incorrect sentences to correct sentences

- Your rule logic is nothing but the steps of converting incorrect sentences into correct sentences
- What elements do I need to take care of?
    - First, you need to think about a very simple way of correcting the mistakes or incorrect sentences
    - Try to make pattern-based rules
    - If pattern-based rule are not possible to derive then check if you can use parsing and/or morphological analyzer results and then check other tools and libraries
    - By the way, there is one catch here. When you defining rules, you also need to think about how feasible the rule logic is for implementation
    - Are the tools available or not? If the tools are available then you can code your rules or the developer can code the rules
    - If the tools aren't available then you need to discard your rules
    - Research is involved when you define a rule and then check whether there are any tools available which coders can use for coding up the defined rule logic
    - The selected tools should be capable of coding the exceptional scenarios for rules
    - Defining rules and researching on tools can be basic tasks for linguists if you have some linguists in your team. If not, then you as coders need to search tools which you can use for coding the rule logic

Without any delay, we will start coding.

Start with simple rules

I have written a script which scrapes the Wikipedia page entitled Programming language.

Click here to open that page: https://en.wikipedia.org/wiki/Programming_language

Extracting the name of the programming languages from the text of the given page is our goal. Take an example: The page has C, C++, Java, JavaScript, and so on, programming languages. I want to extract them. These words can be a part of sentences or have occurred standalone in the text data content.

Now, see how we can solve this problem by defining a simple rule. The GitHub link for the script is:
https://github.com/jalajthanaki/NLPython/blob/master/ch7/7_1_simplerule.py

The data file link on GitHub is:

`https://github.com/jalajthanaki/NLPython/blob/master/data/simpleruledata.txt`

Here our task can be divided into three parts:

- Scraping the text data
- Defining the rule for our goal
- Coding our rule and generating the prototype and result

Scraping the text data

In this stage, we are going to scrape the text from the programming language wiki page and export the content into a text file. You can see the code snippet in *Figure 7.9*:

```python
from bs4 import BeautifulSoup
import requests

def savedatainfile(filecontent):
    file = open("/home/jalaj/PycharmProjects/NLPython/NLPython/data/simpleruledata.txt","a+")
    file.write(filecontent+"\n")
    file.close()

def scrapdata():
    url = 'https://en.wikipedia.org/wiki/Programming_language'
    content = requests.get(url).content
    soup = BeautifulSoup(content,'lxml')
    tag = soup.find('div', {'class' : 'mw-content-ltr'})
    paragraphs = tag.findAll('p')
    for para in paragraphs:
        paraexport = para.text.encode('utf-8')
        print paraexport
        savedatainfile(paraexport)


if __name__=="__main__":
    scrapdata()
```

Figure 7.9: Code snippets for scraping text data

The output of the scraping data is shown in *Figure 7.10*:

A programming language is a formal language that specifies a set of instructions that can be used to produce various kinds of output. Programming languages generally consist of instructions for a computer. Programming languages can be used to create programs that implement specific algorithms.

The earliest known programmable machine preceded the invention of the digital computer and is the automatic flute player described in the 9th century by the brothers Musa in Baghdad, "during the Islamic Golden Age".[1] From the early 1800s, "programs" were used to direct the behavior of machines such as Jacquard looms and player pianos. [2] Thousands of different programming languages have been created, mainly in the computer field, and many more still are being created every year. Many programming languages require computation to be specified in an imperative form (i.e., as a sequence of operations to perform) while other languages use other forms of program specification such as the declarative form (i.e. the desired result is specified, not how to achieve it).

The description of a programming language is usually split into the two components of syntax (form) and semantics (meaning). Some languages are defined by a specification document (for example, the C programming language is specified by an ISO Standard) while other languages (such as Perl) have a dominant implementation that is treated as a reference. Some languages have both, with the basic language defined by a standard and extensions taken from the dominant implementation being common.

Figure 7.10: Output of scraping script

Defining the rule for our goal

Now, if you look at our scraped data, you can find the sentences. Now after analyzing the text, you need to define a rule for extracting only programming language names such as Java, JavaScript, MATLAB, and so on. Then, think for a while about what kind of simple rule or logic can help you to achieve your goal. Think hard and take your time! Try to focus on your thinking process and try to find out the patterns.

If I wanted to define a rule, then I would generalize my problem in the context of the data given to me. During my analysis, I have noticed that the majority of the programming language keywords come with the word language. I have noticed that when language as a word appears in the sentences, then there is a high chance that the actual programming language name also appears in that sentence. For example, the C programming language is specified by an ISO standard. In the given example, the C programming language appears and the word language also appears in the sentence. So, I will perform the following process.

First, I need to extract the sentences which contain language as a word. Now as a second step, I will start to process the extracted sentences and check any capitalized words or camel case words there are in the sentence. Then, if I find any capitalized words or camel case words, I need to extract them and I will put them into the list because most of the programming languages appear as capitalized words or in camel case word format. See the examples: C, C++, Java, JavaScript, and so on. There will be cases where a single sentence contains the name of more than one programming language.

The preceding process is our rule and the logical form of the rule is given here:

- Extract sentences with language as a word
- Then try to find out words in the sentence which are in camel case or capitalized form
- Put all these words in a list
- Print the list

Coding our rule and generating a prototype and result

This example gives you the practical essence of the rule making process. This is our first step so we are not focusing on accuracy very much. I know, this is not the only way of solving this problem and this is not the most efficient way. There are also other efficient ways to implement the same problem, but I'm using this one because I felt this solution is the simplest one and easiest to understand.

This example can help you to understand how rules can be coded and, after getting the result of the first prototype, what next steps you can take to improve your output.

See the code snippet in *Figure 7.11*:

```python
from bs4 import BeautifulSoup
import requests

def savedatainfile(filecontent):
    file = open("/home/jalaj/PycharmProjects/NLPython/NLPython/data/simpleruledata.txt", "a+")
    file.write(filecontent + "\n")
    file.close()

def rulelogic(filecontent):
    programminglanguagelist = []
    with open(filecontent)as file:
        for line in file:
            if 'languages' in line or 'language' in line:
                # print line
                words = line.split()
                for word in words:
                    if word[0].isupper():
                        programminglanguagelist.append(word)
                        # print programminglanguagelist
        print programminglanguagelist

def scrapdata():
    url = 'https://en.wikipedia.org/wiki/Programming_language'
    content = requests.get(url).content
    soup = BeautifulSoup(content, 'lxml')
    tag = soup.find('div', {'class': 'mw-content-ltr'})
    paragraphs = tag.findAll('p')
    for para in paragraphs:
        paraexport = para.text.encode('utf-8')
        savedatainfile(paraexport)
    rulelogic("/home/jalaj/PycharmProjects/NLPython/NLPython/data/simpleruledata.txt")


if __name__ == "__main__":
    scrapdata()
```

Figure 7.11: Code for implementation of rule logic for extracting programming language

The output for the preceding code snippet is as follows:

```
['A', 'Programming', 'The', 'Musa', 'Baghdad,', 'Islamic', 'Golden',
'Age".[1]', 'From', 'Jacquard', 'Thousands', 'Many', 'The', 'Some', 'C',
'ISO', 'Standard)', 'Perl)', 'Some', 'A', 'Some,', 'Traits', 'Markup',
'XML,', 'HTML,', 'Programming', 'XSLT,', 'Turing', 'XML', 'Moreover,',
'LaTeX,', 'Turing', 'The', 'However,', 'One', 'In', 'For', 'Another',
'John', 'C.', 'Reynolds', 'He', 'Turing-complete,', 'The', 'The',
'Absolute', 'The', 'These', 'The', 'An', 'Plankalk\xc3\xbcl,', 'German',
'Z3', 'Konrad', 'Zuse', 'However,', 'John', "Mauchly's", 'Short', 'Code,',
'Unlike', 'Short', 'Code', 'However,', 'At', 'University', 'Manchester,',
'Alick', 'Glennie', 'Autocode', 'A', 'The', 'Mark', 'University',
'Manchester', 'The', 'Mark', 'R.', 'A.', 'Brooker', 'Autocode".',
```

```
'Brooker', 'Ferranti', 'Mercury', 'University', 'Manchester.', 'The',
'EDSAC', 'D.', 'F.', 'Hartley', 'University', 'Cambridge', 'Mathematical',
'Laboratory', 'Known', 'EDSAC', 'Autocode,', 'Mercury', 'Autocode', 'A',
'Atlas', 'Autocode', 'University', 'Manchester', 'Atlas', 'In', 'FORTRAN',
'IBM', 'John', 'Backus.', 'It', 'It', 'Another', 'Grace', 'Hopper', 'US,',
'FLOW-MATIC.', 'It', 'UNIVAC', 'I', 'Remington', 'Rand', 'Hopper',
'English', 'The', 'FLOW-MATIC', 'Flow-Matic', 'COBOL,', 'AIMACO', 'The',
'These', 'The', 'Each', 'The', 'Edsger', 'Dijkstra,', 'Communications',
'ACM,', 'GOTO', 'The', 'C++', 'The', 'United', 'States', 'Ada,', 'Pascal',
'In', 'Japan', 'The', 'ML', 'Lisp.', 'Rather', 'One', 'Modula-2,', 'Ada,',
'ML', 'The', 'Internet', 'Perl,', 'Unix', 'Java', 'Pascal', 'These', 'C',
'Programming', 'Current', "Microsoft's", 'LINQ.', 'Fourth-generation',
'Fifth', 'All', 'These', 'A', 'Most', 'On', 'The', 'The', 'Since',
'Programming', 'Backus\xe2\x80\x93Naur', 'Below', 'Lisp:', 'Not', 'Many',
'In', 'Even', 'Using', 'The', 'C', 'The', 'Chomsky', 'The', 'Type-2',
'Some', 'Perl', 'Lisp,', 'Languages', 'In', "Lisp's", "Perl's", 'BEGIN',
'C', 'The', 'The', 'For', 'Examples', 'Many', 'Other', 'Newer', 'Java',
'C#', 'Once', 'For', 'The', 'There', 'Natural', 'A', 'Results', 'A', 'The',
'Any', 'In', 'In', 'The', 'A', 'For', 'The', 'Many', 'A', 'These', 'REXX',
'SGML,', 'In', 'High-level', 'BCPL,', 'Tcl,', 'Forth.', 'In', 'Many',
'Statically', 'In', 'In', 'Most', 'C++,', 'C#', 'Java,', 'Complete',
'Haskell', 'ML.', 'However,', 'Java', 'C#', 'Additionally,', 'Dynamic',
'As', 'Among', 'However,', 'Lisp,', 'Smalltalk,', 'Perl,', 'Python,',
'JavaScript,', 'Ruby', 'Strong', 'An', 'Strongly', 'An', 'Perl',
'JavaScript,', 'In', 'JavaScript,', 'Array,', 'Such', 'Strong', 'Some',
'Thus', 'C', 'Most', 'Core', 'The', 'In', 'However,', 'Indeed,', 'For',
'Java,', 'Smalltalk,', 'BlockContext', 'Conversely,', 'Scheme',
'Programming', 'But', 'A', 'By', 'While', 'Many', 'Many', 'Although',
'The', 'One', 'The', 'As', 'Because', 'This', 'Natural', 'However,',
'Edsger', 'W.', 'Dijkstra', 'Alan', 'Perlis', 'Hybrid', 'Structured',
'English', 'SQL.', 'A', 'The', 'The', 'A', 'An', 'There', 'It', 'Although',
'Proprietary', 'Some', 'Oracle', 'Corporation', 'Java', "Microsoft's",
'C#', 'Common', 'Language', 'Runtime', 'Many', 'MATLAB', 'VBScript.',
'Some', 'Erlang', "Ericsson's", 'Thousands', 'Software', 'Programming',
'When', 'However,', 'The', 'On', 'A', 'A', 'These', 'Programming',
'Programs', 'In', 'When', 'Unix', 'It', 'One', 'CPU', 'Some', 'For',
'COBOL', 'Fortran', 'Ada', 'C', 'Other', 'Various', 'Combining', 'C,',
'Java,', 'PHP,', 'JavaScript,', 'C++,', 'Python,', 'Shell,', 'Ruby,',
'Objective-C', 'C#.[70]', 'There', 'A', 'Languages', 'Ideas', 'The', 'For',
'Java', 'Python', 'In', 'Traditionally,', 'These', 'A', 'More', 'An', 'By',
'Some', 'A', 'For', 'English', 'Other']
```

Now as you have seen, our basic rule extracted programming languages but it has also extracted junk data. Now think how you can restrict the rule or how you can put in some constraints so it will give us an accurate output. That will be your assignment.

Exercise

Please improvise the preceding output by putting in some constraints (Hint: You can apply some preprocessing and regex can also help you.)

Python for pattern-matching rules for a proofreading application

Now, suppose you want to make a proofreading tool. So, here I will provide you with one very simple mistake that you can find easily in any business mail or in any letter. Then we will try to correct the errors with high accuracy.

The mistake is when people specify a meeting timing in their mail, they may have specified the time as 2pm, or as 2PM, or as 2P.M., or other variations, but the correct format is 2 p.m. or 9 a.m.

This mistake can be fixed by the pattern-based rule. The following is the rule logic.

Suppose the numeric digit of length two starts from 1 to 12. After this numeric digit, if am and pm occurred without a space or without a period, then add the space and the proper period symbol.

I will implement it by using a regular expression.

Source pattern:

```
\b([1-9]|0[1-9]|1[0-2]{1,2})(am)\b
\b([1-9]|0[1-9]|1[0-2]{1,2})(pm)\b
```

Target pattern:

```
r'\b([1-9]|0[1-9]|1[0-2]{1,2})(am)\b',  r'\1 a.m.'
r'\b([1-9]|0[1-9]|1[0-2]{1,2})(pm)\b',  r'\1 p.m.'
```

You can find the code on the GitHub URL at:
https://github.com/jalajthanaki/NLPython/blob/master/ch7/7_2_basicpythonrule.py

The code snippet is given in *Figure 7.12*:

```
import re

inputstring = "Our meeting will be at 5pm tomorrow."
# inputstring = "Our meeting will be schedule at 11am tomorrow."

findpattern_am = re.search(r'\b([1-9]|0[1-9]|1[0-2]{1,2})(am)\b',
                           inputstring, re.M | re.I)
findpattern_pm = re.search(r'\b([1-9]|0[1-9]|1[0-2]{1,2})(pm)\b',
                           inputstring, re.M | re.I)

if findpattern_am:
    print findpattern_am.group()
    print re.sub(r'\b([1-9]|0[1-9]|1[0-2]{1,2})(am)\b', r'\1 a.m.', inputstring)
elif findpattern_pm:
    print findpattern_pm.group()
    print re.sub(r'\b([1-9]|0[1-9]|1[0-2]{1,2})(pm)\b', r'\1 p.m.', inputstring)
else:
    print "Not matched...!"
```

Figure 7.12: Code snippet for pattern-based rule

The output of the preceding code snippet is:

```
Our meeting will be at 5 p.m. tomorrow.
```

Figure 7.13: Output of pattern-based rule

The given example is a basic one, but it helps you to think about how proofreading can be done. Many simple sets of rules can be applied on the data and, according to the pattern, you will get the corrected result.

Exercise

Write a similar kind of rule which helps in correcting the timing pattern 11:30am or 5:45pm to 11:30 a.m. or 5:45 p.m.

Grammar correction

We will make a simple rule about a subject verb agreement rule for simple present tense.

We know that in simple present tense the third-person singular subjects always takes a singular verb with either s/es as the suffix of the verb.

Here are some examples of incorrect sentences:

- He drink tomato soup in the morning
- She know cooking
- We plays game online

We cannot perform a pattern-based correction for these kinds of incorrect sentences. Here, to make a rule, we will parse each sentence and try to check by using the parser result. Can we make any rules? I have parsed sentences to generate the parse result so you can see the parse tree in *Figure 7.14*. This result has been generated by using the Stanford parser:

```
(ROOT
  (S
    (NP (PRP He))
    (VP (VBP drink)
      (NP
        (NP (NN tomato) (NN soup))
        (PP (IN in)
          (NP (DT the) (NN morning)))))
    (. .)))

(ROOT
  (S
    (NP (PRP She))
    (VP (VBP know)
      (NP (NN cooking)))
    (. .)))

(ROOT
  (S
    (NP (PRP we))
    (VP (VBZ plays)
      (NP (NN game))
      (PP (NN online)))
    (. .)))
```

Figure 7.14: Parsing result for example sentences

We need to first extract the **NP**, which either takes the pronouns **PRP/NNP** or **NN**. This rule can be restricted to **PRP** only. We can extract the **PRP** tags from the sentence. After that we need to extract the **VP**. By using the type of pronoun and **VP**, we can suggest the change to the user. I guess you guys remember **NP**, **PRP**, **NNP**, and so on. As we have already shown, these are all kinds of POS tags, in Chapter 5, *Feature Engineering and NLP Algorithm*.

Rule logic:

- Extract the **NP** with the **PRP** tag
- Extract the **VP**
- As per the **PRP**, perform the correction in **VP**

Let's do the coding for this:

 I have installed the Stanford-`corenlp` and `pycornlp` libraries. You have already learned the steps for installing the Stanford parser in `Chapter 5,` *Feature Engineering and NLP Algorithm.*You guys are going to code this. So, it's a complete code challenge. I have a code in which I have extracted the pattern for you for **PRP** and **VBZ/VBP**. Your task is to check whether the combination of **PRP** and **VBP/VBZ** is right or wrong. If it is wrong, then raise an alert. You can find the code at:
`https://github.com/jalajthanaki/NLPython/blob/master/ch7/7_3_SVA`
`rule.py`

You can see the code snippet in *Figure 7.15* and *Figure 7.16*:

```
  13:30:40 as jalaj on jalaj in ~
→ cd stanford-corenlp-full-2016-10-31

  13:30:44 as jalaj on jalaj in ~/stanford-corenlp-full-2016-10-31
→ java -mx2g -cp "*" edu.stanford.nlp.pipeline.StanfordCoreNLPServer
[main] INFO CoreNLP - --- StanfordCoreNLPServer#main() called ---
[main] INFO CoreNLP - setting default constituency parser
[main] INFO CoreNLP - warning: cannot find edu/stanford/nlp/models/srparser/engl
ishSR.ser.gz
[main] INFO CoreNLP - using: edu/stanford/nlp/models/lexparser/englishPCFG.ser.g
z instead
[main] INFO CoreNLP - to use shift reduce parser download English models jar fro
m:
[main] INFO CoreNLP - http://stanfordnlp.github.io/CoreNLP/download.html
[main] INFO CoreNLP -     Threads: 4
[main] INFO CoreNLP - Starting server...
[main] INFO CoreNLP - StanfordCoreNLPServer listening at /0:0:0:0:0:0:0:0:9000
```

Figure 7.15: Stated Stanford corenlp server

I have given you the code but you need to complete it:

```python
from pycorenlp import StanfordCoreNLP
from nltk.tree import Tree

nlp = StanfordCoreNLP('http://localhost:9000')


def rulelogic(sentnece):
    leaves_list = []
    text = (sentnece)

    output = nlp.annotate(text, properties={
        'annotators': 'tokenize,ssplit,pos,depparse,parse',
        'outputFormat': 'json'
    })
    parsetree = output['sentences'][0]['parse']
    print parsetree
    for i in Tree.fromstring(parsetree).subtrees():
        if i.label() == 'PRP':
            print i.leaves(), i.label()
        if i.label() == 'VBP' or i.label() == 'VBZ':
            print  i.leaves(), i.label()


if __name__ == "__main__":
    rulelogic('We plays game online.')
    # 'He drink tomato soup in the morning.'
    # 'We plays game online.   '
```

Figure 7.16: Code which I have given to you but you need to complete

You can see the output of my incomplete code in *Figure 7.17*:

```
(ROOT
  (S
    (NP (PRP We))
    (VP (VBZ plays)
      (NP (NN game))
      (PP (NN online)))
    (. .)))
[u'We'] PRP
[u'plays'] VBZ
```

Figure 7.17: Output of my incomplete code

Template-based chatbot application

Here, we will see how we can build a core engine for a chatbot application which can help a loan applicant to apply for the same. We are generating output in JSON format, so any front-end developer can integrate this output on a website.

Here, I'm using the flask web framework and making web services for each question that our chatbot asks.

You need to install MongoDB if you want to save the user data. The installation steps of MongoDB are in this link:
https://docs.mongodb.com/manual/tutorial/install-mongodb-on-ubuntu/

I have defined functions in the conversationengine.py file. The path of this file on GitHub is:
https://github.com/jalajthanaki/NLPython/blob/master/ch7/chatbot/customscripts/conversationengine.py

You can see the flask web engine code in the flaskengin.py file. The GitHub link is:
https://github.com/jalajthanaki/NLPython/blob/master/ch7/chatbot/customscripts/conversationengine.py

The whole folder and package file path is at:
https://github.com/jalajthanaki/NLPython/tree/master/ch7/chatbot

Flow of code

So, I have written functions in `conversationengine.py` which generate a JSON response according to the questions you have asked and this JSON response can be used by the frontend developer team to display messages on the chatbot UI.

Then, I have written a web service using flask so you can see the JSON response on the web URL specified in JSON itself.

The `conversationengine.py` is the core rule engine with handcrafted rules and codes. See the code snippet in *Figure 7.18*:

```python
def start_converation_action(humanmessage):
    START_CONV_KEYWORDS = ("hello", "hi", "Hi", "Hello")
    START_CONV_RESPONSES = [
        "Please provide me borrower's full name"]
    text = humanmessage
    start_res = ""
    if text.lower() in START_CONV_KEYWORDS:
        # start_res = random.choice(START_CONV_RESPONSES)
        start_conv_json_obj = json.dumps(
            {'message_human': text, 'message_bot': START_CONV_RESPONSES,
             'suggestion_message': ["Please provide me borrower's full name"],
             'current_form_action': "/hi_chat?msg=",
             'next_form_action': "/asking_borowers_full_name?msg=", 'previous_form_action': "/welcomemsg_chat",
             'next_field_type': "text",
             'previous_field_type': "button", "placeholder_text": "Enter borrower's full name",
             "max_length": "255"},
            sort_keys=True, indent=4,
            separators=(',', ': '), default=json_util.default)
    elif text.lower() == "" or text.lower() is None or len(text) == 0:
        start_conv_json_obj = json.dumps({'message_human': text,
                                          'message_bot': defualt_missing_data_error,
                                          'suggestion_message': ["Hi"], 'current_form_action': "/hi_chat?msg",
                                          'next_form_action': "", 'previous_form_action': "/welcomemsg_chat",
                                          'next_field_type': "", 'previous_field_type': "button",
                                          "placeholder_text": "Hi"},
                                         sort_keys=True, indent=4,
                                         separators=(',', ': '), default=json_util.default)
    else:
```

Figure 7.18: Code snippet of conversationengine.py

Here, we have used a keywords list and, responses list to implement chatbot. I have also made customized JSON schema to export the conversation and, if you are from a web development background then you can write JavaScript which will help you to display this JSON on the front end with GUI.

Now, let's look at the web services part in *Figure 7.19*:

```
@app.route('/')
def hello_world():
    return 'Hello from chat bot Flask...!'


@app.route("/welcomemsg_chat")
def welcomemsg_chat():
    welcome_msg = cs.loan_assistant_welcome_msg()
    conversation_list_history.append(welcome_msg)
    # db_handler = mongo.db.chathistory
    # db_handler.insert({"request_user_id": request_user_id, "conversation": conversation_list_history,
    #                    "time": now_india.strftime(fmt)})
    # db_handler.update({"request_user_id": request_user_id}, {
    #     '$set': {"request_user_id": request_user_id, "conversation": conversation_list_history, "time": now_india.strftime(fmt)},
    #     "$currentDate": {"lastModified": True}}, upsert=True)
    resp = Response(welcome_msg, status=200, mimetype='application/json')
    return resp
```

Figure 7.19: Flask web service URLs defined in flaskengin.py

Now, to run the scripts and see the output follow these steps:

1. First run `flaskengin.py`
2. Go to the URL: `http://0.0.0.0:5002/`, where you can see `Hello from chatbot Flask!`
3. You can see the chatbot JSON response by using this URL: `http://0.0.0.0:5002/welcomemsg_chat`
4. You can see the JSON response in *Figure 7.20*:

```
{
    "current_form_action": "/welcomemsg_chat",
    "message_bot": [
        "Hi, I'm personal loan application assistant.",
        "You can apply for loan with help of mine.",
        "To keep going say Hi to me."
    ],
    "message_human": "",
    "next_field_type": "button",
    "next_form_action": "/hi_chat?msg=",
    "placeholder_text": "Hi",
    "previous_field_type": "",
    "previous_form_action": "",
    "suggestion_message": [
        "Hi"
    ]
}
```

Figure 7.20: JSON response of chatbot

5. Now, we are providing suggestions to our human user which will help them analyze what the expected input from them is. So, here, you can see the JSON attribute `suggestion_message: ["Hi"]`. So, the user will see the button with the `Hi` label.

6. If you want to redirect to the next page or next question, then use `next_form_action` URL and put the user argument after `msg = USER ARGUMENT`

7. For example, I am at the `http://0.0.0.0:5002/welcomemsg_chat` page. Now, you can read the `message_bot`. It says you need to say `Hi to bot`

8. You can give your `Hi` response like this:
   `http://0.0.0.0:5002/hi_chat?msg=Hi`

9. When you are on this URL: `http://0.0.0.0:5002/hi_chat?msg=Hi` you can see the bot will ask for your name now you need to enter your name.

10. To enter your name and be redirected to the next question, you need to again check what is the value of the URL for the `next_form_action` attribute

11. Here the value is `/asking_borowers_email_id?msg=`

12. You need to put your name after the = sign so the URL becomes `/asking_borowers_email_id?msg=Jalaj Thanaki`

13. When you use
    `http://0.0.0.0:5002/asking_borowers_full_name?msg=Jalaj%20Thanaki`, you can see next question from the bot.

14. First you need to run the script:
    `https://github.com/jalajthanaki/NLPython/blob/master/ch7/chatbot/flask engin.py` and then you can check the following URLs:

    - `http://0.0.0.0:5002/welcomemsg_chat`
    - `http://0.0.0.0:5002/hi_chat?msg=Hi`
    - `http://0.0.0.0:5002/asking_borowers_full_name msg=Jalaj%20Thanaki`
    - `http://0.0.0.0:5002/asking_borowers_email_id?msg=jalaj@gmail.com`
    - `http://0.0.0.0:5002/mobilenumber_asking?msg=9425897412`
    - `http://0.0.0.0:5002/loan_chat?msg=100000`
    - `http://0.0.0.0:5002/end_chat?msg=Bye`

If you want to insert user data in the MongoDB database, then this is possible and is included in the code but commented.

Advantages of template-based chatbot

- Easy to implement.
- Time and cost efficient.
- Use cases are understood prior to development so user experience will also be good.
- This is a pattern-matching approach, so if users use English and other languages in their conversation then users also get answers because chatbot identifies keywords which he provides in English, and if English keywords match with the chatbot vocabulary, then chatbot can give you answer.

Disadvantages of template-based chatbot

- It cannot work for unseen use cases
- User should process a rigid flow of conversation
- Spelling mistakes by users create a problem for chatbot. In this case, we will use deep learning

Exercise

Develop a template-based chatbot application for a hotel room booking customer support service. Develop some questions and answers and develop the application.

Comparing the rule-based approach with other approaches

The rule-based approach is a very reliable engine which provides your application with high accuracy. When you compare the RB approach with ML approaches or deep learning approaches, you will find the following points:

- For the RB approach, you need a domain expert, while for the ML approach, or for the deep learning approach, you don't need a domain expert
- The RB system doesn't need a large amount of data, whereas ML and deep learning need a very large amount of data

- For the RB system, you need to find patterns manually, whereas ML and deep learning techniques find patterns on your behalf as per the data and input features
- The RB system is often a good approach for developing the first cut of your end product, which is still popular in practice

Advantages of the rule-based system

There are very good advantages to using RB system. The advantages are mentioned as follows:

- Availability: Availability of the system for the user is not an issue
- Cost efficient: This system is cost efficient and accurate in terms of its end result
- Speed: You can optimize the system as you know all the parts of the system. So to provide output in a few seconds is not a big issue
- Accuracy and less error rate: Although coverage for different scenarios is less, whatever scenarios are covered by the RB system will provide high accuracy. Because of these predefined rules, the error rate is also less
- Reducing risk: We are reducing the amount of risk in terms of system accuracy
- Steady response: Output which has been generated by the system is dependent on rules so the output responses are stable, which means it cannot be vague
- The same cognitive process as a human: This system provides you with the same result as a human, as it has been handcrafted by humans
- Modularity: The modularity and good architecture of the RB system can help the technical team to maintain it easily. This decreases human efforts and time
- Uniformity: The RB system is much uniformed in its implementation and its output. This makes life easy for the end user because the output of the system can be easily understood by humans
- Easy to implement: This approach mimics the human thought process, so the implementation of rules is comparatively easy for developers

Disadvantages of the rule-based system

The disadvantages of the RB system are as follows:

- Lot of manual work: The RB system demands deep knowledge of the domain as well as a lot of manual work
- Time consuming: Generating rules for a complex system is quite challenging and time consuming
- Less learning capacity: Here, the system will generate the result as per the rules so the learning capacity of the system by itself is much less
- Complex domains: If an application that you want to build is too complex, building the RB system can take lot of time and analysis. Complex pattern identification is a challenging task in the RB approach

Challenges for the rule-based system

Let's look at some of the challenges in the RB approach:

- It is not easy to mimic the behavior of a human.
- Selecting or designing architecture is the critical part of the RB system.
- In order to develop the RB system, you need to be an expert of the specific domain which generates rules for us. For NLP we need linguists who know how to analyze language.
- Natural language is itself a challenging domain because it has so many exception cases and covering those exceptions using rules is also a challenging task, especially when you have a large amount of rules.
- Arabic, Gujarati, Hindi, and Urdu are difficult to implement in the RB system because finding a domain expert for these languages is a difficult task. There are also less tools available for the described languages to implement the rules.
- Time consumption of human effort is too high.

Understanding word-sense disambiguation basics

Word-sense disambiguation (WSD) is a well-known problem in NLP. First of all, let's understand what WSD is. WSD is used in identifying what the sense of a word means in a sentence when the word has multiple meanings. When a single word has multiple meaning, then for the machine it is difficult to identify the correct meaning and to solve this challenging issue we can use the rule-based system or machine learning techniques.

In this chapter, our focus area is the RB system. So, we will see the flow of how WSD is solved. In order to solve this complex problem using the RB system, you can take the following steps:

- When you are trying to solve WSD for any language you need to have a lot of data where you can find the various instances of words whose meaning can be different from sentence to sentence
- Once you have this kind of dataset available, then human experts come into the picture
- Human experts are used to tag the meaning of a word or words and usually the tags have some predefined IDs. Now, let's take an example: I have the sentences: I went to river bank, and I went to bank to deposit my money.
- In the preceding sentences, the word bank has multiple meanings and the meaning changes as per the overall sentence. So, the human expert is used to tag these kinds of words. Here, our word is bank
- So, the human expert tags the word bank in the river bank sense by using a predefined ID. Assume for now that the ID is 100
- In the second sentence, the word bank is tagged as a financial institution by using the predefined ID. Assume for now that ID is 101
- Once this tag has been given then the next stage has been started, which is either to choose rule-based engine or supervised machine learning techniques
- If we decide to go with the rule-based system then human experts need to come up with a certain pattern or rules which help us to disambiguate the sense of the words. Sometimes, for some words, the expert can find the rule by using a parsing result or by using POS tags, but in most case they can't
- So nowadays, once tagging has been done, the tagged data is used as input to develop a supervised machine learning model which helps humans to identify the senses of the words
- Sometimes only the rule-based system cannot work in the same way only the machine learning approach alone sometimes can't help you. Here is the same kind of case according to my experience. I think the hybrid approach will give you a better result
- After tagging the data, we should build the RB system which handles known situations very well and we also have a situation where we can't define rules. To solve that situation, we need to build a machine learning model.
- You can also use the vectorization concept and deep learning model to solve WSD problems. Your findings on WSD by using deep learning can be a research topic as well.

Discussing recent trends for the rule-based system

This section is a discussion about how the current market is using the RB system. So many people are asking many questions on different forums and they want to know about the future of the RB system, so I want to discuss with you one important question which will help you to learn the future trends of the NLP market and RB system. I have some of the questions that we will look at.

Are RB systems outdated in the NLP domain? I would like to answer this with NO. The RB system has been used majorly in all NLP applications, grammar correction, speech recognition, machine translation, and so on! This approach is the first step when you start making any new NLP application. If you want to experiment on your idea, then prototypes can be easily developed with the help of the RB approach. For prototyping, you need domain knowledge and basic coding skills. You don't need to know high-level mathematics or ML techniques. For basic prototyping, you should go with the RB system.

Can deep learning and ML-based approaches replace the RB based system? This question is quite an open-ended question. I would like to present some facts at this point which will help you to derive your question. Nowadays, we are flooded with data and we have cheap computation power available to us. The AI industry and AI-based projects are creating a lot of buzz. The preceding two points help deep learning and ML approaches to derive accurate results for NLP as well as other AI applications. These approaches need less human effort compared to the RB system. This is the reason why so many people think that the RB system will not be replaced by the deep learning and ML-based systems. I would argue that the RB system is not going to be replaced totally, but it will complement these approaches. Now you ask, how? So, the answer is, I think I would like to go with hybrid approaches which are much more beneficial for us. We can find patterns or predictions with the help of the ML system and then give those predictions to the RB system, and the RB system can validate the prediction and choose the best one for the users. This will actually help us to overcome one major challenge of the RB system, which is the reduction of human effort and time.

For the preceding questions, there is not any right or wrong answers. It is all about how you can see the questions and NLP domain. I just want to leave a thought for you. Think by yourself and try to come up with your own answer.

Summary

In this chapter, we have seen all the details related to the rule-based system and how the rule-based approach helps us to develop rapid prototypes for complex problems with high accuracy. We have seen the architecture of the rule-based system. We have learned about the advantages, disadvantages, and challenges for the rule-based system. We have seen how this system is helpful to us for developing NLP applications such as grammar correction systems, chatbots, and so on. We have also discussed the recent trends for the rule-based system.

In the next chapter, we will learn the other main approaches called machine learning, to solve NLP applications. The upcoming chapter will give you all the details about which machine learning algorithms you need to use for developing NLP applications. We will see supervised ML, semi-supervised ML, and unsupervised ML techniques. We will also develop some of the applications from scratch. So keep reading!

This self-driving car exam

8

Machine Learning for NLP Problems

We have seen the basic and the advanced levels of feature engineering. We have also seen how rule-based systems can be used to develop NLP applications. In this chapter, we will develop NLP applications, and to develop the applications, we will use **machine learning (ML)** algorithms. We will begin with the basics of ML. After this, we will see the basic development steps of NLP applications that use ML. We will mostly see how to use ML algorithms in the NLP domain. Then, we will move towards the features selection section. We will also take a look at hybrid models and post-processing techniques.

This is the outline of this chapter given as follows:

- Understanding the basics of machine learning
- Development steps for NLP application
- Understanding ML algorithms and other concepts
- Hybrid approaches for NLP applications

Let's explore the world of ML!

Understanding the basics of machine learning

First of all, we will understand what machine learning is. Traditionally, programming is all about defining all the steps to reach a certain predefined outcome. During this process of programming, we define each of the minute steps using a programming language that help us achieve our outcome. To give you a basic understanding, I'll take a general example. Suppose that you want to write a program that will help you draw a face. You may first write the code that draws the left eye, then write the code that draws the right eye, then the nose, and so on. Here, you are writing the code for each facial attribute, but ML flips this approach. In ML, we define the outcome and the program learns the steps to achieve the defined output. So, instead of writing code for each facial attribute, we provide hundreds of samples of human faces to the machine. We expect the machine to learn the steps that are needed to draw a human face so that it can draw some new human faces. Apart from this, when we provide the new human face as well as some animal face, it should recognize which face looks like a human face.

Let's take some general examples. If you want to recognize the valid license plates of certain states, in traditional programming, you need to write code such as what the shape of the license plate should be, what the color should be, what the fonts are, and so on. These coding steps are too lengthy if you are trying to manually code each single property of the license plate. Using ML, we will provide some example license plates to the machine and the machine will learn the steps so that it can recognize the new valid license plate.

Let's assume that you want to make a program that can play the game Super Mario and win the game as well. So, defining each game rule is too difficult for us. We usually define a goal such as you need to get to the endpoint without dying and the machine learns all the steps to reach the endpoint.

Sometimes, problems are too complicated, and even we don't know what steps should possibly be taken to solve these problems. For example, we are a bank and we suspect that there are some fraudulent activities happening, but we are not sure how to detect them or we don't even know what to look for. We can provide a log of all the user activities and find the users who are not behaving like the rest of the users. The machine learns the steps to detect the anomalies by itself.

ML is everywhere on the internet. Every big tech company is using it in some way. When you see any YouTube video, YouTube updates or provides you with suggestions of other videos that you may like to watch. Even your phone uses ML to provide you with facilities such as iPhone's Siri, Google Assistance, and so on. The ML field is currently advancing very fast. Researchers use old concepts, change some of them, or use other researchers, work to make it more efficient and useful.

Let's look at the basic traditional definition of ML. In 1959, a researcher named Arthur Samuel gave computers the ability to learn without being explicitly programmed. He evolved this concept of ML from the study of pattern recognition and computational learning theory in AI. In 1997, Tom Mitchell gave us an accurate definition that has been useful to those who can understand basic math. The definition of ML as per Tom Mitchell is: A computer program is said to learn from experience E with respect to some task T and some performance measure P, if its performance on T, as measured by P, improves with experience E.

Let's link the preceding definition with our previous example. To identify a license plate is called task **T**. You will run some ML programs using examples of license plates called experience **E**, and if it successfully learns, then it can predict the next unseen license plate that is called performance measure **P**. Now it's time to explore different types of ML and how it's related to AI.

Types of ML

In this section, we will look at different types of ML and some interesting sub-branch and super-branch relationships.

ML itself is derived from the branch called **artificial intelligence**. ML also has a branch that is creating lot of buzz nowadays called **deep learning**, but we will look at artificial intelligence and deep learning in detail in `Chapter 9`, *Deep Learning for NLP and NLG Problems*.

Learning techniques can be divided into different types. In this chapter, we are focusing on ML. Refer to *Figure 8.1*:

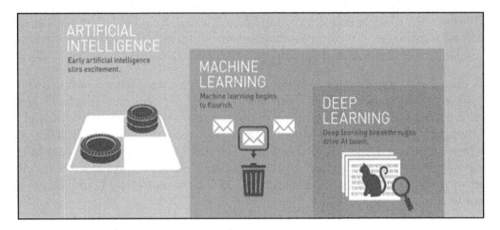

Figure 8.1: Subset and superset relationships of ML with other branches (Image credit: https://portfortune.files.wordpress.com/2016/10/ai-vs-ml.jpg)

ML techniques can be divided into three different types, which you can see in *Figure 8.2*:

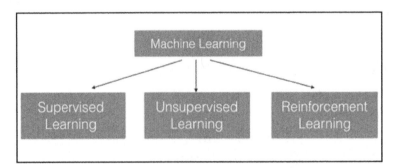

Figure 8.2: Three types of ML (Image credit: https://cdn-images-1.medium.com/max/1018/1*Yf8rcXiwvqEAinDTWTnCPA.jpeg)

We will look at each type of ML in detail. So, let's begin!

Supervised learning

In this type of ML, we will provide a labeled dataset as input to the ML algorithm and our ML algorithm knows what is correct and what is not correct. Here, the ML algorithm learns mapping between the labels and data. It generates the ML model and then the generated ML model can be used to solve some given task.

Suppose we have some text data that has labels such as spam emails and non-spam emails. Each text stream of the dataset has either of these two labels. When we apply the supervised ML algorithm, it uses the labeled data and generates an ML model that predicts the label as spam or non-spam for the unseen text stream. This is an example of supervised learning.

Unsupervised learning

In this type of ML, we will provide an unlabeled dataset as input to the ML algorithm. So, our algorithm doesn't get any feedback on what is correct or not. It has to learn by itself the structure of the data to solve a given task. It is harder to use an unlabeled dataset, but it's more convenient because not everyone has a perfectly labeled dataset. Most data is unlabeled, messy, and complex.

Suppose we are trying to develop a summarization application. We probably haven't summarized the documents corresponding to the actual document. Then, we will use raw and the actual text document to create a summary for the given documents. Here, the machine doesn't get any feedback as to whether the summary generated by the ML algorithm is right or wrong. We will also see an example of a computer vision application. For image recognition, we feed an unlabeled image dataset of some cartoon characters to the machine, and we expect the machine to learn how to classify each of the characters. When we provide an unseen image of a cartoon character, it should recognize the character and put that image in the proper class, which is generated by the machine itself.

Reinforcement learning

The third type of ML is reinforcement learning. Here, the ML algorithm doesn't give you the feedback right after every prediction, but it generates feedback if the ML model achieves its goal. This type of learning is mostly used in the area of robotics and to develop intelligent bots to play games. Reinforcement learning is linked to the idea of interacting with an environment using the trial and error method. Refer to *Figure 8.3*:

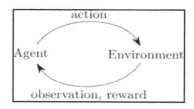

Figure 8.3: Reinforcement learning interacting with environment (Image credit: https://devblogs.nvidia.com/parallelforall/wp-content/uploads/2016/04/aeloop-300x183.png)

To learn the basics, let's take an example. Say you want to make a bot that beats humans at chess. This type of bot would receive feedback only if it won the game. Recently, Google AlphaGo beat the world's best Go player. If you want to read more on this, refer to the following link:

```
https://techcrunch.com/2017/05/24/alphago-beats-planets-best-human-go-player-ke
-jie/.
```

We are not going into detail about this type of ML in this book because our main focus is NLP, not robotics or developing a game bot.

If you really want to learn **reinforcement learning** (**RL**) in detail, you can take up this course:
```
https://www.udacity.com/course/reinforcement-learning--ud600.
```

I know you must be interested in knowing the differences between each type of ML. So, pay attention as you read the next paragraph.

For supervised learning, you will get feedback after every step or prediction. In reinforcement learning, we will receive feedback only if our model achieves the goal. In unsupervised learning, we will never get feedback, even if we achieve our goal or our predication is right. In reinforcement learning, it interacts with the existing environment and uses the trial and error method, whereas the other two types do not apply trial and error. In supervised learning, we will use labeled data, whereas in unsupervised learning, we will use unlabeled data, and in reinforcement learning, there are a bunch of goals and decision processes involved. You can refer to *Figure 8.4*:

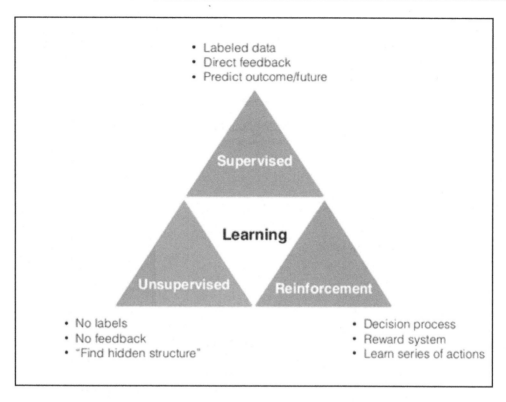

Figure 8.4: Comparison between supervised, unsupervised, and reinforcement learning (Image credit: http://www.techjini.com/wp-content/uploads/2017/02/mc-learning.jpg)

There are so many new things that you will be learning from this section onwards, if you don't understand some of the terminology at first, then don't worry! Just bear with me; I will explain each of the concepts practically throughout this chapter. So, let's start understanding the development steps for NLP applications that use ML.

Development steps for NLP applications

In this section, we will discuss the steps of developing NLP applications using ML algorithms. These steps vary from domain to domain. For NLP applications, the visualization of data does not play that much of a critical role, whereas the visualization of data for an analytical application will give you a lot of insight. So, it will change from application to application and domain to domain. Here, my focus is the NLP domain and NLP applications, and when we look at the code, I will definitely recall the steps that I'm describing here so that you can connect the dots.

I have divided the development steps into two versions. The first version is taking into account that it's the first iteration for your NLP application development. The second version will help you with the possible steps that you can consider after your first iteration of the NLP application development. Refer to *Figure 8.5*:

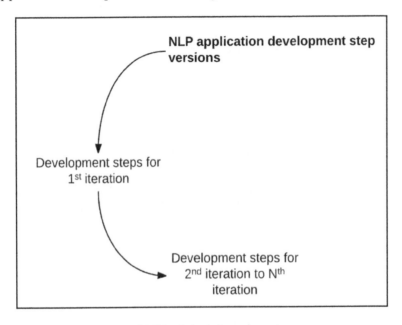

Figure 8.5: NLP application development steps version

Development step for the first iteration

First, we will look at the steps that we can generally use when we develop the first version of the NLP application using ML. I will refer to *Figure 8.6* during my explanation so that you can understand things properly:

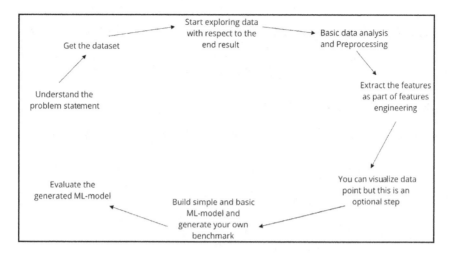

Figure 8.6: The first version and iteration to develop an application using ML algorithms

I'm going to explain each step:

1. The first step of this version is understanding your problem statement, application requirements, or the objective that you are trying to solve.

2. The second step is to get the data that you need to solve your objective or, if you have the dataset, then try to figure out what the dataset contains and what is your need in order to build an NLP application. If you need some other data, then first ask yourself; can you derive the sub-data attributes with the help of the available dataset? If yes, then there may be no need to get another dataset but if not, then try to get a dataset that can help you develop your NLP application.

3. The third step is to think about what kind of end result you want, and according to that, start exploring the dataset. Do some basic analysis.

4. The fourth step is after doing a general analysis of the data, you can apply preprocessing techniques on it.

5. The fifth step is to extract features from the preprocessed data as part of feature engineering.

6. The sixth is, using statistical techniques, you can visualize the feature values. This is an optional step for an NLP application.

7. The seventh step is to build a simple, basic model for your own benchmark.

8. Last but not least, evaluate the basic model, and if it is up to the mark, then good; otherwise, you need more iterations and need to follow another version, which I will be describing in the next section.

Development steps for the second to nth iteration

We have seen the steps that you can take in the first iteration; now we will see how we can execute the second iteration so that we can improvise our model accuracy as well as efficiency. Here, we are also trying to make our model as simple as possible. All these goals will be part of this development version.

Now we will see the steps that you can follow after the first iteration. For basic understanding, refer to *Figure 8.7*:

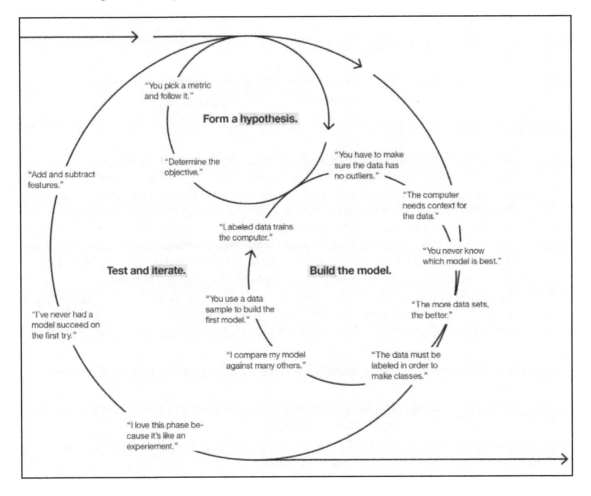

Figure 8.7: ML building cycle

Some of the basic steps for the second iteration are as follows:

1. After the first iteration, you have already built a model, and now you need to improve it. I would recommend you try out different ML algorithms to solve the same NLP application and compare the accuracy. Choose the best three ML algorithms based on accuracy. This will be the first step.

2. As a second step, generally, you can apply hyperparameter tuning for each of the selected ML algorithms in order to achieve better accuracy.

3. If parameter optimization doesn't help you so much, then you need to really concentrate on the feature engineering part and this will be your step three.

4. Now, feature engineering has two major parts: feature extraction and feature selection. So in the first iteration, we have already extracted feature, but in order to optimize our ML model, we need to work on feature selection. We will look at all the feature selection techniques later in this chapter.

5. In feature selection, you basically choose those feature, variable, or data attributes that are really critical or contribute a lot in order to derive the outcome. So, we will consider only important feature and remove others.

6. You can also remove outliers, perform data normalization, and apply cross validation on your input data, which will help you improvise your ML model.

7. After performing all these tricks, if you don't get an accurate result, then you need to spend some time deriving new features and use them.

8. You can reiterate all the preceding steps until you get a satisfactory outcome.

This is how you can approach the development of an NLP application. You should observe your results and then take sensible, necessary steps in the next iteration. Be smart in your analysis, think about all the problems, and then reiterate to solve them. If you don't analyze your result thoroughly, then reiteration never helps you. So keep calm, think wisely, and reiterate. Don't worry; we will look at the previous process when we develop NLP applications using ML algorithms. If you are on the research side, then I strongly recommend you understand the math behind the ML algorithms, but if you are a beginner and not very familiar with math, then you can read the documentation of the ML library. Those who lay between these two zones, try to figure out the math and then implement it.

Now, it's time to dive deep into the ML world and learn some really great algorithms.

Understanding ML algorithms and other concepts

Here, we will look at the most widely used ML algorithms for the NLP domain. We will look at algorithms as per the types of ML. First, we will start with supervised ML algorithms, then unsupervised ML algorithms, and lastly, semi-supervised ML algorithms. Here, we will understand the algorithm as well as the mathematics behind it. I will keep it easy so that those who are not from a strong mathematical background can understand the intuitive concept behind the algorithm. After that, we will see how we can practically use these algorithms to develop an NLP application. We will develop a cool NLP application which will help you understand algorithms without any confusion.

So, let's begin!

Supervised ML

We saw the introduction to supervised machine learning earlier in this chapter. Whatever techniques and datasets we see and use include their outcome, result, or labels that are already given in the dataset. So, this means that whenever you have a labeled dataset, you can use supervised ML algorithms.

Before starting off with algorithms, I will introduce two major concepts for supervised ML algorithms. This will also help you decide which algorithm to choose to solve NLP or any other data science-related problem:

- Regression
- Classification

Regression

Regression is a statistical process that estimates the relationships between variables. Suppose you have a bunch of variables and you want to find out the relationship between them. First, you need to find out which are the dependent variable, and which are the independent variables. Regression analysis helps you understand how the dependent variable changes its behavior or value for given values of independent variables. Here, dependent variables depend on the values of independent variables, whereas independent variables take values that are not dependent on the other variables.

Let's take an example to give you a clear understanding. If you have a dataset that has the height of a human and you need to decide the weight based on the height, this is supervised ML and you already have the age in your dataset. So, you have two attributes, which are also called variables: height, and weight. Now, you need to predict the weight as per the given height. So, think for some seconds and let me know which data attribute or variable is dependent and which is independent. I hope you have some thoughts. So, let me answer now. Here, weight is the dependent data attribute or variable that is going to be dependent on the variable-height. Height is the independent variable. The independent variable is also called a **predictor(s)**. So if you have a certain mapping or relationship between the dependent variable and independent variables, then you can also predict the weight for any given height.

Note that regression methods are used when our output or dependent variable takes a continuous value. In our example, weight can be any value such as 20 kg, 20.5 kg, 20.6 kg, 60 kg, and so on. For other datasets or applications, the values of the dependent variable can be any real number. Refer to *Figure 8.8*:

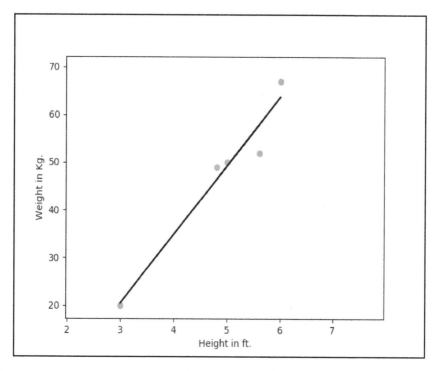

Figure 8.8: Linear regression example

Classification

In this section, we will look at the other major concept of supervised ML, which is called **classification techniques**. This is also called **statistical classification**.

Statistical classification is used to identify a category for a given new observation. So, we have many categories in which we can put the new observation. However, we are not going to blindly choose any category, but we will use the given dataset, and based on this dataset, we will try to identify the best suited category for the new observation and put our observation in this category or class.

Let's take an example from the NLP domain itself. You have a dataset that contains a bunch of emails and those emails already have a class label, which is either spam or non-spam. So, our dataset is categorized into two classes--spam and non-spam. Now if we get a new email, then can we categorize that particular e-mail into the spam or not-spam class? The answer is yes. So, to classify the new e-mail we use our dataset and ML algorithm and provide the best suited class for the new mail. The algorithm that implements the classification is called a **classifier**. Sometimes, the term classifier also refers to the mathematical function which is implemented by the classifier algorithm that maps the input data to a category.

Note that this point helps you identify the difference between regression and classification. In classification, the output variable takes the class label that is basically a discrete or categorical value. In regression, our output variable takes a continuous value. Refer to *Figure 8.9*:

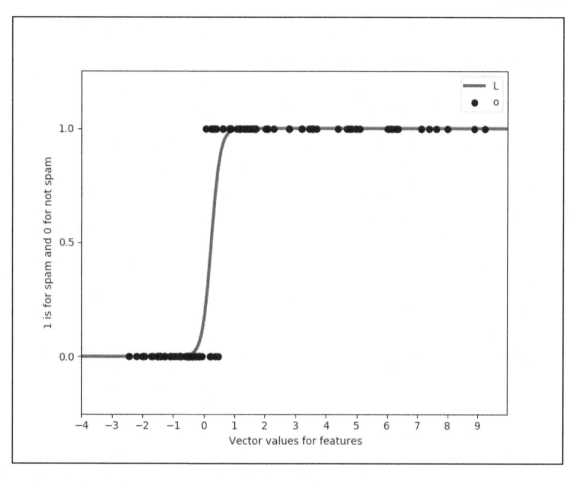

Figure 8.9: Classification visualization for intuitive purposes

Now that we have an idea about regression and classification, let's understand the basic terminology that I am going to use constantly while explaining ML algorithms specially for classification:

- **Instance:** This is referred to as input and generally, they are in the form of vectors. These are vectors of attributes. In the POS tagger example, we used features that we derived from each word and converted them to vectors using `scikit-learns` API `DictVectorizer`. The vector values were fed into the ML algorithm so these input vectors are the instances.

- **Concept:** The concept is referred to as a function that maps input to output. So, if we have an e-mail content and we are tying to find out whether that e-mail content is spam or non-spam, we have to focus on some certain parameters from the instance or input and then generate the result. The process of how to identify certain output from certain input is called **concept**. For example, you have some data about the height of a human in feet. After seeing the data, you can decide whether the person is tall or short. Here, the concept or function helps you to find the output for a given input or instance. So, if I put this in mathematical format, then the concept is a mapping between an object in a world and membership in a set.

- **Target concept:** The target concept is referred to as the actual answer or specific function or some particular idea that we are trying to find. As humans, we have understood a lot of concepts in our head, such as by reading the e-mail, we can judge that it's spam or non-spam, and if your judgments is true, then you can get the actual answer. You know what is called **spam** and what is not, but unless we actually have it written down somewhere, we don't know whether it's right or wrong. If we note these actual answers for each of the raw data in our dataset, then it will be much easier for us to identify which e-mails should be considered as spam e-mails and which not. This helps you find out the actual answer for a new instance.

- **Hypothesis class:** Is the class of all possible functions that can help us classify our instance. We have just seen the target concept where we are trying to find out a specific function, but here we can think of a subset of all the possible and potential functions that can help us figure out our target concept for classification problems. Here, I want to point out that we are seeing this terminology for classification tasks so don't consider the x2 function, because it's a linear function and we are performing classification not regression.

- **Training dataset:** In classification we are trying to find the target concept or actual answer. Now, how can we actually get this final answer? To get the final answer using ML techniques, we will use some sample set, training set, or training dataset that will help us find out the actual answer. Let's see what a training set is. A training set contains all the input paired with a label. Supervised classification problems need a training dataset that has been labeled with the actual answer or actual output. So, we are not just passing our knowledge to the machine about what is spam or non-spam; we are also providing a lot of examples to the machine, such as this is a spam mail, this is non-spam mail, and so on. So, for the machine it will be easy to understand the target concept.

- **ML-model:** We will use the training dataset and feed this data to the ML algorithm. Then, the ML algorithm will try to learn the concept using a lot of training examples and generate the output model. This output model can be used later on to predict or decide whether the given new mail is spam or not-spam. This generated output is called the **ML-model**. We will use a generated ML-model and give the new mail as input and this ML-model will generate the answer as to whether the given mail belongs to the spam category or not-spam category.

- **Candidate:** The candidate is the potential target concept that our ML-model tells us for the new example. So, you can say that the candidate is the predicted target concept by the machine, but we don't know whether the predicted or generated output that is the candidate here is actually the correct answer or not. So, let's take an example. We have provided a lot of examples of emails to the machine. The machine may generalize the concept of spam and not-spam mails. We will provide a new e-mail and our ML-model will say that it's non-spam, however, we need to check whether our ML-model's answer is right or wrong. This answer is referred to as a candidate. How can we check whether the answer generated by the ML-model matches with the target concept or not? To answer your question, I will introduce the next term, that is, testing set.

- **Testing set:** The testing set looks similar to the training dataset. Our training dataset has e-mails with labels such as spam or non-spam. So, I will take the answer that is considered as the candidate and we will check in our testing set whether it is non-spam or spam. We will compare our answer with the testing set's answer and try to figure out whether the candidate has a true answer or false answer. Suppose that not-spam is the right answer. Now, you will take another e-mail and the ML-model will generate a non-spam answer again. We will again check this with our testing set, and this time the ML-model generates a wrong answer- the mail is actually spam but the ML-model misclassifies it in the non-spam category. So the testing set helps us validate our ML-model. Note that the training and testing sets should not be the same. This is because, if your machine uses the training dataset to learn the concept and you test your ML-model on the training dataset, then you are not evaluating your ML-model fairly. This is considered cheating in ML. So, your training dataset and testing set should always be different; the testing set is the dataset that has never been seen by your machine. We are doing this because we need to check the machines ability on how much the given problem can be generalized. Here, generalized means how the ML-model reacts to unknown and unseen examples. If you are still confused, then let me give you another example. You are a student and a teacher taught you some facts and gave you some examples. Initially, you just memorized the facts. So as to check that you got the right concept, the teacher will give a test and give you novel examples where you need to apply your learning. If you are able to apply your learning perfectly to the new example in the test, then you actually got the concept. This proves that we can generalize the concept that has been taught by a teacher. We are doing the same thing with the machine.

Now let's understand ML algorithms.

ML algorithms

We have understood enough about the essential concepts of ML, and now we will explore ML algorithms. First, we will see the supervised ML algorithms that are mostly used in the NLP domain. I'm not going to cover all the supervised ML algorithms here, but I'm explaining those that are most widely used in the NLP domain.

In NLP applications, we mostly perform classification applying various ML techniques. So, here, our focus is mostly on the classification type of an algorithm. Other domains, such as analytics use various types of linear regression algorithms, as well as analytical applications but we are not going to look at those algorithms because this book is all about the NLP domain. As some concepts of linear regression help us understand deep learning techniques, we will look at linear regression and gradient descent in great detail with examples in Chapter 9, *Deep Learning for NLP and NLG Problems*.

We will develop some NLP applications using various algorithms so that you can see how the algorithm works and how NLP applications develop using ML algorithms. We will look at applications such as spam filtering.

Refer to *Figure 8.10*:

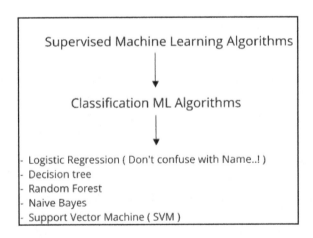

Figure 8.10: Supervised classification ML algorithms that we are going to understand

Now let's start with our core ML part.

Logistic regression

I know you must be confused as to why I put logistic regression in the classification category. Let me tell you that it's just the name that is given to this algorithm, but it's used to predict the discrete output, so this algorithm belongs to the classification category.

For this classification algorithm I will give you an idea how the logistic regression algorithm works and we will look at some basic mathematics related to it. Then, we will look the spam filtering application.

First, we will consider binary classes such as spam or not-spam, good or bad, win or lose, 0 or 1, and so on to understand the algorithm and its application. Suppose I want to classify e-mails into the spam and not-spam category. Spam and not-spam are discrete output labels or target concepts. Our goal is to predict whether the new e-mail is spam or not-spam. Not-spam is also called **ham**. In order to build this NLP application, we will use logistic regression.

Let's understand the technicality of the algorithm first.

Here, I'm stating facts related to mathematics and this algorithm in a very simple manner. A general approach to understanding this algorithm is as follows. If you know some part of ML, then you can connect the dots, and if you are new to ML, then don't worry, because we are going to understand every part:

- We are defining our hypothesis function that helps us generate our target output or target concept
- We are defining the cost function or error function and we choose the error function in such a way that we can derive the partial derivate of the error function so that we can calculate gradient descent easily
- We are trying to minimize the error so that we can generate a more accurate label and classify the data accurately

In statistics, logistic regression is also called **logit regression** or the **logit model**. This algorithm is mostly used as a binary class classifier, which means that there should be two different classes to classify the data. The binary logistic model is used to estimate the probability of a binary response and it generates the response based on one or more predictors or independent variables or features. This is the ML algorithm that uses basic mathematics concepts in deep learning as well.

First, I want to explain why this algorithm is called **logistic regression**. The reason is that the algorithm uses a logistic function or sigmoid function. Logistic function and sigmoid function are synonyms.

We use the sigmoid function as a hypothesis function. What do you mean by hypothesis function? Well, as we saw earlier, the machine has to learn mapping between data attributes and the given label in such a way that it can predict the label for new data. This can be achieved by the machine if it learns this mapping via a mathematical function. The mathematical function is the hypothesis function that the machine will use to classify the data and predict labels or the target concept. We want to build a binary classifier, so our label is either spam or ham. So, mathematically, I can assign 0 for ham or not-spam and 1 for spam or vice versa. These mathematically assigned labels are our dependent variables. Now, we need our output labels to be either zero or one. Mathematically, the label is y and y ε {0, 1}. So we need to choose the hypothesis function that will convert our output value to zero or one. The logistic function or sigmoid function does exactly that and this is the main reason why logistic regression uses a sigmoid function as the hypothesis function.

Logistic or sigmoid function

The mathematical equation for the logistic or sigmoid function is as shown:

$$g(z) = \frac{1}{1 + e^{-z}}$$

Figure 8.11: Logistic or sigmoid function

You can see the plot showing $g(z)$. Here, $g(z)= \Phi(z)$. Refer to *Figure 8.12*:

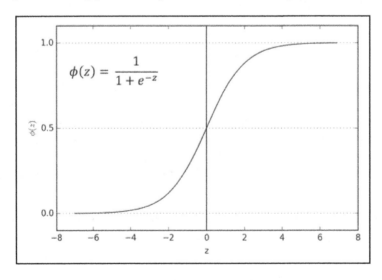

Figure 8.12: Graph of the sigmoid or logistic function

From the preceding graph, you can find the following facts:

- If you have z value greater or equal to zero, then the logistic function gives the output value one
- If you have value of z less than zero, then the logistic function generates the output zero

You can see the mathematical condition for the logistic function as shown:

$$g(z) = \begin{cases} 1 & \text{if } z \geq 0 \\ 0 & \text{if } z < 0 \end{cases}$$

Figure 8.13: Logistic function mathematical property

We can use this function to perform binary classification.

Now it's time to show how this sigmoid function will be represented as the hypothesis function:

$$h_\theta(x) = g(\theta^T x)$$

Figure 8.14: Hypothesis function for logistic regression

If we take the preceding equation and substitute the value of z with $\theta^T x$, then the equation given in *Figure 8.11* is converted to the equation in *Figure 8.15*:

$$h_\theta(x) = g(\theta^T x) = \frac{1}{1 + e^{-\theta^T x}}$$

Figure 8.15: Actual hypothesis function after mathematical manipulation

Here, $h_\theta x$ is the hypothesis function, θ^T is the matrix of the features or independent variables and transpose representation of it, x is for all independent variables or all possible features set. In order to generate the hypothesis equation, we replace the z value of the logistic function with $\theta^T x$.

Using the hypothesis equation, the machine actually tries to learn mapping between input variables or input features and output labels. Let's talk a bit about the interpretation of this hypothesis function. Can you think of the best way to predict the class label? According to me, we can predict the target class label using the probability concept. We need to generate probability for both classes and whatever class has a high probability will be assigned to that particular instance of features. In binary classification, the value of y or the target class is either zero or one. If you are familiar with probability, then you can represent the probability equation given in *Figure 8.16*:

$$P(y = 1 \mid x; \theta) = h_\theta(x)$$
$$P(y = 0 \mid x; \theta) = 1 - h_\theta(x)$$

Figure 8.16: Interpretation of the hypothesis function using probabilistic representation

So those who are not familiar with probability, $P(y=1|x;\theta)$ can be read like this - probability of $y =1$, given x, and parameterized by θ. In simple language, you can say that this hypothesis function will generate the probability value for target output 1 where we give features matrix x and some parameter θ. We will see later on why we need to generate probability, as well as how we can generate probability values for each of the classes.

Here, we have completed the first step of a general approach to understanding logistic regression.

Cost or error function for logistic regression

First, let's understand the cost function or error function. The cost function, loss function, or error function is a very important concept in ML, so we will understand the definition of the cost function.

The cost function is used to check how accurately our ML classifier performs. In our training dataset, we have data and label. When we use the hypothesis function and generate the output, we need to check how near we are to the actual prediction. If we predict the actual output label, then the difference between our hypothesis function output and the actual label is zero or minimum and if our hypothesis function output and actual label are not the same, then we have a big difference between them. If the actual label of an e-mail is spam, that is one, and our hypothesis function also generates the result 1 then the difference between the actual target value and predicted output value is zero, therefore the error in the prediction is also zero. If our predicted output is 1, and the actual output is zero, then we have maximum error between our actual target concept and prediction. So, it is important for us to have minimum error in our prediction. This is the very basic concept of the error function. We will get to the mathematics in some time. There are several types of error functions available, such as r2 error, sum of squared error, and so on. As per the ML algorithm and hypothesis function, our error function also changes.

What will the error function be for logistic regression? What is θ and, if I need to choose some value of θ, how can I approach it? So, here, I will give all the answers.

Let me give you some background on linear regression. We generally use sum of squared error or residual error as the cost function in linear regression. In linear regression, we are trying to generate the line of best fit for our dataset. In the previous example, given height, I want to predict the weight. We first draw a line and measure the distance from each of the data points to the line. We will square these distances, sum them and try to minimize the error function. Refer to *Figure 8.17*:

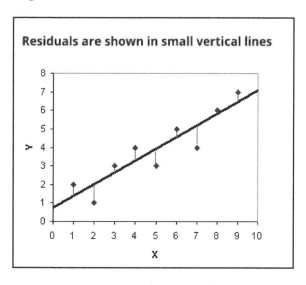

Figure 8.17: Sum of squared error representation for reference

You can see the distance of each data point from the line is denoted using small vertical lines. We will take these distances, square them and then sum them. We will use this error function. We have generated a partial derivative with respect to the slope of line m and intercept b. Here, in *Figure 8.17*, our b is approximately *0.9* and m is approximately two thirds. Every time, we calculate the error and update the value of m and b so that we can generate the line of best fit. The process of updating m and b is called **gradient descent**. Using gradient descent, we update m and b in such a way that our error function has minimum error value and we can generate the line of best fit. Gradient descent gives us a direction in which we need to plot a line. You can find a detailed example in Chapter 9, *Deep Learning for NLP and NLG Problems*. So, by defining the error function and generating partial derivatives, we can apply the gradient descent algorithm that helps us minimize our error or cost function.

Now back to the main question: Can we use the error function for logistic regression? If you know functions and calculus well, then probably your answer is no. That is the correct answer. Let me explain this for those who aren't familiar with functions and calculus.

In linear regression, our hypothesis function is linear, so it is very easy for us to calculate the sum of squared errors, but here, we will use the sigmoid function, which is a non-linear function. If you apply the same function that we used in linear regression, it will not turn out well because if you take the sigmoid function, put in the sum of squared error function, and try to visualize all the possible values, then you will get a non-convex curve. Refer to *Figure 8.18*:

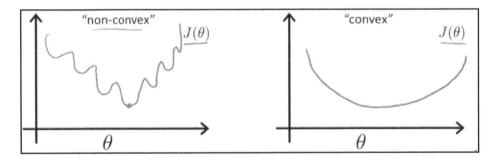

Figure 8.18: Non-convex and convex curve (Image credit: http://www.yuthon.com/images/non-convex_and_convex_function.png)

In ML, we mostly use functions that are able to provide a convex curve because then we can use the gradient descent algorithm to minimize the error function and reach a global minimum. As you can see in *Figure 8.18*, a non-convex curve has many local minima, so to reach a global minimum is very challenging and time-consuming because you need to apply second order or nth order optimization to reach a global minimum, whereas in a convex curve, you can reach a global minimum certainly and quickly.

So, if we plug our sigmoid function into sum of squared error, you get the non-convex function so we are not going to define the same error function that we used in linear regression.

We need to define a different cost function that is convex so that we can apply the gradient descent algorithm and generate a global minimum. We will use the statistical concept called **likelihood**. To derive the likelihood function, we will use the equation of probability that is given in *Figure 8.16* and we will consider all the data points in the training dataset. So, we can generate the following equation, which is called likelihood function. Refer to *Figure 8.19*:

$$
\begin{aligned}
L(\theta) &= p(\vec{y} \mid X; \theta) \\
&= \prod_{i=1}^{m} p(y^{(i)} \mid x^{(i)}; \theta) \\
&= \prod_{i=1}^{m} \left(h_\theta(x^{(i)})\right)^{y^{(i)}} \left(1 - h_\theta(x^{(i)})\right)^{1-y^{(i)}}
\end{aligned}
$$

Figure 8.19: The likelihood function for logistic regression (Image credit: http://cs229.stanford.edu/notes/cs229-notes1.pdf)

Now, in order to simplify the derivative process, we need to convert the likelihood function to a monotonically increasing function. That can be achieved by taking the natural logarithm of the likelihood function, which is called **log likelihood**. This log-likelihood is our cost function for logistic regression. Refer to the following equation in *Figure 8.20*:

$$
\text{Cost}(h_\theta(x), y) = \begin{cases} -\log(h_\theta(x)) & \text{if } y = 1 \\ -\log(1 - h_\theta(x)) & \text{if } y = 0 \end{cases}
$$

Figure 8.20: Cost function for logistic regression

We will plot the cost function and understand the benefits it provides us with. In the *x* axis, we have our hypothesis function. Our hypothesis function range is *0* to *1*, so we have these two points on the *x* axis. Start with the first case, where *y* = *1*. You can see the generated curve that is on the top right-hand side in *Figure 8.21*:

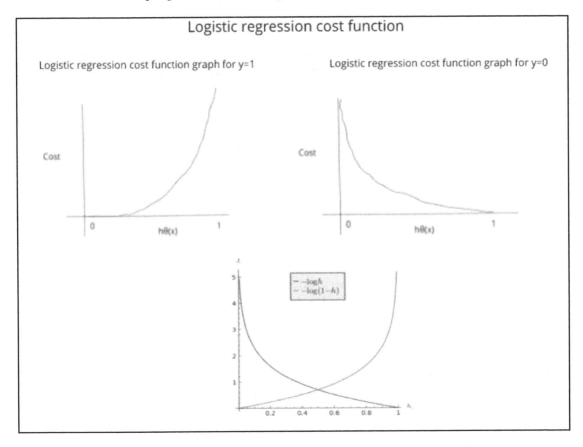

Figure 8.21: Logistic function cost function graph

If you look at any log function plot, then it will look like the graph for error function *y=0*. Here, we flip that curve because we have a negative sign, then you get the curve which we have plotted for *y=1* value. In *Figure 8.21*, you can see the log graph, as well as the flipped graph in *Figure 8.22*:

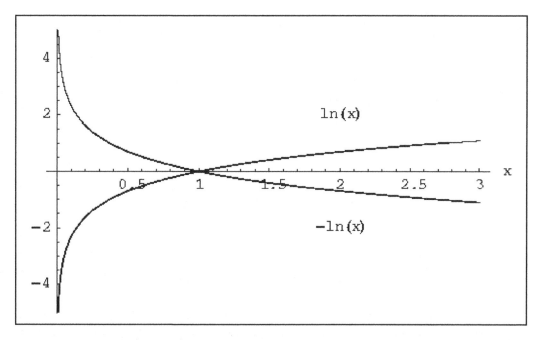

Figure 8.22: Comparing log(x) and -log(x) graph for better understanding of the cost function (Image credit : http://www.sosmath.com/algebra/logs/log4/log42/log422/gl30.gif)

Here, we are interested in the values *0* and *1*, so we are considering that part of the graph that we have depicted in *Figure 8.21*. This cost function has some interesting and useful properties. If the predicted label or candidate label is the same as the actual target label, then the cost will be zero. You can put this as $y = 1$ and if the hypothesis function predicts $H_\theta(x) = 1$ then *cost = 0*; if $H_\theta(x)$ tends to *0*, meaning that if it is more toward the zero, then the cost function blows up to ∞.

For $y = 0$, you can see the graph that is on the top left-hand side in *Figure 8.21*. This case condition also has the same advantages and properties that we saw earlier. It will blow to ∞ when the actual value is 0 and the hypothesis function predicts 1. If the hypothesis function predicts 0 and the actual target is also 0, then *cost = 0*.

Now, we will see why we are choosing this cost function. The reason is that this function makes our optimization easy, as we will use maximum log-likelihood because it has a convex curve that will help us run gradient descent.

In order to apply gradient descent, we need to generate the partial derivative with respect to θ and generate the equation that is given in *Figure 8.23*:

Repeat until convergence

{

$$\theta_j := \theta_j - \alpha \frac{1}{m} \sum_{i=1}^{m} (h_\theta(x^{(i)}) - y^{(i)}) x_j^{(i)}$$

}

Figure 8.23: Partial derivative to perform gradient descent (Image credit:
http://2.bp.blogspot.com/-ZxJ87cWjPJ8/TtLtwqv0hCI/AAAAAAAAAV0/9FYqcxJ6dNY/s1600/gradient+descent+algorithm+OLS.png)

This equation is used to update the parameter value of θ; $\propto$ defines the learning rate. This is the parameter that you can use to set how fast or how slow your algorithm should learn or train. If you set the learning rate too high, then the algorithm cannot learn, and if you set it too low, then it will take a lot of time to train. So you need to choose the learning rate wisely.

This is the end of our second point and we can begin with the third part, which is more of an implementation part. You can check out this GitHub link:

```
https://github.com/jalajthanaki/NLPython/blob/master/ch8/Own_Logistic_Regressio
n/logistic.py
```

This has an implementation of logistic regression and you can find its comparison with the given implementation in the `scikit-learn` library. Here, the code credit goes to Harald Borgen.

We will use this algorithm for spam filtering. Spam filtering is one of the basic NLP applications. Using this algorithm, we want to make an ML-model that classifies the given mail into either the spam or ham category. So, let's make a spam-filtering application. The entire code is on this GitHub link:

https://github.com/jalajthanaki/NLPython/blob/master/ch8/Spamflteringapplica
tion/Spam_filtering_logistic_regression.ipynb

In spam filtering, we will use the `CountVectorizer` API of `scikit-learn` to generate the features, then train using `LogisticRegression`. You can see the code snippet in *Figure 8.24*:

```python
# import and instantiate CountVectorizer (with the default parameters)
from sklearn.feature_extraction.text import CountVectorizer
# instantiate the vectorizer
vect = CountVectorizer()
# learn training data vocabulary, then use it to create a document-term matrix
vect.fit(X_train)
X_train_dtm = vect.transform(X_train)

# equivalently: combine fit and transform into a single step
X_train_dtm = vect.fit_transform(X_train)

# examine the document-term matrix
X_train_dtm

<4179x7456 sparse matrix of type '<type 'numpy.int64'>'
        with 55209 stored elements in Compressed Sparse Row format>

# transform testing data (using fitted vocabulary) into a document-term matrix
X_test_dtm = vect.transform(X_test)
X_test_dtm

<1393x7456 sparse matrix of type '<type 'numpy.int64'>'
        with 17604 stored elements in Compressed Sparse Row format>

from sklearn import linear_model
clf = linear_model.LogisticRegression(C=1e5)

# train the model using X_train_dtm (timing it with an IPython "magic command")
%time clf.fit(X_train_dtm, y_train)

CPU times: user 32 ms, sys: 0 ns, total: 32 ms
Wall time: 32.2 ms

LogisticRegression(C=100000.0, class_weight=None, dual=False,
          fit_intercept=True, intercept_scaling=1, max_iter=100,
          multi_class='ovr', n_jobs=1, penalty='l2', random_state=None,
          solver='liblinear', tol=0.0001, verbose=0, warm_start=False)

# make class predictions for X_test_dtm
y_pred_class = clf.predict(X_test_dtm)
```

Figure 8.24: Spam filtering using logistic regression

First, we perform some basic text analysis that will help us understand our data. Here, we have converted the text data to a vector format using `scikit-learn` API, `Count Vectorizer()`. This API uses **term frequency-inverse document frequency (tf-idf)** underneath. We have divided our dataset into a training dataset and a testing set so that we can check how our classifier model performs on the test dataset. You can see the output in *Figure 8.25*:

```
# calculate accuracy of class predictions
from sklearn import metrics
metrics.accuracy_score(y_test, y_pred_class)

0.98851399856424982

# print the confusion matrix
metrics.confusion_matrix(y_test, y_pred_class)

array([[1205,    3],
       [  13,  172]])

# print message text for the false positives (ham incorrectly classified as spam)
X_test[y_test < y_pred_class]

2340    Cheers for the message Zogtorius. I[]ve been st...
4009    Forgot you were working today! Wanna chat, but...
1497    I'm always on yahoo messenger now. Just send t...
Name: message, dtype: object

# print message text for the false negatives (spam incorrectly classified as ham)
X_test[y_test > y_pred_class]

1777             Call FREEPHONE 0800 542 0578 now!
763     Urgent Ur £500 guaranteed award is still uncla...
3132    LookAtMe!: Thanks for your purchase of a video...
1875    Would you like to see my XXX pics they are so ...
1893    CALL 09090900040 & LISTEN TO EXTREME DIRTY LIV...
4298    thesmszone.com lets you send free anonymous an...
4394    RECPT 1/3. You have ordered a Ringtone. Your o...
4949    Hi this is Amy, we will be sending you a free ...
761     Romantic Paris. 2 nights, 2 flights from £79 B...
19      England v Macedonia - dont miss the goals/team...
2821    INTERFLORA - []It's not too late to order Inter...
2247    Hi ya babe x u 4goten bout me?' scammers getti...
4514    Money i have won wining number 946 wot do i do...
Name: message, dtype: object
```

Figure 8.25: Output of spam filtering using logistic regression

Advantages of logistic regression

The following are the advantages of logistic regression:

- It can handle non-linear effects
- It can generate the probability score for each of the classes, which makes interpretation easy

Disadvantages of logistic regression

The following are the disadvantages of logistic regression:

- This classification technique is used for binary classification only. There are other algorithms which we can use if we want to classify data into more than two categories. We can use algorithms like random forest and decision tree for classifying the data into more than two categories.
- If you provide lots of features as input to this algorithm, then the features space increases and this algorithm doesn't perform well
- Chances of overfitting are high, which means that the classifier performs well on the training dataset but cannot generalize enough that it can predict the right target label for unseen data

Now it's time to explore the next algorithm, called **decision tree**.

Decision tree

Decision tree (DT) is one of the oldest ML algorithms. This algorithm is very simple, yet robust. This algorithm provides us with a tree structure to make any decision. Logistic regression is used for binary classification, but you can use a decision tree if you have more than two classes.

Let's understand the decision tree by way of an example. Suppose, Chris likes to windsurf, but he has preferences - he generally prefers sunny and windy days to enjoy it and doesn't surf on rainy or overcast days or less windy days either. Refer to *Figure 8.26*:

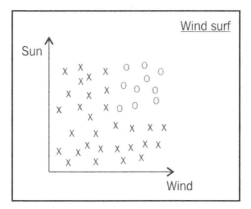

Figure 8.26: Toy dataset to understand the concept (Image credit: https://classroom.udacity.com)

As you can see, *o* (dots) are the happy weather conditions when Chris likes to wind surf and the *x* (crosses) are the bad weather conditions when Chris doesn't like to wind surf.

The data that I have drawn is not linearly separable, which means that you can't classify or separate the red crosses and blue dots just using a single line. You might think that if the goal is just to separate the blue dots and red crosses, then I can use two lines and achieve this. However, can a single line separate the blue dots and red crosses? The answer is no, and that is the reason why I have told you that this dataset is not linearly separable. So for this kind of scenario, we will use a decision tree.

What does a decision tree actually do for you? In layman's terms, decision tree learning is actually about asking multiple linear questions. Let's understand what I mean by linear questions.

Suppose we ask a question: Is it windy? You have two answers: Yes or No. We have a question that is related to wind, so we need to focus on the *x* axis of *Figure 8.26*. If our answer is: Yes, it's windy, then we should consider the right-hand side area that has red crosses as well as blue dots; if we answer: No, it isn't windy, then we need to consider all the red crosses on the left-hand side. For better understanding, you can refer to *Figure 8.27*:

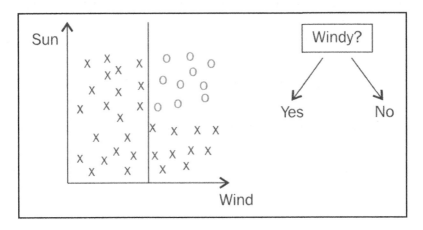

Figure 8.27: Representation of the question: Is it windy? (Image credit: https://classroom.udacity.com/courses/ud120)

As you can see in *Figure 8.27*, I have put one line that passes through the midpoint on the *x* axis. I have just chosen a midpoint, there is no specific reason for that. So I have drawn a black line. Red crosses on the left-hand side of the line represent: No, it's not windy, and red crosses on the right-hand side of the line represent: Yes, it's windy. On the left-hand side of the line, there are only red crosses and not a single blue dot there. If you select the answer, No, then actually you traverse with the branch labeled as No. The area on the left side has only red crosses, so you end up having all the data points belonging to the same class, which is represented by red crosses, and you will not ask further questions for that branch of the tree. Now, if you select the answer, Yes, then we need to focus on the data points that are on the right-hand side. You can see that there are two types of data points, blue dots as well as red crosses. So, in order to classify them, you need to come up with a linear boundary in such a way that the section formed by the line has only one type of data point. We will achieve this by asking another question: Is it sunny? This time, again, you have two possible answers - Yes or No. Remember that I have traversed the tree branch that has the answer of our first question in the form of Yes. So my focus is on the right-hand side of the data points, because there I have data points that are represented in the form of red crosses as well as blue dots. We have described the sun on the *y* axis, so you need to look at that axis and if you draw a line that passes through the midpoint of the *y* axis, then the section above the line represents the answer, Yes, it is a sunny day. All data points below the line represent the answer, No, it is not a sunny day. When you draw such a line and stop extending that line after the first line, then you can successfully segregate the data points that reside on the right-hand side. So the section above the line contains only blue dots and the section below the line, red crosses. You can see the horizontal line, in *Figure 8.28*:

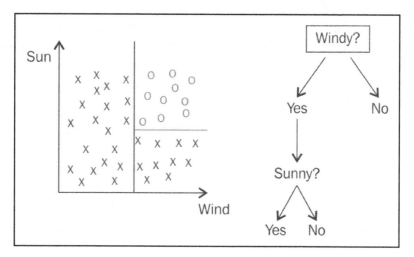

Figure 8.28: Grey line representing the classification done based on the first question

We can observe that by asking a series of questions or a series of linear questions, we actually classify the red crosses that represent when Chris doesn't surf and blue dots that represent when Chris surfs.

This is a very basic example that can help you understand how a decision tree works for classification problems. Here, we have built the tree by asking a series of questions as well as generating multiple linear boundaries to classify the data points. Let's take one numeric example so that it will be clearer to you. Refer to *Figure 8.29*:

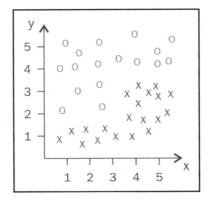

Figure 8.29: See the data points in the 2D graph (Image credit: https://classroom.udacity.com/courses/ud120)

You can see the given data points. Let's start with the *x* axis first. Which threshold value on the *x* axis do you want to choose so that you can obtain the best split for these data points? Think for a minute! I would like to select a line that passes the *x* axis at point **3**. So now you have two sections. Mathematically, I choose the best split for the given data points, that is, x <= 3 and *x* > 3. Refer to *Figure 8.30*:

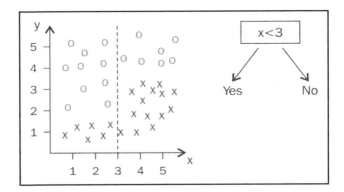

Figure 8.30: See the first linear question and decision boundary graph (Image credit : https://classroom.udacity.com/courses/ud120)

Let's focus on the left-hand side section first. Which value on the y axis would you prefer to choose so that you have only one type of data point in one section after drawing that line? What is the threshold on y axis that you select so you have one type of dataset in one section and the other type of dataset in the other section? I will choose the line that passes through the point **2** on the y axis. So, the data points above the line belong to one class and the data points below the line belong to the other class. Mathematically, $y <= 2$ gives you one class and $y > 2$ gives you the other class. Refer to *Figure 8.31*:

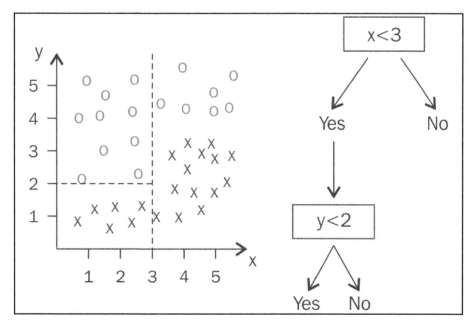

Figure 8.31: See the second linear question and decision boundary graph (Image credit: https://classroom.udacity.com/courses/ud120)

Now focus on the right-hand side part; for that part also, we need to choose a threshold with respect to the y axis. Here, the best threshold for a separation boundary is $y = 4$, so the section $y < 4$ has only red crosses and the section $y >= 4$ has only blue dots. So finally, with a series of linear questions, we are able to classify our data points. Refer to *Figure 8.32*:

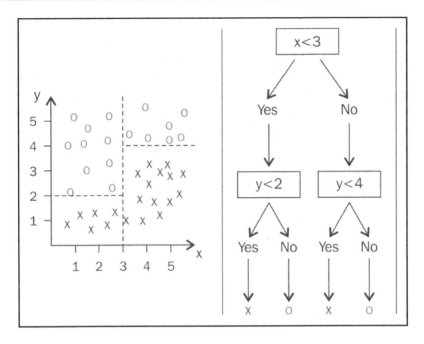

Figure 8.32: The final linear question and decision boundary graph (Image credit: https://classroom.udacity.com/courses/ud120)

Now you get an idea about the algorithm, but there may be a couple of questions in your mind. We have a visualization of the obtaining line, but how does the decision tree algorithm choose the best possible way to split data points and generate a decision boundary using the given features? Suppose I have more than two features, say ten features; then how will the decision tree know that it needs to use the second feature and not the third feature in the first time? So I'm going to answer all these questions by explaining the math behind a decision tree. We will look at an NLP-related example, so that you can see how a decision tree is used in NLP applications.

I have some questions related to decision trees let's answer them one by one. We will use visualization to obtain a linear boundary, but how does a decision tree recognize using which features and which feature value should it split the data? Let's see the mathematical term that is entropy. So, decision tree uses the concept of entropy to decide where to split the data. Let's understand entropy. Entropy is the measure of the impurity in a tree branch. So, if all data points in a tree branch belong to the same class, then entropy $E = 0$; otherwise, entropy $E > 0$ and $E <= 1$. If Entropy $E = 1$, then it indicates that the tree branch is highly impure or data points are evenly split between all the available classes. Let's see an example so that you can understand the concept of entropy and impurity.

We are making a spam filtering application and we have one feature, that is, words and phrases type. Now we will introduce another feature, that is, the minimum threshold count of appearing phrases in the dataset. Refer to *Figure 8.33*:

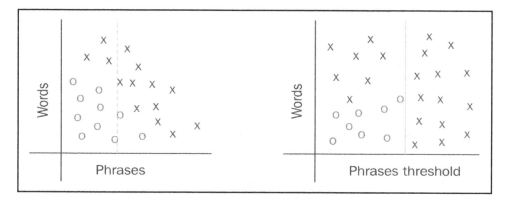

Figure 8.33: Graphs for entropy discussion

Now focus on the right-hand side graph. In this graph, the right-hand side section has only one kind of data points that are denoted by red crosses. So technically, all data points are homogenous as they belong to the same class. So, there is no impurity and the value of entropy is approximately zero. Now if you focus on the left-hand side graph and see its right-hand side section, you will find data points that belong to the other class label. This section has impurity and, thus, has high entropy. So, during the implementation of a decision tree, you need to find out the variables that can be used to define the split points, along with the variables. Another thing that you need to keep in mind is that you are trying to minimize the impurity in the data, so try to split the data according to that. We will see how to choose variables to perform a split in some time.

Now, let's first see the mathematical formula of entropy. Refer to *Figure 8.34*:

$$\textbf{Entropy} = \ \sum_{i=1}^{T} -p_i \log(p_i)$$

Figure 8.34: Entropy mathematical formula (Image credit: http://dni-institute.in/blogs/wp-content/uploads/2015/08/Entrop.png)

Let's see what pi is here. It is the fraction value for a given class. Let's say i is the class. T is the total value of the available class. You have four data points; if two points belong to class A and the other two belong to class B, then $T = 2$. We perform summation after generating log values using the fraction value. Now it's time to perform mathematical calculations for entropy and then I will let you know how we can use entropy to perform splitting on variables or features. Let's see an example to calculate entropy. You can find the data for the example in *Figure 8.35*:

Words	Phrases threshold count	Phrases type	Filtering
Positive meaning words	3	unusual	Spam
Positive meaning words	4	unusual	Spam
Negative meaning words	3	usual	Ham
Positive meaning words	4	usual	Ham

Figure 8.35: The dataset values for spam filtering calculation

If you focus on the **Filtering** column, you have two labels with the value **Spam** and two values with **Ham**-that is *SSHH*. Now answer some of the following questions:

- How many total data rows do we have? The answer is four
- How many times does the data label *S* occur in the **Filtering** column? The answer is two
- How many times does the data label *H* occur in the **Filtering** column? The answer is two
- To generate the fraction value for the class label *S*, you need to perform mathematics using the following formula:
  - *pS = No. of time S occurred / Total no. of data rows = 2/4 = 0.5*
- Now we need to calculate *p* for *H* as well:
  - *pH = No. of time H occurred / Total no. of data rows = 2/4 = 0.5*
- Now we have all the necessary values to generate the entropy. Focus on the formula given in *Figure 8.34*:
  - *Entropy = -pS* $\log_2(pS)$ -pH*$\log_2(pH)$ = -0.5 * log(0.5) -0.5*log(0.5) = 1.0*
- You can do this calculation using Python's math module

As you can see, we get the entropy $E = 1$. This is the most impure state, where data is evenly distributed among the available classes. So, entropy tells us about the state of the data whether classes are in an impure state or not.

Now we will look at the most awaited question: How will we know on which variable or using which feature we need to perform a split? To understand this, we need to understand information gain. This is one of the core concepts of the decision tree algorithm. Let me introduce the formula for **information gain (IG)**:

Information Gain (IG) = Entropy (Parent Node) - [Weight Average] Entropy (Children)

Now let's take a look at this formula. We are calculating the entropy of the parent node and subtracting the weighted entropy of the children. If we perform splitting on the parent node, decision tree will try to maximize the information gain. Using IG, the decision tree will choose the feature that we need to perform a split on. This calculation is done for all the available features, so the decision tree knows exactly where to split. You need to refer to *Figure 8.33*.

We have calculated entropy for the parent node: *E (Parent Node) = 1*. Now we will focus on words and calculate IG. Let's check whether we should perform a split using words with IG. Here, we are focusing on the **Words** column. So, let me answer some of the questions so that you understand the calculations of IG:

- There are how many total positive meaning words? The answer is three
- There are how many total negative meaning words? The answer is one
- So, for this branch, our entropy *E = 0*. We will use this when we are calculating weighted average entropy for the child node

Here, our decision tree looks as given in *Figure 8.36*:

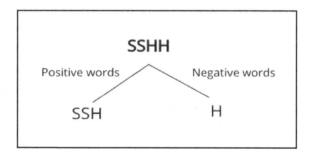

Figure 8.36: Decision trees first iteration

You can see that for the right-hand side node, the entropy is zero so there isn't any impurity in that branch, so we can stop there. However, if you look at the left-hand side node, it has the **SSH** class so we need to calculate entropy for each of the class labels. Let's do it step by step for the left-hand side node:

- *PS* = No. Of *S* label in branch/ Total no. of example in branch = 2/3
- *PH* = No. Of *H* label in branch/ Total no. of example in branch = 1/3
- Now entropy $E = -2/3 \log_2 (2/3) - 1/3 \log_2 (1/3) = 0.918$

In the next step, we need to calculate the weighted average entropy of the child nodes.

We have three data points as part of the left-hand branch and one data point as the right-hand branch, which you can see in *Figure 8.36*. So the values and formula looks as follows:

*Weight average entropy of children = Left hand branch data points / Total no of data points * (entropy for children in that branch) + Right hand branch data points / Total no of data points * (entropy for children in that branch)*

*Weight average entropy of children = [Weight Average] Entropy (Children) =¾ * 0.918 + ¼ * (0) = 0.6885*

Now it's time to obtain IG:

IG = Entropy (parent node) - [Weight Average] Entropy (Children). We have both parts with us-E (Parent Node) = 1 and [Weight Average] Entropy (Children) = 0.6885

So, the final calculation is as follows:

IG = 1 - 0.6885 = 0.3115

Let's focus on the phrase appeared count column and calculate the entropy for phrase count values three, which is $E_{three(3)} = 1.0$, entropy for phrase count values four is $E_{four(4)} = 1.0$; now [Weight Average] Entropy (Children) = 1.0 , IG = 1.0 -1.0 = 0. So, we are not getting any information gain on this split of this feature. So, we should not choose this feature.

Now let's focus on the column of phrases where we have mentioned the phrase category- **Unusual phrases** or **Usual phrases**. When we split data points using this column, we get the **Spam** class in one branch and **Ham** class in another branch. So here, you need to calculate IG on your own, but the *IG = 1*. We are getting the maximum IG. So we will choose this feature for the split. You can see the decision tree in *Figure 8.37*:

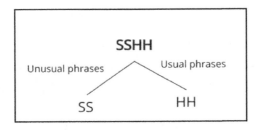

Figure 8.37: Decision tree generated using phrases type feature

If you have a high number of features, then the decision tree performs training very slowly because it calculates IG for each feature and performs a split by choosing the feature that provides maximum IG.

Now it's time to look at the NLP application that uses decision trees. We will redevelop spam filtering but this time, we will use a decision tree.

We have to just change the algorithm for the spam-filtering application and we have taken the same feature set that we generated previously so that you can compare the result of logistic regression and decision tree for spam filtering. Here, we will use the same features that are generated by the `CountVectorizer` API from `scikit-learn`. The code is at this GitHub link:

https://github.com/jalajthanaki/NLPython/blob/master/ch8/Spamflteringapplicatio n/Spam_filtering_logistic_regression.ipynb

You can see the code snippet in *Figure 8.38*:

```python
# import and instantiate CountVectorizer (with the default parameters)
from sklearn.feature_extraction.text import CountVectorizer
# instantiate the vectorizer
vect = CountVectorizer()
# learn training data vocabulary, then use it to create a document-term matrix
vect.fit(X_train)
X_train_dtm = vect.transform(X_train)

# equivalently: combine fit and transform into a single step
X_train_dtm = vect.fit_transform(X_train)

# examine the document-term matrix
X_train_dtm

<4179x7456 sparse matrix of type '<type 'numpy.int64'>'
        with 55209 stored elements in Compressed Sparse Row format>

# transform testing data (using fitted vocabulary) into a document-term matrix
X_test_dtm = vect.transform(X_test)
X_test_dtm

<1393x7456 sparse matrix of type '<type 'numpy.int64'>'
        with 17604 stored elements in Compressed Sparse Row format>

from sklearn import tree
clf = tree.DecisionTreeClassifier(criterion='entropy')

# train the model using X_train_dtm (timing it with an IPython "magic command")
%time clf.fit(X_train_dtm, y_train)

CPU times: user 88 ms, sys: 0 ns, total: 88 ms
Wall time: 89 ms

DecisionTreeClassifier(class_weight=None, criterion='entropy', max_depth=None,
            max_features=None, max_leaf_nodes=None,
            min_impurity_split=1e-07, min_samples_leaf=1,
            min_samples_split=2, min_weight_fraction_leaf=0.0,
            presort=False, random_state=None, splitter='best')

# make class predictions for X_test_dtm
y_pred_class = clf.predict(X_test_dtm)
```

Figure 8.38: Spam filtering using decision tree

You can see the output in *Figure 8.39*:

```
# make class predictions for X_test_dtm
y_pred_class = clf.predict(X_test_dtm)

# calculate accuracy of class predictions
from sklearn import metrics
metrics.accuracy_score(y_test, y_pred_class)

0.97056712132089018

# print the confusion matrix
metrics.confusion_matrix(y_test, y_pred_class)

array([[1184,   24],
       [  17,  168]])
```

Figure 8.39: Spam filtering output using decision tree

As you can see, we get low accuracy compared to logistic regression. Now it's time to see some tuning parameters that you can use to improve the accuracy of the ML-model.

Tunable parameters

In this section, I will explain some tunable `scikit-learn`. You can check the documentation at:

```
http://scikit-learn.org/stable/modules/generated/sklearn.tree.DecisionTreeCl
assifier.html#sklearn.tree.DecisionTreeClassifier.
```

I will explain the following parameters that you can use:

- There is one parameter in `scikit-learn`, which is `criterion`. You can set it as either `entropy` or `gini`. The `entropy` or `gini` are used to calculate IG. So they both have a similar mechanism to calculate IG, and decision tree will perform the split on the basis of the IG calculation given by `entropy` or `gini`.
- There is `min_sample_size` and its default value is `two`. So, the decision tree branch will split until it has more than or equal to two data elements per branch. Sometimes, decision tree tries to fit maximum training data and overfits the training data points. To prevent overfitting, you need to increase the `min_sample_size` from two to more like fifty or sixty.
- We can use tree pruning techniques, for which we will follow the bottom-up approach.

Now let's see the advantages and disadvantages of decision tree.

Advantages of decision tree

The following are the advantages that decision tree provide:

- Decision tree is simple and easy to develop
- Decision tree can be interpreted by humans easily and it's a white box algorithm
- It helps us determine the worst, best, and expected values for different scenarios

Disadvantages of decision tree

The following are the disadvantages that decision tree has:

- If you have a lot of features, then decision tree may have overfitting issues
- You need to be careful about the parameters that you are passing while training

We have seen the shortcomings of decision tree. Decision tree generally overfits the training dataset. We need to solve the problem using parameter tuning or a variant of the decision tree random forest ML algorithm. We will understand the random forest algorithm next.

Random forest

This algorithm is a variant of decision tree that solves the overfitting problem.

Random forest is capable of developing linear regression as well as classification tasks. Here, we are focusing on a classification task. It uses a very simple trick and works very nicely. The trick is that random forest uses a voting mechanism to improve the accuracy of the test result.

The random forest algorithm generates a random subset of the data from the training dataset and uses this to generate a decision tree for each of the subsets of the data. All these generated trees are called **random forest**. Now let's understand the voting mechanism. Once we have generated decision trees, we check the class label that each tree is provided for a specific data point. Suppose that we have generated three random forest decision trees. Two of them are saying some specific data point belongs to class A and the third decision tree predicts that the specific data point belongs to class B. The algorithm considers the higher vote and assigns the class label A for that specific data point.

For random forest, all the calculations for classification are similar to a decision tree. As promised, I will refer to the example that I gave in Chapter 5, *Feature Engineering and NLP Algorithms,* which is the custom POS tagger example. In that example, we used a decision tree. See the code on this GitHub link:

https://github.com/jalajthanaki/NLPython/blob/master/ch5/CustomPOStagger/ownp ostag.py.

Let's revisit the example and understand the features and code given in *figure 8.40*:

```
X, y = transform_to_dataset(training_sentences)
clf = Pipeline([
    ('vectorizer', DictVectorizer(sparse=False)),
    ('classifier', DecisionTreeClassifier(criterion='entropy'))
])

clf.fit(X[:10000],
        y[:10000])   # Use only the first 10K samples if you're running it multiple times. It takes a fair bit :)
```

Figure 8.40: Code snippet for the decision tree algorithm in scikit-learn

Advantages of random forest

The following are the advantages of random forest:

- It helps us prevent overfitting
- It can be used for regression as well as classification

Disadvantages of random forest

The following are the disadvantages of random forest:

- The random forest model can easily grow, which means that if the random subset of datasets is high, then we will get more decision trees, thus, we will get a group of trees, also referred as a forest of decision trees that may take a lot of memory
- For high-dimensional feature space, it is hard to interpret each node of the tree, especially when you have a high number of trees in one forest

Now it's time to understand our next ML algorithm - Naive Bayes.

Naive Bayes

In this section, we will understand the probabilistic ML algorithm that is used heavily in many data science applications. We will use this algorithm to develop the most famous NLP application - sentiment analysis, but before jumping into the application, we will understand how the Naive Bayes algorithm works. So, let's begin!

The Naive Bayes ML algorithm is based on Bayes theorem. According to this theorem, our most important assumption is that events are independent, which is a naive assumption, and that is the reason this algorithm is called **Naive Bayes**. So, let me give you an idea of independent events. In classification tasks, we have many features. If we use the Naive Bayes algorithm, then we assume that each and every feature that we are going to provide to the classifier is independent from each other, which means that the presence of a particular feature of the class doesn't affect any other feature. Let's take an example. You want to find out the sentiment of the sentence, It is very good! You have features such as bag of words, adjective phrase, and so on. Even if all these features depend on each other or depend on the existence of other features, all the properties carried by these features independently contribute to the probability that this sentence carries positive sentiment. This is the reason we call this algorithm Naive.

This algorithm is really simple, as well as a very powerful one. This works really well if you have a lot of data. It can classify more than two classes, so it is helpful in building a multi-class classifier. So, now, let's look at some points that will tell us how the Naive Bayes algorithm works. Let's understand the mathematics and probabilistic theorem behind it.

We will understand Bayes rule first. In very simple language, you have prior probability for some event, and you find some evidence of the same event in your test data and multiply them. Then you get the posterior probability that helps you derive your final predication. Don't worry about the terminology, we will get into those details.

Let me give you an equation first and then we will take one example so that you know what the calculation that we need to do is. See the equation in *Figure 8.41*:

$$P(c \mid x) = \frac{P(x \mid c) P(c)}{P(x)}$$

Likelihood → $P(x \mid c)$

Class Prior Probability → $P(c)$

Posterior Probability → $P(c \mid x)$

Predictor Prior Probability → $P(x)$

$$P(c \mid X) = P(x_1 \mid c) \times P(x_2 \mid c) \times \cdots \times P(x_n \mid c) \times P(c)$$

Figure 8.41: Naive-Bayes algorithm uses Bayes theorem equation (Image credit: http://www.saedsayad.com/images/Bayes_rule.png)

Here, $P(c|x)$ is the probability of class c, class c is the target, and x are the features or data attributes. $P(C)$ is the prior probability of class c, $P(x|c)$ is the estimation of the likelihood that is the probability of the predictor given a target class, and $P(x)$ is the prior probability of the predictor.

Let's use this equation to calculate an example. Suppose there is a medical test that helps identify whether a person has cancer or not. The prior probability of the person having that specific type of cancer is only *1 %*, which means $P(c) = 0.01 = 1\%$ and so $P(not\ c) = 0.99 = 99\%$. There is a *90%* chance that the test will show positive if the person has cancer. So prior probability of $P(Positive\ result\ |\ c) = 0.9 = 90\%$ and there is a *10%* chance that even if the person doesn't have cancer, the result will still show positive, so $P(Positive\ result\ |\ not\ C) = 0.1 = 10\%$.

Now, we need to check whether the person really has cancer. If the result showed positive, that probability is written as $P(c\ |\ Positive\ result)$, and if the person doesn't have cancer but still the result is positive, then that is denoted by $P(not\ c\ |\ Positive\ result)$. We need to calculate these two probabilities to derive the posterior probability. First, we need to calculate joint probability:

Joint $P(c\ |\ Positive\ result) = P(c) * P(Positive\ result\ |\ c) = 0.01\ x\ 0.9 = 0.009$

Joint $P(not\ c\ |\ Positive\ result) = P(not\ c) * P(Positive\ result\ |\ not\ c) = 0.99\ x\ 0.1 = 0.099$

The preceding probability is called **joint probability**. This will be helpful in deriving the final posterior probability. To get the posterior probability, we need to apply normalization:

$P(Positive\ result) = P(c\ |\ Positive\ result) + P(not\ c\ |\ Positive\ result) = 0.009 + 0.099 = 0.108$

Now the actual posterior probability is given as follows:

Posterior probability of $P(c\ |\ Positive\ result) = joint\ probability\ of\ P(c\ |\ Positive\ result)\ /\ P(Positive\ result) = 0.009\ /\ 0.108 = 0.083$

Posterior probability of $P(not\ c\ |\ Positive\ result) = joint\ probability\ of\ P(not\ c\ |\ Positive\ result)\ /\ P(Positive\ result) = 0.099\ /\ 0.108 = 0.916$

If you sum up the Posterior probability of $P(c\ |\ Positive\ result)$ + Posterior probability of $P(not\ c\ |\ Positive\ result)$, it should be = *1*. And in this case, it does sum up to 1.

There is a lot of mathematics going on, so I will draw a diagram for you that will help you understand these things. Refer to *Figure 8.42*:

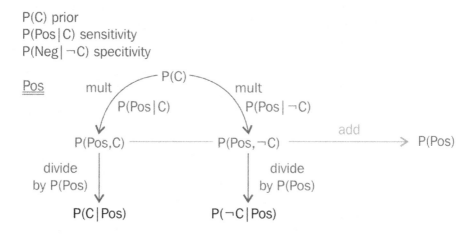

Figure 8.42: Posterior probability calculation diagram (Image credit: https://classroom.udacity.com/courses/ud120/lessons/2254358555/concepts/30144285350923)

We will extend this concept to an NLP application. Here, we will take an NLP-based basic example. Suppose there are two persons - Chris and Sara. We have the e-mail details of Chris and Sara. They both use words such as life, love, and deal. For simplicity, we are considering only three words. They both use these three words at different frequencies.

Chris uses the word love only 1% of the time in his mail, whereas he uses the word deal 80% of the time, and life 1% of the time. Sara, on the other hand, uses the word love 50% of the time, deal 20% of the time, and life 30 % of the time. If we have a new e-mail, then we need to decide whether it is written by Chris or Sara. Prior probability of P(Chris) = 0.5 and P(Sara) = 0.5.

The mail has the sentence Life Deal so the probability calculation is for P(Chris| "Life Deal") = P(life) * P(deal) * P(Chris) = 0.04 and the calculation for P(Sara |"Life Deal") = P(life) * P(deal) * P(Sara) = 0.03. Now, let's apply normalization and generate the actual probability. For this, we need to calculate joint probability = P(Chris| "Life Deal") + P(Sara | "Life Deal") = 0.07. The following are the actual probability values:

P(Chris| "Life Deal") = 0.04 / 0.07 = 0.57

P(Sara| "Life Deal") = 0.03 / 0.07 = 0.43

The sentence Life Deal is more likely to be written by Chris. This is the end of the example and now it's time for practical implementation. Here, we are developing the most famous NLP application, that is, sentiment analysis. We will do sentiment analysis for text data so we can say that sentiment analysis is the text analysis of opinions that are generated by humans. Sentiment analysis helps us analyze what our customers are thinking about a certain product or event.

For sentiment analysis, we will use the bag-of-words approach. You can also use artificial neural networks, but I'm explaining a basic and easy approach. You can see the code on this GitHub link:

```
https://github.com/jalajthanaki/NLPython/blob/master/ch8/sentimentanalysis/sent
imentanalysis_NB.py
```

We will use the `TfidVectorizer` API of `scikit-learn` as well as `MultinomialNB` Naive Bayes. See the code snippet in *Figure 8.43*:

```python
# Create feature vectors
vectorizer = TfidfVectorizer(min_df=5,
                             max_df = 0.8,
                             sublinear_tf=True,
                             use_idf=True)
train_vectors = vectorizer.fit_transform(train_data)
test_vectors = vectorizer.transform(test_data)

clf = MultinomialNB()
t0 = time.time()
clf.fit(train_vectors, train_labels)
t1 = time.time()
prediction = clf.predict(test_vectors)
t2 = time.time()
time_train = t1-t0
time_predict = t2-t1
```

Figure 8.43: Code snippet for sentiment analysis using Naive Bayes

See the output in *Figure 8.44*:

```
Results for NaiveBayes (MultinomialNB)
Training time: 0.003208s; Prediction time: 0.000266s
                precision    recall  f1-score   support

          neg       0.81      0.92      0.86       100
          pos       0.91      0.78      0.84       100

avg / total         0.86      0.85      0.85       200
```

Figure 8.44: Output for sentiment analysis using Naive Bayes

Now it's time to look at some tuning parameters.

Tunable parameters

For this algorithm, sometimes you need to apply smoothing. Now, what do I mean by smoothing? Let me give you a very brief idea about it. Some of the words come in the training data and our algorithm uses that data to generate an ML-model. If the ML-model sees the words that are not in the training data but present in the testing data, then at that time, our algorithm cannot predict things well. We need to solve this situation. So, as a solution, we need to apply smoothing, which means that we are also calculating the probability for rare words and that is the tunable parameter in scikit-learn. It's just a flag--if you enable it, it will perform smoothing or if you disable it, then smoothing will not be applied.

Advantages of Naive Bayes

The following are the advantages that the Naive Bayes algorithm provides:

- You can deal with high-dimensional feature space using the Naive Bayes algorithm
- It can be used to classify more than two classes

Disadvantages of Naive Bayes

The following are the disadvantages of the Naive Bayes algorithm:

- If you have a phrase composed of different words having different meanings, then this algorithm will not help you. You have a phrase, Gujarat Lions. This is the name of a cricket team, but Gujarat is a state in India and lion is an animal. So, the Naive Bayes algorithm takes the individual words and interprets them separately, and so this algorithm cannot correctly interpret Gujarat Lions.

- If some categorical data appears in the testing dataset only and not in the training data, then Naive Bayes won't provide a prediction for that. So, to solve this kind of problem, we need to apply smoothing techniques. You can read about this on this link: https://stats.stackexchange.com/questions/108797/in-naive-bayes-why-bother-with-laplacian-smoothing-when-we-have-unknown-words-i

- Now it is time to look at the last classification algorithm, support vector machine. So, let's begin!

Support vector machine

This is the last but not least supervised ML algorithm that we will look in this chapter. It is called **support vector machine (SVM)**. This algorithm is used for classification tasks as well as regression tasks. This algorithm is also used for multi-class classification tasks.

SVM takes labeled data and tries to classify the data points by separating them using a line that is called the **hyperplane**. The goal is to obtain an optimal hyperplane that will be used to categorize the existing as well as new, unseen examples. How to obtain an optimal hyperplane is what we are going to understand here.

Let's understand the term optimal hyperplane first. We need to obtain the hyperplane in such a way that the obtained hyperplane maximizes the distances to its nearest points of all the classes and this distance is called **margin**. Here, we will talk about a binary classifier. Margin is the distance between the hyperplane (or line) and the nearest point of either of the two classes. SVM tries to maximize the margin. Refer to *Figure 8.45*:

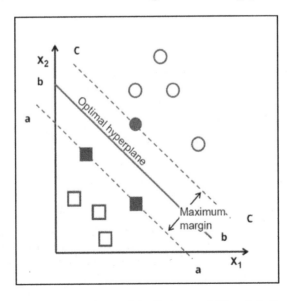

Figure 8.45: SVM classifier basic image (Image credit: http://docs.opencv.org/2.4/_images/optimal-hyperplane.png)

In the given figure, there are three lines *a*, *b*, and *c*. Now, choose the line that you think best separates the data points. I would pick line *b* because it maximizes the margin from two classes and the other lines *a* and *c* don't do that.

Note that SVM first tries to perform the classification task perfectly and then tries to maximize the margin. So for SVM, performing the classification task correctly is the first priority. SVM can obtain the linear hyperplane as well as generate a non-linear hyperplane. So, let's understand the math behind this.

If you have n features, then using SVM, you can draw *n-1* dimensional hyperplane. If you have a two-dimensional feature space, then you can draw a hyperplane that is one-dimensional. If you have a three-dimensional feature space, then you can draw a two-dimensional hyperplane. In any ML algorithm, we actually try minimizing our loss function, so we first define the loss function for SVM. SVM uses the hinge loss function. We use this loss function and try to minimize our loss and obtain the maximum margin for our hyperplane. The hinge loss function equation is given as follows:

$C\ (x,\ y,\ f(x)) = (1 - y * f(x))_+$

Here, *x* is sample data points, *y* is true label, *f(x)* is the predicted label, and *C* is the loss function. What the + sign in the equation denotes is, when we calculate *y*f(x)* and it comes >= 1, then we try to subtract it from *1* and get a negative value. We don't want this, and so to denote that, we put the + sign:

$$C\ (x,y,\ f(x)) = 0 \qquad if\ y * f(x) >= 0$$

$$= 1 - y * f(x) \quad else$$

Now it's time to define the objective function that takes the loss function, as well as a lambda term called a **regularization term**. We will see what it does for us. However, it is also a tuning parameter. See the mathematics equation in *Figure 8.46*:

$$min_w \lambda \| w \|^2 + \sum_{i=1}^{n} (1 - y_i * f(x_i, w))$$

Figure 8.46: Objective function with regularization term lambda

SVM has two tuning parameters that we need to take care of. One of the terms is the lambda that denotes the regularization term. If the regularization term is too high, then our ML-model overfits and cannot generalize the unseen data. If it is too low, then it underfits and we get a huge training error. So, we need a precise value for the regularization term as well. We need to take care of the regularization term that helps us prevent overfitting and we need to minimize our loss. So, we take a partial derivative for both of these terms; the following are the derivatives for the regularization term and loss function that we can use to perform gradient descent so that we can minimize our loss and get an accurate regularization value. See the partial derivative equation in *Figure 8.47*:

$$\frac{\delta}{\delta w_k} \lambda \|w\|^2 = 2\lambda w_k$$

Figure 8.47: Partial derivative for regularization term

See the partial derivative for the loss function in *Figure 8.48*:

$$\frac{\delta}{\delta w_k} \left(1 - y_i \left\langle x_i, w \right\rangle\right)_+ = \begin{cases} 0, & \text{if}_{y_i} \left\langle x_i, w \right\rangle \geq 1 \\ -y_i x_{ik}, & \text{else} \end{cases}$$

Figure 8.48: Partial derivative for loss function

We need to calculate the values of the partial derivative and update the weight accordingly. If we misclassify the data point, then we need to use the following equation to update the weight. Refer to *Figure 8.49*:

$$y_i \left\langle x_i, w \right\rangle < 1$$

Figure 8.49: Misclassification condition

So if y is < 1, then we need to use the following equation in *Figure 8.50*:

$$w = w + \eta\left(y_i x_i - 2\lambda w\right)$$

Figure 8.50: Weight update rule using this equation for the misclassification condition

Here, the long n shape is called eta and it denotes the learning rate. Learning rate is a tuning parameter that shows you how fast your algorithm should run. This also needs an accurate value because, if it is too high, then the training will complete too fast and the algorithm will miss the global minimum. On the other hand, if it is too slow, then it will take too much time to train and may never converge at all.

If misclassification happens, then we need to update our loss function as well as the regularization term.

Now, what if the algorithm correctly classifies the data point? In this case, we don't need to update the loss function; we just need to update our regularization parameter that you can see using the equation given in *Figure 8.51*:

$$w = w + \eta\left(-2\lambda w\right)$$

Figure 8.51: Updating the weight for regularization

When we have an appropriate value of regularization and the global minima, then we can classify all the points in SVM; at that time, the margin value also becomes the maximum.

If you want to use SVM for a non-linear classifier, then you need to apply the kernel trick. Briefly, we can say that the kernel trick is all about converting lower feature space into higher feature space that introduces the non-linear attributes so that you can classify the dataset. See the example in *Figure 8.52*:

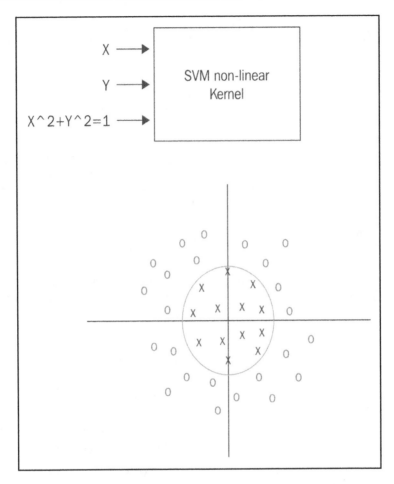

Figure 8.52: Non-linear SVM example

To classify this data, we have **X**, **Y** feature. We introduce the new non-linear feature, $X^2 + Y^2$, which helps us draw a hyperplane that can classify the data correctly.

So, now it's time to implement the SVM algorithm and we will develop the sentiment analysis application again, but this time, I'm using SVM and seeing what the difference is in the accuracy. You can find the code on this GitHub link:

```
https://github.com/jalajthanaki/NLPython/blob/master/ch8/sentimentanalysis/sent
imentanalysis_SVM.py
```

You can see the code snippet in *Figure 8.53*:

```
# Create feature vectors
vectorizer = TfidfVectorizer(min_df=5,
                             max_df = 0.8,
                             sublinear_tf=True,
                             use_idf=True)
train_vectors = vectorizer.fit_transform(train_data)
test_vectors = vectorizer.transform(test_data)

# Perform classification with SVM, kernel=rbf
classifier_rbf = svm.SVC()
t0 = time.time()
classifier_rbf.fit(train_vectors, train_labels)
t1 = time.time()
prediction_rbf = classifier_rbf.predict(test_vectors)
t2 = time.time()
time_rbf_train = t1-t0
time_rbf_predict = t2-t1

# Perform classification with SVM, kernel=linear
classifier_linear = svm.SVC(kernel='linear')
t0 = time.time()
classifier_linear.fit(train_vectors, train_labels)
t1 = time.time()
prediction_linear = classifier_linear.predict(test_vectors)
t2 = time.time()
time_linear_train = t1-t0
time_linear_predict = t2-t1
```

Figure 8.53: Sentiment analysis using SVM

You can find the output in *Figure 8.54*:

```
Results for SVC(kernel=rbf)
Training time: 6.319218s; Prediction time: 0.680047s
                precision    recall  f1-score    support

          neg       0.86      0.75      0.80        100
          pos       0.78      0.88      0.83        100

avg / total         0.82      0.81      0.81        200

Results for SVC(kernel=linear)
Training time: 5.752379s; Prediction time: 0.565493s
                precision    recall  f1-score    support

          neg       0.91      0.92      0.92        100
          pos       0.92      0.91      0.91        100

avg / total         0.92      0.92      0.91        200

Results for LinearSVC()
Training time: 0.034271s; Prediction time: 0.000185s
                precision    recall  f1-score    support

          neg       0.92      0.94      0.93        100
          pos       0.94      0.92      0.93        100

avg / total         0.93      0.93      0.93        200
```

Figure 8.54: Output of SVM

Now it's time to look at some tuning parameters. Let's take a look!

Tunable parameters

Let's check out some of the SVM tuning parameters that can help us:

- `scikit-learn` provides a tuning parameter for the kernel trick that is very useful. You can use various types of kernels, such as linear, rbf, and so on.
- There are other parameters called **C** and **gamma**.
- C controls the trade-off between a smooth decision boundary and classifying the training points correctly. A large value of C gives you more correct training points.
- Gamma can be useful if you are trying to set your margin. If you set high values for the gamma, then only nearby data points are taken into account to draw a decision boundary, and if you have low values for gamma, then points that are far from the decision boundary are also taken into account to measure whether the decision boundary maximizes the margin or not.

Now it's time to look at the advantages and disadvantages of SVM.

Advantages of SVM

The following are the advantages that the SVM algorithm provides to us:

- It performs well for complicated datasets
- It can be used for a multiclass classifier

Disadvantages of SVM

The following are the disadvantages of the SVM algorithm:

- It will not perform well when you have a very large dataset because it takes a lot of training time
- It will not work effectively when the data is too noisy

This is the end of the supervised ML algorithms. You learned a lot of math and concepts, and if you want to explore more, then you can try out the following exercise.

Exercise

- You need to explore **K-Nearest Neighbor (KNN)** and its application in the NLP domain
- You need to explore AdaBoost and its application in the NLP domain

We have covered a lot of cool classification techniques used in NLP and converted the black box ML algorithms to white box. So, now you know what is happening inside the algorithms. We have developed NLP applications as well, so now this is the time to jump into unsupervised ML.

Unsupervised ML

This is another type of machine learning algorithm. When we don't have any labeled data, then we can use unsupervised machine learning algorithms. In the NLP domain, there is a common situation where you can't find the labeled dataset, then this type of ML algorithm comes to our rescue.

Here, we will discuss the unsupervised ML algorithm called K-means clustering. This algorithm has many applications. Google has used this kind of unsupervised learning algorithms for so many of their products. YouTube video suggestions use the clustering algorithm.

The following image will give you an idea of how data points are represented in unsupervised ML algorithms. Refer to *Figure 8.55*:

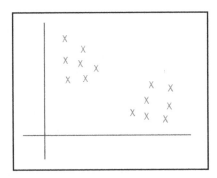

Figure 8.55: A general representation of data points in an unsupervised ML algorithm

As you can see in *Figure 8.55*, the data points don't have a label associated with them, but visually, you can see that they form some groups or clusters. We will actually try to figure out the structure in the data using unsupervised ML algorithms so that we can derive some fruitful insight for unseen data points.

Here, we will look at the k-means clustering algorithm and develop the document classification example that is related to the NLP domain. So, let's begin!

k-means clustering

In this section, we will discuss the k-means clustering algorithm. We will get an understanding of the algorithm first. k-means clustering uses the iterative refinement technique.

Let's understand some of the basics about the k-means algorithm. k refers to how many clusters we want to generate. Now, you can choose a random point and put the centroid at this point. The number of centroids in k-means clustering is not more than the value of k, which means not more than the cluster value k.

This algorithm has the two following steps that we need to reiterate:

1. The first step is to assign the centroid.
2. The second step is to calculate the optimization step.

To understand the steps of the k-means, we will look at an example. Before that, I would like to recommend that you check out this animated image that will give you a lot of understanding about k-means:

`https://github.com/jalajthanaki/NLPython/blob/master/ch8/K_means_clustering/K`
`-means_convergence.gif`.

Now, let's take an example. You have five data points, which are given in the table, and we want to group these data points into two clusters, so k = 2. Refer to *Figure 8.56*:

Data Points	X	Y
A	1	1
B	1	0
C	0	2
D	2	4
E	3	5

Figure 8.56: k-mean clustering data points for calculation

We have chosen point *A(1,1)* and point *C(0,2)* for the assignment of our centroid. This is the end of the assign step, now let's understand the optimization step.

We will calculate the Euclidean distance from every point to this centroid. The equation for the Euclidean distance is given in *Figure 8.57*:

$$\sqrt{\sum_{i=0}^{n}(Xi - X\,mean)^2 + (Yi - Y\,mean)^2}$$

Figure 8.57: Euclidean distance for the k-means clustering algorithm

Every time, we need to calculate the Euclidean distance from both centroids. Let's check the calculation. The starting centroid mean is *C1 = (1,1)* and *C2 = (0,2)*. Here, we want to make two cluster that is the reason we take two centroids.

Iteration 1

For point $A = (1,1)$:

$C1 = (1,1)$ so $ED = Square\ root\ ((1-1)^2 + (1-1)^2) = 0$

$C2 = (0,2)$ so $ED = Square\ root\ ((1-0)^2 + (1-2)^2) = 1.41$

Here, $C1 < C2$, so point A belongs to cluster 1.

For point $B = (1,0)$:

$C1 = (1,1)$ so $ED = Square\ root\ ((1-1)^2 + (0-1)^2) = 1$

$C2 = (0,2)$ so $ED = Square\ root\ ((1-0)^2 + (0-2)^2) = 2.23$

Here, $C1 < C2$, so point B belongs to cluster 1.

For point $C = (0,2)$:

$C1 = (1,1)$ so $ED = Square\ root\ ((0-1)^2 + (2-1)^2) = 1.41$

$C2 = (0,2)$ so $ED = Square\ root\ ((0-0)^2 + (2-2)^2) = 0$

Here, $C1 > C2$, so point C belongs to cluster 2.

For point $D = (2,4)$:

$C1 = (1,1)$ so $ED = Square\ root\ ((2-1)^2 + (4-1)^2) = 3.16$

$C2 = (0,2)$ so $ED = Square\ root\ ((2-0)^2 + (4-2)^2) = 2.82$

Here, $C1 > C2$, so point C belongs to cluster 2.

For point $E = (3,5)$:

$C1 = (1,1)$ so $ED = Square\ root\ ((3-1)^2 + (5-1)^2) = 4.47$

$C2 = (0,2)$ so $ED = Square\ root\ ((3-0)^2 + (5-2)^2) = 4.24$

Here, $C1 > C2$, so point C belongs to cluster 2.

After the first iteration, our cluster looks as follows. Cluster $C1$ has points A and B, and $C2$ has points C, D, and E. So, here, we need to calculate the centroid mean value again, as per the new cluster point:

$C1 = XA + XB / 2 = (1+1) / 2 = 1$

$C1 = YA + YB / 2 = (1+0) / 2 = 0.5$

So new $C1 = (1,0.5)$

$C2 = Xc + XD + XE / 3 = (0+2+3) / 3 = 1.66$

$C2 = Yc + YD + YE / 3 = (2+4+5) / 3 = 3.66$

So new $C2 = (1.66,3.66)$

We need to do all the calculations again in the same way as *Iteration 1*. So we get the values as follows.

Iteration 2

For point $A = (1,1)$:

$C1 = (1,0.5)$ so $ED = Square\ root\ ((1-1)^2 + (1-0.5)^2) = 0.5$

$C2 = (1.66,3.66)$ so $ED = Square\ root\ ((1-1.66)^2 + (1-3.66)^2) = 2.78$

Here, $C1 < C2$, so point A belongs to cluster 1.

For point $B = (1,0)$:

$C1 = (1,0.5)$ so $ED = Square\ root\ ((1-1)^2 + (0-0.5)^2) = 1$

$C2 = (1.66,3.66)$ so $ED = Square\ root\ ((1-1.66)^2 + (0-3.66)^2) = 3.76$

Here, $C1 < C2$, so point B belongs to cluster 1.

For point $C = (0,2)$:

$C1 = (1,0.5)$ so $ED = Square\ root\ ((0-1)^2 + (2-0.5)^2) = 1.8$

$C2 = (1.66, 3.66)$ so $ED = Square\ root\ ((0-1.66)^2 + (2-3.66)^2) = 2.4$

Here, $C1 < C2$, so point C belongs to cluster 1.

For point $D = (2,4)$:

$C1 = (1,0.5)$ so $ED = Square\ root\ ((2-1)^2 + (4-0.5)^2) = 3.6$

$C2 = (1.66,3.66)$ so $ED = Square\ root\ ((2-1.66)^2 + (4-3.66)^2) = 0.5$

Here, $C1 > C2$, so point C belongs to cluster 2.

For point $E = (3,5)$:

C1 = (1,0.5) so ED = Square root ((3-1)^2 + (5-0.5)^2) = 4.9

C2 = (1.66,3.66) so ED = Square root ((3-1.66)^2 + (5-3.66)^2) = 1.9

Here, *C1 > C2*, so point *C* belongs to cluster 2.

After the second iteration, our cluster looks as follows. *C1* has points *A*, *B*, and *C*, and *C2* has points *D* and *E*:

C1 = XA + XB + Xc / 3 = (1+1+0) / 3 = 0.7

C1 = YA + YB + Yc / 3 = (1+0+2) / 3 = 1

So new *C1 = (0.7,1)*

C2 = XD + XE / 2 = (2+3) / 2 = 2.5

C2 = YD + YE / 2 = (4+5) / 2 = 4.5

So new *C2 = (2.5,4.5)*

We need to do iterations until the clusters don't change. So this is the reason why this algorithm is called an **iterative algorithm**. This is the intuition of the K-means clustering algorithm. Now we will look at a practical example in the document classification application.

Document clustering

Document clustering helps you with a recommendation system. Suppose you have a lot of research papers and you don't have tags for them. You can use the k-means clustering algorithm, which can help you to form clusters as per the words appearing in the documents. You can build an application that is news categorization. All news from the same category should be combined together; you have a superset category, such as sports news, and this sports news category contains news about cricket, football, and so on.

Here, we will categorize movies into five different genres. The code credit goes to Brandon Rose. You can check out the code on this GitHub link:

```
https://github.com/jalajthanaki/NLPython/blob/master/ch8/K_means_clustering/K-m
ean_clustering.ipynb.
```

See the code snippet in *Figure 8.58*:

```
from sklearn.cluster import KMeans

num_clusters = 5

km = KMeans(n_clusters=num_clusters)

%time km.fit(tfidf_matrix)

clusters = km.labels_.tolist()
```

Figure 8.58: A short code snippet of the K-means algorithm

See the output in *Figure 8.59*:

Top terms per cluster:

Cluster 0 words: family, home, mother, war, house, dies,

Cluster 0 titles: Schindler's List, One Flew Over the Cuckoo's Nest, Gone with the Wind, The Wizard of Oz, Titanic, Forrest Gump, E.T. the Extra-Terrestrial, The Silence of the Lambs, Gandhi, A Streetcar Named Desire, The Best Years of Our Lives, My Fair Lady, Ben-Hur, Doctor Zhivago, The Pianist, The Exorcist, Out of Africa, Good Will Hunting, Terms of Endearment, Giant, The Grapes of Wrath, Close Encounters of the Third Kind, The Graduate, Stagecoach, Wuthering Heights,

Cluster 1 words: police, car, killed, murders, driving, house,

Figure 8.59: Output of k-means clustering

You can refer to this link for hierarchical clustering:

http://brandonrose.org/clustering.

Advantages of k-means clustering

These are the advantages that k-means clustering provides us with:

- It is a very simple algorithm for an NLP application
- It solves the main problem as it doesn't need tagged data or result labels, you can use this algorithm for untagged data

Disadvantages of k-means clustering

These are the disadvantages of k-means clustering:

- Initialization of the cluster center is a really crucial part. Suppose you have three clusters and you put two centroids in the same cluster and the other one in the last cluster. Somehow, k-means clustering minimizes the Euclidean distance for all the data points in the cluster and it will become stable, so actually, there are two centroids in one cluster and the third one has one centroid. In this case, you end up having only two clusters. This is called the **local minimum** problem in clustering.

This is the end of the unsupervised learning algorithms. Here, you have learned about the k-means clustering algorithm and developed the document classification application. If you want to learn more about this technique, try out the exercise.

Exercise

You need to explore hierarchical clustering and its application in the NLP domain.

Our next section is very interesting. We will look at semi-supervised machine learning techniques. Here, we will get an overview of them. So, let's understand these techniques.

Semi-supervised ML

Semi-supervised ML or **semi-supervised learning** (**SSL**) is basically used when you have a training dataset that has a target concept or target label for some data in the dataset, and the other part of the data doesn't have any label. If you have this kind of dataset, then you can apply semi-supervised ML algorithms. When we have a very small amount of labeled data and a lot of unlabeled data, then we can use semi-supervised techniques. If you want to build an NLP tool for any local language (apart from English) and you have a very small amount of labeled data, then you can use the semi-supervised approach. In this approach, we will use a classifier that uses the labeled data and generates an ML-model. This ML-model is used to generate labels for the unlabeled dataset. The classifiers are used for high-confidence predictions on the unlabeled dataset. You can use any appropriate classifier algorithm to classify the labeled data.

Semi-supervised techniques are a major research area, especially for NLP applications. Last year, Google Research developed semi supervised techniques that are graph-based:

```
https://research.googleblog.com/2016/10/graph-powered-machine-learning-at-googl
e.html.
```

For better understanding, you can also read some of the really interesting stuff given here:
`https://medium.com/@jrodthoughts/google-expander-and-the-emergen`
`ce-of-semi-supervised-learning-1919592bfc49.`
`https://arxiv.org/ftp/arxiv/papers/1511/1511.06833.pdf.`
`http://www.aclweb.org/anthology/W09-2208.`
`http://cogprints.org/5859/1/Thesis-David-Nadeau.pdf.`
`https://www.cmpe.boun.edu.tr/~ozgur/papers/896_Paper.pdf.`
`http://graph-ssl.wdfiles.com/local--files/blog%3A_start/graph_ss`
`l_acl12_tutorial_slides_final.pdf.`

Those interested in research can develop novel SSL techniques for any NLP application.

Now we have completed our ML algorithms section. There are some critical points that we need to understand. Now it's time to explore these important concepts.

Other important concepts

In this section, we will look at those concepts that help us know how the training on our dataset using ML algorithms is going, how you should judge whether the generated ML-model will be able to generalize unseen scenarios or not, and what signs tell you that your ML-model can't generalize the unseen scenarios properly. Once you detect these situations, what steps should you take? What are the widely used evaluation matrices for NLP applications?

So, let's find answers to all these questions. I'm going to cover the following topics. We will look at all of them one by one:

- Bias-variance trade-off
- Underfitting
- Overfitting
- Evaluation matrix

Bias-variance trade-off

Here, we will look at a high-level idea about the bias-variance trade-off. Let's understand each term one by one.

Let's first understand the term bias. When you are performing training using an ML algorithm and you see that your generated ML-model doesn't perform differently with respect to your first round of training iteration, then you can immediately recognize that the ML algorithm has a high bias. In this situation, ML algorithms have no capacity to learn from the given data so it's not learning new things that you expect your ML algorithm to learn. If your algorithm has very high bias, then eventually it just stops learning. Suppose you are building a sentiment analysis application and you have come up with the ML-model. Now you are not happy with the ML-model's accuracy and you want to improve the model. You will train by adding some new features and changing some algorithmic parameters. Now this newly generated model will not perform well or perform differently on the testing data, which is an indication for you that you may have high bias. Your ML algorithm won't converge in the expected way so that you can improve the ML-model result.

Let's understand the second term, variance. So, you use any ML algorithm to train your model and you observe that you get very good training accuracy. However, you apply the same ML-model to generate the output for an unseen testing dataset and your ML-model doesn't work well. This situation, where you have very good training accuracy and the ML-model doesn't turn out well for the unseen data, is called a **high variance** situation. So, here, the ML-model can only replicate the predictions or output that it has seen in the training data and doesn't have enough bias that it can generalize the unseen situation. In other words, you can say that your ML algorithm is trying to remember each of the training examples and, at the end, it just mimics that output on your testing dataset. If you have a high variance problem, then your model converges in such a way that it tries to classify each and every example of the dataset in a certain category. This situation leads us to overfitting. I will explain what overfitting is, so don't worry! We will be there in a few minutes.

To overcome both of the preceding bad situations, we really need something that lies in the middle, which means no high bias and no high variance. The art of generating the most bias and best variance for ML algorithms leads to the best optimal ML-Model. Your ML-model may not be perfect, but it's all about generating the best bias-variance trade-off.

In the next section, you will learn the concepts of *Underfitting* and *Overfitting* as well as tricks that help you get rid of these high bias and high variance scenarios.

Underfitting

In this section, we will discuss the term underfitting. What is underfitting and how is it related to the bias-variance trade-off?

Suppose you train the data using any ML algorithm and you get a high training error. Refer to *Figure 8.60*:

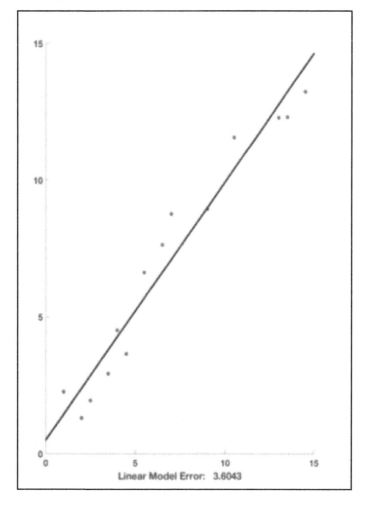

Figure 8.60: Graph indicating a high training error (Image credit: http://www.learnopencv.com/wp-content/uploads/2017/02/bias-variance-tradeoff.png)

The preceding situation, where we get a very high training error, is called **underfitting**. ML algorithms just can't perform well on the training data. Now, instead of a linear decision boundary, we will try a higher degree of polynomials. Refer to *Figure 8.61*:

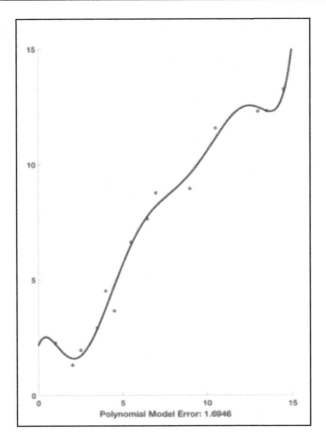

Figure 8.61: High bias situation (Image credit: http://www.learnopencv.com/wp-content/uploads/2017/02/bias-variance-tradeoff.png)

This graph has a very squiggly line and it cannot do well on the training data. In other words, you can say that it is performing the same as per the previous iteration. This shows that the ML-model has a high bias and doesn't learn new things.

Overfitting

In this section, we will look at the term overfitting. I put this term in front of you when I was explaining variance in the last section. So, it's time to explain overfitting and, in order to explain it, I want to take an example.

Suppose we have a dataset and we plot all the data points on a two dimensional plane. Now we are trying to classify the data and our ML algorithm draws a decision boundary in order to classify the data. You can see *Figure 8.62*:

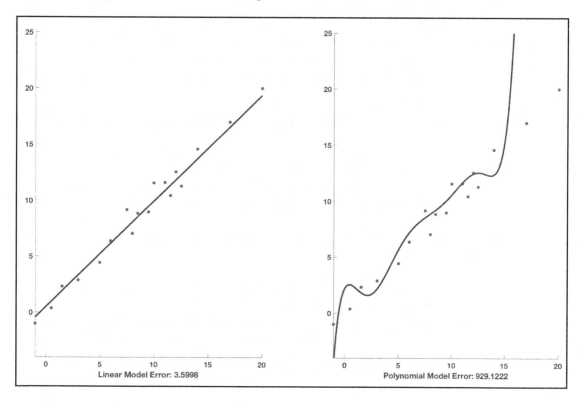

Figure 8:62 Overfitting and variance

(Image credit: http://www.learnopencv.com/wp-content/uploads/2017/02/bias-variance-tradeoff-test-error.png)

If you look at the left-hand side graph, then you will see the linear line used as a decision boundary. Now, this graph shows a training error, so you tune the parameter in your second iteration and you will get really good training accuracy; see the right-hand side graph. You hope that you will get good testing accuracy as well for the testing data, but the ML-model does really bad on the testing data prediction. So this situation, where an algorithm has very good training accuracy but doesn't perform well on the testing data, is called **overfitting**. This is the situation where ML-models have high variance and cannot generalize the unseen data.

Now that you have seen underfitting and overfitting, there are some rules of thumb that will help you so that you can prevent these situations. Always break your training data into three parts:

- 60% of the dataset should be considered as training dataset
- 20% of the dataset should be considered as validation dataset or development dataset, which will be useful in getting intermediate accuracy for your ML algorithm so that you can capture the unexpected stuff and change your algorithm according to this
- 20% of the dataset should be held out to just report the final accuracy and this will be the testing dataset

You should also apply k-fold cross validation. k indicates how many times you need the validation. Suppose we set it to three. We divide our training data into three equal parts. In the first timestamp of the training algorithm, we use two parts and test on a single part so technically, it will train on 66.66% and will be tested on 33.34%. Then, in the second timestamp, the ML algorithm uses one part and performs testing on two parts, and at the last timestamp, it will use the entire dataset for training as well as testing. After three timestamps, we will calculate the average error to find out the best model. Generally, for a reasonable amount of the dataset, k should be taken as 10.

You cannot have 100% accuracy for ML-models and the main reason behind this is because there is some noise in your input data that you can't really remove, which is called **irreducible error**.

So, the final equation for error in an ML algorithm is as follows:

Total error = Bias + Variance + Irreducible Error

You really can't get rid of the irreducible error, so you should concentrate on bias and variance. Refer to *Figure 8.63*, which will be useful in showing you how to handle the bias and variance trade-off:

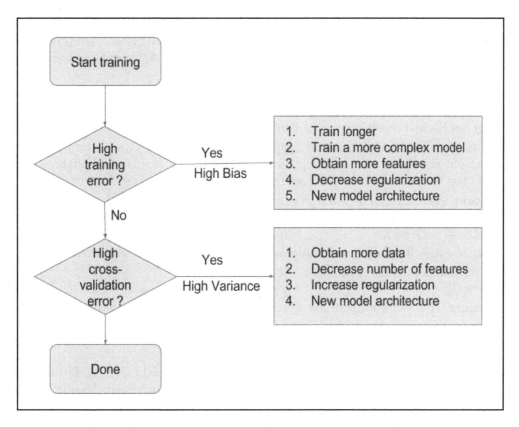

Figure 8.63: Steps to get rid of high bias or high variance situations (Image credit: http://www.learnopencv.com/wp-content/uploads/2017/02/Machine-Learning-Workflow.png)

Now that we have seen enough about ML, let's look at the evaluation matrix, that is quite useful.

Evaluation matrix

For our code, we check the accuracy but we really don't understand which attributes play a major part when you evaluate an ML-model. So, here, we will consider a matrix that is widely used for NLP applications.

This evaluation matrix is called **F1 score** or **F-measure**. It has three main components; before this, let's cover some terminology:

- **True positive (TP)**: This is a data point labeled as A by the classifier and is from class A in reality.
- **True Negative (TN)**: This is an appropriate rejection from any class in the classifier, which means that the classifier won't classify data points into class A randomly, but will reject the wrong label.
- **False Positive (FP)**: This is called a **type-I error** as well. Let's understand this measure by way of an example: A person gives blood for a cancer test. He actually doesn't have cancer but his test result is positive. This is called FP.
- **False Negative (FN)**: This is called a **type-II error** as well. Let's understand this measure by way of an example: A person gives blood for a cancer test. He has cancer but his test result is negative. So it actually overlooks the class labels. This is called FN.
- **Precision**: Precision is a measure of exactness; what percentage of data points the classifier labeled as positive and are actually positive:
  precision=TP / TP + FP
- **Recall**: Recall is the measure of completeness; what percentage of positive data points did the classifier label as positive:
  Recall = TP / TP + FN
- **F measure**: This is nothing but the weighed measure of precision and recall. See the equation:
  F= 2 * precision * recall / precision + recall

Apart from this, you can use a confusion matrix to know each of the TP, TN, FP, and FN. You can use the area under an ROC curve that indicates how much your classifier is capable of discriminating between negative and positive classes. *ROC = 1.0* represents that the model predicted all the classes correctly; area of 0.5 represents that a model is just making random predictions.

If you want to explore the new terms and techniques, you can do the following exercise.

Exercise

Read about undersampling and oversampling techniques.

Now it's time to understand how we can improvise our model after the first iteration, and sometimes, feature engineering helps us a lot in this. In `Chapter 5`, *Feature Engineering and NLP Algorithms* and `Chapter 6`, *Advance Feature Engineering and NLP Algorithms*, we explained how to extract features from text data using various NLP concepts and statistical concepts as part of feature engineering. Feature engineering includes feature extraction and feature selection. Now it's time to explore the techniques that are a part of feature selection. Feature extraction and feature selection give us the most important features for our NLP application. Once we have these features set, you can use various ML algorithms to generate the final outcome.

Let's start understanding the feature selection part.

Feature selection

As I mentioned earlier, feature extraction and feature selection are a part of feature engineering, and in this section, we will look at feature selection. You might wonder why we are learning feature selection, but there are certain reasons for it and we will look at each of them. First, we will see basic understanding of feature selection.

Features selection is also called variable selection, attribute selection, or variable subset selection. Features selection is the process of selecting the best relevant features, variables, or data attributes that can help us develop more efficient machine learning models. If you can identify which features contribute a lot and which contribute less, you can select the most important features and remove other less important ones.

Just take a step back and first understand what the problems are that we are trying to solve using features selection.

Using features selection techniques, we can get the following benefits:

- Selecting the relevant and appropriate features will help you simplify your ML-model. This will help you interpret the ML-Model easily, as well as reduce the complexity of the ML-Model.
- Choosing appropriate features using feature selection techniques will help us improve our ML-Models accuracy.
- Feature selection helps the machine learning algorithms train faster.
- Feature selection also prevents overfitting.
- It helps us get rid of the curse of dimensionality.

Curse of dimensionality

Let's understand what I mean by the curse of dimensionality because this concept will help us understand why we need feature selection techniques. The curse of dimensionality says that, as the number of features or dimensions grows, which means adding new features to our machine learning algorithm, then the amount of data that we need to generalize accurately grows exponentially. Let's see with an example.

Suppose you have a line, one-dimensional feature space, and we put five points on that line. You can see that each point takes some space on this line. Each point takes one-fifth of the space on the line. Refer to *Figure 8.64*:

Figure 8.64: A one-dimensional features space with five data points

If you have two-dimensional feature space, then we need more than five data points to fill up this space. So, we need 25 data points for these two dimensions. Now each point is taking up 1/25 of the space. See *Figure 8.65*:

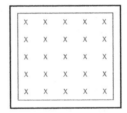

Figure 8.65: A two-dimensional features space with 25 data points

If you have a three-dimensional feature space, which means that we have three features, then we need to fill up the cube. You can see this in *Figure 8.66*:

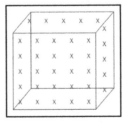

Figure 8.66: A three-dimensional features space with 1/25 data points

However, to fill up the cube, you need exactly 125 data points, as you can see in *Figure 8.66* (assume there are 125 points). So every time we add features, we need more data. I guess you will all agree that the growth in data points increases exponentially from 5, 25, 125, and so on. So, in general, you need Xd feature space, where X is your number of data points in training and d is the number of features or dimensions. If you just blindly put more and more features so that your ML algorithm gets a better understanding of the dataset, what you're actually doing is forcing your ML algorithm to fill the larger features space with data. You can solve this using a simple method. In this kind of situation, you need to give more data to your algorithm, not features.

Now you really think I'm restricting you to adding new features. So, let me clarify this for you. If it is necessary to add features, then you can; you just need to select the best and minimum amount of features that help your ML algorithm learn from it. I really recommend that you don't add too many features blindly.

Now, how can we derive the best features set? What is the best features set for the particular application that I'm building and how can I know that my ML algorithm will perform well with this features set? I will provide the answers to all these questions in the next section *Features selection techniques*. Here, I will give you a basic idea about feature selection techniques. I would recommend that you practically implement them in the NLP applications that we have developed so far.

Feature selection techniques

> *Make everything as simple as possible but not simpler*

This quote by Albert Einstein, is very true when we are talking about feature selection techniques. We have seen that to get rid of the curse of dimensionality, we need feature selection techniques. We will look at the following feature selection techniques:

- Filter method
- Wrapper method
- Embedded method

So, let's begin with each method.

Filter method

Feature selection is altogether a separate activity and independent of the ML algorithm. For a numerical dataset, this method is generally used when we are preprocessing our data, and for the NLP domain, it should be performed once we convert text data to a numerical format or vector format. Let's first see the basic steps of this method in *Figure 8.67*:

Figure 8.67: Filter method for feature selection (Image credit: https://upload.wikimedia.org/wikipedia/commons/2/2c/Filter_Methode.png)

The steps are very clear and self-explanatory. Here, we use statistical techniques that give us a score and based on this, we will decide whether we should keep the feature or just remove it or drop it. Refer to *Figure 8.68*:

		Response	
		Continous	Categorical
Feature	Continous	Correlation	LDA
	Categorical	Anova	Chi-Square

Figure 8.68: Features selection techniques list

Let me simplify *Figure 8.68* for you:

- If feature and response are both continuous, then we will perform correlation
- If feature and response are both are categorical, then we will use Chi-Square; in NLP (we mostly use this)
- If feature are continuous and response is categorical, then we will use **linear discriminant analysis (LDA)**
- If feature are categorical and response is continuous, then we will use Anova

I will concentrate more on the NLP domain and explain the basics of LDA and Chi-Square.

LDA is generally used to find a linear combination of features that characterize or separate more than one class of a categorical variable, whereas Chi-Square is mainly used in NLP as compared to LDA. Chi-Square is applied to a group of categorical features to get an idea of the likelihood of correlation or association between features using their frequency distribution.

Wrapper method

In this method, we are searching for the best features set. This method is computationally very expensive because we need to search for the best features subset for every iteration. See the basic steps in *Figure 8.69*:

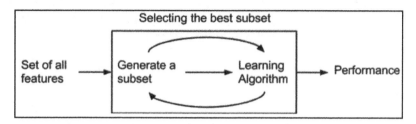

Figure 8.69: Wrapper method steps (Image credit: https://upload.wikimedia.org/wikipedia/commons/0/04/Feature_selection_Wrapper_Method.png)

There are three submethods that we can use to select the best features subset:

- Forward selection
- Backward selection
- Recursive features elimination

In forward selection, we start with no features and add the features that improve our ML-model, in each iteration. We continue this process until our model does not improve its accuracy further.

Backward selection is the other method where we start with all the features and, in each iteration, we find the best features and remove other unnecessary features, and repeat until no further improvement is observed in the ML-model.

Recursive feature elimination uses a greedy approach to find out the best performing features subset. It repeatedly creates the models and keeps aside the best or worst performing features for each iteration. The next time, it uses the best features and creates the model until all features are exhausted; lastly, it ranks the features based on its order of elimination of them.

Embedded method

In this method, we combine the qualities of the filter and wrapper methods. This method is implemented by the algorithms that have their own built-in feature selection methods. Refer to *Figure 8.70*:

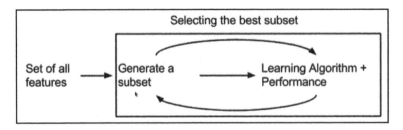

Figure 8.70: Embedded features selection method (Image credit: https://upload.wikimedia.org/wikipedia/commons/b/bf/Feature_selection_Embedded_Method.png)

The most popular examples of these methods are LASSO and RIDGE regression, which has some built-in parameters to reduce the chances of overfitting.

You can refer to these links, which will be very useful for you:
https://www.analyticsvidhya.com/blog/2016/01/complete-tutorial-r
idge-lasso-regression-python/.
http://machinelearningmastery.com/an-introduction-to-feature-sel
ection/.
http://machinelearningmastery.com/feature-selection-in-python-wi
th-scikit-learn/.

We will look at dimensionality reduction in the next section.

Dimensionality reduction

Dimensionality reduction is a very useful concept in machine learning. If we include a lot of features to develop our ML-model, then sometimes we include features that are really not needed. Sometimes we need high-dimensional features space. What are the available ways to make certain sense about our features space? So we need some techniques that help us remove unnecessary features or convert our high-dimensional features space to two-dimensional or three-dimensional features so that we can see what all is happening. By the way, we have used this concept in Chapter 6, *Advance Features Engineering and NLP Algorithms*, when we developed an application that generated word2vec for the game of thrones dataset. At that time, we used **t-distributed stochastic neighbor embedding (t-SNE)** dimensionality reduction technique to visualize our result in two-dimensional space.

Here, we will look at the most famous two techniques, called **principal component analysis (PCA)** and t-SNE, which is used to visualize high-dimensional data in two-dimensional space. So, let's begin.

PCA

PCA is a statistical method that uses an orthogonal transformation to convert a set of data points of possibly correlated features to a set of values of linearly uncorrelated features, called **principal components**. The number of principal components is less than or equal to the number of the original features. This technique defines transformation in such a way that the first principal component has the largest possible variance to each succeeding feature.

Refer to *Figure 8.71*:

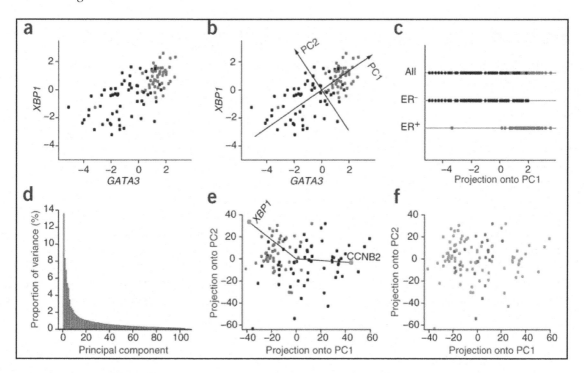

Figure 8.71: PCA (Image credit: https://www.nature.com/article-assets/npg/nbt/journal/v26/n3/images/nbt0308-303-F1.gif)

This graph helps a lot in order to understand PCA. We have taken two principal components and they are orthogonal to each other as well as making variance as large as possible. In *c* graph, we have reduced the dimension from two-dimensional to one-dimensional by projecting on a single line.

The disadvantage of PCA is that when you reduce the dimensionality, it loses the meaning that the data points represent. If interpretability is the main reason for dimensionality reduction, then you should not use PCA; you can use t-SNE.

t-SNE

This is the technique that helps us visualize high-dimensional non-linear space. t-SNE tries to preserve the group of local data points that are close together. This technique will help you when you want to visualize high-dimensional space. You can use this to visualize applications that use techniques such as word2vec, image classification, and so on. For more information, you can refer to this link:

```
https://lvdmaaten.github.io/tsne/.
```

Hybrid approaches for NLP applications

Hybrid approaches sometimes really help us improve the result, of our NLP applications. For example, if we are developing a grammar correction system, a module that identifies multiword expressions such as kick the bucket, and a rule-based module that identifies the wrong pattern and generates the right pattern. This is one kind of hybrid approach. Let's take a second example for the same NLP application. You are making a classifier that identifies the correct articles (determiners - a, an, and the) for the noun phrase in a sentence. In this system, you can take two categories - a/an and the. We need to develop a classifier that will generate the determiner category, either a/an or the. Once we generate the articles for the noun phrase, we can apply a rule-based system that further decides the actual determiner for the first category a/an. We also know some English grammar rules that we can use to decide whether we should go with a or an. This is also an example a of hybrid approach. For better sentiment analysis, we can also use hybrid approaches that include lexical-based approach, ML-based approach, or word2vec or GloVe pretrained models to get really high accuracy. So, be creative and understand your NLP problem so that you can take advantages from different types of techniques to make your NLP application better.

Post-processing

Post processing is a kind of rule-based system. Suppose you are developing a machine translation application and your generated model makes some specific mistakes. You want that **machine translation (MT)** model to avoid these kinds of mistakes, but avoiding that takes a lot of features that make the training process slow and make the model too complex. On the other hand, if you know that there are certain straightforward rules or approximations that can help you once the output has been generated in order to make it more accurate, then we can use post-processing for our MT model. What is the difference between a hybrid model and post-processing? Let me clear your confusion. In the given example, I have used word approximation. So rather than using rules, you can also apply an approximation, such as applying a threshold value to tune your result, but you should apply approximation only when you know that it will give an accurate result. This approximation should complement the NLP system to be generalized enough.

Summary

In this chapter, we have looked at the basic concepts of ML, as well as the various classification algorithms that are used in the NLP domain. In NLP, we mostly use classification algorithms, as compared to linear regression. We have seen some really cool examples such as spam filtering, sentiment analysis, and so on. We also revisited the POS tagger example to provide you with better understanding. We looked at unsupervised ML algorithms and important concepts such as bias-variance trade-off, underfitting, overfitting, evaluation matrix, and so on. We also understood features selection and dimensionality reduction. We touched on hybrid ML approaches and post-processing as well. So, in this chapter, we have mostly understood how to develop and fine-tune NLP applications.

In the next chapter, we will see a new era of machine learning--deep learning. We will explore the basic concepts needed for AI. After that, we will discuss the basics of deep learning including linear regression and gradient descent. We will see why deep learning has become the most popular technique in the past few years. We will see the necessary concepts of math that are related to deep learning, explore the architecture of deep neural networks, and develop some cool applications such as machine translation from the NLU domain and text summarization from the NLG domain. We will do this using TensorFlow, Keras, and some other latest dependencies. We will also see basic optimization techniques that you can apply to traditional ML algorithms and deep learning algorithms. Let's dive deep into the deep learning world in the next chapter!

9
Deep Learning for NLU and NLG Problems

We have seen the rule-based approach and various machine learning techniques to solve NLP tasks in the previous chapters. In this chapter, we will see the bleeding edge subset of machine learning technique called **deep learning** (**DL**). In the past four to five years, neural networks and deep learning techniques have been creating a lot of buzz in the artificial intelligence area because many tech giants use these cutting-edge techniques to solve real-life problems, and the results from these techniques are extremely impressive. Tech giants such as Google, Apple, Amazon, OpenAI, and so on spend a lot of time and effort to create innovative solutions for real-life problems. These efforts are mostly to develop artificial general intelligence and make the world a better place for human beings.

We will first understand the overall AI, in general, to give you a fair idea of why deep learning is creating a lot of buzz nowadays. We will cover the following topics in this chapter:

- How NLU and NLG are different from each other
- The basics of neural networks
- Building NLP and NLG applications using various deep learning techniques

After understanding the basics of DL, we will touch on some of the most recent innovations happening in the deep learning field. So let's begin!

An overview of artificial intelligence

In this section, we will see the various aspects of AI and how deep learning is related to AI. We will see the AI components, various stages of AI, and different types of AI; at the end of this section, we will discuss why deep learning is one of the most promising techniques in order to achieve AI.

The basics of AI

When we talk about AI, we think about an intelligent machine, and this is the basic concept of AI. AI is an area of science that is constantly progressing in the direction of enabling human-level intelligence in machines. The basic idea behind AI is to enable intelligence in machines so that they can also perform some of the tasks performed only by humans. We are trying to enable human-level intelligence in machines using some cool algorithmic techniques; in this process, whatever kind of intelligence is acquired by the machines is artificially generated. Various algorithmic techniques that are used to generate AI for machines are mostly part of machine learning techniques. Before getting into the core machine learning and deep learning part, we will understand other facts related to AI.

AI is influenced by many branches; in *Figure 9.1*, we will see those branches that heavily influence artificial intelligence as a single branch:

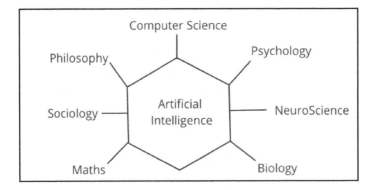

Figure 9.1: AI influence by other branches

Components of AI

First of all, we will see the key components of AI. These components will be quite useful for us to understand that direction the world is going.

According to me, there are two components, that you can see in *Figure 9.2*:

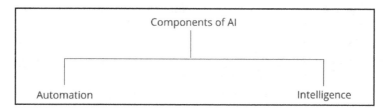

Figure 9.2: Components of AI

Let's see the AI components in detail. We will also see some examples.

Automation

Automation is a well-known component of AI. People around the world work heavily on automation and we have achieved tremendous success in the area of automatic tasks performed by machines. We will look at some examples that are intuitive enough for you to understand the automation concept in AI.

In the automobile sector, we are using automatic robots to manufacture vehicles. These robots follow a set of instructions and perform the definite tasks. Here, these robots are not intelligent robots that can interact with humans and ask questions or respond to human questions, but these robots are just following a set of instructions to achieve great accuracy and efficiency in manufacturing with high speed. So these kinds of robots are examples of automation in the AI area.

The other example is in the area of DevOps. Nowadays, DevOps is using machine learning to automate many human-intensive processes such as, in order to maintain in-house servers, the DevOps team gets a bunch of recommendations after analyzing various logs of servers, and after getting the recommendations, another machine learning model prioritizes the alerts and recommendations. This kind of application really saves time for the DevOps team to deliver great work on time. These kinds of applications really help us understand that automation is a very important component of AI.

Now let's see how intelligence is going to impact the world as part of AI.

Intelligence

When we say intelligence, as humans, our expectations are really high. Our goal is that we really want machines to understand our behavior and emotions. We also want machines to react intelligently based on human actions and all the reactions generated by machines should be in such a way that it mimics human intelligence. We want to achieve this goal since the mid 1900s. Around the globe, many researchers, groups of scientists, and communities are doing a lot of cool research to make machines as intelligent as humans.

We want that after acquiring intelligence, machines will perform majority of the tasks for humans with better accuracy and this is the single broad expectation. During the last four-five years, we have started to successfully achieve this broad goal and, as a result of so many years of efforts, Google recently announced that Google Assistant can hear natural language from humans and interpret the speech signal as accurately as a human. The other example is that the Facebook research group did a very powerful research in order to build a system that is good at applying reasoning for questions and answers. Tesla and Google self-driving cars are a complex AI system but very useful and intelligent. Self-driving cars and chatbots are part of narrow AI. You can also find many other examples on the web, that are coming out now and then.

There are certain subcomponents that can be included as part of intelligence. Refer to *Figure 9.3*:

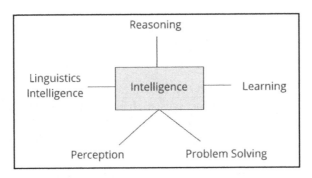

Figure 9.3: Subcomponents of intelligence

Intelligence is a combination of all the components described in the preceding figure. All these components--reasoning, learning, learning from experience, problem solving, perception, and linguistics intelligence--come very naturally to humans but not to machines. So we need the techniques that enable intelligence for machines.

Before learning the name of the techniques that we will use later in this chapter, let's understand the various stages of AI.

Stages of AI

There are three main stages for the AI system. We will see the following stages in detail:

- Machine learning
- Machine intelligence
- Machine consciousness

Before getting into the details of each stage of AI, refer to *Figure 9.4*:

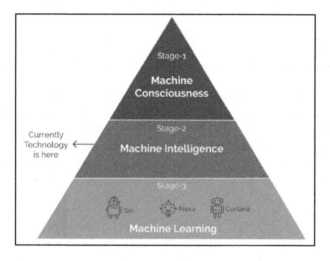

Figure 9.4: Stages of AI (Image credit: https://cdn-images-1.medium.com/max/1600/0*aefkt8m-V66Wf5-j.png)

We will begin from the bottom to the top, so we will understand the machine learning stage first, then machine intelligence, and finally machine consciousness.

Machine learning

You have learned a lot of things about machine learning in the previous chapters, but I want to give you an AI perspective of it in this chapter.

ML techniques are a set of algorithms that explain how to generate or reach the defined output. This kind of algorithm is used by intelligent systems that try to learn from experience. The system that uses MLL algorithms is keen to learn from the historical data or real-time data. So, at this stage of AI, we focus on algorithms that learn patterns or specific structures from the data using features that we have provided to the ML system. To make it clear, let's take an example.

Suppose you want to build a sentiment analysis application. We can use historical tagged data, hand-crafted features, and the Naive Bayes ML algorithm. As a result, we can have an intelligent system that has learned from its learning example--how to provide a sentiment tag for an unseen new data instance.

Machine intelligence

Machine intelligence is again a set of algorithms, but most of the algorithms are heavily influenced by how the human brain learns and thinks. Using neuroscience, biology, and mathematics, the AI researcher came up with a set of advance-level algorithms that help machines to learn from the data without providing hand-crafted features. In this stage, algorithms use unlabeled or labeled data. Here, you just define the end goal, and the advanced algorithms figure out their own way to achieve the expected result.

If you compare the algorithms that we are using at this stage with the traditional ML algorithms, then the major difference is that, in this machine intelligence stage, we are not giving hand-crafted features as input to any algorithm. As these algorithms are inspired by human brains, the algorithm itself learns the features and patterns and generates the output. Currently, the world of AI is in this stage. People across the world use these advanced algorithms that seem very promising to achieve human-like intelligence for machines.

Artificial neural networks (ANNs) and deep learning techniques are used to achieve machine intelligence.

Machine consciousness

Machine consciousness is one of the most discussed topics in AI as our end goal is to reach here.

We want machines to learn the way humans learn. As humans, we don't need a lot of data; we don't take so much time to understand the abstract concepts. We learn from small amounts of data or without data. Most of the time, we learn from our experiences. If we want to build a system that is as conscious as a human, then we should know how to generate consciousness for machines. However, are we fully aware how our brain works and reacts in order to transfer this knowledge to machines and make them as conscious as we are? Unfortunately, right now we aren't aware of this. We expect that in this stage, machines learn without data or with very small amounts of data and use their self-experience to achieve the defined output.

There are a lot of interesting researches going on, and I encourage you to check out this YouTube video of researcher John Searle, who talks about machine consciousness: `https://www.youtube.com/watch?v=rHKwIYsPXLg`. This video may give you a fresh perspective about consciousness in AI.

We have seen the various stages of AI. ANNs and deep learning are a part of the machine intelligence stage. At the end of the *A brief overview of deep learning* section, you have the necessary details that can help you understand why deep learning is the new buzzword in AI.

Now we are going to see the various types of AI.

Types of artificial intelligence

There are three types of AI, as follows:

- Artificial narrow intelligence
- Artificial general intelligence
- Artificial superintelligence

Artificial narrow intelligence

Artificial narrow intelligence (ANI) is a type of AI that covers some of the basic tasks such as template-based chatbot, basic personal assistant application like the initial versions of Siri by Apple.

This type of intelligence is majorly focused on basic prototyping of applications. This type of intelligence is the starting point for any application and then you can improve the basic prototype. You can add the next layer of intelligence by adding artificial general intelligence, but only if your end users really need that kind of functionality. We have also seen this kind of basic chatbot in `Chapter 7`, *Rule-Based System for NLP*.

Artificial general intelligence

Artificial general intelligence (AGI) is a type of AI that is used to build systems that are capable of performing human-level tasks. What do I mean by human-level tasks? Tasks such as building self-driving cars. Google self-driving cars and Tesla autopilot are the most famous examples. Humanoid robots also try to use this type of AI.

NLP-level examples are sophisticated chatbots that ignore spelling mistakes and grammatical mistakes and understand your query or questions. The deep learning techniques seem very promising for the understanding of the natural language by humans.

We are now at a stage where people and communities around the world use basic concepts, and by referring to each other's research works, try to build systems that have AGI.

Artificial superintelligence

The way to achieve **artificial superintelligence (ASI)** is a bit difficult for us because, in this type of AI, we expect that machines are smarter than humans in order to learn specific tasks and capable enough to perform multiple tasks as humans do in their life. This kind of superintelligence is right now a dream for us, but we are trying to achieve this in such a way that machines and systems always complement human skills and will not create a threat for humans.

Goals and applications of AI

This is the time and section where we need to understand the goals and applications for AI in general for various areas. These goals and applications are just to give you an idea about the current state of AI-enabled applications, but if you can think of some crazy but useful application in any area, then you should try to include it in this list. You should try to implement various types and stages of AI in that application.

Now let's see the areas where we want to integrate various stages of AI and make those applications AI-enabled:

- Reasoning
- Machine learning
- Natural language processing
- Robotics
- Implementing general intelligence
- Computer vision
- Automated learning and scheduling
- Speech analysis

You can refer to *Figure 9.5*, which shows many different areas and related applications:

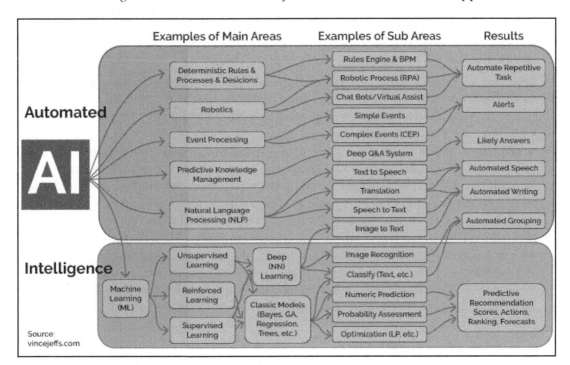

Figure 9.5 : Various areas of AI and applications (Image credit: http://vincejeffs.com/)

Now let's see the applications from some of the areas in the preceding list.

AI-enabled applications

Here, I will give you a brief idea about AI-enabled applications. Some of the applications are related to the NLP domain as well:

- Enabling reasoning for any system will be very exciting stuff. Under this area, we can build a Q/A system that can use the reasoning to derive answers for the asked questions.
- If we can enable the reasoning for an AI-based system, then those systems will be very good at decision making and will improvise the existing decision making system.
- In machine learning, we want the perfect architecture of an ML-based application that can be decided by machines themselves. This is, according to me, an AI-enabled application in ML.

- When we are talking in terms of AI-enabled NLP applications, then we really need NLP systems that can understand the context of human natural language and react and behave more like humans.
- Humanoid robots are the best application to describe an AI-enabled system. Robots should acquire perception, which is a long term AI goal.
- When we are talking about general intelligence, according to me, systems should react more like humans do. Particularly machine reactions should match with real human behavior. After analyzing certain situations, machines should react the same or better than humans.
- Nowadays, computer vision has many applications that give us solid proof that AI will be achieved very soon in this area. The applications are object identification, image recognition, skin cancer detection using image recognition techniques, generating face images from machines, generating text for images and vice versa, and others. All these applications give us concrete proof about AI-driven computer vision.
- Automated learning and scheduling is a kind of building system that works for your personal assistance and manages your schedule. Regarding the AI part, we really expect that every user of the system will get a personalized experience so automating the learning of a person's personal choice is very important for AI-driven scheduling. To achieve this goal, automated learning systems should also learn how to choose the best suited model for a particular user.
- Speech analysis is a different form of NL, but unfortunately, we are not talking about this concept in this book. Here, we are talking about a speech recognition system in terms of a potential AI-enabled area. By enabling AI with this speech recognition area, we can understand the human environment and thinking process that is generated under the effect of a person's sociology, psychology, and philosophy. We can also predict their personality.

After seeing all these fascinating applications, there are three really interesting questions that come to our mind: what are the reasons that lead us to produce AI-driven systems, why the time is so perfect for us to build an AI-driven system, and how can we build an AI-enabled system?

Since the mid 1900s, we are trying to bring intelligence in machines. During this phase, researchers and scientists have given a lot of cool concepts. For example, an artificial neuron, also known as **McCulloch-Pitts model (MCP)**, is inspired by the human brain and the purpose of this concept is to understand the human brain biological working process and represent this process in terms of mathematics and physics. So it will be helpful to implement AI for machines.

They successfully gave the mathematical representation of how a single neuron works, but there is one outcome of this model that wasn't good for training purposes. So researcher Frank Rosenblatt, in his 1958 paper, came up with the *perceptron*, introducing *dynamic weight* and *threshold* concepts. After this, many researchers have developed concepts such as backpropagation and multilayer neural networks based on the earlier concepts. The research community wanted to implement the developed concepts in practical applications, and the first researcher, Geoffrey Hinton, demonstrated the use of the generalized backpropagation algorithm to train multilayer neural networks. From that point, researchers and communities started to use this generalized model, but in the late 1900s, the amount of data was less compared to now and computational devices were slow as well as costly. So we didn't get the expected results. However, with the result that was achieved at the time, the researcher had faith that these are the concepts that will be used to enable an AI-driven world. Now we have a lot of data as well as computation devices that are fast, cheap, and capable enough to process large amounts of data. When we apply these old concepts of ANNs in the current era to develop applications such as a universal machine translation system, speech recognition system, image recognition system, and so on, we get very promising results. Let's take an example. Google is using ANNs to develop a universal machine translation system and this system will translate multiple languages. This is because we have large datasets available and also fast computation capabilities that can help us process the datasets using ANNs. We have used neural networks that are not one or two, but many, layers deep. The result achieved is so impressive that every big tech giant is using deep learning models to develop an AI-enabled system. According to me, data, computational capabilities, and solid old concepts are the key components that are perfect to develop an AI-driven system. You can refer to *Figure 9.6* for a brief history of the neural network:

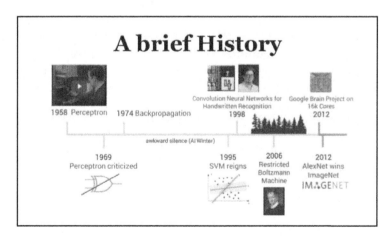

Figure 9.6: History of ANN (Image credit: https://image.slidesharecdn.com/deeplearning-170124234229/95/deep-learning-9-638.jpg?cb=1485303074)

Figure 9.7 will give you an idea about the long term history of neural networks:

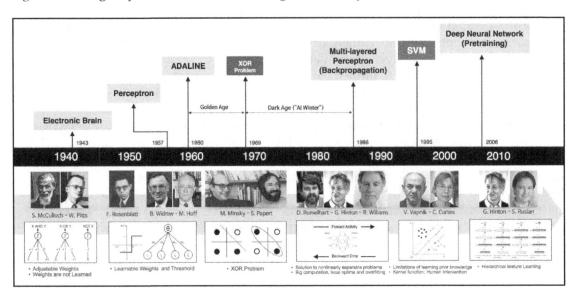

Figure 9.7: History of ANN (Image credit: http://qingkaikong.blogspot.in/2016/11/machine-learning-3-artificial-neural.html)

Now let's move toward the next question: how can we enable AI? The answer is deep learning. This is one of the most favorite techniques to enable AI for non-AI systems. There are a few cases where deep learning is not used to enable AI, but in the NLP domain, deep learning is majorly used to enable AI. To develop general intelligence, we can use deep learning. We get very promising results from this technique. Experiments such as machines generating human faces understands the speech of humans more accurately in a noisy environment, self-driving cars, reasoning for question answer systems are just a few of the experiments. The deep learning techniques are using lots and lots of data and high computational capability to train systems on the given data. When we apply the right deep learning model on a large amount of data, we will get a magical, impressive, and promising result. These are the reasons deep learning is creating lot of buzz nowadays. So I guess now you know why deep learning is the buzzword in the AI world.

Further in this chapter, we will see deep learning techniques in detail and develop NLP applications using deep learning.

Comparing NLU and NLG

We have already seen the NLU and NLG definitions, details, and differences in `Chapter 3`, *Understanding Structure of Sentences*. In this section, we are comparing these two subareas of NLP in terms of an AI-enabled application.

Natural language understanding

Earlier, we have seen that NLU is more about dealing with an understanding of the structure of the language, whether it is words, phrases, or sentences. NLU is more about applying various ML techniques on already generated NL. In NLU, we focus on syntax as well as semantics. We also try to solve the various types of ambiguities related to syntax and semantics. We have seen the lexical ambiguity, syntactic ambiguity, semantic ambiguity, and pragmatics ambiguity.

Now let's see where we can use AI that helps machines understand the language structure and meaning more accurately and efficiently. AI and ML techniques are not much behind to address these aspects of NL. To give an example, deep learning gives us an impressive result in machine translation. Now when we talk about solving syntactic ambiguity and semantic ambiguity, we can use deep learning. Suppose you have a NER tool that will use deep learning and Word2vec, then we can solve the syntactic ambiguity. This is just one application, but you can also improve parser results and POS taggers.

Now let's talk about pragmatics ambiguity, where we really need AGI as well as ASI. This ambiguity occurs when you try to understand the long distance context of a sentence with other previously written or spoken sentences, and it also depends on the speaker's intent of speaking or writing.

Let's see an example of pragmatics ambiguity. You and your friend are having a conversation, and your friend told you long ago that she had joined an NGO and would do some social activity for poor students. Now you ask her how was the social activity. In this case, you and your friend know about what social activities you are talking about. This is because as humans, our brain stores the information as well as knows when to fetch that information, how to interpret it, and what is the relevance of the fetched information to your current conversation that you are having with your friend. Both you and your friend can understand the context and relevance of each other's questions and answers, but machines don't have this kind of capability of understanding the context and speaker's intent.

This is what we expect from an intelligent machine. We want the machine to understand this kind of complex situation as well. Enabling this kind of capability of resolving pragmatics ambiguity is included in MSI. This will definitely be possible in future, but right now, we are at a stage where machines are trying to adopt AGI and using statistical techniques to understand semantics.

Natural language generation

NLG is an area where we are trying to teach machines how to generate NL in a sensible manner. This, in itself, is a challenging AI task. Deep learning has really helped us perform this kind of challenging task. Let me give you an example. If you are using Google's new inbox, then you may notice that when you reply to any mail, you will get three most relevant replies in the form of sentences for the given mail. Google used millions of e-mails and made an NLG model that was trained using deep learning to generate or predict the most relevant reply for any given mail. You can refer to *Figure 9.8*:

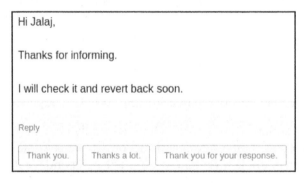

Figure 9.8: Google's new inbox smart reply

Apart from this application, there is another application: after seeing the images, the machine will provide a caption of a particular image. This is also an NLG application that uses deep learning. The task of generating language is less complex than the generation of NL, that is, coherence, and this is where we need AGI.

We have talked a lot about the term, deep learning, but how does it actually work and why is it so promising? This we will see in an upcoming section of this chapter. We will explain the coding part for NLU and NLG applications. We are also going to develop NLU and NLG applications from scratch. Before that, you must understand the concepts of ANN and deep learning. I will include mathematics in upcoming sections and try my best to keep it simple. Let's dive deep into the world of ANN and deep learning!

A brief overview of deep learning

Machine learning is a sub-branch of AI and deep learning is a sub-branch of ML. Refer to *Figure 9.9*:

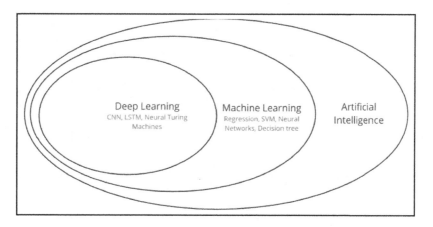

Figure 9.9: Deep learning as a sub-branch of ML

Deep learning uses ANN that is not just one or two layers, but many layers deep, called **deep neural network (DNN)**. When we use DNN to solve a given problem by predicting a possible result for the same problem, it is called **deep learning**.

Deep learning can use labeled data or unlabeled data, so we can say that deep learning can be used in supervised techniques as well as unsupervised techniques. The main idea of using deep learning is that using DNN and a humongous amount of data, we want the machines to generalize the particular tasks and provide us with a result that we think only humans can generate. Deep learning includes a bunch of techniques and algorithms that can help us solve various problems in NLP such as machine translation, question answering system, summarization, and so on. Apart from NLP, you can find other areas of applications such as image recognition, speech recognition, object identification, handwritten digit recognition, face detection, and artificial face generation.

Deep learning seems promising to us in order to build AGI and ASI. You can see some of the applications where deep learning has been used, in *Figure 9.10*:

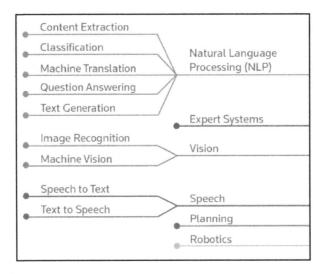

Figure 9.10: Applications using deep learning (Image credit: http://www.fullai.org/)

This section gives you a brief overview about deep learning. We will see many aspects of deep learning in this chapter, but before that, I want to explain concepts that are related to deep learning and ANN. These concepts will help you understand the technicality of deep learning.

Basics of neural networks

The concept of neural networks is one of the oldest techniques in ML. Neural network is derived from the human brain. In this section, we will see the human brain's components and then derive the ANN.

In order to understand ANN, we first need to understand the basic workflow of the human brain. You can refer to *Figure 9.11:*

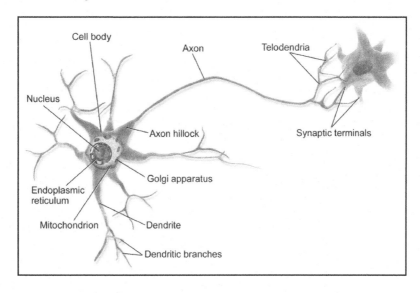

Figure 9.11: Neurons of human brain (Image credit: https://en.wikipedia.org/wiki/File:Blausen_0657_MultipolarNeuron.png)

The human brain consists of an estimated hundreds of billion nerve cells called **neurons**. Each neuron performs three jobs that are mentioned as follows:

- Receiving a signal: It receives a set of signals from its **dendrites**
- Deciding to pass the signal to the cell body: It integrates those signals together to decide whether or not the information should be passed on to the cell body
- Sending the signal: If some of the signals pass a certain threshold, it sends these signals, called **action potentials**, onward via its axon to the next set of neurons

You can refer to *Figure 9.12*, which demonstrate components that are used to perform these three jobs in the biological neural network:

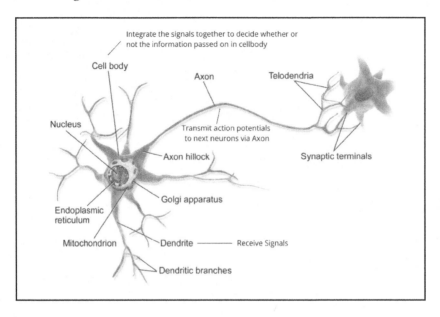

Figure 9.12: Demonstrates the components that performs the three jobs

This is a very brief overview on how our brain learns and processes some decision. Now the question is: can we build an ANN that uses a non-biological substrate like silicon or other metal? We can build it, and then by providing a lot of computer power and data, we can solve the problems much faster as compared to humans.

ANN is a biologically inspired algorithm that learns to identify the pattern in the dataset.

We have seen a brief history of ANN earlier in this chapter, but now it's time to see ANN and its history in detail.

The first computation model of the neuron

In mid-1943, researchers McCulloch-Pitts invented the first computation model of a neuron. Their model is fairly simple. The model has a neuron that receives binary inputs, sums them, and, if the sum exceeds a certain threshold value, then output is one, if not then output is zero. You can see the pictorial representation in *Figure 9.13*:

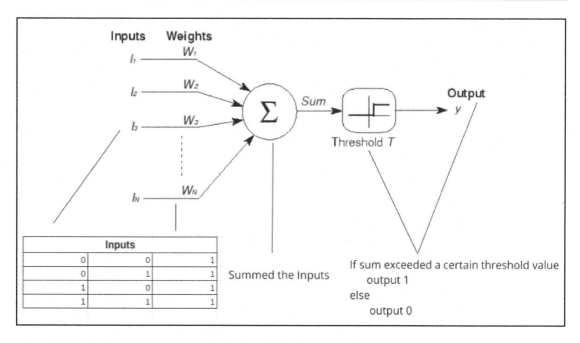

Figure 9.13: McCulloch-Pitts computation model of neuron (Image credit for NN: http://wwwold.ece.utep.edu/research/webfuzzy/docs/kk-thesis/kk-thesis-html/node12.html)

It looks very simple, but as it was invented in the early days of AI, an invention of this kind of model was a really big deal.

Perceptron

After a few years of the invention of the first computational model of neuron, a psychologist named Frank Rosenblatt found out that the McCulloch-Pitts model did not have the mechanism to learn from the input data. So he invented the neural network that was built on the idea of the first computational model of neuron. Frank Rosenblatt called this model the **perceptron**. It is also called a **single-layer feedforward neural network**. We call this model a feed forward neural network because, in this neural network, data flows in only one direction--the forward direction.

Now let's understand the working of the perceptron that has incorporated the idea of having weights on the given inputs. If you provide some training set of input output examples, it should learn a function from it by increasing and decreasing the weights continuously for each of the training examples, depending on what was the output of the given input example. These weight values are mathematically applied to the input such that after each iteration, the output prediction gets more accurate. This whole process is called **training**. Refer to *Figure 9.14* to understand the schematic of Rosenblatt's perceptron:

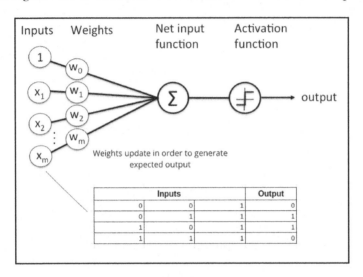

Figure 9.14: Schematic of Rosenblatt's perceptron (Image credit for NN: http://sebastianraschka.com/Articles/2015_singlelayer_neurons.html)

We will see the ANN-related mathematical concepts such as gradient descent, activation function, and loss function in the next section. So get ready for some mathematics!

Understanding mathematical concepts for ANN

This section is very important because ML, ANN, and DL use a bunch of mathematical concepts and we are going to see some of the most important ones. These concepts will really help you optimize your ML, ANN, and DL models. We will also see different types of activation functions and some tips about which activation function you should select. We are going to see the following mathematical concepts:

- Gradient descent
- Activation function
- Loss function

Gradient descent

Gradient descent is a very important optimization technique that has been used by almost any neural network. In order to explain these techniques, I want to give an example. I have a dataset of students' scores and hours of study for each of the students. We want to predict the test scores of a student just by his amount of hours of study. You would say that this looks like an ML linear regression example. You are right; we are using linear regression to make a prediction. Why linear regression and what is the connection with gradient descent? Let me answer this and then we will see the code and some cool visualization.

Linear regression is the ML technique that uses statistical methods and allows us to study relationships between two continuous quantitative variables. Here, those variables are students' scores and students' hours of study. Usually in linear regression, we try to get a line that is the best fit for our dataset, which means that whatever calculation we are doing is just to get a line of the best fit for the given dataset. Getting this line of the best fit is the goal of linear regression.

Let's talk about the connection of linear regression with gradient descent. Gradient descent is the most popular optimization technique that we are using to optimize the accuracy of the linear regression and minimize the loss or error function. Gradient descent is the technique that helps us minimize our error function and maximize our prediction accuracy. The mathematical definition for gradient descent is that it is a first-order iterative optimization algorithm. This algorithm is used to find a local minimum of a function using gradient descent. Each taken step is proportional to the negative of the gradient of the function at the current point. You can think of gradient descent using this real-life example. Suppose you are at the top of a mountain and now you want to reach the bottom that has a beautiful lake, so you need to start descending it. Now you don't know in what direction you should start walking. In this case, you observe the land near you and try to find the way where the land tends to descend. This will give you an idea in what direction you should go. If you take your first steps in the descending direction and each time you follow the same logic, then it is very likely that you would reach the lake. This is exactly what we are doing with the mathematical formula for gradient descent. In ML and DL, we think about everything in terms of optimization so gradient descent is the technique that is used to minimize the loss function over time.

The other example is you have a deep bowl in which you put a small ball from its one end. You can observe that after some time, the ball reduces its speed and tries to reach the base of the bowl. Refer to *Figure 9.15*:

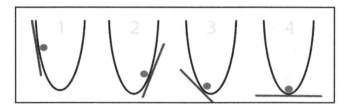

Figure 9.15: Intuition of gradient descent (Image credit: https://iamtrask.github.io/img/sgd_optimal.png)

You must also check out the image given at this GitHub link:
https://github.com/jalajthanaki/NLPython/blob/master/ch9/gradien
tdescentexample/gradient_descent_example.gif

This figure shows the process or steps of getting the line of best fit using gradient descent. It's just the visualization that gives you an overall idea of what we are going to do in the code. By the way, loss function, error function, and cost function are synonyms of each other. Gradient descent is also known as **steepest descent**.

Now let's get to the code and I will explain things as we go. Here, we are not developing a predictive model; we will implement and understand gradient descent. The dataset and code is at
https://github.com/jalajthanaki/NLPython/tree/master/ch9/gradientdescentexample

First of all, let's understand the dataset. It is the dataset of the students' test scores and the amount of hours they studied. We know that between these two attributes, there should be a relationship--the less amount you study, poorer is the score of the student, and the more you study, better the score will be. We will prove the relationship using linear regression. The **X** value means the first column of the dataset, that is, the amount of hours the student studies, and **Y** value means the second column, which is the test score. Refer to *Figure 9.16*:

X points = hours student study	Y Points = Test score
32.5023452695	31.7070058466
53.4268040333	68.7775959816
61.5303580256	62.5623822979
47.4756396348	71.5466322336
59.8132078695	87.2309251337
55.1421884139	78.2115182708
52.2117966922	79.6419730498
39.2995666943	59.1714893219
48.1050416918	75.3312422971

Figure 9.16: Sample data from the dataset

Let's define the main function that is going to read our dataset and some basic hyperparameters. We have also called a function that we will use to compute the errors and actual gradient descent. You can see the code snippet in *Figure 9.17*:

```python
def run():
    # Step 1 : Read data

    # genfromtext is used to read out data from data.csv file.
    points = genfromtxt("/home/jalaj/PycharmProjects/NLPython/NLPython/ch9/gradientdescentexample/data.csv", delimiter=",")

    # Step2 : Define certain hyperparameters

    # how fast our model will converge means how fast we will get the line of best fit.
    # Converge means how fast our ML model get the optimal line of best fit.
    learning_rate = 0.0001
    # Here we need to draw the line which is best fit for our data.
    # so we are using y = mx + b ( x and y are points; m is slop; b is the y intercept)
    # for initial y-intercept guess
    initial_b = 0
    # initial slope guess
    initial_m = 0
    # How much do you want to train the model?
    # Here data set is small so we iterate this model for 1000 times.
    num_iterations = 1000
```

Figure 9.17: Code snippet of gradient descent

You can see the output in *Figure 9.18*:

```
# Step 3 - print the values of b, m and all function which calculate gradient descent and errors
# Here we are printing the initial values of b, m and error.
# As well as there is the function compute_error_for_line_given_points()
# which compute the errors for given point
print "Starting gradient descent at b = {0}, m = {1}, error = {2}".format(initial_b, initial_m,
                                        compute_error_for_line_given_points(initial_b, initial_m, points))
print "Running..."

# By using this gradient_descent_runner() function we will actually calculate gradient descent
[b, m] = gradient_descent_runner(points, initial_b, initial_m, learning_rate, num_iterations)

# Here we are printing the values of b, m and error after getting the line of best fit for the given dataset.
print "After {0} iterations b = {1}, m = {2}, error = {3}".format(num_iterations, b, m, compute_error_for_line_given_points(b, m, points))

if __name__ == '__main__':
    run()
```

Figure 9.18: Output of gradient descent

As you can see in *Figure 9.18*, we have called two functions:
`compute_error_for_line_points()`, which will compute the error between the actual value and predicted value, and `gradient_descent_runner()`, which will calculate the gradient for us. We need to understand first how we are going to calculate errors and then gradient descent.

Calculating error or loss

There are many ways to calculate the error for ML algorithms, but in this chapter we will be using one of the most popular techniques: sum of squared distance error. Now we are going straight into details.

What does this error function do for us? Recall our goal: we want to get the line of best fit for our dataset. Refer to *Figure 9.19*, which is the equation of line slope. Here, *m* is the slope of line, *b* is the *y* intercept, *x* and *y* are the data points--in our case, *x* is the numbers of hours the student studies and *y* is the test score. Refer to *Figure 9.19*:

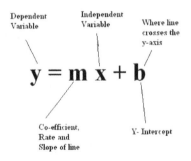

Figure 9.19: Line slope equation (Image credit: https://www.tes.com/lessons/Xn3MVjd8CqjH-Q/y-mx-b)

Using the preceding equation, we are drawing the line and starting with random values of slope m and y intercept b and using our first column data points as value of x so that we get a value of y. In the training data, we already have y values, which means that we know the test score of each student. So for each student, we need to calculate the error. Let's take a very intuitive example; note that we are working with dummy values for explanation. Suppose you get y value of 41.0 by putting a random value of m and b. Now you have the actual value of y, that is, 52.5, then the difference between the predicted value and real value is 11.5. This is just for a single data point but we need to calculate for every data point. So to do this kind of error calculation, we are using sum of squared distance error.

Now how are we calculating the sum of squared distance error and why are we using sum of squared distance error?

So let's begin with the first question, the equation to calculate sum of squared distance error is given in *Figure 9.20*:

$$\text{Error}_{(m,b)} = \frac{1}{N} \sum_{i=1}^{N} (y_i - (mx_i + b))^2$$

Figure 9.20: Equation for calculating sum of squared distance error (Image credit: https://spin.atomicobject.com/wp-content/uploads/linear_regression_error1.png)

As you can see, the last part mx_i+b is the line that we have drawn by choosing a random value of m and b and we can actually put y in place of mx_i+b. So here, we are calculating the difference between the original y value with the generated y value. We are subtracting the original y value and generated y value and squaring this value for each data point. We are squaring the value because we don't want to deal with negative values as we are performing sum after calculating square and we want to measure the overall magnitude. We don't want the actual value as we are trying to minimize this overall magnitude. Now back to the equation; we have calculated the square of the difference of the original y value and the generated y value. Now we are performing summation for all these points; we will use the sigma notation to indicate the summation operation for all the data points in the dataset. By this time, we have the sum value that indicates the error magnitude and we will divide these values by the total number of data points. After this, we will get the actual error value that we want.

You can see the animated image at this GitHub link:

```
https://github.com/jalajthanaki/NLPython/blob/master/ch9/gradientdescentexample
/gradient_descent_example.gif
```

You can see that the line is moving for each iteration in order to generate the line with the best fit for our dataset. We are updating the value of *m* and *b* according to the value of our error. Now, for each timestamp, the line is static and we need to calculate the error. Refer to *Figure 9.21*:

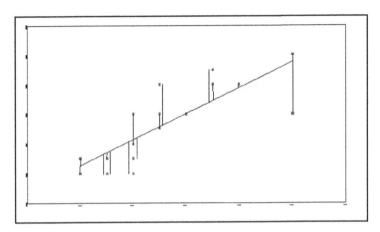

Figure 9.21: Calculating distance between line and data points at given timestamp (Image credit: http://statutor.org/c3/glmregression/IMAG004.JPG)

Now we need to express our intuitive example and equation in a technical manner as per the given equation. Here, we are calculating the distance from each data point to the line that we have drawn, squaring them, summing them all together, and then dividing by the total number of points. So, after every iteration or timestamp, we can calculate our error value and get to know how bad our line is or how good our line is. If our line is bad, then to get the line of best fit, we update the values of *m* and *b*. So the error value provides us with an indication of whether there is a possibility of improvement or not in order to generate the line of best fit. So eventually we want to minimize the value of error that we are getting here in order to generate the line of best fit. How will we minimize this error and generate the line of best fit? The next step is called **gradient descent**.

A couple of reasons for sum of squared error is that, for linear regression, this is the most popular technique to calculate the error. You can also use this if you have a large dataset.

Let's see the coding part and then we will jump to our core part of calculating gradient descent. See the code snippet in *Figure 9.22*:

```python
# y = mx + b
# m is slope, b is y-intercept
# here we are calculating the sum of squared error by using the equation which we have seen in the book.
def compute_error_for_line_given_points(b, m, points):
    totalError = 0
    for i in range(0, len(points)):
        x = points[i, 0]
        y = points[i, 1]
        totalError += (y - (m * x + b)) ** 2
    return totalError / float(len(points))
```

Figure 9.22: Code snippet for calculating sum of squared error

Now let's see the next step--calculating gradient descent.

Calculating gradient descent

Using the error function, we know whether we should update our line in order to generate the line of best fit or not, but how to update the line is what we are going to see in this section. How will we minimize this error and generate the line of best fit? So to answer this question, first of all, let's get some basic understanding about gradient descent and the coding part, where we are just left with our one last function, gradient_descent_runner(). Refer to *Figure 9.23*:

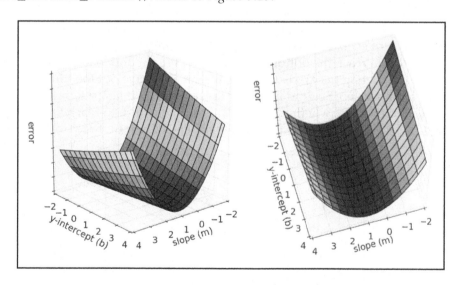

Figure 9.23: A 3D graph for understanding gradient descent (Image credit: https://spin.atomicobject.com/wp-content/uploads/gradient_descent_error_surface.png)

As you can see in *Figure 9.23*, this is a three dimensional graph. These two graphs are the same; their viewing angle is different. So these graphs show all the possible values of slope *m*, *y*-intercept *b*, and *error*. These are pairs of three values including *m*, *b*, and *error*. Here, the *x* axis is a slope value, the *y* axis is a *y*-intercept, and the *z* axis is the error value. We try to get the point where the error is the least. If you see the graph carefully, then you can observe that at the bottom of the curve, the error value is the least. The point where the value is the least is called **local minima** in ML. In complex datasets, you may find multiple local minima; here our dataset is simple so we have a single local minima. If you have a complex and high-dimensional dataset where you have multiple local minima, then you need to do a second-order optimization to decide which local minima you should choose for better accuracy. We are not going to see second-order optimization in this book. Now let's look back to our graph where we can visually identify the point that gives us the smallest error value and the same point also gives us the ideal value of *y*-intercept that is *b* and slope value that is *m*. When we get the ideal value for *b* and *m*, we will put these values in our *y=mx+c* equation and then magic will happen and we will get the line of best fit. This is not the only way to get the line of best fit, but my motive is to give you an in-depth idea about gradient descent so that we can later use this concept in DL.

Now visually, you can see the smallest point where the error is the smallest, but how to reach this point? The answer is by calculating the gradient. Gradient is also called **slope** but this is not the slope value *m* so don't get confused. We are talking about slope in the direction of getting us to that smallest error point. So we have some *b* value and some *m* value and after every iteration, we update these *b* and *m* values so that we can reach that smallest error value point. So in perspective of the three dimensional image, if you are at the top of the curve, for every iteration we calculate the gradient and error and then update the values of *m* and *b* to reach the bottom of that curve. We need to reach to the bottom of the curve and by calculating the gradient value, we get an idea about the direction in which we should take our next step. So gradient is the tangent line that keeps telling us the direction we need to move in, whether it's upward or downward, to reach the smallest error point and obtain ideal *b* and *m* values to generate the line of best fit. Refer to *Figure 9.24*:

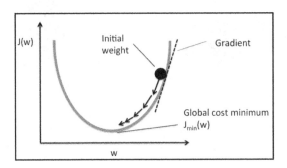

Figure 9.24: Gradient values and direction (Image credit: https://sebastianraschka.com/images/faq/closed-form-vs-gd/ball.png)

Now let's see the last but not least equation of calculating gradient descent. In *Figure 9.25*, you can see the equations of gradient descent that are nothing but a partial derivative of our error function. We have taken the equation of sum of squared error and performed partial derivatives with respect to m and b to calculate gradient descent. The outcome is in *Figure 9.25*:

$$\frac{\partial}{\partial m} = \frac{2}{N} \sum_{i=1}^{N} -x_i(y_i - (mx_i + b))$$

$$\frac{\partial}{\partial b} = \frac{2}{N} \sum_{i=1}^{N} -(y_i - (mx_i + b))$$

Figure 9.25: Equations for calculating gradient descent (Image credit: https://spin.atomicobject.com/wp-content/uploads/linear_regression_gradient1.png)

The left-hand side ∂ symbol is the symbol of partial derivative. Here, we have two equations because we take our error function and generate the partial derivative with respect to variable m, and in the second equation, we generate the partial derivative with respect to variable b. With these two equations, we will get the updated values of b and m.

To calculate the gradient, we need to derive the partial derivative of the error function. For some problems in ML and DL, we don't know the partial derivative of the error function, which implies that we can't find the gradient. So we don't know how to deal with this kind of function. Your error function should be differentiable, which means that your error function should have partial derivatives. Another thing here is that we are using the linear equation, but if you have high-dimensional data, then you can use the non-linear function if you know the error function. Gradient descent doesn't give us the minima when we start for the first time. Gradient just tells us how to update our m and b values, whether we should update with a positive value or negative value. So gradient gives us an idea how to update values of m and b, which means that by calculating the gradient, we are getting the direction and trying to reach the point where we get the smallest error value and best values for m and b.

Now it is time to jump to the code again and finish gradient descent. Refer to *Figure 9.26*:

```python
def step_gradient(b_current, m_current, points, learningRate):
    b_gradient = 0
    m_gradient = 0
    N = float(len(points))
    for i in range(0, len(points)):
        x = points[i, 0]
        y = points[i, 1]
        # Here we are coding up out partial derivatives equations and
        # generate the updated value for m and b to get the local minima
        b_gradient += -(2/N) * (y - ((m_current * x) + b_current))
        m_gradient += -(2/N) * x * (y - ((m_current * x) + b_current))
    # we are multiplying the b_gradient and m_gradient with learningrate
    # so it is important to choose ideal learning rate if we make it to high then our model learn nothing
    # if we make it to small then our training is to slow and there are the chances of over fitting
    # so learning rate is important hyper parameter.
    new_b = b_current - (learningRate * b_gradient)
    new_m = m_current - (learningRate * m_gradient)
    return [new_b, new_m]

def gradient_descent_runner(points, starting_b, starting_m, learning_rate, num_iterations):
    b = starting_b
    m = starting_m
    for i in range(num_iterations):
        # we are using step_gradient function to calculate the actual partial derivatives for error function
        b, m = step_gradient(b, m, array(points), learning_rate)
    return [b, m]
```

Figure 9.26: Code snippet of the actual gradient descent runner function

In the code, we have multiplied m_gradient and b_gradient with the learning rate, so learning rate is an important hyperparameter. Be careful while selecting its value. If you select a very high value, your model may not train at all. If you select a very low value, then it would take a lot of time to train and there is a chance of overfitting as well. Refer to *Figure 9.27*, which provides you with an intuition about a good learning rate:

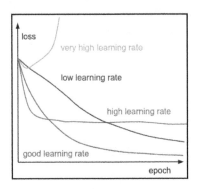

Figure 9.27: Learning rate intuition (Image credit: http://cs231n.github.io/assets/nn3/learningrates.jpeg)

This is it for the coding part of linear regression and gradient descent. Let's run the code and *Figure 9.28* will give you an idea about the output:

```
Starting gradient descent at b = 0, m = 0, error = 5565.10783448
Running...
After 1000 iterations b = 0.0889365199374, m = 1.47774408519, error = 112.614810116
```

Figure 9.28: Code snippet of output

There are types of gradient descent, so let's name a few of them, but we are not going into detail. You can explore gradient descent with momentum, Adagrad, Adam, and so on.

 I will provide you with a link that will be helpful to you if you really want to explore more:
https://www.analyticsvidhya.com/blog/2017/03/introduction-to-gradient-descent-algorithm-along-its-variants/

Now it's time to understand the activation function, so let's begin!

Activation functions

Let's see the activation function first. I want to give you an idea at what stage of ANN we will use this activation function. In our discussion of the perceptron, we said that neural networks will generate an output of one if it exceeds a certain threshold; otherwise, the output will be zero. This whole mechanism to calculate the threshold and generate the output based on this threshold is taken care by the activation function.

Activation functions are able to provide us with values that lie between 0 and 1. After this, using our threshold value, we can generate output value 1 or output value 0. Suppose our threshold value is 0.777 and our activation function output is 0.457, then our resultant output will be 0; if our activation function output is 0.852, then our resultant output will be 1. So, here is how the activation function works in ANN.

Usually, in neural networks, we have a certain weight and input value for each neuron. We are summing them and generating the weighted sum value. When we pass these values through a non-linear function, this non-linear function activates certain numbers of neurons to get the output for a complex task; this activation process of neurons using certain non-linear mathematical functions is known as an **activation function** or **transfer function**. Activation functions map input nodes to the output nodes in a certain fashion using certain mathematical operations.

The purpose of having an activation function in ANN is to introduce non-linearity in the network. Let's understand this step by step.

Let's concentrate on the structure of ANN. This ANN structure can be further divided into three sections:

- **Architecture:** Architecture is all about deciding the arrangement of neurons and layers in the ANN
- **Activities:** In order to generate the output of complex tasks, we need to see the activities of the neurons--how one neuron responds to another to generate complex behavior
- **Learning rule:** When ANN generates the output, we need to update our ANN weight at each timestamp to optimize the output using the error function

Activation function is part of the activities section. As we mentioned, we will introduce non-linearity into the ANN. The reason behind it is that without non-linearity, the ANN can't produce complex behavior to solve complex tasks. Most of the time in DL, we use non-linear activation functions to get the complex behavior. Apart from that, we also want to map our input to the output in a non-linear manner.

If you are not using a non-linear activation function, then the ANN won't give you significant amount of useful output for complex tasks because you are passing out the matrices, and if you are using more than one layer in your ANN with a linear activation function, you get an output that is the summation of the input value, weights, and bias from all the layers. This output gives you another linear function and that means that this linear function converts the behavior of a multi-layer ANN to single-layer ANN. This kind of behavior is not at all useful to solve complex tasks.

I want to highlight the idea of connectionism. The connectionism in ANN is to use neurons that are interconnected with each other and produce complex behavior, just like human brains, and we cannot achieve this kind of behavior without introducing non-linearity in the ANN. Refer to *Figure 9.29* to understand activation function:

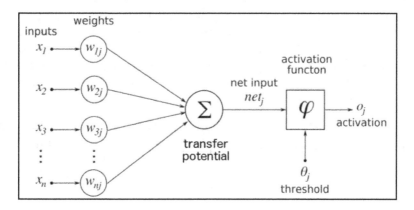

Figure 9.29: ANN with activation function (Image credit: https://cdn-images-1.medium.com/max/800/0*bWX2_ecf3l6lKyVA.png)

Here, we are going to cover these functions mentioned in the preceding image:

- **Transfer potential:** This is the function that aggregates inputs and weights. More specifically, this function performs the summation of inputs and weights
- **Activation function:** This function takes the output of the transfer potential function as input and applies a non-linear mathematical transformation using an activation function
- **Threshold function:** Based on the activation function, the threshold function either activates the neuron or does not activate

Transfer potential is a simple summation function that will perform the summing of inner dot product of the input to the weights of the connection. You can see the equation in *Figure 9.30*:

$$\sum_{i=1}^{n} x_i * w_i$$

Figure 9.30: Summation equation for transfer potential (Image credit: https://cdn-images-1.medium.com/max/800/0*005k9F1JxQ0oKEeM.png)

This transfer potential is generally a dot product, but it can use any mathematical equation such as a multi-quadratic function.

The activation function, on the other hand, should be any differentiable and non-linear function. It needs to be differentiable so that we can calculate the error gradient, and this function has to have a non-linear property to gain complex behavior from the neural network. Typically, we are using the sigmoid function as activation function, which takes the transfer potential output value as input to calculate the final output and then calculates the error between our actual output and the generated one. Then, we will use the concept of calculating the gradient of error as well as applying a backpropagation optimization strategy in order to update the weight of the connection of the ANN.

Figure 9.31 expresses the transfer potential function in terms of theta, also called the **logit**, which we will be using in the equation of the logistic sigmoid activation function:

$$\theta = \sum_{i=1}^{n} X_i * W_i$$

Figure 9.31: Transfer potential output in the form of logit value (Image credit: https://cdn-images-1.medium.com/max/800/0*mPYW0-FKPTOSACPP.png)

You can see the equation of the logistic sigmoid function in *Figure 9.32*:

$$f(\theta) = \frac{1}{1 + e^{-\theta}}$$

Figure 9.32: Logistic sigmoid activation function (Image credit: https://cdn-images-1.medium.com/max/800/0*SwSxznoodb2762_9.png)

The whole idea behind an activation function is roughly modeled the way neurons communicate in the brain with each other. Each one is activated through its action potential if it reaches a certain threshold; then we know whether to activate a neuron or not. The activation function simulates the spike of the brain's action potential. **Deep neural nets (DNN)** are called **universal approximator** functions because they can compute any function at any instance. They can calculate any differentiable linear as well as non-linear function. Now you might ask me when to use this activation function. We will see this in the next paragraph.

There is a variety of activation functions available. Be careful while using them. We should not use any of them just because it sounds new and cool. Here, we will talk about how you know which one you should use. We will see three main activation functions because of their wide usage in DL, although there are other activation functions that you can use.

These three activation functions are mentioned as follows:

- Sigmoid
- Tanh
- ReLU and its variants

Sigmoid

The sigmoid function is very easy to understand in terms of its mathematical concepts. Its mathematical formula is shown in *Figure 9.33*:

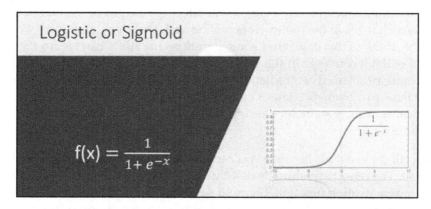

Figure 9.33: Sigmoid function equation (Image credit: https://cdn-images-1.medium.com/max/800/1*QHPXkxGmIyxn7mH4BtRJXQ.png)

As you can see in *Figure 9.33*, the sigmoid function will take the given equation, take a number, and squash this number in the range of zero and one. It produces an s-shaped curve.

This function is the first one to be used in ANN as an activation function because it could be interpreted as the firing rate of neuron--zero means no firing and one is fully saturated firing. When we use this activation function for DNN, we get to know some limitations of this activation function that makes it less popular nowadays.

Some basic problems with these functions are as follows:

- It suffers from the gradient vanishing problem
- It has a slow convergence rate
- It is not a zero-centric function

Let's understand each of the problems in detail:

Vanishing gradient problem: You can find this problem when you are training certain ANNs with gradient-based methods and mostly in ANNs with backpropagation. This problem makes it really hard to learn and tune the parameters of the earlier layers in the ANN. This becomes more problematic when you add more layers to your ANN. If we choose the activation function wisely, then this problem can be solved. I want to give you details about the problem first and then we will discuss the cause behind it.

Gradient-based methods learn the values of parameters by understanding how a small change in the input parameters and weights will affect the output of the NN. If this gradient is too small, then changes in the parameters will be such that they cause very small changes in the output of ANN. In this case, after some iterations the ANN can't learn the parameters effectively and will not converge in the way we want. This is exactly what happens in a gradient vanishing problem. The gradient of the output of the network with respect to the parameters in the early layers becomes very small. You can say that even if there is a large change in the value of the parameters for input layers and weights, this does not provide a big effect in the output.

I'm giving you all these details because you can face this same problem with the sigmoid function as well. The most basic thing is that this vanishing gradient problem depends on the choice of your activation function. Sigmoid squashes the input into a small range of output in a non-linear manner. If you give a real number to the sigmoid function, it will squash that number in the range of [0,1]. So there are large regions of input space that are mapped to a very small range. Even a large change in input parameters will produce a very small change in output because the gradient of this region is small. For the sigmoid function, when a neuron saturates close to either zero or one, the gradient at this region is very close to zero. During backpropagation, this local gradient will be multiplied by the gradient of each layer's output gate. So if the first layer maps to a large input region, we get a very small gradient as well as a very small change in the output of the first layer. This small change passes to the next layer and makes even smaller changes in the second layer's output. If we have a DNN, there is no change in the output after some layers. This is the problem with the sigmoid activation function.

You can refer to the vanishing gradient problem in detail at this link: `https://ayearofai.com/rohan-4-the-vanishing-gradient-problem-ec68f76ffb9b`

Low convergence rate: Due to this vanishing gradient problem, sometimes the ANN with the sigmoid activation function converges very slowly.

 If you really want to dig deep into the vanishing gradient problem, then you can check out this link: `https://cs224d.stanford.edu/notebooks/vanishing_grad_example.html`

Non-zero-centric function: The sigmoid function is not a zero-centric activation function. What this means is that the sigmoid function's output range is [0,1], which means the value of the function's output will be always positive so that makes the gradient of the weights become either all positive or all negative. This makes the gradient update go too far in different directions and this makes optimization harder.

Due to these limitations, the sigmoid function is not used recently in DNNs. Although you can solve these problems using other functions, you can also use the sigmoid activation function only at the last layer of your ANN.

TanH

To overcome the problems of the sigmoid function, we will introduce an activation function named **hyperbolic tangent function (TanH)**. The equation of TanH is given in *Figure 9.34*:

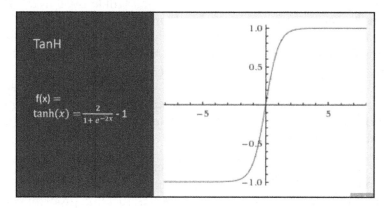

Figure 9.34: Tanh activation function equation (Image credit: https://cdn-images-1.medium.com/max/800/1*HJhu8BO7KxkjqRRMSaz0Gw.png)

This function squashes the input region in the range of [-1 to 1] so its output is zero-centric, which makes optimization easier for us. This function also suffers from the vanishing gradient problem, so we need to see other activation functions.

ReLu and its variants

Rectified Linear Unit (ReLu) is the most popular function in the industry. See its equation in *Figure 9.35*:

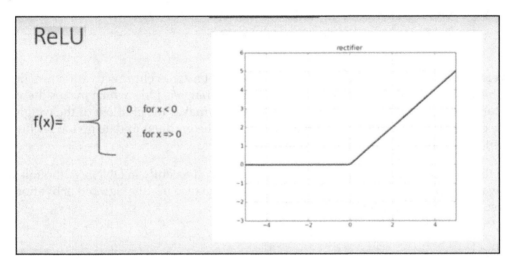

Figure 9.35: ReLu activation function equation (Image credit: https://cdn-images-1.medium.com/max/800/1*JtJaS_wPTCshSvAFlCu_Wg.png)

If you will see the ReLu mathematical equation, then you will know that it is just *max(0,x)*, which means that the value is zero when x is less than zero and linear with the slope of *1* when x is greater than or equal to zero. A researcher named Krizhevsky published a paper on image classification and said that they get six times faster convergence using ReLu as an activation function. You can read this research paper by clicking on http://www.cs.toronto.edu/~fritz/absps/imagenet.pdf. This function is simple and doesn't have any complex computation and is less expensive compared to sigmoid and TanH. This is the reason that this function learns faster. Apart from this, it also doesn't have the vanishing gradient problem.

We used to apply the activation function in each layer present in the DNN. Nowadays, ReLu is used for most of the DNN, but it is applied to the hidden layers of DNN. The output layer should use softmax if you are solving a classification problem because the softmax function gives us the probability for each class. We have used the softmax activation function in the word2vec algorithm. In case of a regression problem, the output layer should use a linear function because the signal goes through unchanged.

Apart from all these wonderful advantages of ReLu, it has one problem: some units of the neural network can be fragile and die during training, which means that a big gradient flowing through a ReLu neuron could cause a weight update that makes it never activate on any data point again. So the gradient flowing through it will always be zero from that point on. To overcome this limitation of ReLu, a variant of ReLu has been introduced--Leaky ReLu. Instead of the function being zero when *x* is less than zero (*x<0*), Leaky ReLu has a small negative slope. Refer to *Figure 9.36*:

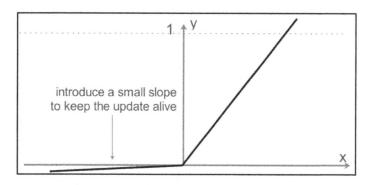

Figure 9.36: Leaky ReLu (Image credit: http://wangxinliu.com/images/machine_learning/leakyrelu.png)

There is another variant called **maxout** that is a generalized form of both ReLu and Leaky ReLu, but it doubles the parameters of each neuron, which is a disadvantage.

Now you know enough about activation functions, so which one should you use? The answer is ReLu, but if too many neurons die, then use Leaky ReLu or maxout. This activation function is applied to the hidden layer. For the output layer, use the softmax function if you are solving a classification problem or linear activation function if you are solving a regression problem. The sigmoid and TanH shouldn't be used in DNNs. This is quite an interesting research area and there is much room to come up with great activation functions.

There are other activation functions out there that you can check out: identity function, binary step function, ArcTan, and so on. Here, we will check the third important concept-- loss functions.

Loss functions

Sometimes, loss functions are also referred to as **cost functions** or **error functions**. A loss function gives us an idea of how good the ANN performs with respect to the given training examples. So first, we define the error function and when we start to train our ANN, we will get the output. We compare the generated output with the expected output given as part of the training data and calculate the gradient value of this error function. We backpropagate the error gradient in the network so that we can update the existing weights and bias values to optimize our generated output. The error function is the main part of the training. There are various error functions available. If you ask me which error function to choose, then there is no specific answer because all ANN training and optimization is based on this loss function. So it depends on your data and problem statement. If you ask somebody which error function you have used in your ANN, then indirectly you are asking them the whole logic of the training algorithm. Whatever error function you will use, make sure that the function must be differentiable. I have listed down some of the most popular error functions:

- Quadratic cost function also known as **mean squared error** or **sum squared error**
- Cross-entropy cost function also known as **Bernoulli negative log likelihood** or **binary cross-entropy**
- Kullback-Leibler divergence also known as **information divergence**, **information gain**, **relative entropy**, or **KLIC**
- Apart from these three, there are many other loss functions such as exponential cost, Hellinger distance, Generalized Kullback-Leibler divergence, and Itakura-Saito distance

In general, we are using sum of square error for regression and cross-entropy for categorical data and classification tasks.

We have seen the most important mathematical and theoretical concepts to develop ANN. In the next section, we will see the implementation of our first ANN. Let's jump to the implementation part.

Implementation of ANN

In this section, we will implement our first ANN in Python using `numpy` as our dependency. During this implementation, you can relate how gradient descent, activation function, and loss function have been integrated into our code. Apart from this, we will see the concept of backpropagation.

We will see the implementation of a single-layer NN with backpropagation.

Single-layer NN with backpropagation

Here, we will see the concept of backpropagation first, then we will start coding and I will explain things as we code.

Backpropagation

In a single-layer neural network, we have input that we feed to the first layer. These layer connections have some weights. We use the input, weight, and bias and sum them. This sum passes through the activation function and generates the output. This is an important step; whatever output has been generated should be compared with the actual expected output. As per the error function, calculate the error. Now use the gradient of the error function and calculate the error gradient. The process is the same as we have seen in the gradient descent section. This error gradient gives you an indication of how you can optimize the generated output. Error gradient flows back in the ANN and starts updating the weight so that we get a better output in the next iteration. The process of flowing back the error gradient in ANN to update weight in order to generate more accurate output is called **backpropagation**. In short, backpropagation is a popular training technique to train a neural network by updating the weight via gradient descent.

All other aspects of calculation and math will be shown in the coding part. So let's code our own single-layer feedforward neural network with backpropagation.

First, we will define the main function and our abstract steps. Here, we will give the input and output values. As our data is labeled, it is a supervised learning example. The second step will be the training, and we will repeat the training to iterate for 10,000 times. We will first start with a random weight and adjust the weight as per the activation function and error function. Refer to *Figure 9.37:*

```
if __name__ == "__main__":

    #Intialise a single neuron neural network.
    neural_network = NeuralNetwork()

    print "Random starting synaptic weights: "
    print neural_network.synaptic_weights

    # The training set. We have 4 examples, each consisting of 3 input values
    # and 1 output value.
    training_set_inputs = array([[0, 0, 1], [1, 1, 1], [1, 0, 1], [0, 1, 1]])
    # Python store output in horizontally so we have use transpose
    training_set_outputs = array([[0, 1, 1, 0]]).T

    # Train the neural network using a training set.
    # Do it 10,000 times and make small adjustments each time.
    neural_network.train(training_set_inputs, training_set_outputs, 10000)

    print "New synaptic weights after training: "
    print neural_network.synaptic_weights

    # Test the neural network with a new situation.
    print "Considering new situation [1, 0, 0] -> ?: "
    print neural_network.think(array([1, 0, 0]))
```

Figure 9.37: Code snippet of the main function for a single-layer ANN

Here, we are using sigmoid as the activation function. We will use the sigmoid derivative to calculate gradient of the sigmoid curve. Our error function is a simple subtraction of the actual output from the generated output. We multiply this error value with the gradient to get the error gradient that helps us adjust the weight of NN. The new updated weight and input again passes through the ANN, calculates gradient descent of the sigmoid curve and error gradient, and adjusts the weight until we get minimum error. Refer to *Figure 9.38* and *Figure 9.39:*

```python
from numpy import exp, array, random, dot


class NeuralNetwork():
    def __init__(self):
        # Seed the random number generator, so it generates the same numbers
        # every time the program runs.
        random.seed(1)

        # We model a single neuron, with 3 input connections and 1 output connection.
        # We assign random weights to a 3 x 1 matrix, with values in the range -1 to 1
        # and mean 0.
        self.synaptic_weights = 2 * random.random((3, 1)) - 1

    # The Sigmoid function, which describes an S shaped curve.
    # We pass the weighted sum of the inputs through this function to
    # normalise them between 0 and 1.
    def __sigmoid(self, x):
        return 1 / (1 + exp(-x))

    # The derivative of the Sigmoid function.
    # This is the gradient of the Sigmoid curve.
    # It indicates how confident we are about the existing weight.
    def __sigmoid_derivative(self, x):
        return x * (1 - x)
```

Figure 9.38: Code snippet of a single-layer ANN

Refer to the following code snippet:

```python
    # We train the neural network through a process of trial and error.
    # Adjusting the synaptic weights each time.
    def train(self, training_set_inputs, training_set_outputs, number_of_training_iterations):
        for iteration in xrange(number_of_training_iterations):
            # Pass the training set through our neural network (a single neuron).
            output = self.think(training_set_inputs)

            # Calculate the error (The difference between the desired output
            # and the predicted output).
            error = training_set_outputs - output

            # Multiply the error by the input and again by the gradient of the Sigmoid curve.
            # This means less confident weights are adjusted more.
            # This means inputs, which are zero, do not cause changes to the weights.
            adjustment = dot(training_set_inputs.T, error * self.__sigmoid_derivative(output))

            # Adjust the weights.
            self.synaptic_weights += adjustment

    # The neural network thinks.
    def think(self, inputs):
        # Pass inputs through our neural network (our single neuron).
        return self.__sigmoid(dot(inputs, self.synaptic_weights))
```

Figure 9.39: Code snippet of ANN

When you run the code, you will get the following result. Refer to *Figure 9.40*:

```
Random starting synaptic weights:
[[-0.16595599]
 [ 0.44064899]
 [-0.99977125]]
New synaptic weights after training:
[[ 9.67299303]
 [-0.2078435 ]
 [-4.62963669]]
Considering new situation [1, 0, 0] -> ?:
[ 0.99993704]
```

Figure 9.40: Output snippet of single layer ANN

Exercise

Build a three-layer deep ANN using numpy as a dependency. (Hint: In a single-layer ANN, we used single layer, but here, you will use three layers. Backpropagation usually uses recursively taken derivatives, but in our one layer demo, there was no recursion. So you need to apply recursive derivatives.)

Deep learning and deep neural networks

Now, just shift from ANN to DNN. In the upcoming section, we will see deep learning, architecture of DNN, and compare the approaches of DL for NLP and ML for NLP.

Revisiting DL

We have seen some basic details about DL. Here, the purpose is just to recall things as a little refresher. ANN that is not two or three layers but many layers deep is called DNN. When we use many layers deep neural networks on lots of data using lots of computing power, we call this process deep learning.

Let's see the architecture of a deep neural network.

The basic architecture of DNN

In this section, we will see the architecture of a DNN. The pictorial representation looks very simple and is defined with some cool mathematical formulas in the form of activation function, activation function for hidden layer, loss function, and so on. In *Figure 9.41*, you can see the basic architecture of a DNN:

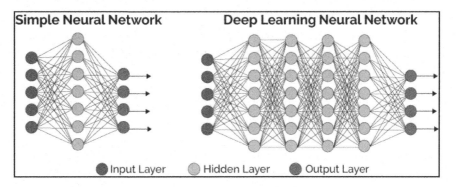

Figure 9.41: Architecture of DNN (Image credit: https://cdn-images-1.medium.com/max/800/1*5egrX--WuyrLA7gBEXdg5A.png)

Now why are we using a multi-layer deep neural network, are there any certain reasons for this, and what is the significance of having many layers?

Let me explain why we are using multi-layer DNNs. Suppose, as a coder, you want to develop a system that identifies the images of fruits. Now you have some images of oranges and apples and you develop a logic such as I can identify images using the color of the fruits and you have also added shape as an identification parameter. You do some coding and are ready with the result. Now if someone tells you that we also have images that are black and white. Now you need to redo your coding work. Some varieties of images are too complex for you, as a human, to code, although your brain is very good at identifying the actual fruit name. So if you have such a complex problem and you don't know how to code or you know less details about the features or parameters that will be helpful for the machine to solve the problem, then you use a deep neural network. There are several reasons and those are mentioned as follows:

- DNN has been derived using the abstract concept of how a human brain works.
- Using DNN, we flip the approach of our coding. Initially, we provided features like color, shape, and so on to the machine to identify the fruit name in the given images, but with DNN and DL, we provide many examples to the machine and the machine will learn about the features by itself. After this, when we provide a new image of a fruit to the machine, it will predict the name of the fruit.

Now you really want to know how DNN can learn features by itself, so let's highlight some points as follows:

- DNN uses a cascade of many layers of non-linear processing units that are used for feature extraction and transformation. Each successive layer of DNN uses the output from the previous layer as input, and this process is very similar to how the human brain transmits information from one neuron to the other. So we try to implement the same structure with the help of DNN.
- In DL, features have been learned using multiple levels of representation with the help of DNNs. Higher levels of features or representation are derived from the lower level of features. So we can say that the concept of deriving features or representation in DNN is hierarchical. We learn something new using this lower level of ideas and we try to learn something extra. Our brain also uses and derives concepts in a hierarchical manner. This different level of features or representation is related to different levels of abstraction.
- Multi-layers of DNN helps the machine to derive the hierarchical representation and this is the significance of having many layers as part of the architecture.
- With the help of DNN and mathematical concepts, machines are capable to mimic some of the processes of the human brain.
- DL can be applied to a supervised as well as unsupervised dataset to develop NLP applications such as machine translation, summarization, question answering system, essay generation, image caption tagging, and so on.

Now we will move to the next section where we will discuss the need of deep learning in NLP.

Deep learning in NLP

The early era of NLP is based on the rule-based system, and for many applications, an early prototype is based on the rule-based system because we did not have huge amounts of data. Now, we are applying ML techniques to process natural language, using statistical and probability-based approaches where we are representing words in form of one-hot encoded format or co-occurrence matrix.

In this approach, we are getting mostly syntactic representations instead of semantic representations. When we are trying out lexical-based approaches such as bag of words, ngrams, and so on, we cannot differentiate certain context.

We hope that all these issues will be solved by DNN and DL because nowadays, we have huge amounts of data that we can use. We have developed good algorithms such as word2vec, GloVe, and so on in order to capture the semantic aspect of natural language. Apart from this, DNN and DL provide some cool capabilities that are listed as follows:

- **Expressibility:** This capability expresses how well the machine can do approximation for a universal function
- **Trainability:** This capability is very important for NLP applications and indicates how well and fast a DL system can learn about the given problem and start generating significant output
- **Generalizability:** This indicates how well the machine can generalize the given task so that it can predict or generate an accurate result for unseen data

Apart from the preceding three capabilities, there are other capabilities that DL provides us with, such as interpretability, modularity, transferability, latency, adversarial stability, and security.

We know languages are complex things to deal with and sometimes we also don't know how to solve certain NLP problems. The reason behind this is that there are so many languages in the world that have their own syntactic structure and word usages and meanings that you can't express in other languages in the same manner. So we need some techniques that help us generalize the problem and give us good results. All these reasons and factors lead us in the direction of the usage of DNN and DL for NLP applications.

Now let's see the difference between classical NLP techniques and DL NLP techniques because that will connect our dots in terms of how DL can be more useful for us to solve NLP domain-related problems.

Difference between classical NLP and deep learning NLP techniques

In this section, we will compare the classical NLP techniques and DL techniques for NLP. So let's begin! Refer to *Figure 9.42*:

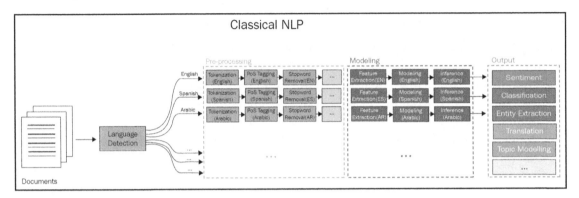

Figure 9.42: Classical NLP approach (Image credit: https://s3.amazonaws.com/aylien-main/misc/blog/images/nlp-language-dependence-small.png)

Refer to *Figure 9.43* for DL techniques:

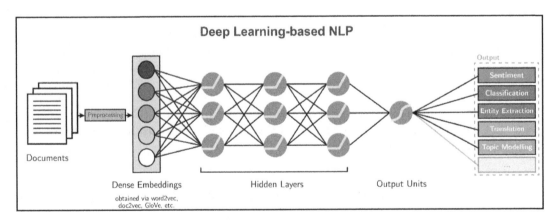

Figure 9.43: Deep learning approach for NLP (Image credit: https://s3.amazonaws.com/aylien-main/misc/blog/images/nlp-language-dependence-small.png)

In classical NLP techniques, we preprocessed the data in the early stages before generating features out of the data. In the next phase, we use hand-crafted features that are generated using NER tools, POS taggers, and parsers. We feed these features as input to the ML algorithm and train the model. We will check the accuracy, and if the accuracy is not good, we will optimize some of the parameters of the algorithm and try to generate a more accurate result. Depending on the NLP application, you can include the module that detects the language and then generates features.

Now let's see the deep learning techniques for an NLP application. In this approach, we do some basic preprocessing on the data that we have. Then we convert our text input data to a form of dense vectors. To generate the dense vectors, we will use word-embedding techniques such as word2vec, GloVe, doc2vec, and so on, and feed these dense vector embedding to the DNN. Here, we are not using hand-crafted features but different types of DNN as per the NLP application, such as for machine translation, we are using a variant of DNN called **sequence-to-sequence model**. For summarization, we are using another variant, that is, **Long short-term memory units.(LSTMs)**. The multiple layers of DNNs generalize the goal and learn the steps to achieve the defined goal. In this process, the machine learns the hierarchical representation and gives us the result that we validate and tune the model as per the necessity.

 If you really want to see the coding of different variants of DNNs, then use this GitHub link:
https://github.com/wagamamaz/tensorflow-tutorial

The next section is the most interesting part of this chapter. We are going to build two major applications: one is for NLU and one is for NLG. We are using TensorFlow and Keras as our main dependencies to code the example. We will understand a variant of DNN such as sequence-to-sequence and LSTM as we code them for better understanding.

Guess what we are going to build? We are going to build a machine translator as part of an NLP application and we will generate a summary from recipes. So let's jump to the coding part! I will give you some interesting exercises!

Deep learning techniques and NLU

This section is coding-based and I will explain concepts as we go. The application that we are building here is one of the main applications in NLU.

There are so many languages spoken, written, or read by humans. Have you ever tried to learn a new language? If yes, then you know how difficult it is to acquire the skill of speaking a new language or writing a new language. Have you ever thought how Google translator is used in order to translate languages? If you are curious, then let's begin developing a machine translation application using a deep learning technique. Don't worry about questions like what type of DNN we will use because I'm explaining things to you in detail. So let's do some translation!

 Note that DL takes a lot of computing power so we are not going to actually train the model, although I will give you details about the training code, we will use the trained model to replicate the results at our end. Just to give you an idea: Google uses 100 GPU for one week continuously to train the language translation model. So we get through the code, understand the concept, use an already trained model, and see the result.

If you want to use any specific version of TensorFlow, you can follow this command. If you want to install TensorFlow 0.12 version, you can install it with the following commands:

```
$ export
TF_BINARY_URL=https://storage.googleapis.com/tensorflow/linux/cpu/tensorflo
w-0.12.1-cp27-none-linux_x86_64.whl
$ sudo pip install --upgrade $TF_BINARY_URL
```

If you want to use the version of TensorFlow then when you run the code please update you import statements. You can use the simple following command to install TensorFlow for CPU. I'm using GPU version only:

```
$ pip install tensorflow
```

If you want to run on GPU, you can use a cloud platform such as Google Cloud, AWS, or any other cloud platform or you need a GPU-enabled computer. To install TensorFlow for GPU, you can follow this link:

https://www.tensorflow.org/install/

Machine translation

Machine translation (MT) is a widely known application in the NLU domain. Researchers and tech giants are experimenting a lot in order to make a single MT system that can translate any language. This MT system is called a universal machine translation system. So the long-term goal is that we want to build a single MT system that can translate English to German and the same MT system should also translate English to French. We are trying to make one system that can help us translate any language. Let's talk about the efforts and experiments done by researchers till date to build a universal machine translation system.

In 1954, the first machine translation demo had been given, which translated 250 words between Russian and English. This was a dictionary-based approach, and this approach used the mapping of words for source and target languages. Here, translation was done word by word and it wasn't able to capture syntactic information, which means that the accuracy was not good.

The next version was interlingual; it took the source language and generated an intermediary language to encode and represent a certain rule about the source language syntax, grammar, and so on and then generated a target language from the intermediary language. This approach was good compared to the first one but soon this approach was replaced by **statistical machine translation (SMT)** techniques.

IBM used this SMT approach; they broke the text into segments and then compared it to an aligned bilingual corpus. After this, using statistical techniques and probabilities, the most likely translation was chosen.

The most used SMT in the world is Google translation, and recently, Google published a paper stating that their machine translation system uses deep learning to generate the great result. We are using the TensorFlow library, which is an open source library for deep learning provided by Google. We will code to know how to do machine translation using deep learning.

We are using movies subtitles as our dataset. This dataset includes both German and English languages. We are building a model that will translate the German language into English and vice versa. You can download the data from `http://opus.lingfil.uu.se/OpenSubtitles.php`. Here, I'm using the pickle format of data. Using `pickle`, which is a Python dependency, we can serialize our dataset.

To begin with, we are using LSTMs network that is used to remember long term and short term dependencies. We are using TensorFlow's built-in `data_utils` class to preprocess the data. Then we need to define the vocabulary size on which we need to train the model. Here, our dataset has a small size of vocabulary so we are considering all the words in the dataset, but we define vocab (vocabulary) size such as 30,000 words, that is, a small set of training dataset. We will use the `data_utils` class to read the data from the data directory. This class gives us tokenized and formatted words from both languages. Then we define TensorFlow's placeholder that are encoders and decoders for inputs. These both will be integer tensors that represent the discrete values. They are embedded into dense representation. We will feed our vocabulary words to the encoder and the encoded representation that is learned to the decoder. You can see the code at this Github link: `https ://github.com/jalajthanaki/NLPython/tree/master/ch9/MT/Machine_Translation_GR _EN`.

Now we can build our model. You can see the code snippets in *Figure 9.44*, *Figure 9.45*, and *Figure 9.46*:

```
# read dataset
X, Y, en_word2idx, en_idx2word, en_vocab, de_word2idx, de_idx2word, de_vocab = data_utils.read_d
ataset('data.pkl')

# inspect data
print 'Sentence in English - encoded:', X[0]
print 'Sentence in German - encoded:', Y[0]
print 'Decoded:\n------------------------'

for i in range(len(X[1])):
    print en_idx2word[X[1][i]],

print '\n'

for i in range(len(Y[1])):
    print de_idx2word[Y[1][i]],
```

Figure 9.44: Code snippet for MT

```
# data processing

# data padding
def data_padding(x, y, length = 15):
    for i in range(len(x)):
        x[i] = x[i] + (length - len(x[i])) * [en_word2idx['<pad>']]
        y[i] = [de_word2idx['<go>']] + y[i] + [de_word2idx['<eos>']] + (length-len(y[i])) * [de_
word2idx['<pad>']]

data_padding(X, Y)

# data splitting
X_train,  X_test, Y_train, Y_test = train_test_split(X, Y, test_size = 0.1)

del X
del Y
```

Figure 9.45: Code snippet for MT

```
input_seq_len = 15
output_seq_len = 17
en_vocab_size = len(en_vocab) + 2 # + <pad>, <ukn>
de_vocab_size = len(de_vocab) + 4 # + <pad>, <ukn>, <eos>, <go>

# placeholders
encoder_inputs = [tf.placeholder(dtype = tf.int32, shape = [None], name = 'encoder{}'.format(i))
 for i in range(input_seq_len)]
decoder_inputs = [tf.placeholder(dtype = tf.int32, shape = [None], name = 'decoder{}'.format(i))
 for i in range(output_seq_len)]

targets = [decoder_inputs[i+1] for i in range(output_seq_len-1)]
# add one more target
targets.append(tf.placeholder(dtype = tf.int32, shape = [None], name = 'last_target'))
target_weights = [tf.placeholder(dtype = tf.float32, shape = [None], name =
'target_w{}'.format(i)) for i in range(output_seq_len)]

# output projection
size = 512
w_t = tf.get_variable('proj_w', [de_vocab_size, size], tf.float32)
b = tf.get_variable('proj_b', [de_vocab_size], tf.float32)
w = tf.transpose(w_t)
output_projection = (w, b)
```

Figure 9.46: Code snippet for MT

Now let's understand this encoder- and decoder-based system. Google recently published a paper where they discuss the system that they integrated into their translation system, that is, **neural machine translation (NMT)**. It is an encoder decoder-based model with the new NMT architecture. Earlier, Google translated from language A to language English and then to language B. Now, Google translator can translate directly from one language to the other. Refer to *Figure 9.47*:

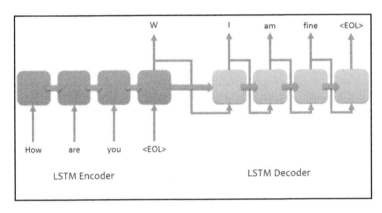

Figure 9.47: LSTM-based encoder and decoder architecture (Image credit:
https://camo.githubusercontent.com/242210d7d0151cae91107ee63bff364a860db5dd/687474703a2f2f6936342e74696e6797069632e636f6d2f333031333674652e706e67)

Now with the existence of NMT, there is no need to memorize phrase-to-phrase translation. With the help of NMT, a translation system can encode semantics of the sentences. This encoding is generalized so that it can translate from Chinese to English, French to English as well as translate language pairs like Korean to Japanese, which has not been seen before.

Now can we use this simple LSTM-based encoder-decoder architecture? We will see some of the fundamental details of the architecture. Refer to *Figure 9.48*:

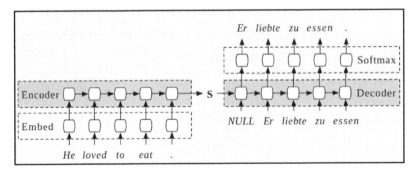

Figure 9.48: LSTM recurrent NN for translation (Image credit: https://smerity.com/articles/2016/google_nmt_arch.html)

We can use LSTM recurrent NN to encode a sentence of language A. The RNN splits a hidden state **S**, as shown in *Figure 9.48*. This **S** represents the vectorized content of the sentence. After that, we pass this vectorized form to the decoder that generates the translated sentence in language B, word by word. It's easy to understand this architecture, isn't it? However, this architecture has some drawbacks. This architecture has limited memory. The hidden state **S** of the LSTM is where we are trying to cram the whole sentence that we want to translate, but here **S** is usually a few hundred floating point numbers long. We need to fit our sentence into this fixed dimensionality and if we force our sentence to fit into this fixed dimensionality, then our network becomes more lossy, which means that we lose some information if we are forcefully fitting our sentence into a fixed size of dimensionality. We could increase the hidden size of LSTMs because their main purpose is to remember long-term dependencies, but if we increase the hidden size, then the training time increases exponentially. So, we should not use an architecture that takes a lot of time to converge.

We will introduce another architecture--attention-based encoder-decoder model. As humans, when we see a long sentence and we need to translate it, then we probably glance back at the source sentence a couple of times to make sure that we are capturing all the details. The human mind iteratively pays attention to the relevant parts of the source sentence. We want the neural network do the same thing for us by letting it store and refer to the previous output of the LST. This increases the storage of our model without changing the functionality of LSTMs. Refer to *Figure 9.49*:

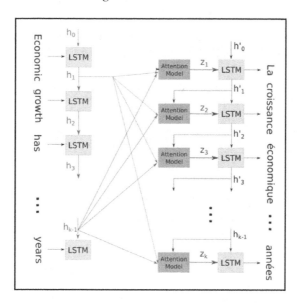

Figure 9.49: Architecture of attention-based NMT (Image credit: https://heuritech.files.wordpress.com/2016/01/trad_attention1.png?w=470)

Once we have the LSTM output from the encoders stored, we can query each output asking how relevant it is to the current computation happening in the decoder. Each encoder output gets a relevancy score that we can convert to a probability score using the softmax activation function. Refer to *Figure 9.50*:

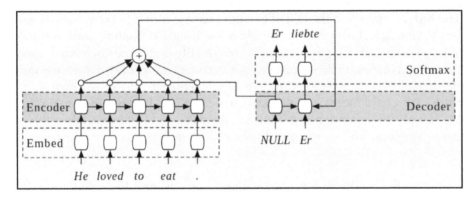

Figure 9.50: SoftMax function to generate the relevance score (Image credit: https://smerity.com/)

Then, we extract a context vector that is the weighted summation of the encoder's output depending on how relevant they are. Now let's get back to the code. To implement this attention-based functionality, we will use TensorFlow's built-in embedding attention sequence-to-sequence function. This function will take encoder and decoder inputs as arguments as well as some additional hyperparameters. This function is the same architecture that we have discussed. TensorFlow has some really great built-in models that we can use easily. Refer to *Figure 9.51* for the code snippet:

```
outputs, states = tf.contrib.legacy_seq2seq.embedding_attention_seq2seq(
                        encoder_inputs,
                        decoder_inputs,
                        tf.contrib.rnn.BasicLSTMCell(size),
                        num_encoder_symbols = en_vocab_size,
                        num_decoder_symbols = de_vocab_size,
                        embedding_size = 100,
                        feed_previous = False,
                        output_projection = output_projection,
                        dtype = tf.float32)
```

Figure 9.51: Code snippet for attention-based sequence-to-sequence model

Refer to *Figure 9.52* for the output of the preceding code:

```
1.
- - - - - - - - - - - - - - - - - - - -
What' s your name
Was ist dein Sohn
- - - - - - - - - - - - - - - - - - - -
2.
- - - - - - - - - - - - - - - - - - - -
My name is
Meine Sohn
- - - - - - - - - - - - - - - - - - - -
3.
- - - - - - - - - - - - - - - - - - - -
What are you doing
Was machst du denn
- - - - - - - - - - - - - - - - - - - -
4.
- - - - - - - - - - - - - - - - - - - -
I am reading a book
Ich bin ein Frühstück
- - - - - - - - - - - - - - - - - - - -
5.
- - - - - - - - - - - - - - - - - - - -
How are you
Wie sind du -
- - - - - - - - - - - - - - - - - - - -
6.
- - - - - - - - - - - - - - - - - - - -
I am good
Ich bin gut
```

Figure 9.52: Output for MT

You can also follow this link, `https://www.tensorflow.org/tutorials/seq2seq`, to run the MT example without making your customized code. This tutorial is an example of French to English and English to French translation system. This is a really easy way to run this example. I would recommend you to use this way because customized code is much complicated to begin with.

1. First, you need to download 2.4GB training `giga-fren.tar` dataset from this link: `http://www.statmt.org/wmt10/training-giga-fren.tar`.
2. Now you need to store this data in the `data_dir` directory and save your trained model time to time. For this, we need to create a checkpoint directory inside `train_dir`.

3. After that, you can execute the following command:

```
python translate.py  --data_dir [your_data_directory] --train_dir
[checkpoints_directory]  --en_vocab_size=40000 --
fr_vocab_size=40000
```

4. If the preceding command takes a lot of memory of the GPU, then execute this command:

```
python translate.py  --data_dir [your_data_directory] --train_dir
[checkpoints_directory]  --size=256 --num_layers=2 --
steps_per_checkpoint=50
```

5. Once your epoch reaches 340 K with batch size 64, you can use the model for translation before that also you can use it but accuracy will as follows:

```
python translate.py --decode  --data_dir [your_data_directory] --
train_dir [checkpoints_directory]Reading model parameters from
/tmp/translate.ckpt-340000>  Who is the president of the United
States? Qui est le président des États-Unis ?
```

Our German to English (GR_EN) translation model gives us a fairly good result and we are doing only one round of training, but if we really want to get the same accuracy that Google has in their translation system, then we need to train this model for several weeks using high computational capability such as 100 GPUs for several weeks continuously running. Here, we are definitely not going to implement that model, but I will explain its working. So let's dive conceptually.

If the output doesn't have sufficient context for the encoded source sentence, then the model won't be able to give us a good translation result. In this case, we need to give the information about the future words so that the encoder output is determined by the words on the left and right. As humans, we use this kind of full context to understand the meaning of the sentence. This will happen on the machine level by including bidirectional encoders so that it contains two **recurrent neural nets** (RNN). One goes forward over the sentence and the other goes backward. So for each word, it concatenates the vector outputs that produce the vector with context of both sides. Refer to *Figure 9.53*:

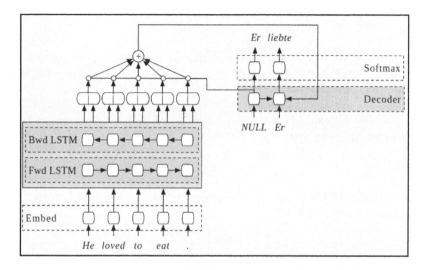

Figure 9.53: Bidirectional RNN architecture for MT (Image credit:
http://img.yantuwan.com/weiyuehao.php?http://mmbiz.qpic.cn/mmbiz_png/KmXPKA19gW81aVM2Gdgrxfsa0vR4YVib2wCIHNabCic1Hr144r4PAuSDMLNMHGgWz12GtibY
dgF1jTvHtuniauHYSw/0?wx_fmt=png)

Google has included lots of layers to the models as well as encoders that have one bidirectional RNN layer and seven unidirection layers. The decoder has eight unidirectional RNN layers. If you add more layers, then the training time increases. Here, we are using only one bidirectional layer. If all layers are bidirectional, then the whole layer would have to finish their computation before other layer dependencies could start their computation. With the help of a unidirection layer, we can perform computation in parallel.

This is all about machine translation. We have generated the machine translation output but still there is more room for improvement. Using DL, we are going to build a single universal machine translation system.

Now let's begin our next part of coding that is based on NLG.

Deep learning techniques and NLG

In this section, we are going build a very simple but intuitive application for NLG. We are going to generate a one-line summary from shot articles. We will see all the details about summarization in this section.

This application took a lot of training time so you can put your model to train on CPU and meanwhile, you can do some other task. If you don't have any other task, then let me give you one.

Exercise

Try to figure out how you can generate a Wikipedia article by just providing some starting character sequences. Don't take me wrong! I'm serious! You seriously need to think on this. This is the dataset that you can use: `https://einstein.ai/research/the-wikitext-long-term-dependency-language-modeling-dataset`. Jump to the download section and download this dataset named **Download WikiText-103 word level (181 MB)**.

(Hint: See this link, `https://github.com/kumikokashii/lstm-text-generator`.)

Don't worry ;after understanding the concepts of summarization, you can attempt this. So let's begin the summarization journey!

Recipe summarizer and title generation

Before jumping into the code, I want to give you some brief background about summarization. Architecture and other technical parts will be understood as we code.

Semantics is a really big deal in NLP. As data increases in the density of the text, information also increases. Nowadays, people around you really expect that you say the most important thing effectively in a short amount of time.

Text summarization started in the 90s. The Canadian government built a system named **forecast generator** (**FoG**) that uses weather forecast data and generates a summary. That was the template-based approach where the machine just needed to fill in certain values. Let me give you an example, **Saturday will be sunny with 10% chances of rain**. The word *sunny* and *10%* are actually generated by FoG.

The other areas are finance, medical, and so on. In the recent world, doctors find the summarization of a patient's medical history very useful and they can diagnose people efficiently and effectively.

There are two types of summary that are given as follows:

- Extractive
- Abstractive

Most summarization tools in the past were of the extractive type; they selected an existing set of words from the article to create a summary for the article. As humans, we do something more; that is, when we summarize, we build an internal semantic representation of what we have read. Using this internal semantic representation, we can summarize text. This kind of summarization is called **abstractive summarization**.

So let's build an abstractive summarization tool using Keras.

Keras is a high-level wrapper for TensorFlow and Theano. This example needs multiple GPUs for more than 12 hours. If you want to reproduce the result at your end, then it shall take a lot of computation power.

These are the steps for the coding part. Here, for the first time, we are using Python 3:

1. Clone the GitHub Repository:
   `https://github.com/jalajthanaki/recipe-summarization`

2. Initialized submodules:

   `git submodule update --init -recursive`

3. Go inside the folder:

   `python src/config.p`

4. Install dependencies:

   `pip install -r requirements.txt`

5. Set up directories:

   `python src/config.py`

6. Scrape recipes from the web or use the existing one at this link:

   `wget -P recipe-box/data https://storage.googleapis.com/recipe-box/recipes_raw.zip; unzip recipe-box/data/recipes_raw.zip -d recipe-box/data`

7. Tokenize the data:

   `python src/tokenize_recipes.py`

8. Initialize word embeddings with `GloVe vectors`:
    1. Get the GloVe vectors trained model:

    ```
    wget -P data http://nlp.stanford.edu/data/glove.6B.zip;
    unzip data/glove.6B.zip -d data
    ```

    2. Initialize embeddings:

    ```
    python src/vocabulary-embedding.py
    ```

9. Train the model:

```
python src/train_seq2seq.py
```

10. Make predictions:

```
use src/predict.ipynb
```

Here, for vectorization, we are using GloVe because we want a global-level representation of the words for summarization, and we are using the sequence-to-sequence model (Seq2Seq model) to train our data. Seq2Seq is the same model that we discussed in the *Machine translation* section. See the code snippets in *Figure 9.54*, *Figure 9.55*, and *Figure 9.56*, and after training, you can see the output in *Figure 9.57*:

```python
def tokenize_recipes(recipes):
    tokenized = []
    N = len(recipes)
    for i, r in enumerate(recipes.values()):
        if recipe_is_complete(r):
            ingredients = '; '.join(parse_ingredient_list(r['ingredients'])) + '; '
            tokenized.append((
                tokenize_sentence(r['title']),
                tokenize_sentence(ingredients) + tokenize_sentence(r['instructions'])))
        if i % 10000 == 0:
            print('Tokenized {:,} / {:,} recipes'.format(i, N))
    return tuple(map(list, zip(*tokenized)))

def pickle_recipes(recipes):
    # pickle to disk
    with open(path.join(config.path_data, 'tokens.pkl'), 'wb') as f:
        pickle.dump(recipes, f, 2)
```

Figure 9.54: Tokenization code snippet

Refer to the following figure for vocab building using GloVe:

```python
FN = 'vocabulary-embedding'
seed = 42
vocab_size = 40000
embedding_dim = 100
lower = False


# read tokenized headlines and descriptions
with open(path.join(config.path_data, 'tokens.pkl'), 'rb') as fp:
    heads, desc = pickle.load(fp)

if lower:
    heads = [h.lower() for h in heads]

if lower:
    desc = [h.lower() for h in desc]

# build vocabulary
def get_vocab(lst):
    vocabcount = Counter(w for txt in lst for w in txt.split())
    vocab = list(map(lambda x: x[0], sorted(vocabcount.items(), key=lambda x: -x[1])))
    return vocab, vocabcount

vocab, vocabcount = get_vocab(heads + desc)
```

Figure 9.55: Vocab building using GloVe

Refer to the following figure to train the model:

```python
# start with a standaed stacked LSTM
model = Sequential()
model.add(Embedding(vocab_size, embedding_size,
                    input_length=maxlen,
                    W_regularizer=regularizer, dropout=p_emb, weights=[embedding], mask_zero=True,
                    name='embedding_1'))
for i in range(rnn_layers):
    lstm = LSTM(rnn_size, return_sequences=True,
                W_regularizer=regularizer, U_regularizer=regularizer,
                b_regularizer=regularizer, dropout_W=p_W, dropout_U=p_U,
                name='lstm_{}'.format(i + 1))
    model.add(lstm)
    model.add(Dropout(p_dense, name='dropout_{}'.format(i + 1)))
```

Figure 9.56: Training of the model

Examples are given in the following figure:

Example 1:

- **Generated:** Chicken Cake
- **Original:** Chicken French - Rochester , NY Style
- **Recipe:** all purpose flour ; salt ; eggs ; white sugar ; grated parmesan cheese ; olive oil ; skinless ; butter ; minced garlic ; dry sherry ; lemon juice ; low sodium chicken base ; ;Mix together the flour , salt , and pepper in a shallow bowl . In another bowl , whisk beaten eggs , sugar , and Parmesan cheese until the mixture is thoroughly blended and the sugar has dissolved . Heat olive oil in a large skillet over medium heat until the oil shimmers . Dip the chicken breasts into the flour mixture , then into the egg mixture , and gently lay them into the skillet . Pan-fry the chicken breasts until golden brown and no longer pink in the middle , about 6 minutes on each side . Remove from the skillet and set aside . In the same skillet over medium-low heat , melt the butter , and stir in garlic , sherry , lemon juice , and chicken base ...

Example 2:

- **Generated:** Fruit Soup
- **Original:** Red Apple Milkshake
- **Recipe:** red apple peeled ; cold skim milk ; white sugar ; fresh mint leaves for garnish ; ;In a blender , blend the apple , skim milk , and sugar until smooth . Garnish with mint to serve .

Figure 9.57: Prediction result of the model

I know that the summarization example will take a lot of computational power and maybe there will be a situation where your local machine does not have enough memory (RAM) to run this code. In that case, don't worry; there are various cloud options available that you can use. You can use Google Cloud, Amazon Web Services (AWS), or any other.

Now you have enough idea about the NLU and NLG applications. I have also put one more application related to the NLG domain at this GitHub Link:
`https://github.com/tensorflow/models/tree/master/im2txt`

This application generates captions for images; this is a kind of combined application of computer vision and NLG. Necessary details are on GitHub so check out this example as well.

In the next section, we will see the gradient descent-based optimization strategy. TensorFlow provides us with some variants of the gradient descent algorithm. Once we have an idea of how all these variants work and what are the drawbacks and advantages of each of them, then it will be easy for us to choose the best option for the optimization of our DL algorithm. So let's understand the gradient descent-based optimization.

Gradient descent-based optimization

In this section, we will discuss gradient descent-based optimization options that are provided by TensorFlow. Initially, it will not be clear which optimization option you should use, but as and when you know the actual logic of the DL algorithm, it will became much clearer to you.

We use a gradient descent-based approach to develop an intelligent system. Using this algorithm, the machine can learn how to identify patterns from the data. Here, our end goal is to obtain the local minimum and the objective function is the final prediction that the machine will make or result that is generated by the machine. In the gradient descent-based algorithm, we are not concentrating on how to achieve the best final goal for our objective function in the first step, but we will iteratively or repeatedly take small steps and select the intermediate best option that leads us to achieve the final best option, that is, our local minima. This kind of educated guess and check method works well to obtain local minima. When the DL algorithm obtains local minima, the algorithm can generate the best result. We have already seen the basic gradient descent algorithm. If you face overfitting and underfitting situations, you can optimize the algorithm using different types of gradient descent. There are various flavors of gradient descent that can help us in order to generate the ideal local minima, control the variance of the algorithm, update our parameters, and lead us to converge our ML or DL algorithm. Let's take an example. If you have function Y = X^2, then the partial derivative of the given function is 2X. When we randomly guess the stating value and we start with value X = 3, then Y = 2(3) =6 and to obtain local minima, we need to take a step in the negative direction--so Y = -6. After the first iteration, if you guess the value X = 2.3, then Y = 2(2.3) = 4.6 and we need to move in the negative direction again-- Y = -4.6--because we get a positive value. If we get a negative value, then we move in the positive direction. After certain iterations, the value of Y is very near zero and that is our local minima. Now let's start with basic gradient descent. Let's start exploring varieties of gradient descent.

Basic gradient descent

In basic gradient descent, we calculate the gradient of loss function with regards to the parameters present in the entire training dataset, and we need to calculate gradient for the entire dataset to perform a single update. For a single update, we need to consider the whole training dataset as well as all parameters so it is very slow. You can see the equation in *Figure 9.58*:

$$\theta = \theta - \eta \cdot \nabla_\theta J(\theta).$$

Figure 9.58: Equation for gradient descent (Image credit: http://sebastianruder.com/optimizing-gradient-descent/index.html#challenges)

You can find the sample logic code for understanding purposes in *Figure 9.59*:

```
for i in range(nb_epochs):
    params_grad = evaluate_gradient(loss_function, data, params)
    params = params - learning_rate * params_grad
```

Figure 9.59: Sample code for gradient descent (Image credit: http://sebastianruder.com/optimizing-gradient-descent/index.html#challenges)

As this technique is slow, we will introduce a new technique called Stochastic Gradient Descent.

Stochastic gradient descent

In this technique, we update the parameters for each training example and label so we just need to add a loop for our training dataset and this method updates the parameters faster compared to basic gradient descent. You can see the equation in *Figure 9.60*:

$$\theta = \theta - \eta \cdot \nabla_\theta J(\theta; x^{(i)}; y^{(i)}).$$

Figure 9.60: Equation for stochastic gradient descent (Image credit: http://sebastianruder.com/optimizing-gradient-descent/index.html#challenges)

You can find the sample logic code for understanding purposes in *Figure 9.61*:

```
for i in range(nb_epochs):
  np.random.shuffle(data)
  for example in data:
      params_grad = evaluate_gradient(loss_function, example, params)
      params = params - learning_rate * params_grad
```

Figure 9.61: Sample code for stochastic gradient descent (Image credit: http://sebastianruder.com/optimizing-gradient-descent/index.html#challenges)

This method also has some issues. This method makes convergence complicated and sometimes updating the parameters is too fast. The algorithm can overshoot the local minima and keep running. To avoid this problem, another method is introduced called Mini-Batch Gradient Descent.

Mini-batch gradient descent

In this method, we will take the best part from both basic gradient descent and stochastic gradient descent. We will take a subset of the training dataset as a batch and update the parameters from them. This type of gradient descent is used for basic types of ANNs.

You can see the equation in *Figure 9.62:*

$$\theta = \theta - \eta \cdot \nabla_\theta J\left(\theta; x^{(i:i+n)}; y^{(i:i+n)}\right).$$

Figure 9.62: Equation for mini-batch gradient descent (Image credit: http://sebastianruder.com/optimizing-gradient-descent/index.html#challenges)

You can find the sample logic code for understanding purposes in *Figure 9.63:*

```
for i in range(nb_epochs):
  np.random.shuffle(data)
  for batch in get_batches(data, batch_size=50):
    params_grad = evaluate_gradient(loss_function, batch, params)
    params = params - learning_rate * params_grad
```

Figure 9.63: Sample code for mini-batch gradient descent (Image credit: http://sebastianruder.com/optimizing-gradient-descent/index.html#challenges)

If we have a high-dimensional dataset, then we can use some other gradient descent method; let's begin with momentum.

Momentum

If all the possible parameters' values surface curves much more steeply in one dimension than in another, then in this kind of case, this are very common around local optima. In these scenarios, SGD oscillates across the slopes. So to solve this oscillation issue, we will use the momentum method. You can see the equation in *Figure 9.64:*

$$v_t = \gamma v_{t-1} + \eta \nabla_\theta J(\theta)$$
$$\theta = \theta - v_t$$

Figure 9.64: Equation for momentum (Image credit: http://sebastianruder.com/optimizing-gradient-descent/index.html#challenges)

If you see the equation, we are adding a fraction of the direction of the gradient from the previous time step to the current step, and we amplify the parameter update in the right direction that speeds up our convergence and reduces the oscillation. So here, the concept of momentum is similar to the concept of momentum in physics. This variant doesn't slow down when local minima is obtained because at that time, the momentum is high. In this situation, our algorithm can miss the local minima entirely and this problem can be solved by Nesterov accelerated gradient.

Nesterov accelerated gradient

This method was invented by Yurii Nesterov. He was trying to solve the issue that occurred in the momentum technique. He has published a paper that you can see at this link:

You can see the equation in *Figure 9.65:*

$$v_t = \gamma v_{t-1} + \eta \nabla_\theta J(\theta - \gamma v_{t-1})$$
$$\theta = \theta - v_t$$

Figure 9.65: Equation for Nesterov accelerated gradient (Image credit: http://sebastianruder.com/optimizing-gradient-descent/index.html#challenges)

As you can see, we are doing the same calculation that we have done for momentum but we have changed the order of calculation. In momentum, we compute the gradient make jump in that direction amplified by the momentum, whereas in the Nesterov accelerated gradient method, we first make a jump based on the previous momentum then calculate gradient and after that we add a correction and generate the final update for our parameter. This helps us provide parameter values more dynamically.

Adagrad

Adagrad is stands for adaptive gradient. This method allows the learning rate to adapt based on the parameters. This algorithm provides a big update for infrequent parameters and a small update for frequent parameters. You can see the equation in *Figure 9.66:*

$$\theta_{t+1} = \theta_t - \frac{\eta}{\sqrt{G_t + \epsilon}} \odot g_t.$$

Figure 9.66: Equation for Adagrad (Image credit: http://sebastianruder.com/optimizing-gradient-descent/index.html#challenges)

This method provides a different learning rate for every parameter at the given timestamp based on the past gradient computed for that parameter. Here, we don't need to manually tune our learning rate although it has a limitation. As per the equation, the learning rate is always decreasing as the accumulation of the squared gradients placed in the denominator is always positive, and as the denominator grows, the whole term will decrease. Sometimes, the learning rate becomes so small that the ML-model stops learning. To solve this problem. the method called Adadelta has come into the picture.

Adadelta

Adadelta is an extension of Adagrad. In Adagrad, we constantly add the square root to the sum causing the learning rate to decrease. Instead of summing all the past square roots, we restrict the window to the accumulated past gradient to a fixed size.

You can see the equation in *Figure 9.67*:

$$\Delta\theta_t = -\frac{\eta}{\sqrt{E[g^2]_t + \epsilon}} g_t$$

Figure 9.67: Equation for Adadelta (Image credit: http://sebastianruder.com/optimizing-gradient-descent/index.html#challenges)

As you can see in the equation, we will use the sum of gradient as a decaying average of all past squared gradients. Here, the running average $E[g^2]_t$ at a given timestamp is dependent on the previous average and the current gradient.

After seeing all the optimization techniques, you know how we can calculate the individual learning rate for each parameter, how we can calculate the momentum, and how we can prevent the decaying learning rate. Still, there is room for improvement by applying some adaptive momentum and that leads us to our final optimization method called **Adam**.

Adam

Adam stands for adaptive momentum estimation. As we are calculating the learning rate for each parameter, we can also store the momentum changes for each of them separately.

You can see the equation in *Figure 9.68*:

$$\hat{m}_t = \frac{m_t}{1 - \beta_1^t}$$
$$\hat{v}_t = \frac{v_t}{1 - \beta_2^t}$$

Figure 9.68: Mean and variance for Adam (Image credit: http://sebastianruder.com/optimizing-gradient-descent/index.html#challenges)

First, we will be calculating the mean of the gradient, then we are going to calculate the uncentered variance of the gradient, and use these values to update the parameters. Just like an Adadelta. You can see the equation of Adam in *Figure 9.69*:

$$\theta_{t+1} = \theta_t - \frac{\eta}{\sqrt{\hat{v}_t} + \epsilon} \hat{m}_t.$$

Figure 9.69: Equation for Adam (Image credit: http://sebastianruder.com/optimizing-gradient-descent/index.html#challenges)

So now you want to know which method we should use; according to me, Adam is the best overall choice because it outperforms the other methods. You can also use Adadelta and Adagrad. If your data is sparse, then you should not use SGD, momentum, or Nesterov.

Artificial intelligence versus human intelligence

From the last one year, you may have heard this kind of question. In the AI world, these kinds of questions have become common. People have created a hype that AI will make humanity vanish and machines will take away all the powers from us. Now let me tell you, this is not the truth. These kinds of threats sound like science-fiction stories. According to me, AI is in its high pace development phase but its purpose is to complement humanity and make human life easier. We are still figuring out some of the complex and unknown truths of this universe that can help us provide more insight on how we can build AI-enabled systems. So AI is purely going to help us. AI will amaze our lives for sure but it is not going to be saturated with its inventions soon. So enjoy this AI phase and contribute to the AI ecosystem in a positive manner.

People have concerns that AI will take away our jobs. It will not take away your job. It will make your job easier. If you are a doctor and want to give your final words on some cancer report, AI will help you. In the Information Technology (IT) industry, there's a concern that AI will replace the coders. If you believe that very soon researchers and tech companies will be able to build machines that are more powerful than humans and that the AI shift will happen soon and machines will take away our jobs, then it is better for you to acquire ML, DL, and AI related skill sets to have jobs, and perhaps you are the last person on this planet who has some job to do! We assume that AI would take away some jobs, but this AI ecosystem will also create so many new jobs. So don't worry! This discussion can be ongoing but I want to really give you guys some time window to think on this.

Summary

Congratulations guys! We have made it to the last chapter! I really appreciate your efforts. In this chapter, you have learned a lot of things such as artificial intelligence aspects that help you understand why deep learning is the buzzword nowadays. We have seen the concept of ANNs. We have seen concepts such as gradient descent, various activation functions, and loss functions. We have seen the architecture of DNN and the DL life cycle. We have also touched on the basics of the sequence-to-sequence model and developed applications such as machine translation, title generation, and summarization. We have also seen the gradient descent-based optimization techniques.

The next sections are Appendices A to C, that will provide you with an overview about frameworks such as hadoop, spark, and so on. You can also see the installation guide for these frameworks as well as other tools and libraries. Apart from this, you can find cheatsheets for many Python libraries that are very handy if you are new to Python. There are some tips from my side if you really want to improve your data science as well as NLP skills. I have also provided Gitter links in the appendices that you can use to connect with me in case you have any questions.

10
Advanced Tools

This appendix focuses on how the various frameworks can be used in NLP applications. We will look at an overview of the frameworks and touch on the basic features and what they do for you. We are not going to see look at a detailed architecture of each framework. Here, the purpose is to get you aware of the different tools and frameworks that can be used together to build various NLP applications. We will also look at visualization libraries that can help you develop a dashboard.

Apache Hadoop as a storage framework

Apache Hadoop is one of the widely used frameworks. Hadoop allows the distributed processing of large datasets across clusters of commodity computers using a simple programming model. Hadoop uses the concept of MapReduce. MapReduce divides the input query into small parts and processes them in parallel to the data stored on the **Hadoop distributed file system (HDFS)**.

Hadoop has the following features:

- It is scalable
- It is cost-effective
- It provides a robust ecosystem
- It provides faster data processing

Hadoop can be used as a storage framework for NLP applications. If you want to store large amounts of data, then you can use a multinode Hadoop cluster and store data on HDFS. So, many NLP applications use HDFS for their historical data. Hadoop sends a program to the data and the data processes it locally. These features give Hadoop good speed. Note that Hadoop performs operations on the disk level, which is slow, but we execute operations in parallel so data processing is fast. Now, you may think that disk operations are slow compared to memory operations, but we have large amounts of data, which will not fit into memory at once. So, this approach of processing data locally and executing operations in parallel, using a multinode cluster, gives us a good throughput.

Hadoop has the following components as part of its core architecture:

- HDFS
- MapReduce
- YARN
- Hadoop common utilities

You can see the architecture of Hadoop in *Figure 01*:

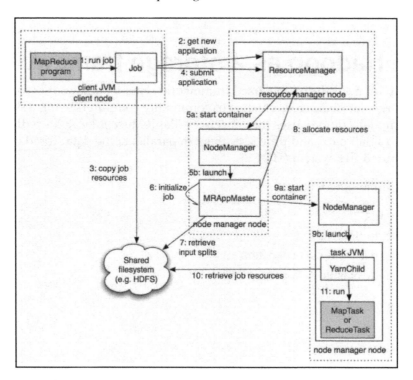

Figure 01: Hadoop 2.x yarn architecture(Image credit: https://github.com/zubayr/big_config/blob/master/hbase/hbase_tuning.md)

You can see the Hadoop ecosystem in *Figure 02*:

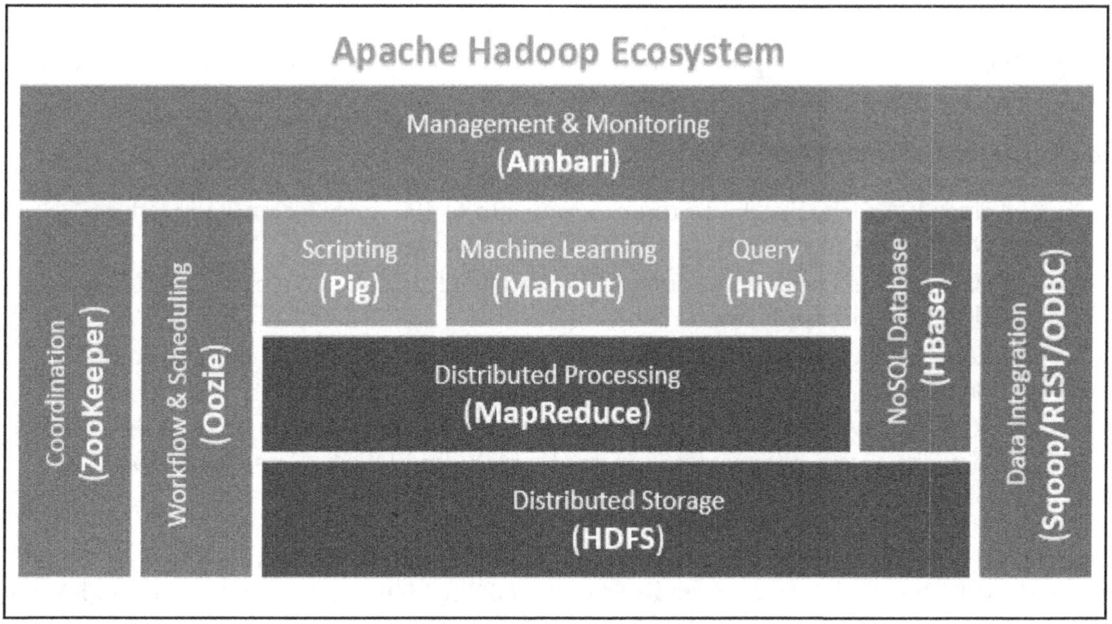

Figure 02: The Hadoop ecosystem (Image credit:
https://s3.amazonaws.com/files.dezyre.com/images/blog/Big+Data+and+Hadoop+Training+Hadoop+Components+and+Architecture_1.png)

For real-time data processing, Hadoop is a bit slow and not very efficient. Don't worry! We have another framework that helps us with real-time data processing.

Many NLP applications use Hadoop for data storage because it can handle data processing very well. On a personal level, I used Hadoop to store my corpus on HDFS. Then, I have used Spark MLlib to develop **machine learning** (ML) algorithms. For real-time data processing, I use Apache Flink.

For experimenting purposes, I have provided you with the steps of setting up a single-node Hadoop cluster. The GitHub link for this is:
`https://github.com/jalajthanaki/NLPython/blob/master/Appendix3/Installationdocs/App3_3_Hadoop_installation.md`.

You can find some of the commands of Hadoop in this document:

- `https://dzone.com/articles/top-10-hadoop-shell-commands`.
- `https://hadoop.apache.org/docs/current/hadoop-project-dist/hadoop-common/FileSystemShell.html`

Apache Spark as a processing framework

Apache Spark is a large-scale data processing framework. It is a fast and general-purpose engine. It is one of the fastest processing frameworks. Spark can perform in-memory data processing, as well as on-disk data processing.

Spark's important features are as follows:

- **Speed**: Apache Spark can run programs up to 100 times faster than Hadoop MapReduce in-memory or 10 times faster on-disk
- **Ease of use**: There are various APIs available for Scala, Java, Spark, and R to develop your application
- **Generality**: Spark provides features of Combine SQL, streaming, and complex analytics
- **Run everywhere**: Spark can run on Hadoop, Mesos, standalone, or in the cloud. You can access diverse data sources by including HDFS, Cassandra, HBase, and S3

I have used Spark to train my models using MLlib. I have used Spark Java as well as PySpark API. The result is you can redirect to the HDFS. I have saved my trained models on HDFS and then loaded them as and when needed. Spark really speeds up your processing time. I have experienced this. The reason behind this is its in-memory processing architecture. Spark architecture is given in *Figure 03*:

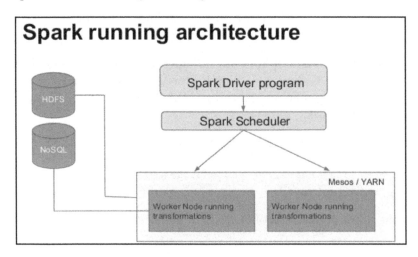

Figure 03: Spark running architecture (Image credit: https://www.slideshare.net/datamantra/spark-architecture)

You can see the Spark ecosystem in *Figure 04*:

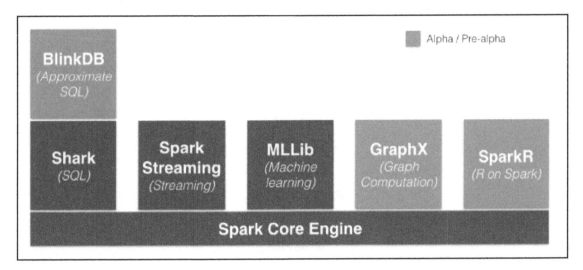

Figure 04: Spark ecosystem (Image credit: http://jorditorres.org/spark-ecosystem/)

You can see the installation steps on this GitHub link:

```
https://github.com/jalajthanaki/NLPython/blob/master/Appendix3/Installationdocs
/App3_4_Spark_installation.md
```

You can find more information on the following links:

- https://jaceklaskowski.gitbooks.io/mastering-apache-spark/content/
- https://www.gitbook.com/book/jaceklaskowski/mastering-apache-spark/d
  etail
- http://spark.apache.org/
- http://spark.apache.org/docs/latest/ml-guide.html
- http://spark.apache.org/docs/latest/mllib-guide.html

Apache Flink as a real-time processing framework

Apache Flink is used for real-time streaming and batch processing. I have told you we should not worry about real-time frameworks. The reason is we have the Flink framework for this.

Flink is an open source stream processing framework for distributed, high-performing, always available, and accurate data streaming applications. You can see more about Flink at `https://flink.apache.org/`.

Flink will definitely provide a very nice future. You can see in *Figure 05*:

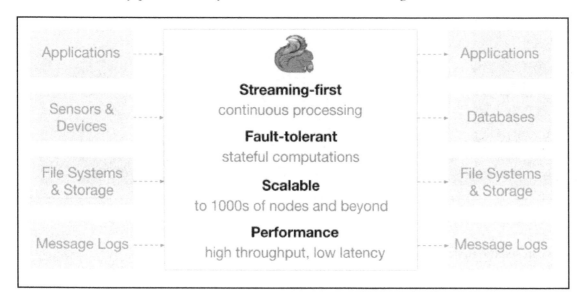

Figure 05: Features of Flink (Image credit: https://flink.apache.org/)

Flink is quite a new framework. If you want to perform real-time sentiment analysis or make a real recommendation engine, then Flink is very useful. You can refer to the following video where you can understand how the HDFS, Flink, Kappa, and lamda architecture has been used. It's a must-see video:

`https://www.youtube.com/watch?v=mYGF4BUwtaw`

This video helps you understand how various frameworks fuse together to develop a good real-time application.

Visualization libraries in Python

Visualization is one of the important activities that is used to track certain processes and the results of your application. We used `matplotlib` in `Chapter 6`, *Advance Feature Engineering and NLP Algorithms*, as well as in other chapters.

Apart from `matplotlib`, we can use various visualization libraries:

- `matplotlib`: It is simple to use and very useful
- `bokeh`: It provides customized themes and charts
- `pygal`: You can make cool graphs and charts with this

You can use the following links to refer to each of the libraries. All libraries have written documentation so you can check them and start making your own charts.

You can find more on `matplotlib` at `https://matplotlib.org/`.

You can find more on `Bokeh` at `http://bokeh.pydata.org/en/latest/docs/gallery.html`.

You can find documentation about `pygal` at
`http://pygal.org/en/stable/documentation/index.html`.

Summary

If you want detailed information regarding these frameworks and libraries, then you can use the Gitter room to connect with me, because in-depth details of the frameworks are out of the scope of this book.

This framework overview will help you figure out how various frameworks can be used in NLP applications. Hadoop is used for storage. Spark MLlib is used to develop machine learning models and store the trained models on HDFS. We can run the trained model as and when needed by loading it. Flink makes our lives easier when real-time analysis and data processing come into the picture. Real-time sentiment analysis, document classification, user recommendation engine, and so on are some of the real-time applications that you can build using Flink. The `matplotlib` is used while developing machine learning models. The `pygal` and `bokeh` are used to make nice dashboards for our end users.

11

How to Improve Your NLP Skills

This appendix will give you more information about how you can improve your skills in NLP. This will also help you update your knowledge.

Beginning a new career journey with NLP

If you are a coder and want to pursue a career in NLP, then keep the following things in mind:

- NLP, as well as AI, is growing so fast that it will not be enough for you to just acquire the skills. You also need to update them.
- Kaggle is one of the best learning platforms for all NLP and data science folks. If you are hearing about this hackathon platform for the first time, then I'm sure that by clicking on this link, you will not be disappointed:
  https://www.kaggle.com/.
- Participate in Kaggle competitions. Learn, discuss, and implement.
- GitHub is your new resume if you are from a coding background. So, try to make new projects and put them on your GitHub.
- Contribute to open source community projects. This will help your thinking process, as well as your coding skills.
- Attend various conferences. Try to explore new ideas and techniques.
- Read research papers and articles.
- Be a part of communities and conversations.
- Ask questions. In short, just unlock yourself.

- Think about the product architecture.
- Combine all your learning and try to see the big picture for your development product.
- If you are thinking that you have learned enough, then think again. Sometimes, use cases, applications, and so on that you have tried are so similar that you don't find things very interesting. Recall all your learning and experiences. Give your thoughts a better and new direction (just like Newton or Einstein. They stopped learning and started thinking and gave us great theories of science). Try to make something useful that impacts others' lives in a positive manner.

Cheat sheets

I'm providing cheat sheets for libraries and frameworks on this link:

`https://github.com/jalajthanaki/NLPython/tree/master/Appendix2/Cheatsheets`

Cheat sheets cover the following libraries, tools, and frameworks. These cheat sheets were not developed by me. I want to give full credit to individual authors who have made the cheat sheets for the following topics:

- Linux books for beginners
- Python
- NumPy
- SciPy
- pandas
- Fask
- scikit-learn
- TensorFlow API at `https://www.tensorflow.org/api_docs/python/`
- TensorFlow cheat sheet at `https://github.com/crscardellino/cheatsheets/blob/master/tensorflow.md` which was made by Cristian Cardellino
- Keras
- PySpark
- Math
- Git
- Linux

Choose your area

After reading all the chapters, you might know enough to decide what you like. Do you want to build core ML stuff? Do you like to work on frameworks such as Hadoop, Spark, and so on? Are you keen on designing architecture? Do you want to contribute to visualization? Think and choose.

You can choose any area from data science or you can be a part of the whole data science product development life cycle. I want to give my example. I have worked with mid-size and start-up organizations. So far, I have had the freedom to explore various areas related to data science, such as proposing a data science product and releasing the product. I used to propose a new product after doing an analysis of business opportunities. I always validate my product proposal by thinking that if we were to make this product, then our end users would use it and, in return, the company that I'm working for will get the positive impact of it. Then, I would start work on the designing part by asking many questions, such as what kind of data will we need, what data resources will we use, what are the critical data points that we need to collect, what will the architecture of the product, what machine learning models will we use, how will we integrate with the existing product be, when will we release it, and so on. If you think like me and want to work on all the areas, as well as on each and every component of the data science product, then it is a very good thing. Just do your work from your heart and with passion. See the big picture as well.

Agile way of working to achieve success

NLP or any other data science-related projects need many iterations to get optimal output. You need to understand the problem statement. After this, to achieve the best result, you need to start with an analysis of your data. After analyzing the data, make a basic prototype. Then validate your model. If it gives you the best result, then you are done; if not, then try to implement different algorithms, do hyperparameter tuning, or change or improve your features set. You need to be agile in your working process. Try to identify your problem or mistake and then do smart iterations. Ask questions on stack overflow. Try to search for answers. This will really help you. Keep yourself updated with all the techniques and tools. There are some libraries that can solve your issue. Look for any paid third-party tool available and try to understand how it works. There are chances that, after using the tool, you could become a master of your product and your product could become more valuable for your end users.

Useful blogs for NLP and data science

Here are some important blogs for NLP and data science:

- http://www.datasciencecentral.com/
- https://nlp.stanford.edu/blog/
- http://www.kdnuggets.com/
- https://nlpers.blogspot.in/
- https://lingpipe-blog.com/lingpipe-home-page/

Grab public datasets

Here is a list of the available datasets:

- Kaggel dataset: https://www.kaggle.com/datasets
- UCI machine learning: http://archive.ics.uci.edu/ml/
- Reddit: https://www.reddit.com/r/datasets/
- An awesome GitHub repository that contains a list of public datasets: https://github.com/caesar0301/awesome-public-datasets
- Google Advanced Search is also handy when you are searching for datasets: https://www.google.co.in/advanced_search

Mathematics needed for data science

If you are from a non-technical background and you want to learn mathematics which could be helpful to you in your NLP or any other data science projects, then you can start learning from this site:

https://www.khanacademy.org/math.

If you want to access reference links, research papers, and books, then you can click on the following GitHub link:

https://github.com/jalajthanaki/NLPython/tree/master/Appendix2

If you want to add something to this page, then feel free to do so. Let's keep continuing this journey.

Summary

This entire section is more about discussing and sharing my views with you. These views may help you go ahead. I have given some suggestions, procedures, and areas that you can check and try to absorb if you like. I have listed down links of some useful blogs and other important links for publicly available datasets. I have also provided cheat sheets for different Python libraries.

12
Installation Guide

This appendix provides you with information related to the installation of Python libraries, as well as single-node Hadoop clusters, and single-node Spark clusters. If you want to ask me questions related to this book or any NLP-related questions, you can join me on Gitter.

Installing Python, pip, and NLTK

Pip stands for pip installs package or pip installs Python.

You can see how to install `pip` and `nltk` at this link:

https://github.com/jalajthanaki/NLPython/blob/master/Appendix3/Installationdocs
/App3_1_Install_python_pip_NLTK.md.

Python has been preinstalled on Linux and macOS. I would recommend you to use Linux OS or macOS as it will be easy to set up any ML-related frameworks.

Installing the PyCharm IDE

You can install the PyCharm community IDE for Linux OS by clicking on this link:

https://github.com/jalajthanaki/NLPython/blob/master/Appendix3/Installationd
ocs/App3_2_Pycharm_installation_guide.md.

Installing dependencies

You can run the following command to install various Python dependencies for NLP projects:

```
sudo pip install -r pip-requirements.txt
```

This is the link for the dependency file:

```
https://github.com/jalajthanaki/NLPython/blob/master/pip-requirements.txt
```

Framework installation guides

Hadoop standalone cluster installation guide:

```
https://github.com/jalajthanaki/NLPython/blob/master/Appendix3/Installationd
ocs/App3_3_Hadoop_installation.md.
```

Spark standalone cluster installation guide:

```
https://github.com/jalajthanaki/NLPython/blob/master/Appendix3/Installationd
ocs/App3_4_Spark_installation.md.
```

TensorFlow installation guide:

```
https://www.tensorflow.org/install/.
```

Drop your queries

If you have any installation-related queries, then you can join me on Gitter using this link:

```
https://gitter.im/NLPython/Installation_queries?utm_source=share-link&utm_mediu
m=link&utm_campaign=share-link
```

If you want to ask coding-related questions or other questions related to this book, then join me in this Gitter room:

```
https://gitter.im/NLPython/Lobby?utm_source=share-link&utm_medium=link&utm_c
ampaign=share-link.
```

Summary

This section's focus area was on giving you details about the installation of various libraries. I have also given the installation steps of various IDE's. To make your life easier, I have developed one pip requirement document. By running the previously given command, you will be able to install Python dependencies. I have given steps to install Hadoop and Spark on your machine, and run both of them in a single-node cluster. You can also get in touch with me if you want to ask me something about installation.

Index

Made in the USA
Coppell, TX
09 June 2020